THE CASE FOR
U.S. NUCLEAR WEAPONS
IN THE 21st CENTURY

THE CASE FOR U.S. NUCLEAR WEAPONS IN THE 21st CENTURY

Brad Roberts

Stanford Security Studies
An Imprint of Stanford University Press
Stanford, California

Stanford University Press
Stanford, California

Printed in the United States of America on acid-free, archival-quality paper

Library of Congress Cataloging-in-Publication Data

Roberts, Brad, author.
    The case for U.S. nuclear weapons in the 21st century / Brad Roberts.
        pages cm
    Includes bibliographical references and index.
    ISBN 978-0-8047-9645-3 (cloth : alk. paper) —
    ISBN 978-0-8047-9713-9 (pbk. : alk. paper)
1. Nuclear weapons—Government policy—United States. 2. Deterrence (Strategy)
3. National security—United States. 4. United States—Military policy. 5. United States—Foreign relations—21st century. I. Title.
    UA23.R59 2015
    355.02'170973—dc23
                                                                    2015016028
ISBN 978-0-8047-9715-3 (electronic)

Typeset by Thompson Type in 10/14 Minion

This volume is dedicated to Thérèse Delpech—a friend, colleague, and mentor taken by cancer too early in life in January 2012. By those who knew her, she is remembered for her clarity of policy vision, her willingness to challenge conventional wisdom and weak leadership, and her deep conviction that the strength of the democracies will be a deciding factor in the battle against savagery in the 21st century, just as it was in the 20th. She was an inspiration, and this volume is guided by her values.

Contents

Acknowledgments ix

Introduction 1

1 The Evolution of U.S. Nuclear Policy and Posture
since the End of the Cold War 11

2 The First New Problem: Nuclear-Armed Regional Challengers 51

3 The New Regional Deterrence Strategy 81

4 The Second New Problem: Relations with Putin's Russia 106

5 The Evolving Relationship with China 141

6 Extended Deterrence and Strategic Stability in Europe 176

7 Extended Deterrence and Strategic Stability in Northeast Asia 197

8 The Broader Nuclear Assurance Agenda 214

9 Conclusions 235

Epilogue: Implications for Future Strategy, Policy,
and Posture Reviews 253

Notes 277

Index 323

Acknowledgments

THIS VOLUME WAS WRITTEN AT STANFORD UNIVERSITY IN 2014. It was my pleasure and honor to serve as a consulting professor and a William Perry Fellow at the Center for International Security and Cooperation (CISAC) from September 2013 to December 2014. I am grateful to the university for this opportunity. I am grateful also to Los Alamos and Lawrence Livermore national laboratories for their support of the fellowship.

The arguments presented here were strengthened significantly through exchanges and debates with the faculty and students at Stanford. I am grateful especially to participants in a manuscript review session at CISAC in October 2014. I had many additional opportunities to review this work with colleagues in multiple academic and research institutions in the United States and elsewhere, which also greatly enriched my thinking. I wish to express special thanks to the following individuals for their willingness to review and critique the manuscript or elements of it: Daniel Altman, Michael Armacost, Ivanka Barshazka, Robert Bell, Coit Blacker, Lynn Eden, Tom Fingar, David Holloway, Miriam John, Vince Manzo, Michael May, Sean McDonald, Michael McFaul, Patrick McKenna, James Miller, Michael Nacht, Jonathan Pearl, Joseph Pilat, Mira Rapp-Hooper, Nicolas Roche, Scott Sagan, William Schlickenmaier, Shane Smith, Jonathan Trexel, Christopher Twomey, Michael Urena, Victor Utgoff, Robert Vince, Ted Warner, James Wirtz, and David Yost. I owe a special debt of gratitude to Linton Brooks and Lewis Dunn for exceptional assistance in developing the ideas contained here.

This work could not have been concluded successfully without the valuable research assistance of Jaclyn Marcatili and Marilyn Harris. And it could not have been published in such fine form without the support of Geoffrey Burns, James Holt, and Margaret Pinette.

More generally, I am indebted to the large community of people, both outside and inside government, and in the United States and abroad, with whom I have discussed and debated for many years our changing world and emerging challenges of deterrence, assurance, and strategic stability. The views expressed here are my own and should not be attributed to any institution with which I am or have been affiliated.

Introduction

T HE UNITED STATES IS ENTERING A PERIOD OF RENEWED debate about nuclear deterrence. That debate will address the most fundamental question: Are U.S. nuclear weapons merely Cold War relics that belong in "the dustbin of history" along with communism and the Soviet Union, or do they make an important and irreplaceable contribution to the national security of the United States?

This debate will be driven by three key factors. The first is the reassessment of U.S. defense strategy after fifteen years of war in Afghanistan and Iraq. A number of questions come into play. Is a shift away from counter-terrorism and counter-insurgency possible for U.S. military planners? Is the intended "rebalance" of security strategy toward Asia possible given widespread instability in the Middle East and Russian assertiveness in Europe? Is limited war with China and/or Russia a serious possibility? Is war with North Korea likely; if so, how might it exploit its new military capabilities to try to secure its interests? Will Iran "go nuclear" and with what implications for U.S. military strategies? What can the United States do to constructively shape developments in the Middle East while insulating itself and its allies and partners from the effects of deep and sustained conflict there? Answers to each of these questions have important implications for U.S. nuclear policy and posture.

Developments in the security environment that call into question some of the premises of U.S. policy since the end of the Cold War also play a role in driving renewed debate. The profound changes in Russia's foreign policy in 2014 have raised fundamental questions about the future role of nuclear weapons in Europe and in U.S.–Russian relations more generally. North Korea's progress in developing weapons capable of reaching the United States highlights an emerging major challenge to U.S. security strategy. China is making significant progress in deploying the key elements of a secure nuclear retaliatory force. Some U.S. allies in Europe, Asia, and the Middle East feel pressured by these developments and are seeking new forms of assurance that the U.S. security commitment to them will remain credible over the long term. New premises might well drive U.S. nuclear policy in new directions.

In addition, policy makers in Washington need to decide whether and how much to invest in keeping U.S. nuclear forces viable. For the last twenty-five years or so, the United States has spent only the money needed to operate and maintain standing nuclear forces. It has not had to modernize or replace them. Over the next twenty-five years or so, the entire remaining triad of delivery systems and inventory of weapons will have to be modernized or replaced in some way. These will be inherently contentious decisions, not least because they come at a time of budget austerity and in competition with the need to renew nonnuclear forces after more than a decade of war in Iraq and Afghanistan.

But the United States is ill prepared for this debate. Most of the stakeholders in the debate about U.S. nuclear deterrence policy and posture made up their minds a long time ago about the big questions. They generally fall into two camps with different core beliefs.

One camp recoils from the horror of nuclear war, sees the risks of nuclear terrorism as high, seeks the abolition of nuclear weapons, and advocates strongly for steps by the nuclear weapons states toward that end. It places a particular onus on the United States to take additional substantial steps at this time to reduce its reliance on nuclear weapons and otherwise lead by example. It makes a passionate case against nuclear weapons and for disarmament.

The other camp accepts nuclear weapons as necessary and useful, sees risks from both states and nonstate actors, and advocates for retention of U.S. nuclear forces sufficient to U.S. military and political purposes. It rejects the notion that abolition would make the world a safer place. It resists continued steps to marginalize nuclear weapons in U.S. security strategy. Its case for nuclear weapons is pragmatic but not passionate in the way of the disarmers.

These two camps do not debate each other so much as they pursue competing agendas. Though there are examples of respectful discourse between them, adherents of each camp are generally contemptuous of the views of the other. Given the long-standing and deep divisions between these two camps, agreement on policy is rare.

One practical result of this divergence has been gridlock in Congress, which has found it difficult to produce decisions in support of any particular nuclear policies. Looking for a way out of this gridlock, in 2007 Congress created a commission, with an equal mix of Democrats and Republicans, and essentially asked it two simple questions. Is there any basis for a renewal of bipartisanship sufficient to sustain U.S. nuclear policy over the longer term? If so, what is it? Despite strong differences of opinion on many matters, members of the Strategic Posture Commission converged on a hopeful note. Policy continuity is possible, they argued, on the basis of a balanced approach that combines political efforts to reduce and ultimately eliminate threats with military efforts to deter existing threats.

Seven years later, a third camp has not coalesced around this balanced approach. This is so despite the fact that the Obama administration embraced this approach and used it as a guide in developing and implementing its nuclear policy. Adherents of the other two camps sometimes praise the virtues of the balanced approach, but rarely are such words followed by deeds of advocacy in support of policy initiatives that depart from the canon of their camp.

This book will not remake these fundamental contours of the U.S. debate on nuclear policy and posture. But it can help to inform the coming debate and to shift it onto more productive grounds. Toward this end, it has a number of objectives.

One is to review and assess the experience of the Obama administration in working to create the conditions that would allow the United States and other states with nuclear weapons to take additional steps in the future to reduce the role and number of such weapons. The administration has made a serious, sustained, and high-level effort toward this end. Yet, despite some important achievements, the overall results are disappointing. The lessons are many.

A second objective is to review and assess the experience of the Obama administration in working to adapt nuclear deterrence to 21st-century purposes. Having declared that nuclear deterrence should be effective so long as nuclear weapons remain, President Obama directed the Department of Defense to ensure that nuclear deterrence will be effective for the problems for which it is relevant in the 21st century. This work has revealed important insights into the particular new challenges of regional conflicts under the nuclear shadow, of extended deterrence, and of strategic stability. The lessons here, too, are many.

A third objective is to review and assess the "balanced approach." The Obama administration has made a good faith effort to implement this approach even as the world around it has changed in significant and worrisome ways. Does it remain valid? If so, what does it require, and what will it require of future administrations?

A final objective is to fill a key gap in the current debate. As it now stands, the case made for U.S. nuclear weapons is not robust. It stands on assertions about the enduring value of nuclear weapons in preventing major power war. Whether nuclear weapons will continue to be effective in preventing limited wars among major powers is an open question. Moreover, this case lacks the fidelity needed to determine which capabilities are needed. This book sets out a somewhat different case for U.S. nuclear weapons, drawn from the preceding analysis.

In support of these objectives, this volume proceeds as follows. It begins with a more complete characterization of the current debate about U.S. nuclear policy and posture than possible in this introduction. Chapter 1 reviews the evolution of U.S. nuclear policy and posture from the end of the Cold War to today, highlighting elements of both change and continuity. It also reviews relevant developments in the external analytical and political communities with an eye to understanding their influences on the policy-making process.

Subsequent chapters explore U.S. efforts to adapt deterrence to 21st-century purposes and to bring into being the conditions necessary to safely take further steps to reduce the role and number of nuclear weapons. Chapter 2 turns to the new strategic problem posed by the proliferation to regional actors like North Korea of nuclear weapons, other weapons of mass destruction, and the long-range missiles to deliver them. I call this "the first new strategic problem" because it is without precedent in the Cold War and because it took shape before some newer problems for the U.S. strategic posture.

This chapter develops a heuristic device for understanding the deterrence challenges for the United States posed by a nuclear-armed North Korea and perhaps by other nuclear-armed regional challengers in the future. It sets out a spectrum of deterrence challenges from the lowest to the highest ends of conflict. This spectrum helps to illuminate the possible ways in which such a conflict might escalate and deescalate and thus the decision points that the United States will want to influence with an eye to inducing adversary restraint.

To better understand how potential U.S. regional adversaries might think about their escalation and deescalation strategies in conflict with the United States, this chapter invokes an old, contentious, but still useful term: *theory of victory*. For historians of nuclear deterrence, this term conjures up Cold War debates about whether leaders in the Soviet Union actually believed that general war involving the large-scale use of nuclear weapons could be fought and won (or believed that a general war in Europe could be fought and won without crossing the nuclear threshold). It also invokes debates about whether the United States could or should have had such a theory during the Cold War. Those are important debates, but they attach a particular meaning to the term that is uniquely associated with the Cold War.

Today, the term is useful for coming to terms with the thinking done by potential U.S. adversaries about how to manage the risks of escalation against a militarily superior foe and otherwise to secure their interests when in conflict or confrontation with the United States. It is difficult to find solid evidence that any such potential adversary believes that it can fight and win a major nuclear war against the United States. But there is some evidence that such potential adversaries have developed nuclear theories of victory over the United States in two senses. The first is in the Clausewitzian sense (in which war is a continuation of politics by other means, and thus victory is a "culminating point" in war when one side chooses to accept an outcome on political terms dictated by the other rather than bear the costs and risks of continued war). The second is in the sense of Sun Tzu (in which war is a failure of policy, and thus victory entails subduing the enemy without fighting).

There is good reason to be skeptical about the theories of victory being developed by potential U.S. adversaries and the available evidence. After all, the leaders of states fearful of U.S. military intervention must convey to U.S. leaders their intentions and capabilities to stand up to the United States. This is a domestic political requirement for them and may also have some international benefits. Moreover, the existing evidence is piecemeal, incomplete, and of varying degrees of credibility. It is difficult to assess whether the available evidence reflects coherent and complete military doctrines and political strategies or instead reflects a mix of wishful thinking and propaganda. Accordingly, it is important to let the evidence speak for itself and to resist knitting together a military logic for nuclear war that political leaders of these countries might find difficult to embrace.

But the cumulative body of available evidence sends a strong message: that a few potential adversaries have thought in a serious and sustained way about conflict with the United States under the shadow cast by nuclear weapons, both theirs and ours. They may believe that they can engage in nuclear coercion and blackmail and that, in extremis, they could resort to nuclear employment and escape conflict with the United States with some of their main interests intact. The United States would be ill served by simply waiting for more evidence. Even as we look for more such evidence, we must begin to come to terms with their potential theories of victory. Our historical experience of nuclear war as unthinkable should not blind us to the possibility that it has been made thinkable for the leaders of countries with a different historical experience and a different strategic problem. After all, history is replete with adversaries acting in ways we see as irrational in light of their interests as we understand them. Their nuclear aggression might seem suicidal to us, and thus implausible, but it might in extremis seem to them to be a risk worth taking to secure regime survival or some other core interest.

Accordingly, Chapter 2 makes the case that there is evidence, albeit imperfect and incomplete, that North Korea's leaders have a small number of nuclear-backed theories of victory. The term is then invoked again in the subsequent analyses of Russia and China, not to suggest that they have nuclear strategies akin to the Soviet Union but to explore their thinking about how to exploit the shadow cast by their nuclear weapons to avoid war with the United States and to prevail if war proves unavoidable. To encompass the thinking of multiple potential U.S. adversaries about this problem, I sometimes refer to "Red theories of victory" as a shorthand.

Chapter 3 sets out the response of the United States to the new strategic problem posed by regional challengers armed with nuclear weapons and long-range delivery systems. It characterizes a continued but changed role for U.S. nuclear weapons in meeting these new challenges in the context of a comprehensive approach to adapting and strengthening regional deterrence architectures. This chapter also sets out a "Blue theory of victory"—another shorthand, in this case encompassing a set of hypotheses about how the United States can manage escalation and deescalation in a confrontation with a nuclear-armed state in a manner that safeguards its interests. This Blue theory, like its Red counterparts, has elements of both Clausewitz and Sun Tzu, in that it is about achieving U.S. objectives in peacetime as in crisis and war. The formulation offered here is the author's and relies on the heuristic device from Chapter 2 (the spectrum of deterrence challenges) to map out the problem space.

The book then turns to the U.S. relationships with Russia and China, in Chapters 4 and 5 respectively. The analysis highlights the similarities and differences between these two cases, not least in terms of their impact on U.S. nuclear policy and posture. Chapter 4 on Russia reviews more than two decades of effort by leaders in both Washington and Moscow to move the bilateral relationship in a positive new direction and the sharp turning point in Russian policy in spring 2014. Chapter 5 on China reviews the parallel history in the U.S.–China relationship and the potential for a future turning point in Chinese policy. The Obama administration has put the spotlight on strategic stability as the organizing concept for the nuclear relationship with both countries, as a counterpoint to a spotlight on deterrence. It has encountered myriad challenges in advancing an agenda to strengthen strategic stability with both countries.

Relations with U.S. allies in Europe and Northeast Asia under the so-called nuclear umbrella are the focus of Chapters 6 and 7 respectively. Extended deterrence is the provision of nuclear-backed security guarantees to U.S. allies (more precisely, to a select group of them). The changed and changing requirements of extended deterrence have been little studied in the United States with the passing of the Cold War. Yet the United States continues to provide security guarantees to more than forty allies in three regions (Europe, Northeast Asia, and the Middle East), and some of them feel strongly pressured by new developments in their security environments, whether those be the ambitions of a newly nuclear-armed neighbor (as in Northeast Asia) or uncertainty about the strategic intentions of a neighboring major power (as in both Europe and Northeast Asia). Some of these allies have returned to fundamental questions about whether the United States is a credible guarantor of their security, especially their security from nuclear threats.

Chapter 8 summarizes the key insights from the preceding two chapters as they bear on the question of the assurance of allies. It invokes the so-called Healey theorem (in reference to a former British defense minister) to the effect that assuring allies that they will escape coercion, aggression, and the costs of war is more politically challenging than deterring potential adversaries. It does so to set out an assessment of the current state of assurance of U.S. allies under the U.S. nuclear umbrella.

This chapter also challenges the reader to think more broadly about the assurance requirements of U.S. nuclear strategy. Other actors require assurance of various forms—including U.S. allies and partners not under the nuclear umbrella, other states that foreswore the right to nuclear weapons when they joined the Nuclear Non-Proliferation Treaty (NPT), even U.S. enemies (who require a unique form of assurance for our deterrence strategies to function as desired). This chapter also considers the unique challenges of assuring the three major powers—the United States, Russia, and China—that their strategic restraint will not be exploited by another power. The chapter concludes with the argument that its possession of nuclear weapons helps to assure the United States that the risks and burdens of international leadership are bearable.

Chapter 9 sets out my conclusions from this work. It draws on the lessons of the Obama administration and its predecessors, as distilled in the intervening chapters, in adapting U.S. deterrence strategies to new circumstances and in trying to create the conditions to (1) make additional substantial changes to the number of nuclear weapons in the U.S. arsenal and to their role in U.S. security strategies and (2) enable other nuclear-armed states to join with us in future steps. Here I argue that the time is not ripe for additional substantial changes. Quite simply, other states are not prepared to join us at this time in such steps, and additional unilateral action would serve the United States poorly.

This argument culminates in a restatement of the case for U.S. nuclear weapons. It derives from the lessons noted in the preceding pages and from the requirements of the Blue theory of victory in both crisis/war and peacetime. It does not contradict the existing case for nuclear weapons. It adds fidelity and amplification drawn from the current security context and in a way that informs choices about needed U.S. capabilities. Significantly, it is not a case for nuclear weapons in perpetuity. Looking twenty-five or fifty years into the future, there is no reason to preclude the possibility of changes in the security environment that could substantially reduce the need for U.S. nuclear weapons. But neither can they be assumed today.

The closing chapter considers implications. This epilogue returns to the opening chapter and asks, "Where do we go from here?" in light of the conclusions and lessons learned. It poses some basic questions about whether the approach to nuclear policy and posture in place since the end of the Cold War still makes sense in today's world and considers potential adjustments.

This short summary of the scope and structure of the book invites a clear statement about what the book is not: It is not a book about every aspect of U.S. nuclear policy and strategy. It does not address a variety of questions that are important but unrelated to questions of U.S. nuclear deterrence policy and posture. What more can be done to strengthen the nonproliferation regime? What more can be done to reduce the risks of nuclear terrorism? What might be the specific elements of a future U.S.–Russian arms control agreement? What should the United States do about the emerging nuclear competition in South Asia? How can it prevent a nuclear tipping point from being crossed in Northeast Asia and the Middle East? Should it try to sustain cooperative threat reduction activities with Russia? How might it expand them with others? These topics belong in any comprehensive discussion of U.S. nuclear policy and strategy, and the argument laid out in this book has implications for many of those questions. However, the focus here is on the key determinants of U.S. deterrence policy and posture.

Nor is this book a comprehensive analysis of all of the conditions that would have to be fulfilled to allow the United States to safely proceed to eliminate its nuclear weapons. A full catalogue of the conditions that would have to be brought into being would include, for example, confidence in a system of international monitoring and compliance enforcement that could be counted on to deal with any aggressor caught surreptitiously producing nuclear weapons. Examining these further conditions is beyond the scope of this volume.[1]

As an analysis of U.S. nuclear policy and posture, this volume draws on my experience in the Obama administration, where I played a leading role in the preparation and implementation of the administration's Nuclear Posture Review as deputy assistant secretary of defense for nuclear and missile defense policy. But it also reaches well beyond this governmental experience, by drawing on insights gained in many years of work as an analyst in the Washington think-tank community. Where I describe and characterize administration policy, I am explicit in doing so. Where I go beyond official policy to amplify or extend ideas with thinking of my own, I do so explicitly. The views expressed here are my personal views and should not be attributed to the Obama administration, the U.S. Departments of Defense and Energy, Stanford University, or any institution with which I have been or am affiliated.

1 The Evolution of U.S. Nuclear Policy and Posture since the End of the Cold War

T O UNDERSTAND THE CURRENT MOMENT IN U.S. NUCLEAR policy and debate, some historical perspective is useful. U.S. nuclear policy used to be at the center of the U.S. national security debate; as it has become marginalized over the last three decades, it has become increasingly difficult to see the elements of continuity and change in U.S. policy and to understand the lessons of past experience for current and future policy.

This chapter begins with a summary of the nuclear inheritance from the Cold War in terms of the policy and posture in place in 1990. It then reviews the evolution of policy and posture with each subsequent presidential administration. This review includes also developments in the nongovernmental expert community that influenced U.S. policy. Following on this chronological overview, the chapter then identifies elements of change and continuity in U.S. nuclear policy and posture over the last twenty-five years. The chapter then pivots to the twenty-five years ahead. It sets out some critical decisions that must be made about the future of U.S. nuclear posture. This analysis highlights the weakness of the intellectual and political foundations on which such decisions will be made.

The Cold War Inheritance

With the collapse of the Soviet Union on Christmas Day 1991, one chapter in U.S. nuclear history ended and another began. At that time, U.S. nuclear policy and posture reflected the long-standing bipolar standoff and decades of technically driven arms competition with the Soviet Union.

Following the modernization of the U.S. nuclear posture in the 1980s, the U.S. nuclear arsenal contained approximately 21,000 weapons in late 1991. The triad of strategic nuclear delivery systems (submarine-launched ballistic missiles [SLBMs], land-based intercontinental-range ballistic missiles [ICBMs], and strategic bombers) was completing a cycle of modernization, along with the associated warheads. U.S. nuclear weapons were also deployed in both Europe and East Asia. This large force was supported by a modern command and control system ensuring presidential control of nuclear operations even under nuclear attack. The overall size and structure of U.S. nuclear forces were a function of the requirements of deterrence of the Soviet Union and Warsaw Pact, with any other contingency deemed a lesser-included problem. The standing force was supported by a robust research, development, and production capacity for both warheads and delivery systems.

In 1990, the United States and Soviet Union were actively pursuing arms control across a broad front, following the thaw in their political relations. The Treaty on Intermediate-range Nuclear Forces (INF) was being implemented, having been agreed in December 1987, leading to the elimination of such weapons from the arsenals of both the Soviet Union and United States. The treaty on Conventional Forces in Europe (CFE) was concluded in November 1990 to reorient military forces away from the Cold War standoff. The first Strategic Arms Reduction Treaty (START) was in negotiation and would ultimately be signed in July 1991.

The deterrence strategy then in place was based on formal presidential guidance provided early in the Reagan administration. That guidance stipulated that:

> The most fundamental national security objective is to deter direct attack—particularly nuclear attack—on the United States and its Allies. Should nuclear attack nonetheless occur, the United States and its allies must prevail. . . . Stated otherwise, we must be prepared to wage war successfully.[1]

This strategy informed the Single Integrated Operational Plan (SIOP) for the employment of U.S. nuclear weapons (which is possible only under the personal authority of the president). That plan's primary purpose was deterrence of attack. If deterrence were to fail and the Soviets to conduct attacks on the United States or its allies, the United States would have sought to use nuclear weapons in ways it hoped would restore deterrence. U.S. attacks would have been conducted not to annihilate the entirety of Soviet society but to put at risk those military, economic, and political assets most valued by Soviet leadership.[2]

The injunction in the strategy to be prepared to "prevail" was hotly contested outside government and anathema to many in the West because it seemed to imply that nuclear wars could be won. It seemed oddly dissonant, coming from a president who also argued publicly that "a nuclear war cannot be won and must never be fought."[3] In a statement explaining this strategy a few years later, one of its principal architects, Leon Sloss, argued as follows: "While it was difficult to foresee anyone winning such a conflict, it seemed far preferable to set a national goal of 'prevailing' rather than, say, 'losing.'"[4] Bernard Brodie made a similar point earlier in the Cold War: "So long as there is a finite chance of war, we have to be interested in outcomes, and although all outcomes would be bad, some would be much worse than others."[5]

Notably, this guidance followed debate about how the new capabilities being developed and deployed would create the conditions for success in war. Critics argued that the United States lacked a theory of victory to guide its investments and ensure that deterrence would be strengthened. In the words of Colin Gray in 1979,

> Our real problem . . . is that the United States (and NATO-Europe) lacks a theory of victory in war (or satisfactory war termination). If, basically, one has no war aims (one has no image of enforced and favorable war termination, or of how the balance of power may be structured in a post-war world), on what grounds does one select a strategic nuclear employment policy, and how does one know how to choose an appropriate strategic posture?[6]

By this definition, a theory of victory is a set of concepts for how to force termination of a war in a manner favorable to one's objectives and to achieve an acceptable post-war balance of power. The preceding Sloss statement would imply that the United States had a narrowly conceived theory of victory. Whether the Soviets had a theory of victory for nuclear war remains in debate.[7]

In the Cold War, the development of U.S. nuclear policy and posture was supported by substantial long-term investment in the associated intellectual infrastructure, with financial resources flowing from the Defense Nuclear Agency and other parts of the nuclear establishment for analytic work on deterrence. The development and implementation of policy was enabled by strong capacities inside government. The president, for example, could turn to his Arms Control and Disarmament Agency for analysis and advice, while the secretary of defense had an assistant reporting directly to him on the technical aspects of nuclear forces. In the legislative branch, the Senate Arms Control Observers Group ensured informed congressional engagement with the executive branch on nuclear treaty issues.

The George H. W. Bush Administration

The George H. W. Bush administration moved quickly to seize the opportunities presented by the end of the Cold War to remake the U.S. nuclear posture and strategy. It made some basic changes to U.S. nuclear deterrence strategy, such as eliminating all targets in the former Warsaw Pact from the U.S. plan.[8] It also tried to shift the focus of leaders in both Washington and Moscow from mutual deterrence to cooperative threat reduction. A primary reason for doing so was concern for the safety and security of nuclear weapons and materials of the former Soviet Union and the possibility that they might fall into the hands of proliferators or terrorists.

To advance this agenda, the Bush administration relied heavily on unilateral pledges to limit and reduce nuclear weapons made on a reciprocal basis with Moscow. Called the Presidential Nuclear Initiatives, such pledges were politically but not legally binding. On September 27, 1991, President Bush announced multiple decisions to remake the U.S. nuclear posture: (1) to stand down from alert all U.S. strategic bombers, (2) to stand down from alert all ICBMs scheduled for deactivation under START, (3) to terminate development of mobile ICBMs, (4) to cancel the replacement program for a modern short-range attack missile for bombers, (5) to consolidate command of all strategic forces under a single commander, (6) to withdraw to the United States all ground-launched short-range weapons deployed overseas and to destroy them along with existing U.S. stockpiles of these weapons, and (7) to cease deployment of tactical nuclear weapons on surface ships, attack submarines, and land-based naval aircraft during "normal circumstances."[9]

On October 5, 1991, Soviet President Mikhail Gorbachev announced reciprocal Russian steps. These included elimination of all nuclear artillery munitions, nuclear warheads for tactical missiles, and nuclear mines; removal of all tactical nuclear weapons from surface ships and multipurpose submarines;

and separation of nuclear weapons from air defense missiles and storing or destroying them. These decisions were reaffirmed following the collapse of the Soviet Union in December 1991 by new Russian President Boris Yeltsin. Yeltsin also went a step further. In response to a second round of U.S. nuclear weapons cutbacks focused on strategic forces, Yeltsin opted to eliminate one-third of Russia's sea-based tactical nuclear weapons, half of its ground-to-air nuclear missile warheads, and half of its stockpile of airborne tactical nuclear weapons.[10]

On the arms control front, the Bush administration secured ratification and entry into force of the START treaty. Implementation proceeded over the decade, leading to reductions by 2001 in deployed U.S. strategic forces of approximately one-third. The Bush administration also negotiated and signed START II, which provided for an additional cut of roughly an additional one-third. The fate of this treaty proved more problematic (as discussed further in the following pages). The administration also helped to negotiate the Lisbon Protocol after the disintegration of the Soviet Union, an agreement among Belarus, Kazakhstan, Russia, and Ukraine ensuring that Russia assumed all Soviet nuclear treaty obligations.

At the same time, the Bush administration became concerned by the revelations about weapons of mass destruction (WMD) in Iraq's arsenal as it moved to expel Iraq from Kuwait in the Persian Gulf War of 1990 and 1991. A defense posture review led by Secretary of Defense Richard Cheney coined the term *rogue state* and began to shift the focus of military planners to the challenge of dealing with regional adversaries armed with WMD and potentially willing to employ them for purposes of regime survival.[11] This invited new questions about the reliability of deterrence, nuclear and otherwise, in meeting new, post–Cold War security challenges.

The Clinton Administration

The Clinton administration arrived in 1993 with a commitment to revamp national strategy in a comprehensive fashion to address the opportunities and challenges presented by the end of the Cold War. An early priority was the development of an updated National Security Strategy. The resulting "National Security Strategy of Engagement and Enlargement" struck a positive note, emphasizing "unparalleled opportunities to make our nation safer and more prosperous."[12] But it also highlighted the emergence of "more diverse" dangers in a changing world and characterized the proliferation of WMD as "a major challenge to our security" that could substantially complicate the effort to engage internationally and enlarge the community of democracies.[13] The strategy also expressed a strong commitment to arms control and non-proliferation and other forms of political cooperation to address and reduce nuclear dangers.

Secretary of Defense Les Aspin came to the Pentagon at this time with a determination to lead a broad reform of defense strategy. For decades, U.S. military forces had been designed primarily for confrontation with an enemy roughly equal in power and influence (a "peer adversary"), now gone. More-over, there was the wake-up call to a new set of problems provided by the war to expel Iraq from Kuwait. Aspin's first major initiative was a bottom-up review (BUR) of defense strategy and capabilities. This review gave a promi-nent place to a new defense counter-proliferation initiative (DCI)—an effort to ensure that U.S. forces would be capable of meeting the military challenges posed by the proliferation of WMD. Aspin was particularly motivated by the role reversal evident in the new security environment: in the past, he argued, the United States had used nuclear weapons to deter the use of force against its interests and allies by the Soviet Union and the Warsaw Pact; looking to the present and future, he argued, the United States was at risk of becoming "the deteree" as regional challengers acquire WMD to thwart its power projection strategy.[14]

On conclusion of the BUR in autumn 1993, Aspin initiated a compre-hensive review of the U.S. nuclear posture—what became the first Nuclear Posture Review (NPR).[15] This was an internal review by the Department of Defense (DOD) of what to do with the inherited Cold War force structure in light of a radically changed security environment. The review set out a new approach to nuclear strategy, summarized as "lead but hedge." The United States would take steps to lead in reducing nuclear dangers, threats, and risks after the Cold War. At the same time, the United States would ensure that it would be well prepared for the possibility of a sudden collapse of political reform in Russia and the reemergence in Moscow of a government hostile to the United States and the West. In his press briefing on the NPR results in September 1994, Aspin's successor, William Perry, expressed his view that "the new posture . . . is no longer based on Mutual Assured Destruction, no longer based on MAD. We have coined a new word for our new posture which we called Mutual Assured Safety, or MAS."[16]

The effort to "lead" focused primarily on working cooperatively with Russia to reduce Cold War–vintage arsenals and contain the risks of unsafeguarded materials and technologies. While it sought to have Russia bring into force the START II treaty negotiated by its predecessor, the Clinton administration also began discussions with Russia on the possibility of a new strategic arms treaty (later referred to informally as START III). As discussed further in Chapter 4, both of these efforts came to naught. It also signed the Comprehensive Test Ban Treaty and sought Senate consent to ratification. But the Senate rejected the CTBT as inadequately verifiable and damaging to the effectiveness of U.S. nuclear forces, though the United States has abided by its provisions in follow up.[17] The effort to hedge focused primarily on maintaining the means to reconstitute dismantled strategic forces if Russia were to choose to abandon the arms control process and reconstitute dismantled forces of its own.

The 1994 NPR expressed a clear continuing role for U.S. nuclear weapons in U.S. security. Specifically, that role was "to deter any future hostile leadership with access to strategic nuclear forces from acting against our vital interests and to convince it that seeking a nuclear advantage would be futile."[18] The review expressed a continued nuclear commitment to NATO but also the need to adapt deterrence concepts to a new international environment. The review also catalogued the many changes to U.S. nuclear forces in the short period since the end of the Cold War. By 1994:

- No nuclear weapons were in the custody of U.S. ground forces.
- Naval nonstrategic nuclear forces were no longer deployed at sea.
- Strategic bombers had been taken off of day-to-day alert.
- The total active warhead stockpile had been reduced 50 percent.
- The number of deployed strategic warheads had been reduced 47 percent.
- The number of deployed nonstrategic nuclear weapons had been reduced by about 90 percent, as had the number of U.S. nuclear weapons in the NATO stockpile.
- The number of nuclear weapons storage locations had been reduced by 75 percent.
- The number of personnel with access to nuclear weapons had been reduced by 70 percent.

- Many delivery systems in development at the end of the Cold War had been terminated, including a new small ICBM and various new tactical missiles.

- The deployment of some new systems had been truncated, including the Peacekeeper ICBM, the B-1 and B-2 bombers, and a new submarine ballistic missile warhead. The planned number of ballistic missile submarines was also reduced from twenty-four to eighteen.

- Multiple weapon systems had been retired without replacement, including nuclear artillery projectiles and nuclear depth bombs.

- Spending on U.S. strategic nuclear forces had been reduced from $47.8 billion in 1984 to $13.5 billion in 1994.

The BUR, DCI, and NPR were followed by the 1994 Quadrennial Defense Review, which introduced the term *major theater wars* as a focus of military planning. Later in the decade, the success of North Korea and others in developing long-range ballistic missiles led to a surprising new political agreement in support of limited national missile defense. The National Missile Defense Act of 1999 stated that it is the policy of the United States to "deploy as soon as is technologically possible an effective National Missile Defense system capable of defending the territory of the United States against limited ballistic missile attack (whether accidental, unauthorized, or deliberate)."[19] The Clinton administration sought changes to the Anti-Ballistic Missile Treaty with Russia to allow an effective limited defense of the U.S. homeland.

In 1997 the administration revised the presidential nuclear guidance. This was the first revision to the guidance after the end of the Cold War (and replaced the guidance put in place by the Reagan administration in 1981). A senior administration official, Robert Bell, reported that the new policy "recognizes that we're at the end of the Cold War and that nuclear weapons now play a smaller role in our nuclear strategy than at any point during the nuclear era."[20] He went on to report that the new guidance "removes . . . all previous references to being able to wage a nuclear war successfully or to prevail in a nuclear war . . . The emphasis in this PDD [Presidential Decision Directive] is therefore on deterring nuclear wars or the use of nuclear weapons at any level, not fighting them."[21]

Administration documents also began to address the problem of tailoring deterrence to deal with the variety of challenges present in the security environment. This followed from assessments that the United States had pursued a "one size fits all" approach to nuclear deterrence in the Cold War and that such an approach is inadequate for a world in which various regional contingencies might give rise to WMD deterrence challenges, thus requiring deterrence approaches "tailored" to different circumstances.[22]

This new agenda of defense policy concerns gave impetus to a new focus in the analytic community on deterrence challenges different from those of the Cold War. Federally funded research and development centers (FFRDCs) produced some initial thinking exploring the challenges of "tailoring" nuclear deterrence for non-Soviet actors and also of protecting allies neighboring the aggressor. Given the times, there was a heavy emphasis on Iraq for these purposes as a model of the new deterrence problem.[23] Other organizations contributed significantly to the effort to rethink U.S. deterrence policy in light of new challenges.[24]

Nonproliferation policy was also a high priority for the Clinton administration. The year 1995 was a critical turning point for the nonproliferation regime, as decisions needed to be taken internationally about whether and how to extend the Non-Proliferation Treaty (NPT). In the lead-up to the review and extension conference, concerns took shape about the possible implications of a breakdown of the regime and the wider spread of nuclear weapons. Negotiators were successful in securing a commitment to extend the life of the treaty indefinitely and without formal conditions. But this did not definitively settle questions about the long-term effectiveness of the regime or about what nuclear weapon states must contribute to the success of the regime, as discussed further in the following pages.[25]

Also of note in this period were institutional changes bearing on the work of the federal government in making and implementing nuclear strategy. In 1997 (and on the occasion of its fiftieth anniversary year), the Defense Nuclear Agency stood down and was replaced by the Defense Special Weapons Agency (and then the Defense Threat Reduction Agency) with a significantly broader mandate and a shrinking budget.[26] In 1999, the Arms Control and Disarmament Agency was merged into the Department of State, ending four decades of independent advice to the president.[27] At the same time, the Senate Arms Control Observers Group ceased to function.[28] Each of these changes had a significant and negative impact on the capacity of the U.S. government to deal with future nuclear policy issues.

Outside government, there was a rising discussion in the 1990s about the new challenges of deterrence in a post–Cold War era marked by the proliferation of weapons of mass destruction and ballistic missiles to regional actors with interests hostile to those of the United States and its allies. The term *second nuclear age* was first coined at this time to catalyze thinking about the new deterrence landscape. Fred Iklé set down a marker in 1996, arguing that "the nuclear drama has reached the conclusion of its first act" and that a future rupture of the nuclear taboo would compel "a revolution in strategic thinking."[29] Additional markers were put down by Keith Payne and Colin Gray, among others.[30] In his 1996 volume *Deterrence in the Second Nuclear Age*, Payne challenged the confidence of American strategists in the effectiveness of deterrence, arguing that "leaders do make decisions based on calculations that are outside the boundaries of deterrence theory, not only, or even primarily because they are limited by psychopathy. Rather, leaders make decisions based on ignorance, misperception, and a misunderstanding of their opponent's values and likely behavior."[31] This led him to the conclusion that:

> U.S. regional policies should take into account the potential for deterrence failure or irrelevance, in the sense of being prepared to frustrate the challenger's military goals and directly enforce U.S. will. Preparation for deterrence failure suggests the need to move toward "deterrence by denial," recognizing that the forces supporting regional deterrence threats should not be too far removed from the forces that actually would prove militarily useful.[32]

Gray echoed Payne's concerns about the unreliability of deterrence but framed the second nuclear age in somewhat different terms, arguing that the "second nuclear age can be seen as a period of interregnum between irregular cyclical surges in the kind of great power rivalry that organizes many strands in the course of strategic history."[33]

This line of argument illuminated shifting thinking in the United States and the West more generally about the changing roles of nuclear weapons. As Laurence Freedman argued,

> Throughout the cold war the concept of deterrence was central to all strategic discourse. . . . As is often the case with orthodoxies, deterrence began to attract the mockery and disgust of the disaffected and hostile. Then, abruptly, with the end of the cold war, it was no longer orthodox. . . . From dominating Western strategic thinking, it moved to the margins.[34]

As these and other experts began to debate the contours of a second nu-clear age, other experts focused on the continued challenges of escaping the first nuclear age. These experts generally adhered to the view that much more could and should be done to reduce the dangers left by Cold War–vintage nuclear arsenals—and that the new threats put no special demands on the U.S. nuclear deterrent.[35] These differences of perspective and priority reflected the emergence of two different camps in the U.S. expert community, each with its own assumptions and policy agenda.[36]

The George W. Bush Administration

Like its predecessor, the new Bush administration sought to start afresh in the making of national security strategy, defense strategy, deterrence strategy, and nuclear policy. It arrived with a deep antipathy to the Clinton administration on many fronts and an abundance of new thinking about how to exercise American power in a changing security environment.

But its efforts to conduct high-level policy reviews and to craft them in the sequence intended by Congress (national security strategy first, then the sub-sidiary military and nuclear reviews) were foiled by circumstance. Its national security strategy was much delayed, not least because of the attacks of 9/11 and the significant rethinking of the objectives and strategies of the administration in the aftermath. The resulting strategy was a powerful reaffirmation of the role of the world's preeminent political, economic, and military power in using its power to shape the world in ways the administration deemed in the best interests of the nation and its allies. Like the Clinton national security strategy, it put emphasis on uncertainty in the security environment as a driver of U.S. security strategy. Unlike the Clinton administration, it put emphasis on what it saw as the urgent need to confront gathering threats "at the crossroads of radicalism and technology. . . . History will judge harshly those who saw this coming danger but failed to act. In the new world we have entered, the only path to peace and security is the path of action."[37] Administration leaders spoke about "a nexus" of terrorism, rogue states, and WMD.[38] Thus the counter-proliferation agenda set out by the Clinton administration was adapted in a manner emphasizing preventative and preemptive action against proliferators.

The administration's NPR came before its national security strategy. It built on a private effort in 1999 and 2000 by a group of Republicans to set out a pathway for the transformation of the U.S. strategic posture to meet the requirements of the so-called second nuclear age. Conducted under Keith Payne's leadership, the study produced a report that became a template for the Bush administration's NPR, not least because so many of its coauthors (including Payne himself) joined the new administration.[39] This report echoed many of the "second nuclear age" ideas, including skepticism about the reliability of deterrence and about arms control. Significantly, the report also reflected the desire of many in this community to take additional steps to further deemphasize nuclear weapons in national security strategy.[40] This template was used by the new Bush national security team to craft its own official NPR.[41]

The incoming administration also had formal guidance from the Congress to conduct a review of the U.S. nuclear posture (there had been no such congressional guidance for the 1994 review). The Congress was concerned about maintaining large standing U.S. nuclear forces as an incentive to persuade Russia to make a decision (to implement START II) it seemed unwilling to make. The resulting official report of the Bush administration's NPR was provided to the Congress but never released in unclassified form. After the classified version was distributed to individuals with the required security clearances, materials appeared on the internet that were allegedly extracts from the classified original. At the unclassified level, the administration provided congressional testimony, a public briefing, and materials in a report by the secretary of defense.[42] A detailed unclassified summary of key points became available in 2005 with an article by Keith Payne, entitled "The Nuclear Posture Review: Setting the Record Straight."[43]

The 2001 NPR was ambitious in scope and thrust and, like so much of the Bush administration's security policy, generated intense debate and strong opposition. There were important innovations on both policy and posture.

On nuclear policy, the 2001 NPR explicitly aligned nuclear strategy with the then-new defense strategy and its four goals: to assure allies, to dissuade potential competitors, to deter aggressors, and to defeat enemies. In this respect, it provided a clear but somewhat different formulation of the role of U.S. nuclear weapons. It also expressed a commitment to further reduce reliance on nuclear weapons and to deemphasize them in U.S. national security strategy. It incorporated thinking in the defense strategy about adapting to uncertainty by shifting from threat-based to capability-based planning (on the argument that in an uncertain environment specific future threats cannot confidently be anticipated, so the United States must instead create the needed suite of capabilities, both nuclear and nonnuclear). It echoed thinking set out elsewhere by the administration about "a new strategic framework" built around an improved relationship with Moscow and an improving but still very uncertain relationship with China (identified as a "potential adversary"). This thinking also rejected formal arms control on the argument that it was an impediment to both reductions and improvements in the political relationship with Russia.[44] It broke important new ground in the practice of deterrence of Russia, with the conclusion that Russia should not be the basis of day-to-day U.S. nuclear deterrence planning.

Changes to deterrence planning were reflected in the step taken in March 2003 to abandon the long-standing Single Integrated Operational Plan (SIOP) in favor of a more flexible approach. This new approach was intended to provide more flexibility for the president for the use of both nuclear and nonnuclear weapons.[45]

On the nuclear posture, the 2001 NPR expressed a commitment to move toward a "new triad" of offensive strike forces (including nuclear, nonnuclear and nonkinetic means), ballistic missile defense (and in theory, though not in practice, other forms of protection), and a responsive infrastructure (enabling agile responses to changing circumstances). It provided a solution to the dilemma posed by Russia's failure to implement START II in the form of a decision to determine the number of deployed weapons sufficient to U.S. purposes and to reduce forces to that level with or without parallel action by Russia. But it also expressed a commitment to maintain a nuclear posture "second to none" (as a form of reassurance to U.S. allies that they need not worry about Russia gaining nuclear superiority over the United States) and sufficiently large so as to dissuade China from considering a "sprint to parity." In a particularly controversial aspect, the 2001 NPR emphasized a shift in priority from sustainment of aging nuclear weapons to "transformation" of both the weapons complex and the arsenal. Although it did not call for new nuclear weapons for new military purposes, as some have claimed, it did call for the capability to "modify, upgrade, or replace portions of the extant nuclear force or develop concepts for follow-on nuclear weapon systems better suited to the nation's needs."[46]

To enable unfettered development of ballistic missile defenses, the administration withdrew from the ABM Treaty—a move strongly opposed by Moscow (and many Democrats).[47] In reaction to shifting U.S. thinking about the role and value of arms control, President Putin was strongly motivated to maintain an arms control framework with the United States. He was successful in persuading President Bush to formulate an agreement based on the planned numerical reductions in the U.S. arsenal. Signed in May 2002, the Strategic Offensive Reductions Treaty (SORT), otherwise known as the Moscow Treaty, committed the two countries to reduce their operationally deployed strategic forces to between 2,200 and 1,700 weapons by December 31, 2012. The START I treaty also remained in force and provided verification mechanisms lacking in SORT.

The numerical limits agreed in the treaty reflected separate thinking by the Bush administration about the needed size of the U.S. nuclear arsenal in light of changing international circumstances. In a communication to the Senate in June 2002, President Bush explained this thinking and linkage:

> On November 13, 2001, I announced the United States plan for such cuts—to reduce our operationally deployed strategic nuclear warheads to a level of between 1700 and 2200 over the next decade. I announced these planned reductions following a careful study within the Department of Defense. That study, the Nuclear Posture Review, concluded that these force levels were sufficient to maintain the security of the United States. In reaching this decision, I recognized that it would be preferable for the United States to make such reductions on a reciprocal basis with Russia, but that the United States would be prepared to proceed unilaterally.[48]

Essentially, the treaty reflected changes to the U.S. stockpile that the Bush administration was making unilaterally, which the Russians then joined in a legally binding framework.

Some amplification of the administration's thinking about nuclear policy came in 2005 in conjunction with the NPT review conference. The administration offered a strong statement of the progress of the United States in implementing Article VI of the Nuclear Non-Proliferation Treaty (NPT). It also sent out its disarmament ambassador, Christopher Ford, with innovative thinking about how to ensure security in a world in which nuclear weapons have been eliminated.[49]

Implementation of the George W. Bush administration's NPR was stymied by many factors. The administration's efforts to begin the modernization of the nuclear arsenal were repeatedly rejected by Congress (as it failed to support plans for the Robust Nuclear Earth Penetrator and the Reliable Replacement Warhead). The effort to develop other elements of the "new triad" was slow and controversial; for example, the effort to develop a system for the prompt delivery of nonnuclear weapons at long ranges was ultimately not supported by the Congress (as it rejected the administration's proposal to replace nuclear with conventional weapons aboard a small number of Trident ballistic missiles aboard submarines). This reflected general opposition within the Congress to much of the Bush administration's national security policy.

Over time, the administration's push for missile defense, doubts about the effectiveness of nuclear deterrence for new problems, and repeated calls to reduce reliance on nuclear weapons contributed to a significant loss of leadership engagement in moving forward the nuclear aspects of the nuclear policy review. Ironically, as the administration was being attacked from outside for seeking new nuclear weapons for new military purposes, there seemed to be very little commitment high inside the administration to maintaining a credible and effective nuclear deterrent.

This loss of leadership focus on the deterrence mission was cast into sharp relief by an incident in August 2007, when an Air Force crew mistakenly loaded a B-52 with six cruise missiles, each loaded with a live nuclear warhead, and then flew them across the country from one air base to another. The nuclear warheads in the missiles were supposed to have been removed before taking the missiles from their storage bunker. Following multiple investigations, both the secretary of the Air Force and the Air Force chief of staff were relieved of their duties by Secretary of Defense Gates. Gates asked former Secretary of Defense James Schlesinger to lead a broader review and offer recommendations. His two reports detailed a significant loss of leadership focus and institutional excellence for nuclear deterrence within the Air Force and much more broadly across the Department of Defense. They also emphasized the corrosive effects of repeated high-level statements about reducing reliance on nuclear weapons.[50]

Late in the Bush administration, the secretaries of defense and energy attempted to renew momentum around the main objectives of the 2001 NPR with an unclassified report on nuclear deterrence (the Gates-Bodman report).[51] The report reviewed the administration's progress in reducing the U.S. nuclear arsenal under the START and SORT treaties and in beginning the needed modernization of the aging nuclear arsenal. The report also asserted that the initiatives of the Bush administration were largely consistent with those of its predecessors, including explicitly the "lead but hedge" strategy of the Clinton administration. But this effort to strike a bipartisan tone fell on largely deaf ears in the Congress, where both sides of the aisle were weary of Bush administration policies and focused increasingly on the change of administrations due in 2009.

In these years there were also important developments outside the U.S. government that would bear on the future of U.S. nuclear policy and posture. One was broadly rising concern about a possible new wave of nuclear proliferation and "tipping points" in Northeast Asia and the Middle East. In 2004, the United Nations Security Council expressed its concern about this problem, with the argument that "we are approaching a point at which the erosion of the non-proliferation regime could become irreversible and result in a cascade of proliferation."[52] There was renewed attention to the conditions that might lead friends and allies of the United States to resume efforts to acquire nuclear weapons or to enhance their capabilities in case of a future decision to do so—concerns that had been set aside when the states joined the NPT in the 1960s.[53] In 2007, a State Department advisory board issued a report on mitigating the risks of such a proliferation cascade, emphasizing a recommitment to the nonproliferation regime.[54]

In some quarters, the perception had taken hold that U.S. policy had veered too far off course from nonproliferation and disarmament and would thus fail to meet these new challenges. Writing in 2007, former Secretaries Henry Kissinger, William Perry, and George Schulz, joined by Senator Sam Nunn (and thus the oft-used shorthand, "Gang of Four") made a forceful public case for renewing the U.S. commitment to the ultimate abolition of nuclear weapons:

> Nuclear weapons today present tremendous dangers but also a historic opportunity. U.S. leadership will be required to take the world to the next stage—to a solid consensus for reversing reliance on nuclear weapons globally as a vital contribution to preventing their proliferation into potentially dangerous hands, and ultimately ending them as a threat to the world. . . . Reassertion of the vision of a world free of nuclear weapons and practical measures toward achieving that goal would be, and would be perceived as, a bold initiative consistent with America's moral heritage.[55]

They argued further that the "first and foremost" objective should be "to turn the goal of a world without nuclear weapons into a joint enterprise" with the leaders of the other nuclear weapon states. And they cautioned that "reliance on nuclear weapons for [deterrence] is becoming increasingly hazardous and decreasingly effective."[56]

The four further elaborated their thinking in a second article in 2008, in which they identified a large number of steps that the United States could take in partnership with Russia and also unilaterally to reduce nuclear dangers associated with their own nuclear deterrents, including further steps to de-alert nuclear forces, discard outdated operational plans, and accelerate cooperation on the security of warheads and fissile materials. They argued in favor of U.S. ratification of the Comprehensive Test Ban Treaty (CTBT). They also argued that "there should be an agreement to undertake further reductions in U.S. and Russian nuclear forces beyond those recorded in the U.S.–Russia Strategic Offensive Reductions Treaty. As the reductions proceed, other nations would become involved."[57]

Their initiative had wide-ranging repercussions in the United States and abroad. Presidential candidates Barack Obama and John McCain both endorsed the goal of a world free of nuclear weapons while they campaigned for the White House.[58] Think tanks in the United States and Europe focused renewed energies on how to accelerate arms control and disarmament processes. They found a new measure of support from the foundation community, willing to invest in nuclear-focused studies for the first time in two decades. A Global Zero movement formed to advance the disarmament objective and gained the participation of influential individuals from around the world.[59] A separate International Commission on Nuclear Non-Proliferation and Disarmament was formed as a joint initiative of the Australian and Japanese governments, with the aim of reinvigorating international efforts on both objectives. An International Campaign to Abolish Nuclear Weapons was also formed to promote negotiation of a treaty banning nuclear weapons within a fixed period of time.

As this work began to gain momentum, there was a refocusing and expansion of work on the so-called second nuclear age. The thinking of various analysts had converged around the proposition that the second nuclear age will be the Asian nuclear age. The need to fit Asia more clearly into the emerging picture of the future nuclear order had started with the nuclear tests conducted by India and Pakistan in 1998 but gained urgency with North Korea's progress in developing and testing nuclear weapons, and China's nuclear modernization program. Thérèse Delpech helped launch this discourse with an essay arguing that "the most complex nuclear questions are located in Asia."[60] Paul Bracken added new momentum to thinking about this problem with a book exploring the impact on regional stability of the proliferation of missiles and WMD into Asia. He argued:

> It is easy to forget just how much the cold war was a European affair that spilled over into regions, and how deeply Eurocentric nearly everything about the first nuclear age really was . . . The second nuclear age is driven by national insecurities that are not comprehensible to outsiders whose security is not endangered. Its metaphors are fundamentally different from those of the cold war, grounded in Munich and the Cuban missile crisis.[61]

A key addition to this discussion came in the form of a 2008 volume entitled *The Long Shadow: Nuclear Weapons and Security in 21st Century Asia*. The editor, Muthiah Alagappa of the East-West Center, offered the important proposition that the effect of nuclear proliferation will ultimately be a stabilizing and positive one, as "Asian countries are not immune to the logic of that [nuclear] revolution."[62]

Not all of the exploration of the "second nuclear age" in this period focused on the Asian nuclear question. Writing in *Foreign Affairs* in 2006, Stephen Rosen argued that "nuclear proliferation is once again at the top of the U.S. national security agenda. Practically all of the discussion about the issue has centered on how to prevent proliferation. . . . few observers have spent much time considering what a postproliferation world would look like."[63] Rosen went on to argue:

> Some future nuclear actors might think that resorting to these weapons would serve their interests. It is not inconceivable, for example, that some state or group might want to show the rest of the world that it is willing and able to violate the most hallowed norms of the international system. Nazi Germany deliberately targeted civilian refugees in Poland in 1939 and in the Netherlands and France in 1940 as part of its strategy of *Schrecklichkeit* (instilling terror) . . . What kind of state might attempt such a thing? If history is any guide, a state that openly rejects the existing international order, considers its opponents to be less than fully human, and seeks to intimidate others. . . . By far . . . the most plausible use of nuclear weapons would involve a nuclear power that found itself on the losing side of a nonnuclear war. Such a state would be faced with a choice not between maintaining peace and initiating nuclear war but between

accepting its impending defeat and gambling that escalation might suddenly end the fighting without defeat.[64]

This exploration of the potential implications of a future use of nuclear weapons is a powerful reminder of how much American thinking about the nuclear future is colored by the expectation that the taboo against use is strong and that nuclear use in the future is unlikely, except perhaps by an irrational nonstate actor. Whether the taboo is durable remains an open question. Whether nuclear use is plausible is also an open question. What is not open is the impact of such use on perceptions—which would be dramatic and widespread.[65]

The Obama Administration

Like the Bush administration's NPR of eight years earlier, the Obama administration's NPR had some important antecedents.

One was the call by the "Gang of Four" for "a bold initiative" to take practical steps toward the long-term goal of nuclear disarmament with the ambition of reinvigorating the nonproliferation effort. This was embraced by candidate Obama and then reflected in the new president's speech in Prague in April 2009, in which he expressed his commitment to "the safety and security of a world free of nuclear weapons." Accordingly, his administration was directed to identify steps that could be taken safely to reduce the role and number of nuclear weapons and to create the conditions for further such steps in the future by the United States and by other nuclear-armed nations. The president also stated in Prague that fulfillment of this objective is a long-term goal—and promised that the U.S. nuclear deterrent would remain safe, secure, and effective until that goal is achieved.[66] Accordingly, his administration was directed to identify steps to ensure nuclear deterrence would remain effective for the problems for which it is relevant in the current period.

The Obama administration also received specific direction from the Congress, which obliged it to undertake a review of nuclear policy and posture. But in contrast to its guidance in 2000, in 2007 the Congress cast the requirement in the broadest possible terms, directing that the incoming administration conduct a review encompassing not just deterrence but also arms control, nonproliferation, and nuclear security more generally. The Congress accordingly also directed an interagency review, with the Department of Defense in the lead. This direction reflected the sense of many in Congress that U.S. nuclear policy and strategy had fallen into disarray and that they could no longer effectively come to agreement about specific investment decisions in the absence of some better understanding of the larger policy framework.

In a bid to ensure that its own debate about the next NPR would be well informed, the Congress in 2007 stood up a bipartisan Commission on the Strategic Posture of the United States. With former Secretary of Defense Perry as chair and former Secretary of Defense Schlesinger as vice chair, the group was tasked with offering advice and recommendations on the future of U.S. nuclear deterrence. More broadly, the Congress was looking for advice on whether a renewal of bipartisanship was possible following a decade of increasingly acrimonious debate and, if so, on what basis. The Commission issued its report in spring 2009, just as the Obama administration's internal review was gearing up. It concluded that a bipartisan approach is possible and must be built on a balanced approach that encompasses both political measures such as arms control and nonproliferation to reduce nuclear threats with military measures to ensure that deterrence is effective for the problems for which it is relevant in the 21st century. Put differently, the commission argued that the traditional approach to nuclear policy that draws on different political and military tools to address different problems but in an integrated, coherent way should remain the basis of nuclear policy. The report also expressed the view that "the conditions that might make possible the global elimination of nuclear weapons are not present today and their creation would require a fundamental transformation of the world political order."[67]

The report was influential within the administration, not least because many of the advisers supporting the commission found roles in the Obama administration (including Ashton Carter, Michele Flournoy, James Miller, and this author, among others). One early sign of its influence was the balanced view reflected in the Prague speech.

The final NPR antecedent was the ongoing effort by Secretary Gates to implement the recommendations of the Schlesinger panel (not to be confused with the aforementioned Strategic Posture Commission). These recommendations were aimed at restoring leadership focus and institutional excellence for nuclear deterrence in the Air Force, in his Office of the Secretary of Defense, and more generally at leadership levels in the national security community. The panel stated that a presidential commitment to ensure that nuclear deterrence would remain effective so long as nuclear weapons remain was essential to making any progress at all in restoring focus and excellence.

The Obama administration's NPR ran from April 2009 until release of the report in April 2010. Roughly speaking, it ran in three phases. The first phase used working groups to identify issues and options and to do the supporting analysis with interagency teams. The second phase used the formal interagency process to prepare specific topics for leadership review. The final phase was deliberative and decisional, as the president and his national security team worked through each of the high-level topics and then the draft report.

In contrast to its predecessor, the Obama administration encouraged inputs from all interested stakeholders, including allies, nongovernmental organizations, and other states and organizations, with an eye to ensuring a comprehensive analysis of issues. The Obama administration chose not to prepare a classified report. It saw an unclassified report as better able to generate broad understanding of its policies and objectives. It also sought to avoid the difficulties of the Bush administration in addressing concerns about a classified but leaked report.

Like its predecessors, the Obama administration sought to align its nuclear policy with its National Security Strategy. That strategy identified a mix of positive and negative trends in the security environment and set out explicitly "an approach from the world as it is to the world we seek," including "a just and sustainable international order . . . based on rights and responsibilities." It highlighted a commitment to renewing American leadership, not least by renewing the sources of strength at home. It also argued that "America has not succeeded by stepping outside the currents of international cooperation" and promised to strengthen and modernize old alliances while building new and deeper partnerships and strengthening international standards and institutions.[68]

The 2010 NPR report set out five main goals:

1. To strengthen efforts to prevent nuclear proliferation and nuclear terrorism.
2. To reduce the role of nuclear weapons in U.S. strategy.
3. To ensure strategic stability while reducing the number of nuclear weapons.
4. To strengthen extended deterrence and assurance.

5. To maintain a safe, secure, and effective deterrent so long as nuclear weapons remain.

In support of the first goal, the report defined a "whole-of-government" approach (involving a broad range of actors in the U.S. government) aimed at strengthening both cooperation with international partners and the defense-in-depth of the United States. Implementation has been carried out through cooperative programs of the Departments of Defense, State, and Energy, with a sustained presidential-level focus on issues of nuclear material safety and security.

In support of the effort to reduce the role of nuclear weapons, the report identified changes to the declaratory policy of the United States, more narrowly circumscribing the role of nuclear weapons. The role was characterized as follows:

> The fundamental role of U.S. nuclear weapons, which will continue as long as nuclear weapons exist, is to deter nuclear attack on the United States, our allies, and our partners . . . The U.S. would only consider the use of nuclear weapons in extreme circumstances to defend the vital interests of the United States or its allies and partners. . . . Nuclear forces will continue to play an essential role in deterring potential adversaries and reassuring allies and partners around the world.[69]

The NPR also stated that the United States would not use or threaten to use nuclear weapons against nonnuclear weapon states that are party to the NPT and in compliance with their nuclear nonproliferation obligations. In reformulating this aspect of U.S. declaratory policy, the administration also dropped Cold War–vintage conditions created to deal with deterrence of the Warsaw Pact (and threatening U.S. nuclear attacks on states allied with nuclear-armed enemies), resulting in the so-called clean assurance. But the administration rejected the advice of many advocates of a "sole purpose" formulation, by which the United States would state that the sole purpose of nuclear weapons is to deter nuclear attack. It rejected this advice on the basis of an assessment that in a narrow set of cases the vital interests of the United States and its allies can also be jeopardized by nonnuclear means.

In support of the effort to ensure strategic stability while reducing the number of nuclear weapons, the report defined a pathway forward for arms reductions in partnership with Russia as a part of the effort to "reset" bilateral relations and dialogues with both Russia and China aimed at ensuring stable strategic relationships. This was an early administration priority, as the existing arms control framework was due to expire early on its watch (START I was due to expire in December 2009, and SORT was due to expire in December 2012). The administration was then successful in negotiating a New START Treaty with Russia and in securing the advice and consent of the U.S. Senate to ratification. Initial work was also undertaken on a potential follow-on agreement that would accomplish U.S. objectives in both continuing reductions in strategic weapons while also agreeing to new restraints on both nondeployed and nonstrategic weapons.

In support of the effort to strengthen extended deterrence and assurance, the report set out a comprehensive approach to strengthening regional deterrence architectures. This approach includes a nuclear component tailored to each region where the United States provides security guarantees. That tailored component is underpinned by the ability to forward deploy nuclear weapons with a nonstrategic delivery system into any region in support of U.S. security guarantees.

In support of the effort to maintain a safe, secure, and effective deterrent, the administration followed the advice of the Strategic Posture Commission in setting out a pathway for sustaining the life of existing nuclear weapons (as opposed to building new ones) while modernizing the nuclear complex. It also highlighted the continuing need for leadership focus and institutional excellence for nuclear deterrence, including at NATO.

On its release, the 2010 NPR Report received an endorsement from Secretaries Perry and Schlesinger in their roles as leaders of the Strategic Posture Commission.[70] It was less warmly endorsed by advocates of more immediate and far-reaching changes to U.S. policy and posture. These advocates had hoped for both more unilateral action to reduce the U.S. nuclear posture (such as the withdrawal of remaining U.S. nuclear weapons from Europe) and the adoption of a declaratory policy stating that the sole purpose of U.S. nuclear weapons is to deter nuclear attack.[71]

Perhaps the most controversial aspect of the Obama administration's NPR was its restatement of the president's intention to take practical steps toward the long-term goal of a world free of nuclear weapons. This was intended to signal clearly the intention of the United States to fulfill its obligations under Article VI of the NPT to join with the other nuclear weapon states in eliminating their nuclear weapons in the context of general and complete disarmament. This restatement was seen as necessary and useful. It was seen as necessary for addressing domestic and international concerns about American leadership of the global nonproliferation and disarmament effort. It was seen as useful to renewing international engagement on nonproliferation, counter-terrorism, and arms control. It also proved controversial with those who interpreted it as a sign that President Obama would compromise the requirements of a safe, secure, and effective deterrent in the interests of accelerating abolition.

New Deterrence Guidance

On release of the NPR report in April 2010, the administration's focus shifted from policy formulation to policy implementation. Interagency and other consultative mechanisms developed during the NPR were then adapted to ensure timely and effective implementation. The dialogues with domestic partners were sustained, and there was a broad effort to brief interested audiences on Capitol Hill and elsewhere on the results of the review and the supporting logic. Building on consultations conducted with allies during the NPR, mechanisms for dialogue on nuclear deterrence were institutionalized where they did not exist (with allies in Northeast Asia), were renewed where they had lapsed (in 2010 a dialogue with France was renewed), or otherwise reinvigorated (long-running dialogues with NATO and separately with the United Kingdom).

A key follow-on task was the development of new written guidance from the president to the Department of Defense on how to align military planning with the results of the policy review and with presidential intent as reflected in U.S. declaratory policy on the use of nuclear weapons. Beginning in 2011, the administration conducted a White House–led process of review and deliberation. This work focused on understanding the elements of presidential guidance; options for aligning guidance with NPR commitments to deterrence, assurance, and strategic stability; and how to achieve U.S. and allied objectives if deterrence fails.

In June 2013, the president issued new guidance to the military—a classified document. At the same time, the White House provided an unclassified report to Congress characterizing that guidance.[72] That report affirms many long-standing aspects of U.S. deterrence policy while also introducing some important new aspects.

The report affirms that only the president has the authority to employ U.S. nuclear weapons. No other political figure or military leader has that authority so long as the president is able to exercise it.

The report affirms the U.S. intention to comply with the Law of Armed Conflict in its development of nuclear employment plans and specifically with the principles of discrimination and proportionality. The principle of discrimination obliges the United States to distinguish between civilian and combatant targets. The principle of proportionality obliges the United States to ensure that any harm inflicted on noncombatants is not excessive in relation to the concrete and direct military advantage anticipated by an attack on a military objective.[73]

The report affirms that deterrence depends on the ability to convince any potential adversary that the adverse consequences of its further actions will far outweigh any potential benefit. This requires putting at risk what the decision makers in adversarial countries most value. The report clearly reflected the administration's rejection of minimum deterrence as inadequate to current deterrence requirements. Minimum deterrence is a mode of deterrence that depends on the threat of nuclear retaliation alone and makes no effective accommodation for the principles of discrimination and proportionality or for a theory of deterrence that depends on putting at risk those things most valued by enemy leadership. The advocates of minimum deterrence for the United States have argued that "deterrence today would remain stable even if retaliation against only ten cities were assured."[74] But retaliation against cities would violate the principles of discrimination and proportionality, and thus U.S. deterrence strategy requires being able to put at risk other assets in an enemy country that enemy leaders would not want to lose.

The report also affirms continuation of the existing alert posture of U.S. forces. Since the decisions of the George H. W. Bush administration to take one leg of the triad off alert (the bombers) and to reduce the alert posture of a second leg (by reducing the fraction of the ballistic missile submarine fleet on alert), no administration has seen it as necessary or useful to take additional steps in this direction. The report reflects the guidance to the Department of Defense to retain an ability to launch U.S. nuclear forces when under attack. But it also directed the department to examine "further options" to reduce the role of "launch under attack," on the argument that there is a "significantly diminished possibility of a disarming surprise nuclear attack."[75]

The report also reflects the administration's assessment that another one-third reduction of deployed strategic forces could be undertaken by the United States and Russia without damaging strategic stability. The report reaffirms administration intent to proceed with such reductions only in the context of parallel Russian reductions. This reflects the administration's commitments to avoid large disparities in the strategic forces of Russia and the United States (even if not adhering to strict numerical parity) and to strengthen partnership with Russia in support of strategic stability.

The report also sets out the president's direction to "focus on more likely 21st century contingencies" than a major bolt-out-of-the-blue attack by a nuclear peer or near peer. As the White House argued at the time, "The potential for a surprise, disarming nuclear attack is extremely remote."[76] But the report does not identify specific alternative contingencies. It simply asserts that "the threat of global nuclear war has become remote, but the risk of nuclear attack has increased."[77] Of note, the 2014 Quadrennial Defense Review (QDR) highlights the challenges of addressing regional conflicts in which local adversaries armed with WMD attempt to escalate their way out of failed conventional aggression.[78]

The significant elements of continuity, and the absence of additional information about "21st century contingencies," helped to generate criticism of the report from the advocates of more dramatic changes in the U.S. deterrence posture.[79] Others criticized it as going too far in the direction of the "flawed vision" of disarmament.[80]

As in the prior two administrations, there were important developments during this time in the community outside government that affected policy development. There were three developments of note. The first was a renewal of focus in think tanks and elsewhere on how to continue nuclear reductions in partnership with Russia, with alternative concepts emerging for various steps, both incremental and bold.[81] This generated valuable new insights into the potential impact of the possible future move to lower numbers of deployed nuclear weapons on strategic stability and extended deterrence. This work highlighted the ways in which allies could become anxious about the credibility of extended deterrence (especially if capabilities uniquely associated with that role are eliminated) and strategic stability (if arms control leads to a fundamental shift in strategic balance by changing China's calculus and inducing it to seek parity).[82]

The second development in the external environment was a dramatic rise in the currency of discussion about nuclear disarmament. This was reflected in continued advocacy by the Gang of Four as well as a flurry of new studies on specific topics and sustained high-level advocacy in Washington and other Western capitals for policies consistent with the global zero agenda.[83]

The Gang of Four continued to advocate for practical steps to move toward a nuclear-free world. In March 2011, they argued against nuclear deterrence, because it "is becoming increasingly hazardous and decreasingly effective," and in favor of steps they deem necessary to begin moving toward "a safer and more stable form of deterrence":

> Nations should move forward together with a series of conceptual and practical steps toward deterrence that do not rely primarily on nuclear weapons or nuclear threats to maintain international peace and security. . . . Continued reliance on nuclear weapons as the principal element is encouraging, or at least excuse, the spread of these weapons, and will inevitably erode the essential cooperation necessary to avoid proliferation, protect nuclear materials, and deal effectively with new threats. . . . Changes to extended deterrence must be developed over time by the U.S. and its allies working closely together.[84]

In 2013, the four again weighed in, arguing that "Washington should carefully examine going below New START levels of warheads and launchers, including the possibility of coordinated mutual actions with Russia."[85] On a seemingly independent note, Henry Kissinger argued together with Brent Scowcroft that "nuclear weapons will continue to influence the international landscape as part of strategy" and that "strategic stability is not inherent with low numbers."[86]

The new studies in the external environment took varied approaches. Some examined the potential for, and implications of, nuclear abolition.[87] A group of studies explored dramatic steps toward zero, including U.S. adoption of a minimum deterrence posture akin to that of China's.[88] In other cases, the practical aspects of maintaining stability in the case of very deep cuts were examined.[89] Some individuals made the case for the elimination of nuclear weapons, on the argument that their effectiveness as deterrents is unproven and the risks of retaining them outweigh any potential benefits.[90]

In this time frame, a significant new international movement took shape to examine and address the humanitarian impact of nuclear weapons.

Periodic international conferences drew broad participation by states and NGOs. In his summary of the second conference in Mexico City in February 2014, the conference chair asserted that the use of nuclear weapons "would violate international humanitarian law and thus they should be banned."[91] This assertion suggests that the effort to understand the humanitarian impact of nuclear weapons has been co-opted by those who seek to criminalize the possession of nuclear weapons. But this effort jeopardizes the step-by-step approach to disarmament long advocated by the United States, built on pragmatic actions by the nuclear weapon states as political circumstances permit but including also actions by non–nuclear weapon states to fulfill the obligations of the NPT.

In addition in this time frame, other major international advocacy groups produced reports recommending various actions. The International Commission on Nuclear Non-proliferation and Disarmament called on the United States and Russia to take dramatic steps to reduce the role of nuclear weapons in their security strategies—and on others to join the process.[92]

The Global Zero Movement produced two reports that generated political attention. One was an "action plan" mapping out a four-phased process culminating in the elimination of nuclear weapons globally by 2030. The report asserted that "any residual benefits of nuclear weapons are now overshadowed by the growing risk of proliferation and the related risk of nuclear terrorism" and that there is a "growing international nonproliferation consensus" in support of Global Zero.[93] Recalling the assessment of the 2009 Strategic Posture Commission report that the creation of the conditions for disarmament would require "a fundamental transformation of the world political order," of note the report offered a single observation that "nations will confront profound and complex security issues" as they implement the plan.[94] Self-characterized as a "practical, end-to-end strategy," the plan promises only that the Global Zero Commission will examine such issues. It provides no arguments whatsoever about how a denuclearized world would be monitored and policed to ensure compliance.

The other Global Zero Movement report focused on U.S. nuclear policy and posture. It provided an illustrative future U.S. nuclear policy and architecture "built on a series of possible, desirable steps."[95] Those steps include retiring ICBMs and thereby moving to a dyad, eliminating U.S. nuclear weapons in Europe, and bringing China, Britain, and France into the nuclear reductions process. In assessing the security environment, it argues that (1) "a severe deterioration of geostrategic relations between the United States and either Russia or China . . . is a remote possibility," (2) "international cooperation on missile defense can be achieved . . . and would complete the transition from MAD to mutual awareness, warning, and defense," and (3) that the assurance requirements of U.S. allies can be met "amply" with U.S. strategic forces, rendering the military utility of U.S. nuclear weapons in Europe "practically nil."[96] The report characterized U.S. nuclear planning as "driven largely by inertia and vested interests left over from the Cold War."[97] It argued further that "a strong case can be made that unilateral U.S. deep cuts and de-alerting coupled with strengthened ballistic missile defense and conventional capabilities would not weaken deterrence . . . and would lay the groundwork for increasing security cooperation" with Russia.[98] It concluded that there is an "alternate deterrence construct for the 21st century" in which "security, previously organized around bilateral confrontation, increasingly depends on multilateral cooperation."[99]

The advocacy of such positions to the Obama administration has been energetic and continuous. The recommendations have been received with an open mind and a sympathetic ear. From an administration perspective, the recommendations generally fell into two categories. One set was practical and well aligned with the administration's sense of what it might accomplish on its four- or eight-year watch. Others were much more aspirational and to a significant extent founded on perceptions of the security environment or existing U.S. deterrence practices that were inconsistent with the perceptions of the administration.

Thus some of the recommendations were found wanting. The Global Zero Movement reports, for example, were particularly misaligned with administration thinking. The "severe deterioration" of security relations with Russia deemed highly unlikely by the authors of the report on U.S. nuclear policy in 2012 in fact occurred in 2014. The effort to secure missile defense cooperation with Russia has been a bitter disappointment. Some U.S. allies reject the idea that they would be adequately assured if the United States were to retire its capabilities to deploy nuclear weapons into their regions. De-alerting proposals seem to increase risk without adding benefit. And a White House that had just led a lengthy and thorough review of deterrence requirements was hardly likely to agree that deterrence planning is driven by inertia or vested interests.

Accordingly, the administration has not implemented the Global Zero agenda. It rejects time-bound disarmament (as envisioned in the plan to disarm by 2030). It rejects further steps to reduce the role and number of nuclear weapons without creating the conditions that make it safe to do so. It has not neglected efforts to sustain the balanced approach. It has updated political guidance to align deterrence practices with 21st-century requirements. It has worked with the Congress to fund key warhead modernization actions. It sees a security environment a good deal more challenging, even hostile, than does the Global Zero Movement.

The third development in the external environment came somewhat as a backlash to the second. Counterpoints emerged to some of the main tenets of the disarmament agenda. Frank Miller argued that "nuclear weapons have made war among the Great Powers too dangerous."[100] Richard Mies argued that they should be retained as a form of insurance against uncertainty in the security environment.[101] Others have argued that nuclear weapons have an "enduring value" that transcends historical eras.[102] It would be inaccurate to suggest that there was a debate, as the two different points of view were rarely juxtaposed side-by-side.

This case for nuclear weapons is sometimes buttressed by a story told by Pentagon tour guides at the historical display on the Pacific war and in particular the exhibit on the Hiroshima and Nagasaki bombings. Sitting in boxes somewhere in a Pentagon storeroom are Purple Hearts ordered late in World War II for the 1,000,000 American casualties expected in the planned invasion of Japan; today, many of these awards remain, despite drawing on the supply in 1945 and through seven subsequent decades.[103]

Elements of Continuity and Change across Three NPRs

In sum, for three decades or so since the end of the Cold War, American presidents have been at work on the project of remaking U.S. nuclear policy and posture. The three nuclear posture reviews of this period are marked by elements of both continuity and change.[104] This analysis highlights a few of the most striking elements.

The first and most obvious element of continuity is that each president has wanted to move dramatically away from "Cold War thinking" and to reduce reliance on nuclear deterrence in U.S. security strategy and on nuclear weapons in U.S. military strategy. Each has taken practical, specific steps to do so.

Second, each president has wanted to accomplish additional nuclear reductions, on the argument that the large arsenals inherited from the Cold War are not the kind of arsenals needed today. There is also a great deal of continuity in terms of the capabilities administrations have chosen to preserve.[105]

Third, each administration has pursued a strategy for stability with Russia and to an extent China, while in each case recognizing the potential for military flashpoints with both. Strategic stability remains of high strategic value for the United States, especially in the context of a "changed and changing" security environment. To be sure, different administrations have defined the requirements of strategic stability differently.

Fourth, each administration has wanted confidence that, whatever the reduced role of nuclear deterrence in today's security environment, the nuclear deterrent will be effective for the problems for which it is relevant. What to do if deterrence fails is a question with which every president must come to terms. And every president wants the best possible options and means to deal with any mounting crisis under a nuclear shadow. For twenty-five years administrations have worked to understand the nature of the new challenges posed by the proliferation of weapons of mass destruction and the potential for new forms of regional conflict with a nuclear dimension, whether with regional actors or major powers.

A final element of continuity relates to the deterrence of state sponsored terrorism. Especially after 9/11, U.S. leadership has been highly motivated to reduce the risks of nuclear terrorism. Toward that end, the United States maintains a policy of clearly holding at risk any state sponsors of nuclear terrorism. This policy was articulated forcefully by the Bush administration in 2008:

> The United States has made clear for many years that it reserves the right to respond with overwhelming force to the use of weapons of mass destruction against the United States, our people, our forces and our friends and allies. Additionally, the United States will hold any state, terrorist group, or other non-state actor fully accountable for supporting or enabling terrorist efforts to obtain or use weapons of mass destruction, whether by facilitating, financing, or providing expertise or safe haven for such efforts.[106]

This language was repeated essentially verbatim in the 2010 NPR Report as a way of signaling continuity of American leadership resolve.

The elements of change are equally striking. One key change is in perceptions of the security environment. Over time, perceptions of the security environment have clearly shifted, as reflected in the different national security strategies of each administration. From a nuclear perspective, the key shift is from an environment seen in the 1990s as largely benign and trending in the right direction (in terms of the demands it puts on the U.S. strategic military posture) to one marked by the rising salience of nuclear terrorism and proliferation, of new nuclear-armed regional challengers, and of potential regional conflicts with the major powers.

A second element of change is in the shift from a narrow focus on nuclear arsenals to a broad focus on "whole-of-government" approaches. The first NPR was narrowly focused on the future of U.S. nuclear forces in the immediate aftermath of the Cold War. The second was more broadly about the relationship between nuclear strategy and defense strategy. The third was the broadest in scope.

A third element of change is in the role of arms control. The Clinton and Obama administrations sought arms control with Russia because of the perceived values of legally binding reductions and of the benefits of predictability and transparency. They also strongly supported the nonproliferation regime as a multilateral arms control mechanism. The George W. Bush administration, on the other hand, rejected arms control as a barrier to the needed political transformation of the relationship with Russia. And it was generally skeptical of the nonproliferation regime and invested political capital in it only episodically. Moreover, the two Bush administrations were willing to take unilateral actions to reduce the U.S. arsenal, whereas the two Democratic administrations were not.

A fourth element of change is in the rising salience of extended deterrence and the assurance of allies. The 1994 NPR addressed issues related to the number of U.S. nuclear weapons in Europe, but this was largely an exercise in shrinking the existing force structure. The 2001 NPR included the assurance of allies as a policy priority and criterion for determining the needed size and shape of U.S. nuclear forces. The 2009 NPR went much further in setting out a strategy for strengthening regional deterrence and for meeting the assurance requirements of U.S. allies.

A fifth and final element of change is in the rising emphasis on the need to modernize aging forces. In the 1990s, a "peace dividend" was easy to harvest from the nuclear account. The Presidential Nuclear Initiatives essentially froze the modernization process in a bid to end the arms race. In the 2000s, initial modernization steps needed to be taken but ran into the political roadblock generated by concerns about the George W. Bush administration's national security policy. The Obama administration has had to do more than either of its predecessors to lay the financial and political foundations of a long-term strategy to sustain and modernize the force while also creating the political conditions to avoid a renewal of arms racing with Russia and/or China.

The Modernization Question

Modernization is the next big question in U.S. nuclear policy. During the Cold War, U.S. nuclear forces were modernized on a continuing basis in competition with the Soviet Union, so that new nuclear warheads, new delivery systems, and new command-and-control capabilities regularly replaced their aging predecessors. With the end of the Cold War, this process stopped. For the last twenty-five years or so, the United States has spent essentially just the money needed to operate and maintain standing forces. Moreover, as part of its strategy to end the nuclear confrontation following the end of the Cold War, the George H. W. Bush administration retired the newest generation of ballistic missiles; today, the *newest* ICBM in the existing force was placed in the ground in 1971. Additionally, the replacement of B-52s by B-2 bombers was curtailed, with only twenty B-2 bombers coming into nuclear service. The *newest* B-52 in the existing force came into service in 1962. The *newest* U.S. nuclear warhead went into service in 1989.

Accordingly, although the forces are maintained adequately to ensure operational effectiveness today, they are also aging well past their original intended service lives. Over the next two decades, the entire remaining inventory will have to be modernized in some way. The triad of delivery systems will have to be modernized or replaced. Every nuclear bomb and missile warhead is either being rebuilt now or will have to be rebuilt to extend its service life or replaced with something new. The associated command-and-control system that ensures presidential control of all decisions to employ nuclear weapons must also be modernized.

During the Cold War, the United States spent significant resources to develop, maintain, and modernize nuclear forces—on average approximately 20 percent of defense spending.[107] The cycle of sustainment and modernization ahead, assuming it is completed, will not require investments at Cold

War levels. The force is much smaller today than in decades past, and there is no significant competitive aspect driving an arms race and a need for significant qualitative improvements. But it won't be inexpensive, with estimates ranging from \$500 billion to \$1 trillion over the next two to three decades.[108] These are large sums. But they are only approximately 5 percent of projected defense spending over the same period.[109] By way of comparison, the portion of the defense budget currently spent to maintain and operate nuclear forces is approximately 2 percent.[110]

But the requirement for these new investments comes at a time of significant austerity in the federal budget and many competing demands on U.S. defense spending, including the need to rebuild conventional forces after the long wars in Iraq and Afghanistan. Accordingly, there is considerable political pressure to avoid nuclear spending as each new spending decision comes to a head in the budget process.

The Shifting Political Context

The United States is ill prepared to face this modernization question. This is a problem with multiple aspects.

Part of the problem is that nuclear deterrence has been "normalized" in the defense policy process. In the past, nuclear investment decisions were made by a small number of senior leaders in the executive and legislative branches of government with deep personal knowledge. That generation and that moment are gone. For a certain interim period, political support for investments to sustain existing capabilities was won on the basis of special pleading by the advocates of specific capabilities, usually in the U.S. Navy or Air Force. That period too is now gone. Today, nuclear weapons compete with other military capabilities for resources and leadership attention.

Part of the problem is an unhealthy partisanship that often frustrates coherent U.S. action. On nuclear policy, as elsewhere in the national political discourse, the extremes tend to squeeze out the broad middle. The national debate about nuclear deterrence, to the extent there is one, tends to be dominated by voices from the two opposing camps, in a tone that many others hear as shrill, condescending, and disconnected from real-world concerns. Few people or institutions have seen it as possible or even necessary to try to bridge this divide.[111]

Accordingly, partisanship has settled over the executive–legislative debate about nuclear policy much as it has settled over so many other aspects of the national debate. Healthy partisanship should be welcomed—because informed debate leads to improved policy, deeper consensus, and continuity in U.S. policy across administrations. Unhealthy partisanship that questions motives and competence works against all of those goals and undermines the needed leadership focus—and is much in evidence today.

To illustrate this point, consider the ratification of the New START treaty. The bipartisan Strategic Posture Commission unanimously recommended in 2009 that the new administration seek to take with Russia "a modest step . . . to rejuvenate the process and ensure that strategic arms control survives the end of START I at the end of 2009" and that it then "begin the process of exploring challenges to deeper reductions."[112] Substantive debate by the Senate, including the views of treaty opponents, is to be welcomed as a part of the ratification process. Any treaty deserves full scrutiny. Support for the treaty was broad and deep, including from former commanders of U.S. Strategic Command and U.S. allies. It was also bipartisan in character; one indicator was support from all living secretaries of State and Defense of both parties.[113] Yet when the vote was taken in 2012, only thirteen of the forty-four Republicans serving in the Senate voted in favor of ratification, despite the adoption of two provisions addressing stated reservations. There was a certain irony in the fact that the party that ten years earlier heavily supported the Moscow Treaty (a treaty one paragraph in length with a single obligation and no verification provisions) vigorously opposed New START for its supposed lack of comprehensiveness and weak verification.[114] This leaves a strong impression of an effort by opposition leadership to deny the president a political success rather than to turn back a treaty somehow detrimental to the national interest.

Partisan differences have not, however, prevented congressional support for Obama administration initiatives to sustain the life of existing nuclear warheads and to increase funding for the National Nuclear Security Administration at a time of shrinking federal budgets. This experience stands in sharp contrast to the failure of the George W. Bush administration to fund replacement warheads. The effort to build such support has illustrated the changing nature of American politics, as new coalitions had to be formed to account for changing priorities within the parties (as some Republican deficit hawks abandoned their commitment to strong defense spending and as some Democratic disarmers endorsed warhead sustainment).

An additional part of the problem is what might be called the advocacy mismatch. On the one hand, disarmament advocates are well organized and energetic in making their case that modernization decisions are unnecessary, unwise, or unaffordable.[115] In autumn 2014 past supporters of President Obama began to attack him for his lack of progress in cutting weapons, calling on him to "suspend plans to develop a new arsenal" and arguing that "upgrades could allow future presidents to rapidly expand the nation's atomic forces and have already set a bad example for other nations."[116]

On the other hand, advocacy for investments in the nuclear deterrent is nearly nonexistent. The budget proposals of the Obama administration to begin the modernization process have been supported by a relatively small group of interested Democrats and Republicans. There is essentially no external advocacy for investments in the nuclear deterrent of the kind coming from the advocates of disarmament.

Moreover, a key constituency has been largely silent in this debate: those advocates of a renewed focus on disarmament as a long-term objective who also argue that the conditions do not now exist for the United States to safely make additional substantial changes to its posture. This constituency does not oppose retention of a safe, secure, and effective nuclear arsenal; but neither does it advocate for the investments needed to ensure the arsenal meets those requirements. Additionally, it does little to rebut the use of its arguments in favor of additional U.S. steps toward disarmament by the opponents of modernization. There are some rare and important exceptions. In 2010, the Gang of Four called for investments in the nuclear weapons complex (though conspicuously not in delivery systems).[117] In 2014, William Perry lent his voice to the case for modernization of U.S. nuclear forces in his role as cochair of the 2014 National Defense Panel Report.[118]

The advocacy mismatch reflects the weakness of the case so far made for U.S. nuclear weapons in the 21st century. This case has not been made in a politically salient way by anyone other than serving officials. Nongovernmental voices in favor of nuclear deterrence are few and far between. The case they make for nuclear deterrence rests on their presumed "enduring value" as insurance against the return of major power war. This case may be sound but it doesn't go very far politically. It isn't helpful in informing decisions about what capabilities, and how many of them, are needed. It is also unhelpful in motivating the needed convergence of opinion on a long-term investment strategy that is politically viable. It is not intellectually and politically competitive in a "normalized" defense planning process that requires investments for nuclear deterrence to compete with investments for other defense capabilities. A better case is needed.

Modernization and Disarmament

Underlying these political divisions is a fundamental substantive question: Can the United States expect to make additional substantial reductions to the role and number of nuclear weapons in the foreseeable future?

Different answers to this question derive in part from different assessments of how much progress has been made in the past twenty-five or so years in moving away from the Cold War inheritance. Surveying the many elements of continuity in U.S. nuclear policy and posture reviewed in the previous pages, some conclude that more substantial steps to remake the U.S. nuclear deterrent should and could have been taken by now. Others, surveying the many elements of change in U.S. nuclear policy and posture, worry that there have already been too many changes.

To a certain extent, this is a debate about timelines. President Obama argued in Prague that the timeline is long and that nuclear disarmament may not occur in his lifetime. Others argue that it will never occur. The Global Zero Commission argues that it could occur by 2030. These differences of view often devolve into a quasi-theological debate about whether the conditions can ever be created to safely eliminate nuclear weapons. This is a debate that cannot be settled now. The relevant question is whether we can expect to need the nuclear deterrent beyond the service life of the weapons and delivery systems now aging out and well into or through the service life of their potential replacement systems.

From my perspective, each of the last four administrations has taken practical and significant steps away from Cold War approaches to nuclear policy and posture. Four presidents have occupied the White House since the end of the Cold War, and more secretaries of defense have passed through the Pentagon. The cumulative effect of evolutionary changes over twenty-five years has been significant, and, in my view, U.S. policy and posture are now well aligned with the requirements of the security environment as it exists.

The changes to the arsenal itself are unmistakable. The overall U.S. nuclear arsenal has shrunk by more than 75 percent between 1990 and 2014. The number of deployed strategic nuclear warheads has been reduced by about

80 percent. The number of deployed nonstrategic nuclear weapons has been reduced by more than 90 percent.

Retention of the triad and rejection of the doctrine of minimum deterrence have fueled the perception outside government that there has been little or no meaningful change in the intellectual underpinnings of nuclear deterrence. This is a misperception. The shift from a concern about global to regional nuclear wars, the shift from deterrence to strategic stability as the central organizing concept in relations with Russia and China, the increased reliance on nonnuclear means of strategic deterrence, and the reformulation of extended deterrence in a new security environment all attest to the degree of change.

But different answers to the fundamental question above derive also in part from different assessments of what more can be done in the near term to further reduce the role and number of U.S. nuclear weapons, regardless of past progress. In facing this question in the Obama administration NPR, we made a distinction between steps that could safely be taken in light of existing conditions and steps that might be possible in the future if the conditions could be created. In 2009, the relevant existing conditions were a positive change in the political relationship with Russia and a willingness in Moscow to put in place another arms control agreement, as well as changes in the security environment that enabled the adoption of the "clean" negative security assurance. In discussing the conditions for future steps, the 2010 NPR argued as follows:

> The conditions that would ultimately permit the United States and others to give up their nuclear weapons without risking greater international instability and insecurity are very demanding. Among those are the resolution of regional disputes that can motivate rival states to acquire and maintain nuclear weapons, success in halting the proliferation of nuclear weapons, much greater transparency into the programs and capabilities of key countries of concern, verification methods and technologies capable of detecting violations of disarmament obligations, and enforcement measures strong and credible enough to deter such violations. Clearly, such conditions do not exist today. But we can—and must— work actively to create those conditions.[119]

Conspicuously, this formulation does not embrace the view of the Strategic Posture Commission that the creation of such conditions requires a "fundamental transformation of the world political order." Nor does it embrace the view of the Global Zero Movement that the conditions to take dramatic additional steps already exist. It simply affirms the commitment of the Obama administration to use the means available to it to work to bring into being those conditions necessary for further progress toward the long-term goal of eliminating nuclear weapons globally. This has been dismissed as reckless utopianism by some[120] but might be better thought of in the spirit of "pragmatic idealism" espoused by one-time Secretary of War Henry L. Stimson (as a guide to American leadership for peace building after World War II).

This brings us to the key questions: Do the conditions exist today that would allow the United States to safely take additional substantial steps to reduce the role of nuclear weapons in its security strategies and the number of nuclear weapons in its arsenal? If they do not exist today, can they reasonably be expected to be brought into being soon enough to avoid the modernization of some or all U.S. nuclear forces? What lessons follow from this experience about the case against nuclear weapons and for nuclear disarmament? What lessons follow for the case for U.S. nuclear weapons? What does this case imply about the needed U.S. nuclear posture?

The disarmament literature has described many such conditions, including the following:

- Other states with nuclear weapon must be prepared to join the United States in moving away from reliance on nuclear weapons.
- All states must be prepared to join in a solid and durable political consensus against nuclear weapons.
- Russia and China in particular must be willing to join the United States in taking the next steps. As a first step, Russia must be willing to join the United States in moving below New START levels. And it must be willing to cooperate with the United States and NATO on missile defense and strategic stability more generally.
- It must be possible to make changes to extended deterrence that eliminate the requirement for the nuclear umbrella to U.S. allies. This implies that it must be possible to meet the assurance requirements of U.S. allies solely with the strategic assets of the United States.
- Existing U.S. deterrence practices must be replaced by an alternative deterrence construct for the 21st century.

The experience of the Obama administration and its predecessors provides useful insights into whether or not such conditions exist or can be brought into being in the near to medium term. That experience encompasses efforts to adapt nuclear deterrence to a changed and changing security environment as well as efforts to create the political conditions that would accelerate movement away from cold war nuclear confrontation. Chapters 2 through 8 explore different facets of this experience from the perspective of what they reveal about the existence or viability of the conditions listed in the preceding paragraphs. Chapter 9 will summarize lessons learned, and the Epilogue will consider implications.

2 The First New Problem

Nuclear-Armed Regional Challengers

A SOLID AND DURABLE INTERNATIONAL POLITICAL CONSENSUS against nuclear weapons will not be possible if additional states seek and deploy them. Accordingly, a top priority for U.S. policy makers has been to prevent the emergence of additional nuclear-armed states, largely but not exclusively within the framework of the Nuclear Non-Proliferation Treaty (NPT). Given incomplete success in this effort, U.S. policy makers have also focused on adapting deterrence to ensure that it remains effective in dealing with the problems posed by nuclear proliferation to those who might challenge U.S. interests.

U.S. efforts to prevent the emergence of additional nuclear-armed states have deep roots. The United States has worked with other like-minded countries to inhibit the spread of nuclear weapons to additional states ever since the advent of the nuclear era in the 1940s. To a remarkable degree, this effort has been a success as the number of nuclear-armed states remains far fewer than often feared, and tipping points leading to cascades of proliferation have been successfully avoided. But nonproliferation has not been a complete success, as three countries remain outside the nonproliferation treaty regime (Israel, India, and Pakistan), while other countries have illicitly pursued weapons programs from within the regime (Iraq, Iran, Libya, North Korea, and Syria among them). Conspicuously, this latter list consists of states whose leaders are (or were) deeply opposed to the U.S. role in their region and fearful of U.S.

ambitions to overturn their rule. Also conspicuously, at this writing only one of these states has actually proved willing and able to cross the nuclear threshold and begin to assemble a small nuclear force—North Korea. The problem of nuclear proliferation to regional challengers is magnified by the simultaneous proliferation of ballistic missiles, which gives regional actors strategic reach of a kind they have not previously enjoyed.

Their pursuit of these capabilities recalls the famous 1992 commentary on the rout of Iraq from Kuwait by former Chief of Staff of the Army of India General K. Sundarji, who argued that "the lesson of Desert Storm is, don't mess with the United States without nuclear weapons."[1] This invites an obvious question: How might regional challengers like Saddam Hussein "mess with" the United States *with* nuclear weapons? More broadly, how might they use their nuclear weapons once in hand? This volume takes a broad definition of the term *use*, to include both operational employment of nuclear weapons and threats to employ them, whether explicit or implicit. Such threats can be thought of as casting a "shadow" over a conflict of potential conflict, with the hope of inducing restraint by an adversary. Writing early in the nuclear era, Paul Nitze aptly characterized this function:

> Whether or not atomic weapons are ever used in warfare, the very fact of their existence, the possibility that they could be used, will affect all future wars. . . . The situation is analogous to a game of chess. The atomic queens may never be brought into play; they may never actually take one of the opponent's pieces. But the position of the atomic queens may still have a decisive bearing on which side can safely advance a limited-war bishop or even a cold war pawn.[2]

How do regional challengers to U.S.-backed regional orders think about positioning their "atomic queens" to shape confrontation and conflict with the United States? And how do they think about bringing their "atomic queens" into play operationally—if at all?

Answers to these questions are needed to ensure that the United States and its allies can defend their interests against nuclear-backed regional challengers. Answers to these questions will also shape how the U.S. strategic posture will evolve in coming years, with important implications for U.S. relations with both its allies and with Russia and China.

Answers to these questions have also been difficult to come by. States pursuing illicit weapons programs generally do not clearly explain their intentions or capabilities. They have learned the arts of concealment, denial, and deception. This makes them challenging targets for intelligence agencies. Accordingly, the U.S. government has had problems understanding the proliferation threat and must continue to improve its capabilities to do so.[3]

To better understand this new problem, and its implications for U.S. nuclear policy and posture, this chapter proceeds as follows. It begins with a brief survey of what is known about the thinking of key proliferators in the Middle East about how to use nuclear weapons in conflicts with the United States. Various countries took the lesson from the Persian Gulf War of 1990–1991 that they too might have to contend with future Desert Shields, Desert Storms, and U.S. regime removal strategies.[4] This survey illustrates the very different degrees to which different countries that have or may be pursuing nuclear weapons appear to have thought about how to use them to secure their interests in such an eventuality.[5]

The chapter then turns to North Korea. Given North Korea's progress in developing both nuclear weapons and the missiles to deliver them at all ranges, it is an especially important case study. The chapter reviews key developments in North Korean nuclear capabilities and assesses what is known about North Korean nuclear intentions. It explores the available evidence for insights into North Korean thinking about using nuclear weapons for purposes of deterrence and defense. It posits the existence of a North Korean theory of victory, derivative of Nitze's chess analogy, based on nuclear blackmail and brinksmanship and invoking the thinking of both Clausewitz and Sun Tzu. It suggests the possibility that other regional challengers to the United States and its allies might develop or be developing analogous theories of victory. As a label and shorthand, it is useful to refer to these as a "Red theory of victory," to express a generic, adversarial set of concepts.

The chapter then uses this theory of victory to derive the deterrence challenges for the United States and its allies and partners posed by regional challengers armed with nuclear weapons and long-range ballistic missiles. For now, these challenges are present only in the case of North Korea; should efforts to prevent Iran's acquisition of nuclear weapons fail, such challenges could be present in that case—and possibly others still later. These challenges are arrayed across a spectrum defined by different phases of conflict and degrees of escalation, with an eye to illuminating specific deterrence challenges as opposed to generic ones. This analysis highlights the emergence of a new set of deterrence challenges associated with forms of escalation by regional challengers that they may believe fall beneath the threshold of a U.S. nuclear response. It also sets the foundation for an exploration in the following chapter of the requirements of successfully meeting these challenges.[6]

The Middle East Problem Set

At various times in recent decades, four potential regional challengers to U.S. interests in the Middle East have sought nuclear weapons and ballistic missiles: Iraq, Iran, Libya, and Syria. Looking to the future, there is considerable uncertainty about which countries might renew or discover an interest in these capabilities.

Little or nothing is known about the leadership intentions of Libya and Syria that might have guided their use of nuclear weapons for political or military purposes—or both—had they succeeded in building them. Libya began its pursuit of nuclear weapons with Colonel Mu'ammar Qadhafi's coup in 1969 and seems to have been animated primarily by resentment over the 1967 defeat of the Arabs by Israel. Qadhafi's call for Libyan nuclear weapons became more frequent in the 1990s, and Libya's development activities accelerated, including through cooperation with Dr. A. Q. Khan, a leader of the Pakistan nuclear weapons program who provided technical assistance to several countries, including Iran and North Korea in addition to Libya. Beginning in 1999, but especially after the 9/11 attacks, Qadhafi made overtures to the West that finally resulted in Libya's renunciation of its nuclear program in December 2003 in exchange for relief from economic sanctions.[7]

The Syrian ambition is even more difficult to characterize. Syria is a signatory to the Nuclear Non-Proliferation Treaty (NPT) and has civilian nuclear research facilities monitored by the International Atomic Energy Agency (IAEA). On September 6, 2007, Israel bombed a site in Syria that it characterized as a nuclear reactor under construction. Western press reports indicated that North Korea had recently shipped to Syria a reactor for a nuclear weapon program. Following the strike, the Syrians completely sanitized the site, making investigation pointless. The Bush administration subsequently asserted that the U.S. government was convinced that the struck site was a covert facility not intended for peaceful purposes. The IAEA also concluded that the destroyed building was "very likely" a nuclear reactor.[8]

For understanding how leaders might use nuclear weapons these two cases reveal little. Iraq is an entirely different case. Saddam Hussein's thinking about the potential uses of nuclear weapons and other weapons of mass destruction has come into clearer focus after a period following the U.S. invasion of Iraq in 2003 of uncertainty and recrimination about the uses and misuses of Western intelligence.[9] Analysis done in 2004 by the Iraq Survey Group and by independent analysts reveals that Iraqi leadership thinking about the potential uses of Iraqi nuclear weapons passed through four main phases.

The first phase was as the program took shape in the 1980s. At this time, the Iraqi Ministry of Defense issued instructions for the operational employment of weapons of mass destruction. These instructions characterized nuclear weapons as practical tools of war for the tactical and operational levels of war and clearly stated that nuclear war was both survivable and winnable. The manual explicitly rejected the notion that nuclear weapons would be weapons of last resort or primarily political weapons for deterrence.[10] The second phase was during the initial confrontation with the United States and the U.S.-led coalition in Desert Shield and Desert Storm. At this time, biological weapons were predeployed to various locations and authority for their use predelegated to attack any targets in range as punishment for a coalition march on Baghdad. (Some Iraqis reportedly took the lesson that these weapons were successful in deterring that action.[11]) The third phase was in the lead-up to the war to remove Hussein from power a decade later, when he refrained from any explicit or implicit threat to use such weapons because this would alienate those in the international community whose support he needed.[12] The fourth and final phase was in preliminary thinking done by Hussein and others in Iraq about reconstitution of Iraqi WMD programs at some future time and for purposes of deterrence, primarily of Iran.[13]

This brief review illustrates the potential evolution of leadership intentions over time and in changing circumstances. It also illustrates the important role of chemical and biological weapons and long-range missiles in adversary leadership thinking about how to secure certain operational advantages against a U.S.-led coalition that is conventionally superior but depends on power projection to gain that superiority.

Iran is the country of obvious high salience today from the perspective of its proliferation potential and nuclear ambitions. Like the leaders of Libya, Syria, and Iraq, Iran's leadership has perceived a need to improve its overall deterrence posture. Whether it has also decided that having a tested and deployed nuclear arsenal is essential to this posture remains an open question at this writing in 2014 and will remain a long-term question even if it fully restores its compliance with its NPT obligations.

Even in the absence of nuclear weapons, Iran's developing military posture and assertiveness in the Middle East present important deterrence challenges for the United States and its allies in the region and in Europe. Iran has pursued a strategy for strengthening its deterrence posture that is heavily reliant on weapons of mass destruction and long-range delivery systems (as part of what has been called a "mosaic" defense).[14] It now has options to strike anywhere within its region and into large parts of Europe, while it also continues to develop the capabilities to reach the United States.

Leaders in Tehran have a deep antipathy toward the United States, referred to by Iran's Supreme Leaders as "the Great Arrogance," and perceive Iran to be in a state of war with the United States.[15] They are also contemptuous of some of their neighbors. This contempt is born of deep historical grievance and is reflected in a strong desire to right the dominant political narrative.

Iranian leaders continue to deny that the country's nuclear program has any military aspect. It is hardly surprising, therefore, that Iranian leaders and analysts have said essentially nothing about the potential role of nuclear weapons in Iranian security and military strategies. Accordingly, major uncertainties attach to our understanding of Iranian capabilities and intentions.[16]

Whether Iran would pursue a strategy of nuclear confrontation with the United States if it crosses the nuclear threshold is a matter of intense debate among U.S. analysts.[17] Many believe Iran's leaders would not be emboldened to challenge the United States in new ways. A recent RAND study concluded that "the Islamic Republic will remain a revisionist state for the foreseeable future, but its intent and ability to challenge American power in the Middle East will be limited even if it obtains nuclear weapons."[18] Ken Pollack argues that Iranian leaders may be "aggressive, anti-American, and murderous" but have always pulled back when threatened with severe retaliation, as they would be—and as they understand they would be—if they were actually to employ nuclear weapons.[19] Accordingly, he characterizes concerns about Iranian nuclear employment as a red herring and the risks of nuclear blackmail as slight.

Others predict that Iran will become more aggressive with nuclear weapons.[20] While not taking a position on this particular issue, Henry Kissinger has recently emphasized that the Iranian revolution was conceived and is sustained "in the name of an assault against the entire regional order and indeed the institutional arrangements of modernity."[21] He also describes Iran as a key protagonist in "two forms of civil war in the Middle East . . . one between Muslim regimes that were members of the Westphalian state system and Islamists who consider statehood and the prevailing institutions of international order an abomination to the Quran; and another between Shias and Sunnis across the region."[22]

In the absence of direct evidence, the problem for U.S. deterrence strategy is the problem of uncertainty. As one recent study by the Center for Strategic and Budgetary Assessments has concluded, "It is unclear how a nuclear-armed Iran would weigh the costs, benefits, and risks of brinksmanship and escalation."[23] Another recent RAND study echoes this conclusion but argues that pathways to such a confrontation do exist:

> While Iran's historical behavior, national security interests, and military planning suggest that it is likely to be cautious in undertaking any military action against U.S. military forces in the region, plausible paths to U.S.–Iran conflict exist. Iran's military doctrines and conventional capabilities provide it with alternatives to using nuclear weapons in a conflict, and given the overwhelming superiority of both U.S. conventional and nuclear forces, any Iranian use of nuclear weapons would hold enormous risks for Iran. Thus, Iran is likely to use nuclear weapons only under a narrow set of circumstances that would revolve around Iran viewing itself as vulnerable to U.S. conventional military defeat and threatened as a regime by U.S. conventional military operations.[24]

An additional, uniquely Iranian factor is the potential impact of theocratic interests on the exercise of nuclear strategy, deterrence, and brinksmanship. Michael Eisenstadt, among others, takes the view that interests of the state will guide Iranian nuclear strategy choices, while recognizing the possibility that there are countering views in the Iranian core leadership that might put Islamic interests in righting the moral course of history ahead of Iranian interests in securing the interests of the state.[25]

This catalogue of potential U.S. nuclear adversaries in the Middle East would not be complete without some consideration of the Islamic state that has gained significant ground in 2014. Its way of warfare is founded on the most brutal techniques, as directed by a training manual entitled "The Management of Savagery," which extols the virtues of "vexation and exhaustion" through the use of brutal techniques to gain mastery over political opponents and thereby consolidate control.[26] It is a reflection of a movement that has issued a declaration of war against the existing world order, seeks the eventual global implementation of its religious views, emphasizes purity over stability, and is now engaged in a war of both religious and geopolitical ambition with the aim of turning the global historical narrative in its preferred direction.[27] Among many others, Kissinger cautions against complacency: "In a failure of imagination, many Western elites find revolutionaries' passions inexplicable and assume that their extreme statements must be metaphorical or advanced merely as bargaining chips."[28]

If such a state, or elements of it, were to gain control of nuclear weapons, it seems likely that their thinking about how to use such weapons would not be governed by the interests and perspectives that have guided the thinking of nuclear weapon states so far in history. So far, nuclear history has yet to include the experience of nuclear weapons falling into the hands of groups with revolutionary and messianic visions and potentially willing to employ nuclear weapons not for the purposes of operational or deterrence benefit but to fundamentally shift the dominant historical narrative in favor of a radically different vision. The closest parallel experience was with China's acquisition of nuclear weapons as it still espoused radical Marxist philosophy. Over time, fears that a revolutionary China would use its nuclear weapons for revolutionary purposes gave way to an understanding that the Communist Party of China sought primarily to have nuclear weapons to safeguard the revolution and their grip on power and not to try to remake the international system.[29] If a radical, nuclear-armed caliphate emerges, we can hope that its leaders will be motivated by similar purposes, while we prepare for the possibility that they might not and take whatever measures might be possible to prevent their acquisition of nuclear weapons or preempt their employment of them.

North Korea and the New Austin, Texas, Problem

The Obama administration, likes it predecessors, has sought political agreement with Pyongyang to roll back the North Korean nuclear program in the context of a broader settlement of outstanding political issues on the Korean peninsula. Despite these efforts, North Korea continues to make progress in developing nuclear weapons and the missiles to deliver them at increasingly long ranges. This progress has major implications for the deterrence strategies of the United States and its allies. Indeed, it has been a key driver of developments in U.S. military posture for the last two decades, as multiple presidential administrations in the United States have sought to ensure that deterrence will be effective against such adversaries. North Korea may yet undergo a political transformation of a kind that leads to a decision to relinquish these capabilities. But barring some fundamental change in the situation, the world must for the foreseeable future deal with a nuclear-armed North Korea.[30]

Nuclear sabers were rattled loudly over the Korean peninsula in spring 2013. Kim Jong Un renounced the sixty-year-old armistice and made explicit new nuclear threats against both Japan and the United States.[31] In an effort to assure its allies of the continued reliability of the U.S. nuclear umbrella, the United States flew nuclear-capable bombers into Korean airspace. As a part of its strategic messaging in response, Pyongyang released videos and photographs. The videos included one of a young man dreaming of his role in leading North Korean nuclear strikes on New York City and returning to Pyongyang a hero.[32] The photographs included one of Kim Jong Un meeting with his senior military leadership in front of a large wall display of the flight trajectories of North Korean missiles into the American homeland, with Austin, Texas, among the most visible of the targets in the photo.[33]

This image is presumably intended to send a message of deterrence to the United States, by implying that North Korean leaders have both the capability and intent to conduct such nuclear strikes against the American homeland. During the Cold War, the United States received analogous deterrence messages from the Soviet Union, albeit in a very different context, defined above all by nearly global bipolar division and a risk of Armageddon-like nuclear war. How should the changed context be understood and with it the capabilities and intentions of North Korea?

On capabilities, the general picture is not crystal clear, but its main elements are well understood. As its conventional military posture has disintegrated over the last two decades, North Korea has transformed its strategic posture with the introduction of missiles of ever-longer range and with the development of nuclear weapons.[34] It is developing both fixed and mobile missiles capable of reaching the United States and the nuclear warheads to go with them.[35] It will soon have the ability to credibly threaten to attack the Republic of Korea (RoK), Japan, U.S. bases in the region, Hawaii and Alaska, and the rest of the American homeland with both conventional and nuclear warheads and perhaps also chemical and biological weapons. North Korea's nuclear capabilities continue to develop and improve, not least with the deployment of mobile missiles that are more difficult to target and strike than missiles at fixed launch sites.[36] And although its conventional forces are no longer capable of a major invasion and occupation of the entire peninsula, they continue to possess certain key strengths, including the ability to destroy Seoul with artillery fire and the ability to employ special forces behind enemy lines to disrupt and delay military operations by the Republic of Korea and the United States.

The fact that the picture is not crystal clear is not an accident. North Korea, like many other states, has deliberately obscured its capabilities.[37] In fact, the technical sophistication and reliability of these new weapons is in dispute, not least because North Korea has not had a practice of rigorously and publicly testing new capabilities, in contrast for example to Iran's missile program (with which North Korea has cooperated).[38] North Korea has also not established as a general practice the declaration of new capabilities as they are deployed, so there may be a mismatch between what is generally understood to be in the field and what is actually in the field.

On leadership intentions, the general picture is known but also not crystal clear. North Korea's leadership appears to be pursuing a foreign and defense policy with two main objectives. The first is to compel the United States to alter its strategic calculus in a manner that allows a political settlement on the Korean peninsula along the lines preferred by leaders in Pyongyang (that is, reunification of the peninsula under its leadership). The second is to be prepared to defend its interests in case of renewed military action on the peninsula, including ensuring survival of the regime.[39]

North Korea's Case for Nuclear Weapons

North Korea has made a public case that its new nuclear capabilities are for a fundamentally defensive purpose. When it declared itself a nuclear weapon state in 2005, the North Korean government stated as follows:

> The U.S. disclosed its attempt to topple the political system in [North Korea] at any cost, threatening it with a nuclear stick. This compels us to take a measure to bolster its [sic] nuclear weapons arsenal in order to protect the ideology, system, freedom and democracy chosen by its people . . . [North Korean nuclear weapons] will remain [a] nuclear deterrent for self defense under any circumstances.[40]

This was echoed in subsequent statements, including, for example:

A people without [a] reliable war deterrent are bound to meet a tragic death and the sovereignty of their country is bound to be wantonly infringed upon. . . . [North Korea's] nuclear weapons will serve as [a] reliable war deterrent for protecting the supreme interests of the state and the security of the Korean nation from the U.S. threat of aggression.[41]

The bloody lesson of the war in Iraq for the world is that only when a country has physical deterrence forces and massive military deterrence forces that are capable of overwhelmingly defeating any attack by state-of-the-art weapons, can it prevent war and defend its independence and national security.[42]

It has been shown to the corners of the earth that Libya's giving up its nuclear arms . . . was used as an invasion tactic to disarm the country by sugarcoating it with words like "the guaranteeing of security" and the "bettering of relations." Having one's own strength was the only way to keep the peace.[43]

In 2013, Kim Jong Un presided over the formulation of a law "consolidating the position of North Korea as a nuclear weapon state." That law stipulates that "the DPRK shall take practical steps to bolster up the nuclear deterrence and nuclear retaliatory strike power both in quality and quantity to cope with the gravity of the escalating danger of the hostile forces' aggression and attack."[44] An associated Central Committee report directed that:

The People's Army should perfect the war method and operation in the direction of raising the pivotal role of the nuclear armed forces in all aspects concerning the war deterrence and the war strategy, and the nuclear armed forces should always round off the combat posture.[45]

In summer 2014, Kim Jong Un's pronounced that "the time has gone forever when enemies threatened and intimidated us with atomic bombs."[46]
This progress in developing and fielding capabilities and the high-level official statements about North Korean nuclear strategy indicate that North Korean leaders have given attention to the possibility of armed confrontation with the United States under the nuclear shadow and have developed some ideas about how to bring North Korea's new "nuclear queens" into play to safeguard their interests when in conflict with the United States. According to one media source, North Korean military planning anticipates various possible pathways to nuclear war.[47] But does it also have a theory of victory—that is, a coherent set of ideas about how to achieve desired political objectives and

to induce U.S. restraint in time of crisis and war? The scant information given in the preceding paragraphs suggests three potential theories of victory, each with its own set of implied premises.[48]

Winning in "Peacetime"

Bear in mind that North Korea rejects the notion that it lives in peace with the United States, the Republic of Korea, and Japan. Indeed, as already noted, in 2013 it abrogated the armistice of nearly sixty years and declared itself again at war. But obviously this is not a hot war, in the sense of ongoing combat operations. North Korean leaders may believe that the nuclear means now at their disposal give them the means to win this long cold war by turning history in their preferred direction and achieving the result denied them now for more than six decades.

This theory of victory must include at least two key premises. The first is that the United States, its allies, and the international community more generally are prepared to accept North Korea as a nuclear weapon state and to recognize it formally as such. The second is that America's "hostile intentions" can be negated with a strong deterrent, resulting in new, less hostile intentions and indeed a U.S. willingness to cooperate on a political settlement of the conflict on the peninsula on terms favorable to Pyongyang. An additional premise of this theory may be that the will of the United States and its allies to stick to their current policies can be stressed to the breaking point through periodic provocations aimed at creating public fear, political stress, and crisis fatigue.

This theory of victory in "peacetime" requires no overt role for nuclear weapons, either nuclear threats or actual nuclear attacks. Their role is in the background as powerful "queens." This is a theory of victory in the spirit of Sun Tzu—aimed at subduing the enemy without fighting. As Toshi Yoshihara and James R. Holmes have argued, "Aspiring local hegemons consider nuclear weapons a trump card for deterring great power intervention in their neighborhoods, and thus as an enabler for plans to reshape regional orders."[49]

What evidence is there to support the existence of this theory of victory? The official statements set out in the previous paragraphs are one indicator. North Korea's aggressiveness at the conventional level following tests of its nuclear weapons also fits with this theory. The case can be made that North Korea's progress in developing its strategic deterrent has increased the willingness of its leaders to act aggressively at the conventional level, with provocations such as the sinking of a South Korean naval vessel (the *Cheonan*) in March 2010 and the shelling of Yeonpyeong Island in November 2010. On the other hand, dangerous and provocative behavior is nothing new for a North Korean regime that does not accept the legitimacy of the government in Seoul and sees itself as in a state of continuing war. Recall the long history of provocations against the South, including open attacks of various kinds, commando raids, submarine incursions, intrusions into and infiltrations across the demilitarized zone, assassination missions, airplane hijackings, and kidnappings.[50] But prior provocations never ran the risk of escalating to nuclear war.

This recalls what in the Cold War came to be called the stability-instability paradox. In this concept, stability refers to the achievement of a relationship of mutual nuclear vulnerability and deterrence by a newly nuclear-armed state with a nuclear-armed adversary. The instability refers to actions taken in the context of mutual nuclear vulnerability at the conventional level that would not otherwise have been contemplated because of unacceptable risks of an escalatory response by the enemy. The paradox refers to the fact that stability at the strategic level may generate instability at the conventional level.[51] A common view in South Korea and Japan is that North Korean conventional provocations are driven by this stability–instability paradox.

From an American perspective, this theory of victory is not credible but may seem so to North Korean leaders. The premises are ill-founded from an American perspective, but the strategy may seem sound to a North Korean leadership convinced that it has the "nuclear queens" needed to "mess with the United States."

Winning a Total War Begun by the United States

A second potential theory of victory may be reflected in North Korean thinking about fighting and winning a major war with a significant nuclear dimension but begun by the United States. Some North Korean sources allege that such thinking has been done in Pyongyang. One source asserts that:

> North Korea's war plan in case of a U.S. attack is total war, not the "low intensity limited warfare" or "regional conflict" talked about among the Western analysts. North Korea will mount a total war if attacked by the United States. . . . North Korea expects no help from China, Russia, or other nations in case of war with the U.S. It knows it will be fighting the superpower alone. North Korea's total war plan has two components: massive conventional warfare and

weapons of mass destruction. . . . North Korea will mount strategic nuclear attacks on the U.S. targets. . . . North Korea's war plan goes beyond repulsing U.S.
attackers and calls for the destruction of the United States. . . . [Artillery] can
rain 500,000 conventional and biochemical shells per hour on U.S. troops near
the DMZ. . . . Today few nations have military assets strong enough to challenge
the U.S. military. . . . Both Russia and China lack the political will to face down
the U.S. In contrast, North Korea has not only the military power but also the
political will to wage total war against the United States. North Korea has made
clear that it will strike all U.S. targets with all means, if the U.S. mounts military
attacks against North Korea. That North Korea's threat is no bluff can be seen
from aggressive actions taken by North Korea since the Korean War armistice.

The North believes it will win a war and plans to annihilate Japan . . . if
the United States meddles in it . . . The North can turn the South into a sea of
flame and annihilate it by using nuclear and chemical weapons and rockets. . . .
They [North Korea] will use them [nuclear weapons] if South Korea starts
a war. . . . They intend to devastate Japan to prevent the United States from
participating.[52]

The cited source is not authoritative in the way that statements by officials are.
On the other hand, it is highly unlikely that independent views on so sensitive a topic would be permitted at an institute in Pyongyang. The propaganda
value of such statements is unmistakable. But we should accept also the possibility that there may be some in Pyongyang's profoundly isolated and insecure
community who adhere to such views.

What key premises might inform such thinking? It is difficult to imagine
that North Korean leaders could seriously contemplate this notion of victory,
not least because they do not have the means for extended nuclear war fighting or for the total annihilation of the United States. But even in the absence
of a plausible theory of victory in major war, North Korean leaders may see
a reason to attack the United States by nuclear means. They have frequently
expressed, in personal terms, a desire to directly "punish" or "bloody" the
United States and its allies if war occurs.[53] As one North Korean senior figure
has argued, "The DPRK is resolute and determined . . . we will fight to the
end. . . . the U.S. might win such a war, killing half our people, but it would not
win the minds of the people."[54]

In this theory of victory, North Korean nuclear weapons obviously play a
central operational role. They would be employed as instruments of Armaged-

don. They would also presumably have a role in trying to deter U.S. nuclear counter-attack and to deter formation of a coalition intent on regime removal.

From an American perspective, this theory of victory is again not credible. Total war launched by North Korea would be a total disaster for North Korea, unifying the world community to ensure that the regime in Pyongyang is no longer a danger to anyone and leaving the United States no choice but to use its most powerful tools decisively toward that end. We should accept, however, that vengeance is a powerful motivator and that North Korean leaders may, like other leaders before them, believe that gravely wounding their enemy in retribution may be a form of victory in its own right, even if the war itself is a lost cause.

Winning a Limited War through Blackmail and Brinksmanship

A third potential theory of victory may be reflected in North Korean thinking about initiating a less-than-total war and fighting it to a point where it is able to achieve some significant new political gain, whether a favorable political settlement of the outstanding dispute or merely a weakening of its enemies while safeguarding its own control. Such a theory would include some or all of the following elements.

A key premise would have to be that North Korea can achieve a quick operational advantage in a manner that puts the burden of escalation onto the United States. It must believe that it could achieve a military fait accompli on the peninsula, such as capturing some portion of the demilitarized zone and neighboring territories to the South while taking Seoul "hostage" by overtly threatening it with attack with the massive arsenal of artillery located within range of Seoul. Special operations forces could play a central role for the North in disrupting the military response of the RoK and United States to the unfolding crisis, as might attacks on critical military targets in the South with chemical and biological weapons. Prompt success in achieving this goal would put the U.S.–RoK alliance in the situation of deciding whether it would be willing to pay the high cost of reversing the aggression. In the North Korean theory of victory, it would not.

But this premise alone is insufficient. This third potential theory of victory would not be complete without some notion of how to manage the risks of escalation if the United States and its allies choose to contest the fait accompli and do not acquiesce to the political preferences of the North. North Korea may look for ways to expand the war geographically, by attacking targets at more distance—especially the bases in Japan that fly the flag of the United Nations and host the conventional forces of the UN Command that would then be mobilizing for the conventional defense of South Korea (this is referred to as *horizontal escalation*). It may also increase the intensity of its attacks, including with conventional weapons, chemical weapons, and/or biological weapons (this is referred to as *vertical escalation*). It may look for ways to expand the war into the new domains of cyberspace and outer space (this might be referred to as *lateral escalation*).[55]

Thus, a key premise would have to be that American restraint can be induced by pressuring its allies. Such pressure would come in the form of limited strikes by North Korea to impress on their allies their vulnerability along with the threat of more to come. It may see a particular opportunity in targeting Japan, as political relations between Japan and South Korea are strained and North Korean leaders may believe that the Japanese public would not want to bear high costs for the defense of South Korea. In this version of the North Korean theory of victory, limited nonnuclear strikes backed by overt nuclear threats would suffice to induce this restraint.

A related premise would have to be that American restraint can be induced by reminding the United States of the vulnerability of its own homeland to attack. Actual attack ought to seem excessively risky to leaders in North Korea, but threats to attack, supported by preparations to do so, might seem useful to them. Moreover, it is possible that they may calculate that attacks on U.S. forces in the region, on their military headquarters in Hawaii, and on remotely located U.S. missile defenses in the Aleutian Islands would not run the same risks as attacks on the continental United States and especially urban centers there.

This then invokes the question of whether North Korea might also see the limited employment of nuclear weapons at this point in a conflict as both necessary and effective in inducing the desired U.S. restraint. For this to be so, it must imagine forms of nuclear attack that would be somehow crippling to the political will of the allies or crippling to their military operations but unlikely to incite a nuclear response from the United States. North Korean leaders may believe, for example, that limited nuclear strikes on South Korea or Japan would bring rapid war termination on their terms, as the coalition collapses and the United States is forced to choose between fighting alone and suing for peace. In the language of the Cold War, North Korea's leaders may believe that they can "decouple" the United States from the defense of the Republic of Korea by clearly putting the American homeland in jeopardy.

The dilemma they face is that their threats to employ nuclear weapons might not seem credible to us in view of our overwhelming capacity to respond. Yet to be successful, nuclear blackmail requires both the credible demonstration of resolve and the credible demonstration of restraint. The resolve relates to the willingness to make good on an escalatory threat and the restraint relates to the willingness not to inflict punishment if terms are met. To be credible, the resolve must be demonstrated. Limited nuclear attacks that North Korea might deem as falling beneath the U.S. response threshold could be seen as useful for this purpose, in addition to whatever operational purposes they might serve. Some analysts have highlighted attack scenarios falling well short of comprehensive North Korean nuclear strikes on a wide array of targets, including for example by smuggling a weapon into a port on a trawler.[56] As Keir Lieber and Daryl Press have argued, "The key to coercion is the hostage that is still alive: half a dozen South Korean or Japanese cities, which Kim could threaten to attack unless the Combined Forces Command accepted a cease-fire."[57]

This is a theory of victory that uses the "nuclear queens" as tools of blackmail and brinksmanship. It is not a theory of fighting or winning a major nuclear war. In this sense, it is primarily a nuclear theory of victory and not primarily a theory of nuclear victory.

As set out here, this theory fits a scenario in which North Korea calculates that a war of this kind would serve its interests and thus initiates the war. It may also fit a scenario in which North Korea miscalculates its way into war. This is a scenario that would devolve from the first theory of victory discussed earlier and the North's use of conventional provocations to try to break the resolve of the U.S.–RoK alliance to stay its course. Such provocations could result in military actions by the allies that are unexpected by Pyongyang and lead it to react in ways that precipitate broader combat operations. In this pathway to conflict, North Korea might find itself scrambling to try to secure some fait accompli.

What evidence is there to support the existence of such a theory of victory? The evidence is incomplete and mixed. In the conventional military domain, the emphasis of North Korean military planning appears to have shifted over time from an emphasis on a large conventional invasion to retake the peninsula (essentially, a replay of its aggression in 1950) to an emphasis on more limited operations aimed at decisive strategic effects through the use of special operations forces, missiles armed with both conventional weapons and weapons of mass destruction, cyberattacks, and artillery attacks on Seoul.[58] Pyongyang's apparent confidence in nuclear weapons as "a reliable war deterrent" hints at a possible role for those weapons in containing U.S. and South Korea military action. The official statement about the role of nuclear weapons in "rounding off the combat posture" suggests a more limited role for North Korean nuclear weapons than envisaged in the total war scenario.

From an American perspective, this theory of victory may well seem plausible to North Korean leaders. After all, brinksmanship is nothing new to them. What's new is the introduction of the "nuclear queen." The risks may seem manageable, on the basis of the premises set out earlier. If this strategy results in North Korean nuclear attack, this seems plausible on only a limited basis, in ways North Korea might see as sufficient to its purpose of demonstrating its resolve without running significant risk of counter-escalation by the United States, given the vulnerability of the U.S. homeland to counterattack. This is the theory of victory that comes closest to the spirit of Clausewitz and the use of force to reach a "culminating point" when an enemy not fully subdued accedes to the preferences of the victor in establishing the conditions of peace, conditions aligned with the victor's original political objectives.[59] By this logic, North Korea's theory of victory reflects the conviction that it can force termination of a war in a manner favorable to its political objectives and establishing an acceptable post-war balance of power despite the asymmetry of power vis-à-vis the United States and its allies.

Historical experience lends some credibility to this view. As Paul Huth and Bruce Russett argued in 1988, the local balance of power, both conventional and nuclear, was more determinative of crisis outcomes than comprehensive nuclear superiority or conventional supremacy that can be amassed over time.[60] And as Robert Rauchhaus argued in 2009, nuclear-armed states have been less likely to face the escalation of disputes than nonnuclear states.[61]

From an American perspective again, how plausible are the two pathways to such limited war, the one of calculation and the other of miscalculation? First, is it possible that North Korea's leaders might make a choice for limited premeditated war with an explicit nuclear shadow? On the one hand, North Korean leadership has been astute at conducting provocations without precipitating war and thus seems unmotivated to go to war. On the other hand, reunification of the Fatherland on its terms remains a top priority for North Korean leadership. The regime's continued pursuit of this goal is a key basis of its political legitimacy. The unsettled conflict from the 1950s (the Fatherland Liberation War, as it is known in the North) continues to have a significant role in shaping leadership views and may yet serve as a catalyst for military action.[62]

Moreover, there is an important and at this time unanswerable question about the ambitions of Kim Jong Un. As a young and apparently very confident man, potentially with decades of rule of North Korea in front of him, can he possibly be satisfied with mere preservation of the status quo on the peninsula as his future legacy? How might the successful fielding of a small nuclear force affect his strategic calculus and his willingness to take risks and bear costs with the hope of righting history, as he sees it? And can we assess with confidence his actual intentions? Skepticism is warranted.

How plausible is the miscalculation pathway? The potential for miscalculation by the North appears to be significant. Writing in 2014, Patrick Cronin highlighted the significant potential for miscalculation by the leadership in Pyongyang and concluded that "the risks on the peninsula have not been this significant since the early 1990s."[63] Those risks, he argues, derive in part from "an increasingly perceived need among the North Korean leadership for Pyongyang to demonstrate strength."[64]

To assess that this particular theory of victory is credible from a North Korean perspective is not the same as arguing that it would be effective if put to the test. There is a good deal of wishful thinking here. Moreover, there is much that the United States and its allies can do to erode North Korean confidence in this theory—as will be argued in Chapter 3.

On the Plausibility of North Korean Nuclear Employment

A North Korean theory of victory based on blackmail and brinksmanship backed by nuclear threats seems plausible to outside experts for at least two reasons. One is the long practice of blackmail and brinksmanship by North Korea. The other is our own Cold War history. As Richard Betts has argued in surveying the history of nuclear crises in the early Cold War, U.S. leaders sometimes made nuclear threats without apparent significant concern that they might have to make good on them.[65]

But should a theory of blackmail and brinksmanship that requires limited nuclear strikes to establish the credibility of resolve also seem credible to outside experts? Are the potential pathways to nuclear employment described earlier plausible?

An important cautionary note about the validity of such pathway analysis was struck by McGeorge Bundy in the late 1960s. Surveying the work of civilian strategists trying to understand how the Soviet Union and United States might employ nuclear weapons in war, he observed that they had failed to capture the deep reluctance of political leaders to move down any pathway that might potentially result in nuclear attack on their nation:

> There is an enormous gulf between what political leaders really think about nuclear weapons and what is assumed in complex calculations of relative "advantage" in simulated strategic warfare. Think-tank analysts . . . are in an unreal world. In the real world of real political leaders . . . a decision that would bring even one hydrogen bomb on one city in one's own country would be recognized in advance as a catastrophic blunder.[66]

Bearing in mind this advice, some American analysts dismiss any possibility of nuclear employment by North Korea as a strategic blunder of epic proportions. They assess that North Korean nuclear employment is not plausible under any circumstances, arguing that it would automatically result in the annihilation of Pyongyang and the end of the current regime.[67]

A second cautionary note comes from Stanley Hoffman, who argued in 1965 that nuclear crises would come to substitute for wars as determinants of the distribution of power and influence in the international system.[68] Matthew Kroenig has defined a nuclear crisis as follows:

> In a nuclear crisis, a state exerts coercive pressure on its adversary by raising the risk of nuclear war until one of the participating states prefers to capitulate rather than run any additional risk of catastrophe. A standoff between nuclear-armed opponents is a nuclear crisis whether or not nuclear weapons are used, are explicitly threatened, or are the subject of the dispute, because the very existence of nuclear weapons and the possibility that they could be used have a decisive bearing on bargaining dynamics.[69]

In Hoffman's assessment, while nuclear enemies might make ferocious threats to shape a crisis, their actual propensity to make good on such threats would be low. Bearing in mind this advice, we might reasonably anticipate a long string of future crises precipitated by North Korea but no serious prospect that any of them will become actual armed combat, let alone nuclear conflict.

These two cautionary notes need to be put in context. Bundy was reacting to scenarios for nuclear wars involving tens, hundreds, and thousands of nuclear weapons and also major wars on a continental or even global scale. He was also reflecting the maturation of thinking of political leaders in Washington after more than two decades of managing Cold War nuclear crises. He also had some basis for believing that leaders in Moscow thought in ways understood by leaders in Washington. Today's circumstances are quite different. Scenarios for regional nuclear conflict would involve far more limited types of nuclear attacks (and potentially none on the United States itself). With the possible exception of the Persian Gulf War of 1990–1991, there has been no political-military crisis understood by American political leaders as a nuclear crisis with lessons for how to manage current risks. And there is little evidence to think that leaders in Pyongyang think the way leaders in Washington do (on the contrary).

And Hoffman was writing largely about the behaviors of major powers in a balance of power system centered in Europe and contending with each other in a circumstance in which any local conflict was likely to escalate almost automatically to major conventional and major nuclear war. The only mode of confrontation that would enable survival was brinksmanship and bargaining but not war. In today's world, we have to contemplate the possibility of nuclear crises in a very different context from that of the Cold War.

Given the different context today, some American analysts see North Korean nuclear employment as plausible in some circumstances.[70] They make four key arguments. First, regional conventional wars will almost automatically invoke questions of regime survival, especially if they involve nuclear threats by the regional challenger. This problem will be aggravated by an American way of conventional war that puts a premium of the massive early use of air power and other means to deprive an enemy of his ability to control his armed forces. In the words of Keir Lieber and Daryl Press,

> Weak states face powerful incentives to use nuclear weapons if they find themselves in a conventional war against a much stronger adversary. . . . The logic of coercive nuclear escalation is well understood by countries around the world. Coercive nuclear escalation is not a theoretical possibility; it is reflected

in the defense plans and nuclear employment doctrines of several nuclear-armed states.[71]

Senior U.S. intelligence officials have supported the hypothesis that North Korea might employ nuclear weapons for purposes of regime survival. For example, in February 2009, then Director of National Intelligence Dennis Blair argued in congressional testimony that "Pyongyang probably views its nuclear weapons as being more for deterrence, international prestige, and coercive diplomacy than for war fighting and would consider using nuclear weapons only under certain narrow circumstances . . . [including when] it perceived the regime to be on the verge of military defeat or risked an irretrievable loss of control."[72]

As already noted, leaders in Pyongyang apparently assess the United States as intending to use force to "topple the political system" in the North. An important question is how early in such a war that perception might form. If late in the conflict, nuclear employment by the North might be a last-ditch move in desperation in the closing phases of a conflict. If early in the conflict, nuclear employment by the North might come early and in a way that would surprise many.

The second argument in support of the plausibility of North Korean nuclear employment is about the asymmetry of stake. A leader's political stakes in a conflict are a key determinant of his or her willingness to run risks, including in nuclear crises.[73] In today's world, an asymmetry of stake as perceived by regional actors may give them confidence in their ability to manage the risks of escalation in a "game" of brinksmanship. In war of the kind worried about by McGeorge Bundy, nuclear employment called into question the sovereignty and survival of both governments and societies. In war of the kind imaginable today with regional adversaries, their sovereignty and survival may be at risk, thus creating a vital interest for them, whereas the stake of the United States may be quite important but not vital because its sovereignty and survival are not at risk. Thus, from their perspective, they may have a greater willingness to run nuclear risks and pay the costs of escalation than the United States and its allies. As David Ochmanek and Lowell Schwartz have argued, "The weaker side has, in a sense, achieved escalation dominance."[74] In the words of Victor Utgoff and Michael Wheeler, "The theory of nuclear victory posits that a restrained nuclear war might be initiated if a state thought it could win a stake it values highly but believes its opponent would sacrifice rather than defend at the cost of suffering even a very few nuclear strikes."[75]

But contests of resolve are inherently unpredictable. Neither adversary can know in advance how much resolve the other actually has to win or defend a specific stake. One or both could end up being surprised that the resolve proved higher or lower than calculated. To initiate a conflict on the Korean peninsula and begin to escalate it, Pyongyang would have to calculate that the United States has less resolve to defend the status quo than Pyongyang has to alter it.[76] Historical experience suggests that newly nuclear-armed states go through a period of testing the resolve of their adversaries and of calibrating their degree of risk aversion—which may be precisely the behavior now in evidence by North Korea.[77]

An additional complication is that resolve and perceptions of stake often change in conflict, in a manner that typically makes war more prolonged and unpredictable than expected.[78] This seems especially likely as a political-military crisis transitions into war and as a conventional war transitions into a nuclear war. Pyongyang may not fully understand the stake that would be created by the United States by its employment of nuclear weapons and thus may miscalculate its way into a war with terrible consequences.

The third argument in support of the plausibility of North Korean nuclear employment is simply that the kind of nuclear regional wars that can be imagined today would not involve the massive exchange of large nuclear arsenals and thus may have a much lower threshold to nuclear employment. As Jeffrey Larsen has argued, "If nuclear weapons are used in a future conflict, that use is likely to be limited in ways that contrast sharply with the Cold War assumptions of a massive exchange of thousands of weapons."[79] The risks of nuclear employment thus cannot be judged in the same way that they were in the context of massive exchanges between nuclear arsenals numbering in the tens of thousands.

The fourth argument is that North Korean leaders may not see U.S. threats to employ nuclear weapons as credible. Their potential skepticism may derive from revelations by leaders of the administrations of Presidents George H. W. Bush and Bill Clinton that they would likely not have made good on the implied nuclear threat had Saddam crossed their red lines.[80] North Korean leaders may also believe that they have significantly reduced the likelihood of U.S. nuclear strikes on their nuclear forces by locating them in areas neighboring China, in a manner that might be seen as increasing U.S. risks of military action.[81]

Of note, the North Korean nuclear threat to the American homeland has been sufficiently credible in the eyes of senior American policy makers to motivate bipartisan support to spend approximately $5 billion per year for nearly two decades to develop and deploy a missile defense capable of protecting the United States from this threat. Developments in North Korean capabilities were seen in 2012 as sufficiently worrying to motivate a decision to increase protection of the homeland from North Korean ballistic missile attack.[82]

The New Spectrum of Deterrence Challenges

With the advent of North Korean nuclear weapons and long-range strike capabilities, we are entering a new, more dangerous phase with North Korea. New nuclear crises seem likely, each intended by North Korea to convey a risk of nuclear war. Whether through calculation or miscalculation, such crises might result in actual armed confrontation, combat operations, and escalation of various kinds. These risks cannot be fully calibrated but cannot be ignored. North Korean leaders appear to have thought about how to manage the risks of escalation in a conflict with the United States through nuclear and other threats, though whether they actually have one or more theory of victory vis-à-vis the United States cannot be known definitively.

On the central question of whether North Korean leaders might actually conduct nuclear attacks, the U.S. policy maker is presented with an uncertainty: North Korean nuclear attack cannot be ruled out. But neither should it be ruled in. Although we cannot say definitely whether North Korea would employ nuclear weapons, we can understand something of when, why, and how, based on the pathway analysis given in the preceding pages. As a practical matter, the United States must take steps to reduce the risks of North Korean nuclear use, whatever they may be, while also preparing for the possibility of use and the need to restore deterrence if North Korea proceeds to limited nuclear strikes (while holding something in reserve) aimed at demonstrating the credibility of its nuclear threats.

Toward this end, the United States needs an analytical model to fully map out the problem space and to identify where and how U.S. deterrence practices might be relevant and effective in eliciting restraint by North Korean leaders. Drawing on the pathway analysis in the preceding discussion, it is possible to catalogue and organize the particular decisions North Korean leaders might make that the United States must be effective in influencing to induce

North Korean restraint. It is useful to think of a broad spectrum of deterrence challenges in regional conflict under the nuclear shadow defined by different phases of conflict and degrees of escalation.[83] Those challenges come in three distinct sets along this spectrum:

1. Gray zone: At the low end of the conflict spectrum are provocations and confrontations just below the level of armed conflict. These encompass, for example, North Korea sinking the *Cheonan* or the shelling of Yeonpyeong Island in 2010.[84] War is not underway, but conflict is present, and military-backed coercion is being attempted, whether explicit or implied.

2. Red zone: In the middle of the spectrum are what might be termed "red zone" threats—conflicts involving actual combat operations and efforts by regional actors to try to exploit nuclear and missile capabilities to their advantage with actions that they calculate or hope to be beneath the U.S. nuclear response threshold (U.S. declaratory policy notwithstanding). Along the spectrum, this zone appears to be growing in size and relevance as these new capabilities are developed and fielded.

3. Black-and-white zone: At the opposite, high end of the spectrum are nuclear attacks on the homeland of the United States. Think of this as the "black-and-white zone," where any attack by nuclear means on the homeland of the United States or an ally should be understood as resulting in a devastating U.S. response, likely nuclear.

In the gray zone, the key points are decisions by North Korean leaders whether or not:

1. To conduct conventional provocations.
2. To conduct cyber attacks on civilian and military targets as a form of coercion.
3. To test and otherwise display new capabilities as a way to send messages of resolve and vulnerability.
4. To initiate military operations for a fait accompli.

This fourth decision (to cross from the gray zone into the red zone) might be taken if Pyongyang were to assess that it would be possible to take its "hostage" quickly and to impose high costs on the United States and its allies if they were to seek to reverse it.

In the red zone, Pyongyang's key decision points are as follows:

5. If the fait accompli is not quickly achieved by military means, to employ chemical and/or biological weapons for operational benefits (to degrade U.S. projection of U.S. and allied conventional forces through contaminated bases) and for strategic purposes (to signal a willingness to escalate to more lethal means against additional targets).

6. If this strategy fails to produce the desired political results, to pressure the hostage with additional punishment. On the Korean peninsula, this could involve some rocket and artillery fire into Seoul.

7. If this strategy fails, to retaliate by conventional means for attacks conducted by the United States and its allies. In a Korean conflict, this could involve attacks on or off the peninsula, including on bases and other targets in Japan (Japan hosts eight bases under UN Command in support of the defense of Korea).

8. If the political and military strategy is failing, to conduct a limited nuclear attack with an eye to demonstrating its resolve but in a manner calculated to make U.S. nuclear retaliation unlikely (in Pyongyang's assessment). North Korea might believe that such an attack could break the alliance (by inducing the RoK to sue for peace before the United States is prepared to do so). It might believe that it can greatly reduce if not eliminate the risk of U.S. retaliation with the very limited employment of a nuclear weapon as a way to signal resolve but without killing any or many (such as an offshore demonstration shot or a high-altitude burst for its electromagnetic pulse effects). Presumably this type of action would also be accompanied by a threat of more North Korean nuclear attacks if the allies do not sue for peace on the North's terms.

In the black-and-white zone, North Korea would face the following decisions:

9. To threaten or conduct limited nuclear attacks on military and/or civilian targets in South Korea or Japan, with the threat of more to come.

10. If this fails to induce the desired restraint of the United States and its allies, to threaten or conduct limited nuclear attacks on U.S. military facilities in the American homeland engaged in military operations against North Korea (for example, Pacific Command headquarters in Honolulu or missile defense facilities in Alaska).

11. And if the United States employs nuclear weapons in retaliation, to respond or not with additional nuclear attacks of its own, whether on U.S. bases and forces in the region or on the American homeland. The purpose here might be to persuade the United States that the costs of continuing the war outweigh the potential benefits. Alternatively, the purpose might simply be to exact revenge on a hated enemy as the regime's final act in a war it is poised to lose in any case.

This sequence of decisions implies that the employment of nuclear weapons by North Korea for lethal effect on enemy military and political targets would come only late in a failed conventional conflict. But, as noted earlier, North Korean leaders may calculate that regime survival would automatically be at risk in any renewed war on the Korean peninsula and thus may contemplate employment of nuclear weapons early in a conflict to shock Washington and Seoul into suing for peace. This perception of a need for and value in employing nuclear weapons early in a conflict may be reinforced by fears that the United States would be successful in preemptively eliminating those capabilities.

Each decision in this hierarchy would involve assessments of the resolve of the United States and its allies to continue in an escalating conflict, as well perhaps as assessments of Pyongyang's own resolve. Each new action by Pyongyang can be understood as a test of the separate or collective resolve of Washington, Seoul, and Tokyo. In the preceding scenario, Kim Jong Un would be making choices to signal his resolve to safeguard his interests even in an escalating conflict, while testing the resolve of the alliance arrayed against him to remain intact. The United States would act to signal its resolve to safeguard its allies and forces and the American homeland, while testing the resolve of Kim Jong Un to remain committed to aggression and escalation.

These are inherently competitive and risky strategies.[85] Any such competitive testing of resolve would bring to the fore in the decision-making process the stake each side perceives in the conflict—and the perceived stake of the adversary. Presumably each side begins with the premise that its stake is more substantial. For North Korea, a vital interest would seem to be at stake—regime survival. For the United States, the vital interest of an ally or allies would be at stake—their long-term viability under a political outcome dictated by the North if the United States were to concede. As argued in the preceding pages, North Korean leaders may believe that their vital interest is the more compelling, thus lending credibility to their escalatory threats in their eyes.

Accordingly, a key danger is the potential for miscalculation of resolve.[86] To escalate by any means seems to require a conviction that the other side lacks the resolve to retaliate or to counter-escalate. As argued in the preceding paragraphs, leaders in North Korea may calculate that their resolve is superior to that of the United States and its allies. They may see resolve of the United States and its allies as relatively weak or absolutely weak—perhaps because of a belief that democracies are paper tigers or so casualty averse as to avoid escalation at all costs. They may calculate that America is in decline and no longer ready to pay a significant price to defend the interests at stake on the Korean peninsula. They may calculate further that as the supposed true heirs to Korean history, their victory against the United States is inevitable. Conversely, the United States and its allies may calculate that the resolve in Pyongyang is weak, perhaps because of a belief that nuclear war is unwinnable and thus will not actually be fought.

Moreover, in tests of resolve, bluffs are often employed. This creates the additional risk of miscalculation derived from a decision to dismiss as a bluff a statement of resolve that is no bluff at all.

This suggests that the challenges of managing escalation in a regional conflict with a nuclear-armed aggressor are numerous. Such adversaries may engage in deliberate acts of escalation, as argued earlier. But escalation may be inadvertent, if it results from an action that was not intended to be escalatory but is perceived as such by the other side. And escalation may be accidental, if it results from actions that were not deliberate (but often occur in the fog of war). Deliberate escalation may be "manageable" if the adversary decision maker conducts a deliberate assessment of benefit, cost, and risk, whereas inadvertent and accidental escalation are inherently less "manageable."[87]

The decisions catalogued here are illustrative of the actual decisions that North Korean leaders would face in trying to secure their interests in a political-military confrontation with the United States. There is little evidence to confirm that leaders or planners in Pyongyang have thought systematically about such decisions. But this analytic framework is needed to inform the development of U.S. deterrence strategies vis-à-vis North Korea and any other potential nuclear adversary that might attempt to bring "nuclear queens" into play in an effort to "mess with the United States." Without such a framework, the United States cannot adequately understand how potential enemy leaders calculate the benefits, costs, and risks of various courses of action—a calculus that our deterrence strategies seek to influence.

Conclusions

A new strategic problem for the United States has taken shape since the end of the Cold War. The problem has taken various forms in the Middle East over the last two decade but has taken its clearest and most compelling form in Northeast Asia, where the emergence of a nuclear-armed North Korea with the means to deliver nuclear weapons at long range is rewriting the strategic landscape.

Political agreements with proliferators may yet alleviate this new problem by eliminating the North Korean nuclear threat and preventing the emergence of new regional threats. After all, the United States, along with many other nations working within the nonproliferation regime and outside it, seeks a political settlement with Pyongyang that would roll back its capabilities and bring it back into the NPT. A different regime in Pyongyang might finally abandon its nuclear arsenal to join the community of nations. Korean reunification may yet occur in a way that enables a reunified Korea to join the international consensus against nuclear weapons. The United States also leads a strong international coalition to promote the full and effective implementation of the NPT.

But efforts to eliminate this new problem entirely seem unpromising at this time. Prolonged stalemate with North Korea and long-term uncertainty about Iran's nuclear future seem more likely to amplify than attenuate proliferation pressures. Moreover, other leaders of regional powers may yet find their own reasons to seek "nuclear queens" of their own to "mess with the United States"—or some other country—and pursue their own visions of regional order.

The evidence strongly suggests that North Korea has thought about how to use its new "nuclear queens" to secure its control, to advance its interests in its long-running confrontation with the United States and South Korea, and perhaps even to achieve a settlement on its terms of the long-running conflict on the peninsula. This thinking encompasses ideas about how to persuade the United States to come to the negotiating table willing to cut a deal. It also encompasses ideas about how to manage the risks in war of escalation by the

United States. There is no clear evidence that North Korea has a theory of victory in a war with the United States involving extended nuclear war fighting. But there is evidence, albeit incomplete, that North Korea has various theories of victory. Of these, the most plausible in U.S. eyes must by the theory built on nuclear blackmail and brinksmanship, rather than nuclear war fighting. There is some reason to think, however, that North Korean leaders may believe that they can employ nuclear weapons on a limited basis to demonstrate their resolve and thus to prevail in a limited war with the United States, South Korea, and Japan. To prevail means, in this context, to survive a conflict with their political aims achieved and other interests intact.

North Korean capabilities and concepts can be used to map out a spectrum of deterrence challenges for the United States and its allies. Especially troubling are those new deterrence challenges associated with what I have called the red zone—a category of decisions by leaders in Pyongyang to escalate conflicts in ways that they may believe fall beneath the likely U.S. response threshold. Although this spectrum of deterrence challenges has analogues in the Cold War, it is not merely a Cold War vestige. It requires meaningful solutions suited to the current context. It requires also adapting the old logic of limited nuclear war to this new problem. This is the subject of the following chapter.

3   The New Regional Deterrence Strategy

THE EMERGENCE OF THIS NEW PROBLEM HAS BROUGHT WITH it some new thinking in the United States about how to respond. This thinking is driven by two basic policy imperatives.

The United States must ensure that everything possible is done to preserve the decades-long nonuse of nuclear weapons. If North Korean leaders perceive potential pathways to the successful employment of nuclear weapons, everything must be done to block those pathways.

The United States must also be mindful of precedents. From the perspective of a country with security commitments in three regions and with a global concern about nuclear order, the success of North Korea's theory of victory, whether in peacetime or war, would be highly damaging. Successful North Korean blackmail of the United States and its allies would set precedents of a far-reaching kind, calling into question the credibility of U.S. security guarantees more generally. The wrong choices by the United States and its allies in a military crisis with North Korea under the nuclear shadow could tip the security environment in a dangerous new direction. To be coerced into appeasing a nuclear-backed challenger or to accept defeat in a regional war with some nuclear aspect could have wide-ranging repercussions for the international situation after such a war. The wrong choices could also lead to the "nuclear cascade" long feared by policy makers. How? A failure of U.S. deterrence, or the wrong U.S. responses to such a failure, could embolden others to seek capabilities of their own with which to challenge the United States and U.S.-guaranteed regional orders. A failure of assurance of key allies could similarly lead them to conclude that they can no longer count on the U.S. nuclear umbrella to protect them.

With an eye on this emerging problem, the United States has made some basic strategic choices. To a significant extent, these are common across administrations since the end of the Cold War and enjoy bipartisan support. In its national strategy, the United States has chosen to remain engaged, not retreat into isolationism, and to modernize its alliances for 21st-century purposes. In its military strategy, it has chosen to project power in support of its international commitments and to maintain strong capabilities for deterring and defeating potential regional aggressors.

An additional choice is key: the United States has rejected a mutual deterrence relationship with North Korea—and with any other regional challenger to the United States and its allies. It has done so in part because of an abiding concern that a multipolar world based on the principle of mutual nuclear vulnerability could be deeply unstable. And it has done so in part because of a concern that U.S. nuclear threats may not be credible or effective across the full spectrum of deterrence challenges. They may lack credibility for gray zone and red zone conflicts. U.S. nuclear threats may not be effective for reducing the coercive value of aggressor nuclear threats and against leaders who calculate that an asymmetry of stake lends credibility to their threats. Heavy reliance on nuclear threats is also not reassuring to allies, who seek protection and assurance in addition to deterrence. Reliance on nuclear threats alone would also be unhelpful to the effort to strengthen international cooperation for nonproliferation and disarmament.

Accordingly, the United States has been pursuing a comprehensive approach to strengthening regional deterrence architectures. It is doing so not just in Northeast Asia, where the North Korean threat is now taking shape, but also in Europe and the Middle East. In the latter two regions, the commitment to strengthen regional deterrence architectures follows from two factors. One is the proliferation of ballistic missiles into the region, including but not limited to Iran. Iran has an aggressive research, development, and deployment program for ballistic missiles and is an active exporter. It has the capability to target all countries in the Middle East and much of southern Europe and will soon have the capability to reach all of Europe. The second factor is the increased reliance on deterrence by the United States and its allies at a time of economic difficulty and fiscal austerity for many and the concomitant inability to maintain large standing forces capable of promptly defeating local aggression. These architectures are also the foundation on which additional responses would be built if Iran and/or other states in the Middle East were to decide to acquire and deploy nuclear weapons.

This chapter reviews the elements of this comprehensive approach with an eye to clarifying the desired deterrence and other benefits. Particular attention is paid to the multiple contributions of missile defense to the overall strategy. The chapter also sets out a counterpart Blue theory to the Red theory described in the preceding chapter.

The Comprehensive Approach to Strengthening Regional Deterrence Architectures

This comprehensive approach has been formulated in largely similar ways by each of the presidential administrations since the Cold War, with the Obama administration going the furthest in setting out the details of the approach in the policy reviews and strategic documents it set out early on its watch.[1] Key elements of this approach are the following:

- Political partnerships between the United States and its allies and partners that are strong and effectively focused on cooperative action on challenges to the interests of one, both, or all allies/partners.[2]
- Conventional forces capable of acting quickly and decisively in defense of the interests of the United States and its allies/partners.
- Deployment of conventional strike capabilities, including a long-range prompt component.
- Deployment of ballistic missile defense in two dimensions: (1) protection against regional threats to U.S. forces and U.S. allies/partners and (2) protection of the American homeland against limited strikes from countries like North Korea and Iran.
- Improved resilience against attacks in the cyber and space domains.[3]
- A nuclear component tailored to the unique historical, geographical, and other features of each region where the nuclear "umbrella" is extended.[4]

- Unambiguous statements of political intent by the United States to defend its interests and those of its allies and partners.

The comprehensive approach to strengthening regional deterrence clearly embeds the nuclear component of the strategy in a larger construct. As Wade Huntley has described it, "The nuclear umbrella has become the pinnacle of a security dome."[5]

From a deterrence perspective, the values of this comprehensive approach are cumulative and synergistic across the spectrum of deterrence challenges described in the preceding chapter. As argued there, for deterrence in a regional context to be effective, it must be capable of influencing in a decisive manner the adversary's assessments of resolve and restraint at each of the decision points in the spectrum of deterrence challenges. They are cumulative in that each element makes its own contribution to the spectrum of challenges. They are synergistic in that contributions in one area help to compensate for weaknesses in others.

The deterrence value of strong political partnerships between and among allies is fundamental. Such strength is critical to undermining the adversary's calculus that it can drive wedges into alliances, split the United States from its allies, and compel it to fight on alone without their support. It also lends credibility to the U.S. promise to come to the defense of an ally when that ally's vital interests are put at risk by a regional aggressor.

Equally fundamental is the deterrence value of conventional forces capable of acting quickly and decisively. The existence of such forces undermines the adversary's confidence that a military fait accompli can be quickly won or that efforts to reverse it will be possible only at high cost over a long period of time. Locally deployed forces also play an important role as a trip wire, as their lives would be at stake in any aggressor attempt to create a fait accompli and their deaths would compel strong and decisive U.S. action. Maintaining such favorable balances in any given locale is increasingly difficult as U.S. and allied defense spending has fallen. This puts a premium on maintaining a forward U.S. military presence and access agreements as well as forces that are globally deployable with relative speed to complement in-place regional assets. This highlights also the important role of the conventional forces of U.S. allies and partners in maintaining local deterrence.

The deterrence values of conventional strike capabilities derive fundamentally from the credibility they bring to the threat of preemptive or preventive strikes by the United States and/or its allies and partners. As a gray zone conflict begins to transition into the red zone, the specific deterrence challenges there may not be effectively met with threats of nuclear preemption. It may just not seem credible to regional adversaries that the United States would initiate nuclear war in the circumstances the regional challenger is then creating. Prompt conventional strike capabilities are much more credible in this role. If seen to be effective at putting at risk the adversary's most potent military tools (and thus its means to manage escalation), as well as the leadership and its tools of political control, such capabilities have high deterrence leverage in the early phases of a regional aggressor's attempts to establish the credibility of its coercive threats.[6]

Although the United States has talked about prompt conventional strike capabilities for decades, it does not have an acquisition program in place.[7] Instead, it has focused on research and development, exploring different delivery systems (whether based on land or sea) and different warheads (whether traditional in design or hyperglide). The conclusion of the research and development phase has been delayed by the budget reductions required by the 2011 Budget Control Act.[8] Until a specific design is chosen, debate about its operational and strategic effects, including on stability with Russia and China, is entirely conjectural. The United States may end up with only a few such systems with a range sufficient to strike in countries lacking strategic depth. Alternatively, it may end up with many such systems with much longer range. Time, technology, and finances will shape the resulting force, as well as military strategy.

The deterrence values of ballistic missile defense are elaborated in further detail in the following discussion, as they are multiple, complex, and often misunderstood. A thorough review of those values is necessary to understand the ways in which missile defense can and cannot substitute for nuclear weapons in regional deterrence architectures.

The deterrence values of resilience against attack in the cyber and space domains are relatively simple and straightforward, as an adversary that can identify and exploit vulnerability in those domains will be tempted to do so, whereas one that cannot will not. A key related question is whether deterrence operates at all in the cyber and space domains. On the one hand, given the difficulty of attributing attacks conducted there, challengers may assess that such attacks are relatively risk free. On the other hand, if such attacks occur in the context of an ongoing and escalating conflict, attribution may be made in the absence of definitive technical proof on a strictly political judgment that the current adversary has escalated (or merely shifted) conflict into a new domain. There is also an important argument that adversaries may be self-deterred from extending conflict into these domains because of their own vulnerability to counteractions in those and other domains.[9]

The deterrence values of the nuclear component are narrow but specific. They may bear little if at all on adversary decisions in the gray zone, because the threat of nuclear response to conventional provocations short of major war is not likely to be credible. They should bear clearly on adversary decisions in the black-and-white zone, as there can or should be little doubt that the United States would respond to nuclear attacks on its homeland with nuclear retaliation. A key caveat to this assertion is that the United States might not choose to retaliate by nuclear means if it were to assess that the conflict could promptly be terminated on terms favorable to the United States and its allies and partners even in the absence of nuclear retaliation. The credibility of U.S. nuclear threats for the deterrence of adversary choices in the red zone cannot be clearly established. But U.S. declaratory policy is clear that nuclear employment would be considered when and if an adversary threatens the vital interests of the United States or its allies or partners. Those interests are left undefined, in part to reinforce uncertainty in the aggressor's mind about precisely where U.S. red lines might lie.

High-level statements of political intent play an essential role in reducing the risks of adversary miscalculation and thus reinforcing deterrence. Toward this end, presidential-level formulations of declaratory policy for nuclear use are an essential requisite. But, additionally, they must be reinforced by public and private statements by American political and military leaders. Such statements are required in times of crisis but also in other times, so that continuity of American purpose is understood.

On the Deterrence and Other Values of Ballistic Missile Defense

To characterize the deterrence values of ballistic missile defense (BMD), it is necessary to understand the current state of U.S. missile defense capability. With the systems in hand and in current development, it is possible for the United States and its allies to have a defense in depth from attacks by states like North Korea. Defenses against regional ballistic missiles have been developed, successfully tested, and deployed.[10] Defenses against intercontinental-range missiles were deployed during the George W. Bush administration and provide some protection of the homeland (as discussed further in the following pages). But those deployments occurred before development and testing were complete, and the systems in place have a number of reliability and other performance problems.[11]

As a general proposition, the existing homeland defense posture is effective against small numbers of early generation intercontinental-range ballistic missiles. Early generation missiles are relatively unsophisticated technically, meaning that they take longer to ready to launch, are slower in flight, lack missile defense counter-measures, and, if not the result of a rigorous development and testing program, may lack reliability. An early generation missile force, as opposed to an early generation missile, is likely to be relatively small in number. Later generation missiles fly sooner, faster, further, and more reliably; may have missile defense counter-measures along with multiple warheads; and are likely to exist in numbers sufficient to enable the kind of salvo launches that can overwhelm either sensors or interceptors or both. The shortcomings of current U.S. BMD systems and existing technologies in dealing with counter-measures and large raid sizes are well known.[12]

Hence missile defenses can be deployed and effective against early generation threats from countries like North Korea but cannot be effective against the large and mature forces of Russia and China. This analysis is the basis of the American assessment that BMD technical options are available that promise stabilizing as opposed to destabilizing benefits.

Accordingly, the Obama administration set out as national policy in its 2010 Ballistic Missile Defense Review (BMDR) the commitments to (1) maintain an advantageous defensive posture of the homeland against limited strikes by countries like North Korea and Iran and (2) field regional defenses in partnership with U.S. allies in each region where it offers security guarantees in a manner that is phased to incorporate improving capabilities and adaptive to changing circumstances and geographies.[13] In follow-up to the BMDR, the administration and its regional partners have made substantial progress toward the latter objective.[14] The administration has also taken subsequent decisions to adjust the homeland posture in the light of new information about the threat, by implementing certain hedge capabilities identified in the BMDR (for example, by emplacing additional Ground-Based Interceptors in available silos once technical fixes are confirmed).[15]

With this defense-in-depth portfolio of improving missile defenses, what then are the particular strategic values of BMD in this comprehensive approach to strengthening regional deterrence? And what other values should be accounted for in a comprehensive stock-take of BMD strategic values?[16]

In an emerging political-military crisis, one potentially transitioning from the gray zone to the red zone, missile defense has various strategic values. It:

1. Creates uncertainty about the outcome of an attack in the mind of the attacker.

2. Increases the raid size required for an attack to penetrate, thereby undermining a strategy of firing one or two and threatening more, thus reducing coercive leverage (while increasing the likelihood of retaliation).

3. Provides some assurance to allies and third-party nations of some protection against some risks of precipitate action by the aggressor.

4. Buys leadership time for choosing and implementing courses of action, including time for diplomacy.

5. Reduces the political pressure for preemptive strikes.

In short, BMD helps to put the burden of escalation in an emerging crisis onto the adversary, thus helping to free the United States and its allies from escalation decisions that might seem premature.

When a crisis has become a hot war and where testing of adversary intent and resolve is underway in the red zone, missile defense again has various strategic values. It:

6. Helps to preserve freedom of action for the United States and its partners by selectively safeguarding key military and political assets.

7. Reinforces the enemy's incentive to keep some missiles in reserve for later use, thereby increasing the time and opportunity to attack the adversary's missile force with kinetic and nonkinetic means, potentially eliminating its capacity for follow-on attacks or for achieving decisive political or military effects.

8. Reduces or eliminates the vulnerability of allies, thus reinforcing their intent to remain in the fight.

If and as a regional adversary begins to contemplate possible nuclear attacks on the American homeland, perhaps only in revenge, missile defense:

9. Significantly reduces if not eliminates the vulnerability of the U.S. homeland to one or a few shots, thus taking the adversary's "cheap shot" off the table (that is, that adversary will not be able to shoot very few weapons while threatening to shoot many more but will have to contemplate a much larger initial salvo that will seem to the attacked state less like blackmail than all-out nuclear war—something that should be deterrable by other means).

10. Reduces the vulnerability of the U.S. homeland to repeat attacks, thus reinforcing its intention to remain in the fight.

A catalogue of the strategic values of BMD must also include an assessment of its contributions in peacetime to the foundations of effective deterrence in crisis and war. In this context, it:

11. Provides opportunities for close defense cooperation among the United States and its allies and security partners.

12. Signals the resolve of the United States and its allies/partners to stand up to coercion and aggression (regional missile defense can be demonstrated in live testing with our partners to demonstrate that resolve).[17]

13. Erodes the perceived potential effectiveness for both military and political purposes of nascent ballistic missile capabilities.

14. Imposes additional costs and uncertainty on those considering the acquisition of nuclear weapons to challenge U.S. regional guarantees.

15. Encourages engagement with Russia and China to slow or halt missile proliferation in both its quantitative and qualitative aspects (as the alternative is a steady increase in the quality and quantity of U.S. defensive capabilities, an outcome they wish to avoid).

16. Provides nonnuclear allies a means to contribute to the strengthening of extended deterrence, thereby reducing incentives to acquire nuclear deterrents of their own.

This catalogue identifies sixteen specific strategic values of missile defense. Some of them are direct to the deterrence challenge, some indirect, and some are relevant only to related challenges. Of note, U.S. allies participating in the BMD project have identified and elaborated many of these strategic values.[18] In the language of strategy, BMD reinforces the comprehensive approach by lowering the cost and risk of our continued resolve and by raising the cost and risk for the challenger, essentially by taking his "cheap shots" off the table and requiring him to resort to larger salvo shots that undermine a blackmail strategy of doing a little damage while threatening to do more. Missile defense also has important assurance values, especially for those allies who might be targeted by an adversary's efforts to split them from the United States.

This is not to argue that missile defense is a panacea or without some potentially negative aspects. It is not a panacea in the sense that it is not a substitute for all of the other elements of the comprehensive approach to strengthening regional deterrence architectures. Its potentially negative aspects include the following: North Korea and other regional challengers may respond with a major buildup of missiles in a bid to overwhelm U.S. and allied defenses and/or with the development and deployment of advanced means to penetrate missile defenses. They may also generate responses in the military postures of Russia and China that pose new threats to the United States and its allies. But for nearly two decades now, there has been bipartisan support in the United States for missile defense in the parameters set out in the preceding paragraphs because the benefits for deterrence are seen as outweighing these potential risks.

On the Value of U.S. Homeland Defense for Regional Deterrence

In a missile defense strategy that clearly distinguishes between capabilities for homeland defense and for regional defense with allies, it is important to be clear about the value for regional deterrence of missile defense of the American homeland. As a general matter, protection of the U.S. homeland from long-range missile strikes by countries like North Korea and Iran reinforces the credibility of U.S. extended deterrence guarantees. If the United States is not vulnerable, regional adversaries will not be credible in threatening to put the American homeland at risk in an effort to "decouple" the United States from the defense of its allies by deterring U.S. military action with threats to the homeland. Thus, homeland protection strengthens regional deterrence by helping to ensure that the United States has the freedom to employ whatever means it chooses to respond to aggression by regional challengers without risk of escalation to strikes against its homeland. It also provides a measure of assurance to the United States sufficient to enable sustained political and military engagement in East Asia and elsewhere at a time of rising threat from missile attack—engagement that has significant deterrence benefits. As discussed in further detail in Chapters 6 and 7, it also strengthens the assurance of allies; especially in East Asia but also in Central and Southern Europe, allies are worried about the decoupling effect of long-range ballistic missile threats to the U.S. homeland.

This way of thinking runs counter to the view often expressed a decade ago by some allies that protection of the American homeland has a decoupling effect by allowing the United States to sit out a regional conflict rather than be drawn into it by a regional enemy's provocative threats to the homeland.[19] In fact, homeland defense would work in service of two very different national security strategies—one of isolation and disengagement and one of power projection and forward engagement. The choice of all U.S. administrations since the Cold War has been clear.

A key counter-argument to this way of thinking must be evaluated. The counter-argument is that the strategic values set out in the preceding paragraphs require that the United States and its allies achieve complete defense dominance over regional actors and, further, that doing so is essentially impossible as they are able to improve their forces both qualitatively and quantitatively more rapidly that the defense can improve. With this view in mind, it might be argued further that regional aggressors with missile programs are successfully pursuing a cost-imposing strategy toward the United States and its allies, leading the United States and its allies to squander resources endlessly on a competition they cannot hope to win.

Of course this line of analysis assumes that the two competitors in an offense–defense competition have roughly equivalent capacities to bear costs. The economy of the United States, despite its many difficulties, is outsized compared to all others and continues to generate significant wealth, including significant investments in military capabilities. An offense–defense competition between North Korea or Iran (or both) and the United States would be uneven in this fundamental respect.

But more significantly, the strategic values set out in the preceding paragraphs do not require defense dominance. They do not require that regional defenses perform perfectly or outnumber attacking forces. If my characterization of the Red theory of victory in limited war is valid, then the missile threat that must be "defeated" can be understood at various thresholds. For a regional aggressor to attempt to coerce neighbors, threats to fire many missiles and thus start a big war may be dismissed as not credible. To prevail in an unfolding conventional conflict that has not reached "total" war, the regional aggressor might well seek to keep significant capability in reserve with the hope of "managing" escalation. Only in a last-gasp effort to exact revenge might a regional actor be likely to fire any and all remaining ballistic missiles.

The implication of this way of understanding the problem is that defense dominance is not required. Even limited defenses can take the "cheap shots" off the table and negate the credibility of the threat of limited use.

On Tailoring

Like its predecessors, the Obama administration has tailored this comprehensive but general approach to the specific requirements of individual regions and actors. The argument that the approach must be tailored follows from an assessment that deterrence strategies operate differently in different contexts and will be effective only if attuned to unique requirements. Moreover, they must reflect the specific threats in being and not just generic threats. The tailoring is done with respect to individuals being influenced, the decisions they face, and the capabilities they have.[20]

The application of this general approach is at its most explicit in Northeast Asia, where the United States has worked with its two close allies to define, refine, and implement this approach, as discussed further in Chapter 7. In Europe, "tailoring" has proceeded in the context of NATO's efforts to adapt its deterrence and defense posture to a changed and changing security environment, as discussed further in Chapter 6. In the Middle East, "tailoring" has proceeded along two tracks—one in partnership with Israel to safeguard its long-term security and the other in partnership with the Gulf Cooperation Council to safeguard the security and independence of states there. In this region, the emphasis falls heavily on the nonnuclear elements of the regional deterrence architecture. In both Northeast Asia and Europe, tailoring must also reflect a balanced approach to deterrence of regional aggression and strategic stability with the neighboring major power. The nature of the needed balance in each region is discussed in more detail in Chapters 6 and 7, following separate discussion of the strategic stability challenges with Russia and China.

The "tailoring" is particularly important for the nuclear component of the comprehensive strategy. The concept of tailoring the nuclear deterrent was first set out by the Clinton administration, as it began the project of better understanding the strategy personalities of new WMD-armed strategic actors in the security environment.[21] The George W. Bush administration further elaborated the concept. In the Cold War, it argued, the United States had a single nuclear deterrence strategy that was essentially global in its application, whereas in today's more complex security environment, with very different challenges for which nuclear deterrence is relevant, it is not possible to think that "one size fits all." That is, it is not possible to think that the United States could have a single nuclear deterrence strategy that would be equally effective in different regions and vis-à-vis actors different in value, interest, and orientation than the familiar ones of the Cold War. Accordingly, the Bush administration defined a requirement to tailor deterrence to unique factors in each region and relationship, including history, geography, political context, and so on.

And this approach was embraced by the Obama administration.[22] The 2010 NPR explicitly endorsed this concept, on the argument that this is an essential part of an updated approach to nuclear strategy aligned with 21st-century requirements. The precise character of the nuclear tailoring done with allies and partners is elaborated in Chapters 6 and 7. But a key general point must be made here—about the particular regional deterrence values of different elements of the U.S. nuclear deterrent.

The U.S. nuclear triad underwrites the U.S. commitment to extend nuclear deterrence on behalf of its allies. It provides the U.S. president with the means to employ one or more nuclear weapons on behalf of an ally or partner anywhere in the world within a very short period of time. The United States supplements the triad with nuclear weapons that can be forward deployed with nonstrategic delivery systems into the regions where it offers security guarantees. These weapons are sometimes misnamed as tactical weapons, implying that like nuclear artillery or nuclear land mines, their function is to enable tactical success on the battlefield against a conventionally superior power. Such tactical weapons have long since been retired from the U.S. arsenal. A more accurate name is forward-deployable nonstrategic nuclear weapons (NSNW) (because of their association with delivery systems not defined by treaty as strategic).

NSNW serve two primary deterrence purposes that cannot be served by the strategic triad. Their regional deployment, whether permanently as in Europe or in time of crisis (potentially) as in Northeast Asia or elsewhere, serves as a clear signal of the shared resolve of the United States and its allies/partners to employ nuclear weapons. As a substitute, bombers would be effective signals of U.S. resolve but would fall short as signals of collective allied resolve. And, after all, it is precisely this collective resolve that the Red theory of victory suggests an adversary would seek to test and/or destroy in the red zone. As one East Asian military leader commented in a not-for-attribution discussion of U.S. nuclear signaling in the Korean peninsula, "American bombers are perfect for displaying American resolve but not for displaying the collective resolve of the alliance that we can expect leaders in Pyongyang to directly test."

The other unique deterrence purpose of NSNW derives from the fact that the employment of regionally based nuclear weapons in war by the United States might not be seen to be inviting or legitimizing a nuclear retaliatory strike on the American homeland in the way that a nuclear attack from the territory of the United States might. It is in the interest of the United States and its allies that a regional aggressor think of escalation to an attack on the American homeland as a very significant and thus risky step, certain to generate decisive U.S. retaliation, and not as part of a tit-for-tat exchange of strikes on homelands begun by the United States with a strike from its homeland. Whether an enemy struck by a U.S. nuclear weapon would perceive a meaningful distinction in its launch point is not knowable.

In prior times, the United States met the requirement for regional deterrence with a mix of tactical and intermediate-range weapons in addition to forward-deployable nonstrategic weapons. In the 1980s it eliminated the intermediate-range systems in the context of the Treaty on Intermediate-range Nuclear Forces (INF). In the 1980s and 1990s it withdrew and eliminated nearly all of its tactical weapons. Today, the only means available for underwriting the commitment to a tailored nuclear component in the regional deterrence architecture are the weapons that can be delivered from aircraft—that is, either strategic bombers carrying nuclear bombs or cruise missiles or fighter-bombers certified for the delivery of nuclear bombs. Whether and how this posture might suffice to meet future requirements are discussed further in Chapters 6 and 7.

Are There Substitutes for the Nuclear Component?

In this comprehensive approach, questions naturally arise about the extent to which other capabilities can substitute for the nuclear component, thereby reducing further U.S. and allied reliance on nuclear weapons. Three forms of substitution are conceivable: by missile defenses, by prompt conventional strike capabilities, and through conventional supremacy.

The argument that missile defenses can substitute for nuclear deterrence in the regional equation hinges largely on their value in demonstrating tangibly a link between the United States and its allies. For example, in Europe U.S. nuclear weapons are maintained in part on the argument that they provide clear evidence of a transatlantic link and thus of direct American military engagement if ever a European ally's security is jeopardized. Missile defense cooperation among the United States, Poland, and Bulgaria (among others) is also an affirmation of this transatlantic link. In East Asia, where U.S. nuclear weapons are not maintained, missile defense cooperation plays a positive role in signaling the linkage between the United States and its allies. Indeed, the very close missile defense cooperation between the United State and Japan sends a clear message of peacetime and wartime linkage.

But, as argued earlier in the review of the deterrence contributions of individual elements of the comprehensive approach, nuclear weapons contribute some unique values to the regional deterrence equation that cannot be replaced by missile defense. Such defense can take off the table "cheap shots" against the United States and its allies and partners but cannot effectively deter larger-scale nuclear attacks—a problem for which U.S. nuclear forces are uniquely relevant. Nuclear weapons also "cast a shadow" over decisions in the red zone because they invoke for the adversary questions about what price it might yet pay for an act of aggression in a way that defensive measures of the attacked party do not. Thus the Obama administration, like its predecessors, has argued that missile defense is a complement to nuclear deterrence and not a substitute.

The argument that prompt conventional strike capabilities can substitute for the nuclear component hinges on the possible effectiveness of these weapons in destroying specific targets with the certainty of nuclear weapons but with no collateral radiological damage. The increased accuracy of these weapons does allow some reduced reliance on nuclear weapons for destroying particularly important targets.

But conventional strike systems do not carry with them the same political message to an adversary who has put at risk a vital interest of the United States or an ally. The "shock-and-awe" air campaign at the start of the invasion of Iraq in March 2003 proved unsuccessful in affecting "the will, perception, and understanding of the adversary to fight," though this does not preclude their future effectiveness against adversaries with only a few strategic assets that are not well protected.[23] Nuclear weapons open up an entirely different realm of warfare, one that presents the adversary with the image of the sudden and complete loss of any and all assets he may value.

The argument that conventional supremacy can substitute for the nuclear component in the comprehensive strategy is also sometimes made. Here, the case was stronger twenty years ago than it is today. In the 1990s, the United States had inherited large standing conventional forces from the Cold War—forces that had been improved through a long process of innovation in competition with a peer adversary. As the Cold War wound down, it was easy and prudent to reduce reliance on nuclear weapons while increasing reliance on conventional supremacy in the deterrence equation. Today, those large standing forces have been reduced substantially through a long period of war and budgetary attrition. The qualitative edge remains, but not as before, as U.S. forces have become increasingly vulnerable in many if not all of the domains where they operate (air, land, sea, cyber, and space). Local conventional supremacy depends on limited forward presence and substantial power projection capability, meaning that it is globally available but in practice locally extant in few places—and available only if time allows. Thus the common post–Cold War calculus that the deterrence burden could easily be shifted from nuclear to conventional means has given way to a more problematic situation.

Toward a Blue Theory of Victory

If a nuclear-armed regional challenger believes that it can engage in nuclear blackmail, nuclear brinksmanship, and potentially even limited nuclear employment to prevail over the United States and its allies, then the United States and its allies must also have a theory of victory. If a regional challenger believes that it can deter and defeat the United States and its allies by escalating and deescalating a conflict on its terms, then the United States and its allies must have a strategy for countering adversary escalation and deescalation that negates adversary strategy, achieves preferred political results, and strips away adversary confidence in its theory. If there is a Red theory, there must be a Blue theory illuminating how it would be possible to effectively negate Red coercion and brinksmanship with threats, actions, and a posture that promises to be more effective in producing Red decisions consistent with U.S. interests than is Red's strategy in trying to generate Blue decisions consistent with its interests. More precisely, there must be Blue theories for the different scenarios and challenges, which can be knit together into a single body of ideas about how to use U.S. "nuclear queens" and other tools in the deterrence toolkit to ensure that no challenger is successful in its efforts to "mess with the United States."

Such a Blue theory is in development. It has not been elaborated in any official or unofficial document. But it can be inferred from the strategy, policy, and posture reviews of the Obama administration and from the comprehensive strengthening approach described earlier. It also builds on work done in the 1990s on the dynamics of major theater wars against WMD-armed adversaries and more recent work on limited nuclear war. Drawing on these sources, and filling in some analytical gaps along the way, I see the theory as encompassing the following key ideas about the successful exercise of American influence at each of the key decision points along the spectrum of deterrence set out earlier.[24]

Successful Deterrence in the Gray Zone

In military confrontations short of actual war, the objectives of U.S. deterrence strategy would be to prevent provocations, blunt attempts at coercion, and deter a decision to strike for a military fait accompli.

Thus the first premise in the Blue theory of victory is that provocations will over time come to be seen by the regional challenger as counterproductive. Red's repeated efforts to generate fear and anxiety will not produce the intended result (capitulation by the United States and its allies). Instead, the challenger will repeatedly discover that the United States and its allies are confident in their ability to protect themselves, to respond as they deem appropriate and necessary at times of their choice, to deter escalation to higher levels of conflict, and to prevail if deterrence at lower levels fails.

The second premise is that the challenger's attempts at coercion can be negated with some self-protection. The challenger may persist in threats, but with diminished expectation of a successful result. This aspect of the Blue theory of victory follows from an assessment that the credibility of Red's threats can be stripped of their coercive potential with a strategy that takes the "cheap shots" off the table. By providing missile defense protection against attacks with small numbers of missiles and by fielding means to attack such missiles ready to attack, Blue strips away the credibility of Red's threats to fire one or two as demonstrations of resolve, compelling Red instead to contemplate much larger attacks. Such large attacks would be seen not as demonstrations of resolve in support of a blackmail strategy but as a major act of war by Red of a kind demanding a decisive military reply from Blue. A similar argument can be made with regard to protection against chemical and biological attack, which drives up significantly the scale of attack needed to have an operational effect. The same can be argued with limited missile defense protection of the American homeland; whatever hope the adversary might have of decoupling the United States from the defense of its allies ought to be undermined if the United States can protect itself from limited attacks. Blue resilience against Red cyberattacks could help to demotivate Red attempts. Moreover, Blue cyberattacks on Red in moments of mounting crisis could have the advantage of conveying to Red that it has vulnerabilities it does not understand and an inability to ensure the initiative in war, thus shaking its confidence in its risk calculus.

The third premise of this Blue theory of victory is that the United States and its allies can deny Red the fait accompli it seeks. It can do so with the use of local conventional forces, the rapid inflow of additional forces, and rapid and significant punishment by conventional and perhaps nonkinetic means. This could also involve significant Blue use of special forces to hinder Red's military operations and would likely also require effective measures to suppress Red's use of its own special forces to hinder Blue. Additionally, this deterrence function can be reinforced with steps to impress on the regional challenger the political and economic costs that would result from such escalation to war.

Successful deterrence of regional challengers by the United States and its allies in this gray zone equates with the strategy of "subduing the enemy without fighting." Thus there is one further premise here: if the United States is confident that it can successfully win a contest of resolve with a nuclear-armed challenger in the gray zone, then the adversary will recognize that confidence, change its strategic calculus, and seek conciliation rather than confrontation with the United States. The United States seeks to create the conditions that persuade regional challengers to not threaten their neighbors and to modify their approaches to national security so that they become more cooperative and less combative. Among those conditions is the U.S. ability to effectively coerce such states to adopt policies and behaviors that it prefers.[25]

A key assumption of this Blue theory is that the United States and its allies will remain in agreement about how to manage the threats and other provocations of the regional challenger and will be able to present a strong image of solidarity to that challenger.

Successful Deterrence in the Red Zone

In regional wars that have gone from cold to hot, the primary U.S. deterrence objective is to induce the challenger to choose restraint over escalation when faced with military and political failure.

A key premise of the Blue theory at this phase of conflict must be that the United States can respond meaningfully to any form of escalation that Red may believe falls beneath the U.S. nuclear response threshold. The United States has multiple means to put at risk political, military, economic, and other assets valued by Red leadership, and an escalating war only releases the restraints on the exercise of that full power potential.

A second premise is that deterrence can be restored if it falters once early in a regional conflict. More precisely, if a regional challenger decides to conduct a very limited nuclear attack with few or no casualties as a way to signal his resolve, the United States and its allies will be able to act in a sufficiently purposeful and effective way as to induce the challenger from making further nuclear attacks and indeed to recognize the depth of his miscalculation. A limited nuclear response by the United States might be seen as necessary and useful toward this end. Other responses by the United States might also be seen as effective, if they are seen as credible demonstrations of U.S. intentions to respond with more of the military means available to it if the challenger chooses to continue to escalate a conflict, whether vertically or horizontally.

A key assumption here is that the United States will, as promised, treat an attack on the vital interest of an ally as an attack on a vital interest of its own. A related assumption is that U.S. allies will be reassured by this understanding and not choose courses of action in regional war that diverge from the preference of the United States.

The Blue theory at this stage of a conflict must also include the idea that the United States need not engage in a prolonged tit-for-tat exchange of nuclear weapons limited to the region. Continued nuclear attack by the challenger would not be seen as limited nuclear war by the United States or its allies. Instead, it would be seen as calling into question the deterrence effectiveness of the limited response strategy of the United States and as legitimizing its use of more of the conventional and nuclear tools available to it to try to prevent the conflict from escalating further. If Red continues to use nuclear weapons in the region, Blue will employ more of the means available to it to impress on Red the extent of its miscalculation and the depth of Blue's resolve and also to eliminate to the extent possible any remaining Red capabilities.

Successful Deterrence in the Black-and-White Zone

If the regional challenger cannot induce the desired military restraint and political acquiescence of the United States and its allies with acts of escalation in the war zone and in the broader theater, he will then face choices about whether to broaden the war to military and/or political targets in countries allied with the United States and in the United States itself. At this phase of conflict, the objective of U.S. deterrence strategy must be to prevent such limited or larger-scale attacks on the U.S. homeland or on the homelands of its allies. This is characterized here as the black-and-white zone for the simple fact that there should be no doubt about the will or ability of the United States to respond to such attacks with nuclear attacks of its own. U.S. presidents have made every effort to be very clear on this point. Five key premises guide the Blue theory of victory at this level of conflict.

First, the strategic imbalance favoring the United States will suffice to persuade Red that the risks and costs of U.S. retaliation will far outweigh any potential gain. A regional war that expands to nuclear attacks on U.S. regional allies or the United States itself will no longer look much limited from the U.S. perspective. Political constraints on the use of American military power in a limited regional war would begin to give way as a war expands in this way, playing to American strengths as the power with superior conventional and nuclear means.

Second, Blue threats to employ nuclear weapons under specific conditions will be seen by Red as credible. Moreover, these threats will (according to the theory) become more credible if and as the conflict escalates and the risks to Blue increase. This premise derives from an assessment that the asymmetry of stake will come to increasingly favor Blue as such a conflict unfolds—in precisely an opposite manner to that of the Red theory. In the Red theory, the asymmetry favors the challengers (whose interests at risk are vital, involving as they do regime survival, whereas those of Blue are important but not vital in the same way). In the Blue theory, the asymmetry shifts to favor Blue. A war that involves questions about nuclear employment will bring lessons for the post-war environment that the United States will have compelling interests in settling in ways it considers favorable. It will want to demonstrate that nuclear aggression will never be rewarded. It will want to demonstrate that it did everything within its means to prevent a great human tragedy. It will want to demonstrate that it was not the victim of nuclear bullying and also engaged in none of its own bullying. It will want to demonstrate that its power was sufficient to achieve a just result. In a regional war under the nuclear shadow involving the United States, a desire to shape the peace to follow will shape fundamentally U.S. choices in war and will invoke U.S. interests that the aggressor may not well understand at first but that will rapidly be made clear. And this will lend credibility to U.S. threats.[26]

Third, if the United States must resort to the employment of nuclear weapons, it will be able to do so in a manner that is effective in achieving U.S. operational and political objectives. Indeed, achievement of carefully chosen operational objectives can demonstrate to the enemy that it has tragically miscalculated U.S. resolve and will only lose more of what it values (whether political control, military means, or economic resources) if it does not immediately deescalate the conflict.

Fourth, if the United States must resort to the employment of nuclear weapons, it will be able to do so in a manner that is consistent with the rule of law and the principles of discrimination and proportionality. This reflects an assessment that, in a war forced on us by a nuclear-armed regional challenger, the United States will be able to find the right balance of resolve and restraint in managing the crisis and prosecuting the war such that its actions are seen as just and the political fallout after termination of the war are such that its reputation as a reliable guarantor and also as a steward of nuclear order is intact if not improved.

Fifth, ballistic missile defense protection of the U.S. homeland and of U.S. allies strips away the credibility of nuclear blackmail by a regional challenger at this level. Those regional challengers that might seek in desperation to persuade the United States to sue for peace (by attacking it with one nuclear-armed long-range missile while threatening more to follow if the United States does not quickly acquiesce) will instead have to contemplate larger-scale attacks to overwhelm U.S. missile defenses. This would be seen in the United States not as blackmail but as all-out war.

Sixth, if the United States is prosecuting such a regional nuclear conflict together with one or more nuclear-armed allies, these allies will prove willing and able to act in concert with the United States to defend common interests, rather than at odds in a manner that adds complexity and instability.

Key Blue Assumptions

Like the Red theory, this Blue theory is informed by a set of assumptions (beyond those already specified). A key assumption is that both Red and Blue calculate rationally their interests and the benefits, costs, and risks of different courses of action. This is a necessary assumption that is not fully warranted on the basis of historical experience.[27] The potential for inadvertent and accidental Red escalation has already been noted; the United States and its allies must also be aware of how they may contribute to such results. Forrest Morgan has argued that leaders of Western nations have tended to overestimate their interests, especially early in a conflict, while underestimating the level of effort that is required to obtain those interests.[28] An additional complicating factor is the weak unity of command of these regional adversaries.[29] The presence of nuclear risks may be sufficient, however, to ensure that such calculations are carefully conducted.

A related assumption is that Blue can understand the decision calculus of Red sufficiently to tailor its deterrence strategy. This assumes that decision makers can be identified, their values and modes of communication understood, and messages crafted that they will understand as credible. An important counter-argument has been made to the effect that tailoring is not possible so long as the decision-making calculus of key individual leaders remains so opaque.[30] As noted earlier, knowledge of adversarial capabilities and intentions remains imperfect—but there is enough fidelity to enable some planning for deterrence that can be fine-tuned if and as additional knowledge becomes available.

A further assumption is that the United States will be effective in operating in multiple domains in a manner that integrates effects on adversary decision makers to achieve the desired political decision. Cross-domain deterrence presents many new challenges for U.S. military and political leaders.[31]

Countering Blackmail Strategies and Winning Wars

To be clear: the Blue theory sketched out here is not a theory of nuclear war fighting. It is a theory for effectively negating the blackmail and brinksmanship strategies of nuclear-armed regional challengers. It targets U.S. political and military resources (and those of its allies) on the key decision points along the spectrum of deterrence, with an eye to ensuring that decisions to cross from the gray to the red zone and from the red to the black-and-white zone never seem sufficiently attractive to the challengers to take those steps.

But this is also a theory of limited nuclear war. Jeffrey Larsen and Kerry Kartchner have defined *limited nuclear war* as "a conflict in which nuclear weapons are used in small numbers and in a constrained manner in pursuit of limited objectives."[32] The United States must have a set of ideas about how to meet this challenge, not least because having such a theory, and being seen to have confidence in it, helps to further reduce the odds that it will ever be put to the test in crisis and war. After all, there are red lines in U.S. nuclear declaratory policy that, if crossed by an adversary, will invoke questions about whether and how to employ U.S. nuclear weapons in response (or even in anticipation, if the threat is convincingly seen as imminent). In this circumstance, the U.S. military will be called on to employ such weapons to achieve political and military objectives set by the president. Such employment must be guided by a set of ideas about how to restore deterrence at the lowest possible cost and in a manner consistent with U.S. interests and those of its allies. This Blue theory is thus a collection of ideas about how to keep a limited war limited by reducing the risks of deliberate, inadvertent, and accidental escalation in a regional conflict with a nuclear-armed regional challenger. It is informed by a clear understanding of the key escalation thresholds in what is otherwise understood to be the "fog of war" and of how to influence the types of decisions an enemy leader would actually face in trying to act on the basis of his theories of victory.[33]

This focus on the potential escalation and deescalation dynamics of nuclear wars that are limited in nature is a departure from the general practice of thinking about nuclear war as unlimited war. In the Cold War, it was very difficult to separate the two. But in today's world, the conditions that made them inseparable no longer exist. Limited regional nuclear war without the prospect of major global nuclear war is plausible in the circumstances that exist today and must be taken seriously as a problem of U.S. military and political strategy if we are to reduce its risks and contain its escalation if it occurs.

Such wars bring with them particular challenges of intrawar deterrence (that is, how to restore deterrence once it has failed in war), deescalation, and war termination. Barry Posen, among others, has argued for a renewed focus on intrawar deterrence in this new era.[34] Kerry Kartchner and Michael Gerson have argued that "revisiting the theory of escalation . . . in the context of the new and emerging conditions of the post–Cold War world is essential to improving our capacity for preventing and deterring crises."[35] They assess that the management of nuclear crises will be more challenging in the future than it was in the past, concluding that "whereas the United States . . . might enjoy escalation dominance over many states at the very highest levels of conflict, including general nuclear war, a future opponent might have the capabilities and resolve to dominate at the lower level."[36]

The only alternative to having a Blue theory of victory is to rely on U.S. military supremacy alone as a general deterrent. This has the virtue of greatly simplifying the problem for U.S. deterrence planning. It also appeals to those who think that American military strength translates automatically into successful deterrence. After all, many in the U.S. expert community want to believe that any adversary foolish enough to begin a competition for escalation with the United States would rapidly find itself trumped if not vanquished by a country that enjoys conventional supremacy above all and nuclear supremacy above almost all. When confronted with the possibility that adversaries might actually have ideas, plans, and capabilities for engaging in such competition, and might doubt America's resolve to defend a stake they seek, it is common for Americans to respond with the convictions that "they wouldn't dare" and "we'll turn them into a glass parking lot" (that is, we'll attack them with nuclear weapons until there is nothing left of them). These are not theories of victory. They are a form of wishful thinking. They are a dangerous convenience that let people off the hook of thinking through what actions might be required if these assumptions prove wrong. If deterrence proves unreliable and the United States must then act without some theory of victory, its use of force would likely look, in retrospect, heavy-handed, clumsy, and excessively brutal. Alternatively, it would have to sacrifice through inaction its interests and those of its allies. This hardly serves American interests in achieving a just result in a conflict that can serve as the basis for an enduring peace.

Conclusion

Faced with a new problem posed by nuclear proliferation to regional challengers to U.S.-backed orders, the United States has rejected mutual nuclear deterrence as the basis of the relationship with such countries. It has set out a comprehensive approach to strengthening regional deterrence architectures to negate the deterrence and coercive potential of newly nuclear-armed regional challengers. It has begun to develop a theory of victory for confrontations with such states, a theory in the spirit of both Clausewitz and Sun Tzu (that is, for achieving successful deterrence in crisis and war and for achieving U.S. political objectives in circumstances other than crisis and war).

This comprehensive approach and this theory of victory do not rely heavily or even primarily on U.S. nuclear means to address this new threat. But nuclear weapons play a unique role for dealing with this new problem. There is no current prospect of alternative nonnuclear means becoming so robust as to enable the abandonment of nuclear weapons for a few but essential purposes.

4 The Second New Problem

Relations with Putin's Russia

SINCE THE END OF THE COLD WAR, LEADERS OF EACH U.S. presidential administration have sought to remake the political relationship with Russia in a way that reduces and ultimately eliminates as one of its defining elements the Cold War–vintage nuclear balance of terror. The Clinton administration talked about moving away from mutual assured destruction (MAD) as the basis of the political relationship and toward mutual assured security.[1] The George W. Bush administration talked about moving nuclear weapons out of the foreground and into the background of the political relationship.[2] The Obama administration attempted to "reset" the political relationship in part by shifting the focus away from mutual deterrence and onto shared interests in strategic stability and a stronger nonproliferation regime. It also sought to stimulate broader discussion of the requirements of mutual assured stability.[3]

Russia's leaders have not embraced these efforts. On the contrary, the political relationship between Russia and the United States—indeed, between Russia and the West as a whole—took a dramatic turn for the worse in 2014. It is now clear that leaders in Moscow feel not only threatened by the United States and NATO but encircled and humiliated. They also feel threatened by so-called color revolutions (popular democratic uprisings in post-Soviet states). Moreover, Russia's leaders remain deeply wedded to nuclear deterrence and see American efforts to move away from mutual deterrence as dangerous. That danger stems, in their view, from an expectation that the United States and NATO would exploit a weakened Russian deterrence posture by using force to endanger core Russian interests. Russian military planning remains centrally focused on the possibility of war with the West, while the West has only begun, in the wake of Russia's military annexation of Crimea, to rethink the basic premises that have led it to set aside Russia as a military problem for the last twenty-five years.

There seems no basis for expecting another dramatic reversal of Russian policy for many years to come. So the United States and its Western allies are left with a host of major new policy questions. What goals should inform U.S. and Western policy? Is there any point in adhering to a positive long-term vision? What can and should be done to accommodate the more adversarial quality now evident in Russia's relations with the West? What role should deterrence have in these relations? Is dialogue with Russia on nuclear issues helpful or harmful to long-term objectives? Can any progress be expected in nuclear arms control and nuclear security cooperation more generally? Or has the history of bilateral arms control come to an end?

To find answers to these questions, this chapter begins with a review of U.S. policy objectives since the end of the Cold War and of the ensuing results in the political and military domains. This includes an assessment of the effort to shift the focus from mutual deterrence to strategic stability. It then turns to implications for U.S. policy and posture, primarily but not exclusively in the nuclear domain.

Multiple "Resets" from 1989 to 2014

The fall of the Berlin Wall ushered in an era of change and hope in the West's relations with Russia. President Putin's speech to the Duma of March 18, 2014, put an exclamation point on the end of that era, as he set out his grievances about the impact of those changes on Russia's interests and his loss of hope for a better relationship with the West.

Throughout this period, U.S. policy objectives toward Russia remained fairly constant. As Angela Stent has argued, "There has been far more continuity in Russian policy between Democratic and Republican administrations than many would admit."[4] She argues further that there have been multiple "resets" by both Washington and Moscow, as new leaders have tried to renew momentum toward more positive results following a period of difficulty and disappointment. In her words, "Washington's repeated cycle of high hopes followed by disappointments have been mirrored in Moscow," where this history is read as confirming that "the United States has disregarded Russia's interests."[5]

The George H. W. Bush administration managed the challenges of the collapse of the Warsaw Pact and the Soviet Union and the emergence of fifteen Soviet successor states while working cautiously to reinvent the relationship with Moscow. It put a particular priority on the need to work with four of those successor states to secure the nuclear weapons they inherited (Russia, Belarus, Ukraine, and Kazakhstan), with the goal of ensuring that only Russia remained a nuclear weapon state. It sought also to promote economic cooperation with Russia and to build a positive relationship between NATO and Russia.[6]

The George H. W. Bush administration also moved aggressively with the Presidential Nuclear Initiatives to remake the nuclear deterrence relationship with Russia and to end Cold War–vintage nuclear alert practices. It put in place the Nunn-Lugar Cooperative Threat Reduction program. This program created a partnership between the United States and Russia (and later others) to strengthen Russian control of its nuclear weapons, materials, and expertise to reduce the risk of their diversion to illicit purposes. It completed the negotiation of and signed START I to accomplish a reduction in strategic nuclear deployments of approximately one-third. It also negotiated and signed START II, calling for additional reductions and, more important, the elimination of ICBMs with multiple warheads. But the administration's general caution toward Russian reform was received badly in Moscow, and this first "reset" proved partial and brief.

The Clinton administration was more ambitious politically, not least because of the direct personal engagement of President Clinton in efforts to develop the relationship with his Russian counterpart and to root Russia more firmly in the West. In 1993, he set out his vision of "a strategic alliance with Russian reform," arguing that "the danger is clear if Russia's reforms turn sour—if it reverts to authoritarianism or disintegrates into chaos."[7] The administration sought to broaden the relationship with Russia beyond the military dimension with various efforts to improve political and economic cooperation and also to encourage the development of democratic institutions, norms, and processes in Russia. With an eye to improving Russia's relations with the West more generally, the administration also promoted the establishment in 1997 of the NATO–Russia Permanent Joint Council.

In the nuclear domain, a primary focus of the Clinton administration was to increase cooperative efforts with Russia to secure its nuclear materials, weapons, and technologies, as the scale of the needed effort became clearer. It also promoted ratification and entry into force of START II, with the U.S. Senate consenting to ratification in January 1996, and set out some initial thinking about START III. It discussed with Moscow possible responses to emerging missile threats from the Middle East and Northeast Asia in a manner that would be consistent with the commitments of the 1972 U.S.–Soviet Anti-Ballistic Missile Treaty and reached agreement in September 1997 on how interceptors for these emerging threats would be distinguished from banned interceptors for strategic missiles.[8]

But this ABM Demarcation Agreement did not enter into force. Moreover, the Russian Duma failed on multiple occasions to support ratification of the START II treaty (though for reasons that had less to do with the substance of the treaty than with ballistic missile defense and the dysfunctions of Russia's young democratic institutions).[9] The Duma ultimately ratified START II in 2000 but on the condition that the U.S. Senate approve the ABM Demarcation Agreement, which proved impossible. Russia withdrew from START II in 2002 when the United States withdrew from the ABM Treaty.[10]

From the Russian perspective, this was a period of mounting frustration and disappointment. NATO military action in the former Yugoslavia was seen in Russia as an insult, especially the bombing campaign against Serbia, a Russian ally. As Angela Stent has argued, "It appeared to be more important for Russia to oppose what NATO was doing than to help solve a major humanitarian crisis in Europe."[11]

NATO also took in three new members during this period—Poland, the Czech Republic, and Hungary, all former Soviet allies—over strenuous Russian objections. This followed a period of intense Western debate about the virtues of expansion and the potential damage done to relations with Russia (which made the resulting decision to expand all the more obvious to Moscow as a decision to ignore Russia's interests). Moscow criticized this expansion as contrary to a promise made to it in 1990 when Germany reunified. Citing available evidence, many in the West conclude that no such promise was made.[12] Russia proved reluctant to accept invitations to cooperate more fully with Western institutions, especially NATO and the European Union, on the argument that it was being welcomed essentially as a junior partner. Its economy was in free fall, with many in Moscow believing that the West engineered the experiment in free markets to weaken Russia. By the end of his term in December 1999, President Boris Yeltsin reportedly felt betrayed by the Clinton administration and believed that the United States was treating Russia as a defeated power rather than as an equal.[13]

The George W. Bush administration arrived with an ambition to put the relationship with Russia on an entirely new footing. Writing during the 2000 presidential campaign, Condoleezza Rice argued, "We will always have interests that conflict" because Russia is a great power but also that "Russia is no longer our enemy."[14] The potential for partnership with Russia took clearer shape with the 9/11 attacks and the Bush administration's efforts to build a coalition to confront the new threat. The administration's National Security Strategy set out a very bold vision for relations with Russia (and China):

> Today, the international community has the best chance since the rise of the nation-state in the seventeenth century to build a world where great powers compete in peace instead of continually prepare for war. Today, the world's great powers find ourselves on the same side—united by common dangers of terrorist violence and chaos.[15]

In an attempt to secure those dividends, the Bush administration set out "a new strategic framework" encompassing "new concepts of deterrence that rely on both offensive and defensive forces," withdrawal from the ABM Treaty, further nuclear reductions, and cooperation to confront emerging threats.[16] The new framework also reflected the president's conviction, clearly stated during the campaign, that Cold War arms control treaties are a barrier to the needed rapid changes (primarily reductions) to U.S. nuclear forces and to the desired improvement in political relations with Russia.[17]

President Putin seized the opportunity presented by the 9/11 attacks to pursue his own reset with the United States.[18] Putin traveled to the United States in November 2001, promised active cooperation in the war on terror, facilitated the flow of U.S. and NATO military forces into Afghanistan through Central Asia, and sat around the campfire at the Bush home in Crawford, Texas. He also told Bush that he needed a treaty to implement additional nuclear reductions, and the two countries quickly converged on the Strategic Offensive Reductions Treaty (SORT) or Moscow Treaty, signed during Bush's visit to Moscow in May 2002 (a treaty of one paragraph in length and lacking verification provisions).

President Putin's broader goal was to secure recognition by the United States of Russia's interests across a diverse set of issues. These included Russian interests in what Russians have called the "near abroad" along Russia's western and southern periphery, in the European security order more generally (including NATO expansion), and in legally binding arms control constraints on the United States, among other topics. He was responding in part to a broadly based fear of humiliation among Russian elites, following the collapse of Soviet/Russian power and a decade of triumphalist rhetoric from some Westerners.[19]

But on one issue after another, Putin was disappointed.[20] Over his objections, and within a year, Washington had proceeded to withdraw from the ABM Treaty and to enlarge NATO a second time (with addition of the three Baltic states, former Soviet republics). It had acquiesced to an arms control treaty with Moscow (SORT) but only of extremely modest character. By the end of 2005, Putin also had failed to gain Washington's support for his preference on policy toward Iraq and Iran, in the trade relationship (with Cold War–vintage Jackson-Vanik legislative constraints remaining in place), and in the color revolutions. As became clear only much later, President Putin was also increasingly alarmed by the "freedom agenda" of the Bush administration and its willingness to lend moral and other support to popular prodemocracy uprisings in former Soviet states.

This led to a period of reassessment in Moscow, which culminated in a forceful speech by President Putin to the Munich conference on security policy on February 10, 2007. He made good on his stated intent "to say what I really think about international security problems."[21] To wit:

- "Today we are witnessing an almost uncontained hyper use of force—military force—in international relations, force that is plunging the world into an abyss of permanent conflicts."
- "We are seeing a greater and greater disdain for the basic principles of international law."
- "One state and, of course, first and foremost the United States, has overstepped its national borders in every way."
- "NATO expansion does not have any relation with the modernization of the Alliance itself or with ensuring security in Europe. On the contrary, it represents a serious provocation that reduces the level of mutual trust."

- "We should talk about establishing a whole system of political incentives and economic stimuli. . . . we are open to cooperation."
- "We are well aware of how the world has changed and we have a realistic sense of our own opportunities and potential. And of course we would like to interact with responsible and independent partners with whom we could work together in constructing a fair and democratic world order that would ensure security and prosperity not only for a select few, but for all."

Putin's indictment was clear. But so too was the offer of renewed cooperation toward shared goals. The speech generated some discussion among narrow circles in Washington and Europe, more for its tone than substance, and no broad reassessment of the West's approach to Russia resulted. The only visible high-level official response came from Secretary of Defense Robert Gates who, in remarks the following day in Munich, argued that "one Cold War was enough" and again set out the American commitment to continue to work with Moscow to deepen its partnership with the West.[22]

Three additional developments further aggravated Russia's relations with the West. One was the Bush administration's 2007 decision to create in Europe a third site for protection of the American homeland from ballistic missile attack (the first two being in Alaska and California), with facilities in Poland (the interceptors) and the Czech Republic (the radar). This elicited vehement Russian opposition, with public complaints about the supposed impact on Russia's nuclear deterrent and private complaints about the stationing of such forces on the territories of two of Moscow's former allies. Another was the April 2008 Bucharest summit statement by NATO that it "welcomes Ukraine's and Georgia's Euro-Atlantic aspirations for membership in NATO. We agreed today that these countries will become members of NATO."[23] The third was Putin's April 2008 decision to intervene militarily in Georgia, not least as a signal to the West that he would not accept further NATO expansion.

In 2009, President Obama reframed the effort to move relations with Russia forward onto cooperative approaches to shared interests. As Angela Stent has argued, "The Obama administration in its first term did manage to press the [reset] button and improve both the atmospherics and the substance of the relationship," but with avowedly limited objectives that were more or less fully achieved by 2012. This reset began with a willingness to engage Russia on its concerns about strategic stability and arms control and reflected a belief that the missile defense challenge could be dealt with "firmly, pragmatically, and diplomatically."[24] The development of Russia policy occurred within the framework of a broader effort to renew U.S. partnerships with other countries as a remedy to the perceived excesses of unilateralism by the prior administration. It reflected a desire to go beyond the efforts of prior administrations to renew cooperation with Russia by taking seriously its interests and addressing its concerns about U.S. policy and practice in a manner consistent with U.S. interests.

Presidents Obama and Medvedev got off to a solid start with a meeting in London in April 2009, where they agreed to an agenda of cooperative activities, including negotiation of a replacement for the START I treaty that was due to expire in December 2009. In another bid to broaden the relationship beyond its narrow security focus, they created a Bilateral Presidential Commission. Cooperation on both Iran policy and the war in Afghanistan were strengthened. There were also early signs that the two might find some common ground on approaches to strategic stability and strategic cooperation.[25] They built on this relationship in Moscow in July 2009, where they agreed on the major parameters of what would become the New START Treaty. But New START proved more difficult to negotiate than many in the Obama administration had expected. A key sticking point was ballistic missile defense, as discussed further in subsequent paragraphs.

Assessing the new state of U.S.–Russian relations in 2009, American experts were writing optimistically that "the era of organizing their relationship on the basis of threat and competition with each other is giving way to one shaped by the utility of cooperation."[26] But the Obama reset was short lived. Stent has argued that it was over by the summer of 2013 and was punctuated by Putin's return to the Russian presidency.[27] A key factor was what Prime Minister Putin perceived to be NATO's aggressive action in Libya, beyond the terms of its mandate, which Putin interpreted as a signal that President Obama was just as willing as his predecessor to police up the international order and assert hegemonic U.S. ambitions.[28]

In 2010 Russia's updated military doctrine identified NATO as the primary danger to Russia. One Russian commentator, Fyodor Lukyanov, characterized Putin's views in this period:

> In the 10 years since the Iraq war, Putin's worldview has only strengthened and expanded. Now he believes that the strong not only do what they want, but also

fail to understand what they do. From the Russian leadership's point of view, the Iraq war now looks like the beginning of the accelerated destruction of regional and global stability, undermining the last principles of sustainable world order. Everything that's happened since—including flirting with Islamists during the Arab spring, U.S. policies in Libya, and its current policies in Syria—serves as evidence of the strategic insanity that has taken over the last remaining superpower.[29]

Putin's campaign to return to the presidency in 2012 prominently featured anti-Americanism. His 2013 Foreign Policy Concept set out many of the complaints in his Munich speech. That concept stated Putin's primary objectives: "ensuring the security of the country, protecting and strengthening its sovereignty and territorial integrity, and securing its high standing in the international community as one of the influential and competitive poles in the modern world."[30] Putin also supported a military buildup, which he explained as a necessary response to NATO enlargement and U.S. missile defenses.[31] He welcomed Edward Snowden to Russia later that year, in what was widely interpreted as a direct affront to President Obama. Following the Obama administration's decision to cancel a presidential visit to Moscow in September 2013, Putin characterized his relationship with Obama as follows: "We hear each other and understand the arguments. But we simply don't agree. I don't agree with his arguments and he doesn't agree with mine."[32]

On March 18, 2014, President Putin addressed the Russian Duma to make his case for the annexation of Crimea. His remarks also conveyed—in a clear and compelling manner—the hardening of his views about the West and a shift in focus from concern about Western disrespect for Russian interests to concern about actual Western hostility and aggression.[33] Key points include the following:

- "After the dissolution of bipolarity on the planet, we no longer have stability. Key international institutions are not getting any stronger; on the contrary, in many cases, they are sadly degrading. Our western partners, led by the United States of America, prefer not to be guided by international law in their practical policies, but by the rule of the gun. They have come to believe in their exclusivity and exceptionalism, that they can decide the destinies of the world, that only they can ever be right. They act as they please: here and there, they use force against sovereign states, building coalitions based on the principle 'If you are not with us, you are against us.' To make this aggression look legitimate, they force the necessary resolutions from international organizations, and if for some reason this does not work, they simply ignore the UN Security Council and the UN overall."

- "There was a whole series of controlled 'color' revolutions. Clearly, the people in those nations, where these events took place, were sick of tyranny and poverty, of their lack of prospects; but these feelings were taken advantage of cynically. Standards were imposed on these nations that did not in any way correspond to their way of life, traditions, or these peoples' cultures. As a result, instead of democracy and freedom, there was chaos, outbreaks in violence and a series of upheavals. The Arab Spring turned into the Arab Winter."

- "We are constantly proposing cooperation on all key issues; we want to strengthen our level of trust and for our relations to be equal, open and fair. But we saw no reciprocal steps. On the contrary, they have lied to us many times, made decisions behind our backs, placed us before an accomplished fact."

- "In short, we have every reason to assume that the infamous policy of containment, led in the 18th, 19th and 20th centuries, continues today. They are constantly trying to sweep us into a corner because we have an independent position, because we maintain it and because we call things like they are and do not engage in hypocrisy. But there is a limit to everything. And with Ukraine, our western partners have crossed the line, playing the bear and acting irresponsibly and unprofessionally."

- "If you compress the spring all the way to its limit, it will snap back hard. You must always remember this."

A few weeks later, at the annual Moscow conference on international security hosted by the Russian Ministry of Defense, officials of the Putin government launched tough political attacks on the United States, naming it as an enemy of the state and arguing that its support for so-called color revolutions among the post-communist states was a new form of warfare, requiring a military response from Russia. The Russian military later updated its military doctrine to reflect some of these themes.[34] In October 2014, President Putin spoke to a gathering of a private discussion group, the Valdai Club, under a banner translated as "new rules or a game with no rules," and spoke of an historic turning point in jettisoning the corrupt order preferred by the West and rebuilding order on a new set of principles preferred by Moscow.[35]

In a fundamental sense, the period of searching for deeper cooperation with Russia on the basis of shared interests has come to an end. The final reset of the series was Putin's, with his promise to "snap back hard" against a perceived strategy of containment and contempt ostensibly being pursued by the West and especially the United States.[36] He characterizes U.S. policy toward Russia in late 2014 as "nothing but hostile" and a form of blackmail that could lead to nuclear war.[37]

After the spring 2014 turning point, there has been a rising debate in the West about how we came to this point and the degree to which Western policy contributed to the situation and might in retrospect have been made differently.[38] This important debate is beyond the scope of this analysis. That said, there is much the West might have done differently to accommodate Russian interests as now perceived in Moscow, including not expanding the NATO alliance. But this would have involved abandoning the project of building a post–Cold War order based on a Europe "whole and free." A European order less than whole and free would have had many sources of instability and incipient conflict and thus would also have been difficult to align with Russia's interests in regional stability.

In sum, 2014 proved to be a fundamental turning point in U.S.–Russian relations and in Russia's relations with the West more generally. Developments in Russian external policy have been driven by a rising sense of grievance and vulnerability and by leadership anxiety about the potential spillover effects on Russian political stability of successful popular uprisings in post-Soviet states. A return to business as usual is not likely so long as President Putin remains in power.[39] Further confrontation seems inevitable.[40]

The new trajectory remains unclear, except that the adversarial aspect can no longer be avoided by the West. We are left now with a set of fundamental questions about the implications of the choices made in Moscow in 2014. What else might follow, beyond the military-backed annexation of Crimea, in the "snap back hard" strategy? Will Moscow initiate new military action to suppress color revolutions in other former Soviet states? How far will its promise to protect Russian-speaking peoples be extended? Will it use military means, whether direct or indirect (that is, special forces), against members of the NATO alliance? What additional unilateral steps might it take in an attempt to remake the post–Cold War European security order? Will its foreign and security policies become fully zero-sum in its relations with the West, or will opportunities for cooperation remain? What will be the consequences for Russian political stability of long-term efforts to control and suppress political dissent?

A final question is simply: Might the developments of 2014 prove short lived, with a more rapid return to the trajectory of improving relations sooner rather than later? This possibility should not be ruled out and indeed should remain an objective of Western policy. There is too much at stake to simply settle back into confrontational patterns. Moreover, by late 2014 there was evidence that the Russian economy is in deep trouble and that President Putin is losing some public support.[41] Whenever he finally departs the political scene, President Putin seems likely to ensure that his successor builds on rather than dismantles his legacy. Whether that will be possible in the circumstance is an open question.

These questions will not be answered in the short term. In the meantime, the United States and the West more generally must adapt their security policies and postures to these new realities—including the significant measure of future uncertainty.

The Nuclear Dimension: Converging or Diverging Visions?

As this narrative suggests, efforts to remake the U.S.–Russia nuclear relationship have been at the center of U.S. efforts to remake the political relationship. Each U.S. administration over the last twenty-five years, whether Republican or Democrat, has sought to move away from Cold War approaches to the military relationship with Russia, to reduce the large nuclear force structures built up during the Cold War, and to find some new footing for secure and stable strategic relations other than the nuclear balance of terror. As in the Cold War, the United States has seen talking about the nuclear relationship and arms control as a way to stay focused on shared interests even in difficult political times.

But Russia has been reluctant to embrace this agenda—and increasingly so. The narrative above implies that this reluctance has two main explanations. One is that disagreements about unrelated topics have reduced Moscow's willingness to make deals with Washington. The other is that misperceptions and miscommunication about U.S. missile defenses have contributed

significantly to a lack of trust and therefore progress. In fact, the lack of progress in transforming the nuclear relationship as many in the United States
(and Russia) would have wished has far deeper sources. Twenty-five years of
formal and informal discussions and negotiations between the two countries have brought into focus these deeper rifts.[42] This analysis highlights five
such factors.

First, the two countries see different strategic challenges in the post-bipolar
global order. As Chapters 1 through 3 attest, the United States has been highly
focused on the instabilities associated with the proliferation of nuclear weapons and long-range missiles to regional actors who do not accept the regional
order safeguarded in part by the United States. It is adapting its strategic military posture, including with the introduction of nonnuclear means of defense
and strike, so as to ensure that these regional challengers are not capable of
strategically destabilizing actions. So far at least, it has by-and-large concluded that responses in the strategic military postures of Russia and China
to maintain the status quo ante (that is, the balance of strategic military forces
before the United States began its adaptations for the regional challengers)
do not require corresponding developments in the U.S. strategic military
posture—if and until those Russian or Chinese responses themselves somehow undermine strategic stability.

Russia in contrast sees the strategic challenges of a multipolar, "poly-
centric" world. And accordingly it rejects the U.S. claim that adaptations in
the U.S. strategic posture are about regional challengers. President Putin sees
the United States as seeking to enhance its unipolar moment and to encircle
and contain Russia, not least by imposing a security order in Europe inimical
to Russian interests.[43] As he argued in March 2014, "After the dissolution of
bipolarity on the planet, we no longer have stability."[44]

Some Russians—both official and unofficial—have also criticized the
United States for what they believe to be its ambition to gain strategic dominance by military means. They assert that the United States is trying to escape
the nuclear revolution in world politics by gaining the means to employ conventional weapons against Russia while negating its nuclear deterrent with
preemptive and protective means.[45] Indeed, official Russian documents lodge
a similar complaint:

> Threats to military security include the policies of a number of leading foreign
> countries directed at achieving predominant superiority in the military sphere,

primarily in terms of strategic nuclear forces, but also by developing high-precision, informational, and other high-technology means of conducting armed warfare, strategic non-nuclear arms, by unilaterally creating a global missile defense system and militarizing space, which could lead to a new arms races.[46]

Disagreements about ballistic missile defense (BMD) are a testament to this point. The United States seeks protection against limited ballistic missile strikes from countries like North Korea and Iran, including for its deployed forces and allies, and has clearly stated its intent not to undermine strategic stability with Russia or China. Toward these ends, it has chosen technical approaches to missile defense that promise to be effective in providing the desired protection against limited strikes without credibly threatening to negate potential large-scale strikes from Russia or China.[47] The official Russian view is that missile defense of the American homeland and of NATO from threats emanating from the Middle East is a threat to Russia's deterrent.[48]

The Obama administration, like its predecessor, recognized Russian concerns about missile defense in Europe and, like its predecessor, took steps to try to address Russian concerns. To address concerns about the operational effectiveness against Russian forces of BMD in Europe, the Obama administration continued the efforts begun in the Bush administration to negotiate an agreement with Russia that would have permitted the discussion of classified information related to the performance of both radars and interceptors. In Washington's view, such a discussion would have gone far to address Russian technical and operational concerns. While trying to improve bilateral cooperation, the administration also welcomed Russia's desire to cooperate on BMD in the NATO context and sought to improve this cooperation. And of course the Obama administration shifted from the Bush administration's "third site" for missile defense in Europe to the phased, adaptive approach. This shift was warranted by the desire and ability to provide improved protection for U.S. forces earlier and more affordably than the "third site" approach, while also providing improved opportunities for allied participation. But the phased, adaptive approach also replaced sensors and interceptors capable of operations deep into Russia with sensors and interceptors not capable of such operations, without any compromise to the defense of Europe or North America. The administration also recognized that its ten-year plan for phased adaptive missile defense in Europe left open important questions about developments in future decades. It argued that bilateral and multilateral cooperation would be more effective than confrontation in laying the foundations for missile defense decisions by future U.S. administrations consistent with an approach to strategic stability shared with Russia.

But Russia proved unwilling to conclude a deal to discuss classified performance information. The bilateral track went nowhere. Russia energetically used the NATO–Russia Council mechanism to press its case against the European Phased Adaptive Approach. Secretary of Defense Robert Gates concluded quite early in the Obama administration that "a slim chance [for missile defense cooperation with Russia] had become no chance."[49] By 2012 there was a widespread perception inside the Obama administration and alliance that Russia's policy toward missile defense in Europe was shaped increasingly by political factors (its resentment toward the West and hostility toward NATO) rather than by substantive technical or operational concerns. Russia called repeatedly for cooperation without apparently having made a decision to cooperate. Additional measures that would have helped to address long-term Russian concerns about NATO BMD in the 2020s and beyond were rejected.[50] Its only substantive proposal for cooperation—for a division of labor on missile defense protection of Europe according to different sectors—was widely interpreted as confirmation of the new factors guiding Russian policy, calling as it did to shift from NATO to Russia the responsibility to provide missile defense protection of its former allies.[51]

In sum, for nearly two decades, the United States has been trying to address Russian concerns about ballistic missile defense.[52] Over this time Russian opposition has only deepened.

Of note, Russia is well along in modifying its military posture to ensure that its nuclear forces will remain operationally effective against U.S. and NATO BMD.[53] Accordingly, some influential Russian experts have also concluded that "the United States has not, and in the foreseeable future will not have, a strategic missile defense system capable of fending off a retaliatory counter-strike . . . by Russian strategic nuclear forces."[54] In defending his decision to act on Crimea, President Putin has stated that it was "partially prompted" by continued disagreements on missile defense, because of its "offensive potential" against Russia.[55]

The second factor working against a positive transformation of the strategic relationship is the difference of views about the requirements of strategic stability. Russia and the United States have an abiding commitment to strategic stability, but they disagree about how to define it and what it requires. The last time Washington and Moscow shared a definition of strategic stability was just as the Cold War was ending. This was in the form of an agreed joint statement associated with the START treaty in 1990: "Strategic stability was understood as such a balance of strategic forces of the USSR and the U.S. (or such state of the two powers' strategic relations) where there were no incentives for a first strike."[56] Since then, there appears to be at least a partial divergence of thinking.[57]

In thinking about the requirements of strategic stability in the relationship with Russia, the United States continues to rely on concepts born in the Cold War. As Thomas Schelling argued in 1960, "It is not the 'balance'—the sheer equality or symmetry of the situation—that constitutes mutual deterrence; it is the stability of the balance. The balance is stable only when neither, in striking first, can destroy the other's ability to strike back."[58] Harold Brown provided an update in 1979: "In the interests of stability, we avoid the capability of eliminating the other side's deterrent, insofar as we might be able to do so. In short, we must be quite willing—as we have been for some time—to accept the principle of mutual deterrence, and design our defense posture in light of that principle."[59]

Russia has two similar but not identical concepts of its own, one broad and one narrow (this according to a leading Russian specialist, Vladimir Dworkin).[60] The broad definition characterizes a state in which a series of political, economic, military, and other steps are taken by opposing coalitions such that neither is able to commit military aggression. The narrow definition characterizes a state of relations among the strategic forces of the two protagonists and of the relations between the states themselves, that features a fairly equal balance of military capabilities that neither would attempt to alter or gain supremacy over the other for a long period of time.[61]

These different concepts add both precision and confusion to the bilateral dialogue. They add precision in the sense that they illuminate the multiple factors bearing on perceptions of strategic stability. They add confusion in the sense that in common usage the shorthand is typically a substitute for the more specific meaning, and thus people end up having the misimpression that they are talking about the same thing when they use the same term. Additionally, all of these definitions are rooted in a time when mutual deterrence was the inescapable fact of a bipolar confrontation under the risks of nuclear Armageddon—and thus, to Americans at least, they seem misaligned with a world that has changed in so many respects.

Some Russian analysts have concluded that the term *strategic stability* is unhelpful and that a focus on it is counter-productive in moving political and strategic military relations forward to some new basis—a view shared by some Westerners.[62]

The third factor working against a positive transformation of the strategic relationship is that the requirements of strategic stability are becoming more complex. This stems from a mutual appreciation of the potential for miscalculation and inadvertent escalation in the new domains of military competition, namely cyber and space. Accordingly, U.S. and Russian experts disagree about the essential elements of a potential future bargain on reciprocal strategic restraint. As the two have begun to discuss the potential parameters of a future follow-on to the New START agreement, they have taken fundamentally different views of the implications of the new complexity. The Obama administration has come to the view that an additional reduction of approximately one-third of the deployed force of strategic nuclear weapons would be possible, assuming parallel reductions by Russia, and that there is no need to account for missile defenses or nonnuclear strike systems during the life of the notional treaty. The Putin government has come to the view that everything is connected to everything and that a new arms control agreement is possible only if it encompasses restraints on U.S. defenses, nonnuclear strike systems, weapons based in space for the attack of Earth, and counter-space capabilities, among other factors. Some Russians believe that Russia conceded too much in New START by not securing restrictions on U.S. defense and U.S. nonnuclear strike capabilities.[63]

Fourth, the two countries share a conviction that arms control agreements can have stabilizing benefits. But they disagree on whether the agreement the other might strike would in fact be beneficial.

For decades, the two have valued arms control for its various contributions to strategic stability. Arms control agreements have been seen as providing predictability and transparency in the developments of the strategic postures of what remain the two dominant nuclear weapon states in terms of quantitative measures. That predictability and transparency is valued not just by the parties to the agreements but by U.S. allies and other stakeholders in the strategic restraint of Russia and the United States. Arms control is also a mechanism for addressing concerns that each side has about particular attributes of the other's force structure that it considers destabilizing.[64] For example, the Obama administration has clearly signaled its desire for a follow-on to the

New START Treaty that accomplishes not only additional reductions in deployed strategic weapons but also somehow accounts for the troubling disparities in the arsenals of nonstrategic weapons, while addressing the Russian fear that U.S. nondeployed weapons provide a breakout capability that Russia could not match.[65] That break-out capability derives from the fact that the United States could redeploy stored warheads to delivery systems from which they have been removed. In the current force structures of the two countries, the United States enjoys a significant advantage in this regard.

President Putin's 2013 Foreign Policy Concept leaves open the door to further arms control with the United States but only in a much broader process than the historic bilateral nuclear negotiations and with a move to multilateralism.[66] But President Putin himself seems less open:

> We should not tempt anyone by allowing ourselves to be weak. It is for this reason that we will under no circumstances surrender our strategic deterrent capability, and indeed will in fact strengthen it. It was this strength that enabled us to maintain our national sovereignty during the extremely difficult 1990s when, let's be frank, we did not have anything else to argue with.[67]

The Obama administration takes a different view of the needed next step and the pathway to bringing additional nuclear-armed states into the arms control process. As already stated, it seeks an additional one-third reduction in deployed strategic offensive forces as well as some constraints on Russia's arsenal of nonstrategic and nondeployed weapons. In the long-term vision of further progress toward the elimination of nuclear weapons, the Obama administration anticipates a future stage of arms control that involves the other nuclear weapon states—but it does not see that as a necessary precondition to taking an additional round of reductions bilaterally with Russia. Also as a general principle, the United States rejects any legal constraints on its future development of ballistic missile defenses, with the argument that doing so would ultimately leave American naked in the face of threats from newly armed regional actors.

There appears to be little convergence in these two approaches.[68] This has a significant implication for the United States and the West more generally: the era of bilateral nuclear reductions that began in the mid-1980s may well come to an end when New START expires in 2021 (or 2026 if the single five-year extension is agreed by both parties, as permitted by the treaty). It may happen beforehand, if one or both parties choose to withdraw from the treaty.[69]

Thus it is hardly surprising that the two nations have had fundamentally different ideas about whether and how to align the nuclear relationship with the evolving political context. For more than two decades, the United States has held to the view that the two countries can and should move away from mutual deterrence and mutual assured destruction (MAD) as the organizing concepts for the nuclear relationship and toward a relationship based on mutual assured stability or mutual assured security. Toward this end, the United States has set out various ideas about the elements of such a modified relationship, including the residual deterrent component.[70] After all, in such a relationship, deterrence would play a continuing but subsidiary role. With the fundamental shift in U.S. views of the "new political context" occasioned by developments in spring 2014, there is an open question now for the United States about whether and how to attempt to further proceed down this pathway.

In contrast, for more than two decades Russia's leaders have by and large held to the view that any movement away from mutual deterrence and MAD is dangerous because the United States would be free, in the Russian estimate, to indulge its ideological instincts and employ force in a manner that, sooner or later, will jeopardize vital Russian interests.

The fifth and final insight from twenty-five years of dialogue on these topics is that disagreements have proven persistent. Disagreements on missile defense, for example, scuttled START II, delayed New START, and appear to be a major barrier to a follow-on to New START (they also blocked progress at Reykjavik in 1986). Indeed, in recent years it seems that disagreements have deepened. In these areas, dialogue has deepened understanding but not confidence or trust. As President Putin has argued, "We have lost trust . . . [and] we believe it was not our fault."[71] It is unclear what further dialogue on these topics might yet accomplish so long as Russia's leaders adhere to the vision articulated in March 2014.

In sum, progress in putting the nuclear relationship onto a new footing has been stymied by multiple factors: misaligned perceptions of the security environment, misaligned concepts of strategic stability, misaligned visions of a potential future arms control bargain, different degrees of attachment to mutual deterrence, and a lack of political trust. But the problem is even more complicated than that. Washington and Moscow now have fundamentally different ideas about the possibility of war. Russian leadership has come increasingly to the conviction that war with NATO is a real possibility, whereas the West (including Washington) has stuck to the view that NATO is an alliance without enemies. In 2014, this misalignment of perception emerged starkly, and Western and U.S. views began to shift.[72]

Back to the Problem of War—and Deterrence

The experiences of the two leaderships in Washington and Moscow led them to two very different views of the military dimension of the relationship. Until 2014, Washington had been disappointed and frustrated by the chronic failure to strengthen political and economic cooperation, but it has not felt militarily threatened by Russia. In contrast, Putin has felt humiliated, encircled, provoked by color revolutions, and threatened by the United States and NATO. Until Putin's March 2014 speech and forced annexation of Crimea, Washington thought little about future military threats from Russia, whether to the American homeland or to American allies. In sharp contrast, Russian military leadership has been focused for nearly two decades on the potential for military confrontation with the United States and NATO. These different orientations have reinforced the divergence of thinking about the role of nuclear deterrence in the 21st century in the U.S.–Russia relationship.

Russia has figured little if at all in the periodic U.S. reviews of defense strategy undertaken since the Cold War. The Quadrennial Defense Review issued by the Department of Defense in 1997 struck a note of cautious optimism about Russia, emphasizing its increasing cooperation with the West on a broad set of security challenges, while noting also major uncertainty about Russia's political and economic future.[73] The 2001 QDR highlighted increased opportunities for cooperation after 9/11, arguing that Russia "shares some important security concerns with the United States. . . . Yet at the same time, Russia pursues a number of policy objectives contrary to U.S. interests."[74] The 2014 QDR report, released in March shortly before Russian military action in Ukraine, maintained a hopeful tone, though it deemphasized possibilities for cooperation, arguing that "Russia's multi-dimensional defense modernization and actions that violate the sovereignty of its neighbors present risks. We will engage Russia to increase transparency and reduce the risk of military miscalculation."[75]

As these various defense strategy reviews attest, however problematic relations with Russia might have been throughout this period, no American president has attached significant priority to armed confrontation with Russia as a major planning factor for U.S. defense strategy. Instead, and especially after 9/11, U.S. military planning has focused primarily on the challenges of innovating rapidly to prevail in ongoing counter-terrorism and counter-insurgency operations.

Similarly, until spring and summer 2014, NATO took a largely benign view of the challenges of life with its Russian neighbor. For example, the alliance's Strategic Concept adopted in Lisbon in 2011 reflects the assessment that "the Euro-Atlantic area is at peace and the threat of a conventional attack against NATO territory is low. . . . The alliance does not consider any country to be its adversary."[76] Concerning NATO–Russia relations, it went on to argue that:

> Cooperation is of strategic importance as it contributes to creating a common space of peace, stability and security. NATO poses no threat to Russia. On the contrary: we want to see a true strategic partnership between NATO and Russia, and we will act accordingly, with the expectation of reciprocity from Russia. . . . Notwithstanding differences on particular issues, we remain convinced that the security of NATO and Russia is intertwined.[77]

Accordingly, for the last decade and longer, NATO put its military focus elsewhere: on counter-insurgency operations in Afghanistan, crisis management in the Mediterranean, and strengthened mechanisms for cooperative security.

Russia has featured as a problem of U.S. and Western defense strategy only in one important respect: as a country with the capability to annihilate by nuclear means the United States (and any of its allies). As the nuclear posture reviews of each post–Cold War administration attest, the United States has sought to ensure that no Russian leader will ever conclude that a nuclear attack on the United States or its allies would be anything but a catastrophe for Russia. This objective has had more to do with Russian capabilities than Russian intentions. As the Obama administration argued in June 2013:

> The threat of global nuclear war has become remote. . . . Although differences between our countries continue to arise and Russia continues to modernize its nuclear forces, Russia and the United States are no longer adversaries, and the prospects of military confrontation between us have declined dramatically. At the same time, Russia remains the United States' only peer in nuclear weapons capabilities.[78]

The president's 2013 guidance to the Department of Defense for planning the potential employment of nuclear weapons reiterated the commitment of the administration "to improve strategic stability by demonstrating that it is not our intent to negate Russia's strategic nuclear deterrent, or to destabilize the strategic military relationship with Russia."[79] It also recognizes "the significantly diminished possibility of a disarming surprise nuclear attack" and accordingly directs the department to examine how to continue to adapt the U.S. deterrent posture to this new reality.[80]

This guidance also underscores the fact that the basic parameters of the U.S. nuclear deterrent—its overall size and mix of capabilities—are a function of the commitment to strategic stability with Russia:

> Although the need for numerical parity between the two countries is no longer as compelling as it was during the Cold War, large disparities in nuclear capabilities could raise concerns on both sides and among U.S. allies and partners, and may not be conducive to maintaining a stable, long-term strategic relationship, especially as nuclear forces are significantly reduced. We therefore continue to place importance on Russia joining us as we move to lower levels of nuclear weapons.[81]

The guidance further specifies that the United States should be prepared to deal with "geopolitical surprise." More precisely, the guidance directs that the United States maintain warheads in storage that could be "uploaded" onto delivery systems in response to a deterioration in the international landscape. This hedge is needed to ensure that the United States has an effective deterrent even if relations with another nuclear-armed state unexpectedly become significantly more adversarial.[82]

In sum, until spring 2014, the United States and its European allies had thought little if at all about military threats from Russia, whether to the American homeland or in Europe. In sharp contrast, Russian leadership has focused heavily on the potential for military confrontation with the United States and NATO. Apparently President Putin has come to quite different ideas about the role of nuclear deterrence in the 21st-century U.S.–Russia relationship.

While noting the opportunities for cooperation with the United States and the West more generally, President Putin's national security documents put the emphasis on the dangers and risks posed by the United States and NATO. In those documents, WMD proliferation to regional actors is seen as a problem for Russia but not as a threat in the way the United States perceives it. China is seen as a rising potential danger but not as a problem of immediate security concern as it is for the United States in the Western Pacific. Rather, those documents emphasize Mr. Putin's assessments that:

- The post–Cold War Euro-Atlantic security order is built on "bloc mentality" that perpetuates division and Russian isolation.
- Russia's efforts to cooperate with NATO on equal terms have failed to improve the relationship with the West.
- The United States has put itself above the rule of law, exercises hegemonic dominance with "the rule of the gun," and seeks to contain Russia and impose on it "junior partnership" in support of American ambitions. Indeed, the United States is seen as a dangerous power, willing to infringe vital Russian interests, with NATO as its useful tool.
- It is his duty to "snap back hard," to protect Russian speaking peoples wherever they may reside, and to push back against an unjust order.
- So-called color revolutions are a military threat to Russia, not least because of presumed Western subterfuge in support of them, and require a military response.[83]

Russia's Theory of Victory

Russian military leaders have been thinking seriously about the prospects for military confrontation with the United States since at least the late 1990s. NATO's operations in Kosovo in 1999 had a major impact on thinking in military circles in Russia. As Stephen Blank argued in 2000,

> Russian military apprehensions have grown with the collapse of Russian power, the augmentation of the power of the United States and NATO, Kosovo, the Anglo-American bombing campaign against Iraq, the Revolution in Military Affairs, and the onset of information warfare and operations. Kosovo was the last straw since it united many of the most feared military and political elements of the threat. . . . [It] became a moment of truth for Russia that rendered efforts to work with NATO toward equal security "totally worthless."[84]

The Russian General Staff, Blank argued, concluded that "Kosovo is a template for future NATO strategy."[85] In follow up to the Kosovo war, Russia issued a new security concept emphasizing a rising possibility of direct aggression against Russia and a "transitional" military doctrine that was designed to shift the focus onto this new problem.[86] These documents arrived just as Vladimir Putin started his first term as Russian president in 2000. Reform of the Russian military has been a leadership priority ever since.[87] Fifteen years later, what is the result?[88]

Russian military planning has a strong focus on local and regional conflicts rather than global conflict.[89] In the words of the 2013 Russian Foreign Policy Concept, there is a "reduced risk of large-scale war, including a nuclear one."[90] As President Putin argued in 2012:

> The probability of global war between nuclear powers is not high because that would mean the end of civilization. As long as the "powder" of our strategic nuclear forces created by the tremendous efforts of our fathers and grandfathers remains dry, nobody will dare launch a large-scale aggression against us.[91]

This planning reflects the fact that Russia perceives military dangers from many directions, reflecting "a more acute sense of insecurity and vulnerability."[92] Russian military planners address the potential for wars in four main "strategic directions" around Russia's periphery (which they define as a territory with air, sea, and land dimensions and strategically important assets). These are the Eastern direction covering the Asia-Pacific, the Central Asian direction covering Central Asia, the Southern direction covering the Caucasus and the wider Middle East, and the Western direction covering Europe. In each strategic direction, groups of forces are organized under combined commands to conduct military operations.[93] These are analogous to the geographic combatant commands used to organize U.S. military forces globally.

As perceived in Moscow, the dangers and threats posed by NATO are particularly acute and growing more so. NATO's efforts to move its military infrastructure closer to Russia's borders and to endow the alliance's forces with global functions are defined as threats to Russia and accordingly its military doctrine has focused on the challenge of defeating a conventionally superior nuclear-armed alliance.[94] This sense of vulnerability has something to do with Russian domestic politics and an expectation and fear of U.S. efforts to meddle in Russian internal affairs by promoting color revolutions among its neighbors. It has something also to do with the perceived stability of a ruling class that has built its success in part on corruption and covert deals to secure personal advantage.[95]

Ironically, Russian leadership views of NATO's military effectiveness swung sharply to the negative in 2014. In the words of *Pravda* in autumn 2014:

The West, having discarded Russia, had been cutting its tanks and destroying its tactical nuclear weapons. Russia, feeling its own weakness, kept all tanks and tactical nuclear weapons. . . . While the West, lulled by sweet day-dreams of the liberal "end of history," castrated its armed forces to the point when they could be good for leading colonial wars with weak and technical backward enemies. The balance of forces in Europe has changed in Russia's favor.[96]

Additionally, although Russian military doctrine is characterized as having a defensive character, "It calls for preemptive military actions (including a preemptive use of nuclear weapons), as well as mostly offensive strategy."[97] In limited wars, the primary missions of the Russian military are to seize and hold territory and to conduct standoff operations with both conventional warheads and what it calls "substrategic" nuclear weapons.[98]

Furthermore, the integration of capabilities for substrategic nuclear operations is an essential element of Russian concepts for regular warfare, as opposed to unlimited warfare and strategic deterrence.[99] This reflects, in part, the increased reliance on nuclear weapons Moscow had to accept twenty years ago as a compensation for conventional weakness after the collapse of the Soviet military. As Yury Federov has put it:

> While the role of nuclear weapons in Western security thinking is more modest than it was during the Cold War, Russian strategic thinking is evolving in a different direction. Russian military, political, and bureaucratic elites consider nuclear weapons to be the main foundation of Russian security and see them as an instrument that ensures Russia's national interests. . . . As the second largest nuclear power in the world, Russia hopes to strengthen its international influence by relying on its nuclear assets.[100]

In recent years, the developers of Russian military strategy and doctrine have addressed the challenge of linking the role of nonstrategic weapons in regular warfare with new Russian thinking about the requirements of victory in local and regional conflicts.[101] They have explored the roles of different nuclear capabilities in supporting Russian regional nuclear deterrence objectives: operational-tactical nuclear weapons from nonstrategic delivery platforms, operational-tactical weapons from strategic delivery platforms, and the employment of strategic weapons from strategic delivery platforms. They have also explored the value of a new generation of nuclear weapons that could be employed with less collateral damage. In the words of an authoritative Russian figure, "The principal trend has consistently been in the direction of reducing yield and enhancing accuracy of warheads. . . . alongside this trend, experts have been developing various concepts of limited nuclear war and different controlled nuclear conflicts."[102] Another influential Russian analyst writing in 2014 argued that "a sort of nuclear euphoria is sweeping the country. Whereas we might expect such comments from Kremlin spin doctors whipping up anti-Western hysteria, now even senior officials have joined the nuclear bandwagon in all earnestness."[103]

A particularly alarming Russian assessment of the role of nuclear war in Putin's worldview comes from Andrei Piontkovsky, a Russian scientist and political writer. In his view, Putin believes he can win a war with NATO with limited nuclear strikes:

> That belief is based on Putin's assumption that the logic of mutual assured destruction which prevented a major war between Russia and the West has broken down because of divisions within the West about how to respond to Russian use of a limited nuclear strike . . . [such that] the other side does not respond lest that lead to mutual suicide.[104]

Piointkovsky goes on to argue that "Putin does not seek the destruction of the hated United States, a goal that he could achieve only at the price of mutual suicide. Instead, his goals are significantly more modest: the maximum extension of the Russian world, the destruction of NATO, and the discrediting and humiliation of the United States as the guarantor of the security of the West."[105] Forrest Morgan has drawn a similar conclusion: "Whereas strategic parity made Cold War leaders cautious, it could lead today's leaders to place more faith in stability than is warranted. Moscow might gamble on hopes that fears of escalation would make the West shy of confronting a Russian military intervention."[106]

How far this thinking about nuclear employment has been translated into actual operational plans cannot be known by those outside Russian leadership circles. Dmitry Adamsky, an expert on Russian military doctrine, argues that this thinking has not gone very far:

> The set of ideas pertaining to regional deterrence are vague, not coherently formulated, not codified doctrinally, and not calibrated among different parts of the Russian strategic community. . . . Declarative doctrinal documents assume but do not spell out the causal mechanism of "nuclear deterrence," do not explain how to calculate a "pre-set deterrence damage," and how to dominate escalation without provoking a nuclear response. They are ambiguous in defining

such key terms of nuclear posture as nuclear threshold, situation critical for national security, existence of the state, de-escalation, limited nuclear use, and demonstrative nuclear strike. Interpretation was left, by default, to the echelons below national leadership, who rigorously explored this vague terminology in professional journals.[107]

Others assess it to be well advanced, even if still incomplete.[108] An authoritative Swedish analysis concludes as follows:

> Russia's strategic and sub-strategic (tactical) nuclear weapons provide strategic deterrence and complement conventional forces in regular warfare. . . . Russia has sub-strategic nuclear forces in all strategic directions. There are nuclear-capable short-range ballistic missile brigades and artillery units in all MDs [military districts]. Al fleets include anti-ship missiles and coastal defence missiles with nuclear potential. More importantly, there are attack or bomber aircraft regiments based in each strategic direction. Half of these are furthermore estimated to be able to redeploy to other strategic directions in a matter of a few days. There are nuclear storage facilities available in all strategic directions. . . . Russia is assessed to have sufficient sub-strategic nuclear warfare capabilities for operations aimed at seizing or holding territory in all strategic directions.[109]

A final result of nearly two decades of evolution in Russian strategic thought is that Russian military reform continues to explore thinking about the future of warfare and to develop the means to conduct what it characterizes as hybrid or no-contact warfare—a realm in which cyber means feature prominently.[110] These new forms of warfare are assessed to require asymmetric responses by Russia in these new domains and to promise both operational and strategic benefits. Timothy Thomas has argued that Russian military planners believe that cyberwarfare can lead to strategic capitulation by the enemy.[111] Of note, in recent years Russia has created military commands for cybersecurity and aerospace defense, focusing and expanding its capabilities to operate in those domains.[112]

These initiatives align with a new element of Russian military doctrine: reflexive control. As defined by Timothy Thomas,

> The theory is similar to the idea of perception management, except that it attempts to control more than manage a subject. Reflexive control is defined as a means of conveying to a partner or an opponent specially prepared information to incline him to voluntarily make the predetermined decision desired by

the initiator of the action. . . . The decision itself must be made independently. A "reflex" itself involves the specific process of imitating the enemy's reason or imitating the enemy's possible behavior and causes him to make a decision unfavorable to himself.[113]

Doubts remain about how much more reform Russia must yet accomplish to be effective in a major war with NATO. But Russia's progress is impressive and close watchers have argued that Westerns have still not understood the "sheer scale of change."[114]

This shift in planning and thinking in Moscow implies that Russia, too, has been putting together a theory of victory for potential future war with the United States (and NATO). It is a theory about a particular conflict—not general nuclear war or general war with NATO but a regional war in which Moscow hopes to achieve its operational and political objectives quickly at the conventional level while having credible capabilities to manage the risks of escalation against a conventionally superior, nuclear-armed alliance. Such as it can be derived from available official statements and literature and associated analysis, this theory appears to have some important similarities to, but also some key differences from, the theory of victory discussed in Chapter 2.

The Russian theory apparently begins with an effort to create a military fait accompli on the ground. In the words of one leading Russian military official, "The reaction time for the transition from political-diplomatic measures to the use of armed force has been maximally reduced."[115] With the rising Russian concern about color revolutions and NATO's possible intervention in them, Russia seeks the ability to quash such revolutions before NATO can take the decision and assemble the forces to act. Russian special forces ("little green men"), disinformation, and propaganda all play important roles in this fait accompli strategy.

The Russian theory of victory also includes a significant dimension related to countering possible escalatory responses by the United States and NATO. Russia has developed both horizontal and vertical options to counter and disincentivize Western escalation. Horizontal escalation would encompass standoff strikes on targets beyond the immediate zone of hybrid combat but within the "strategic direction." Vertical escalation would encompass strikes by both nuclear and nonnuclear means (whether kinetic or nonkinetic). Unlike the North Koreans, the Russians also have a significant capability for lateral escalation into the cyber and space domains.

Nonstrategic nuclear weapons apparently play a central role in Russian thinking about how to deter and defeat the West (unlike the North Korean case, where such weapons appear to play no such role). Actual employment would apparently be preemptive in nature and intended to deescalate a conflict. Presumably this follows from the calculus of Russian leadership that their employment of nuclear weapons against NATO forces would signal their resolve and alert Western decision makers to the asymmetry of stake, as Russian leaders perceive it, while being sufficiently limited not to risk a strategic response.[116] In this assessment, the asymmetry of stake favors Russia because any conflict between NATO and Russia would jeopardize vital Russian interests whereas it would involve important but not vital NATO or U.S. interests. The employment of a limited but unspecified number of substrategic nuclear weapons might thus be seen as helpful in containing escalatory responses by the West.[117] Some Russians have also described an effort to calibrate the amount of "tailored damage" that would be needed to induce the desired restraint by NATO rather than inciting it to further military action.[118]

Perhaps recognizing a risk that nuclear employment might not motivate restraint from the attacked countries and their allies, Russian military planners have added a new tool to the escalation-management toolkit: "prenuclear deterrence." Andrei Kokoshin describes this as follows:

> Many experts and politicians have long doubted the value of nuclear threshold reduction, rightly believing that alongside reduction of the threshold any threat to use nuclear weapons becomes less ponderable . . . [This] requires consideration of other additional measures aimed at enhancing the cogency of deterrence and, consequently, its effectiveness. There are such opportunities, for example, in the area of use of long-range high-precision weapons of various types and weapons with conventional warheads, including high-precision warheads, using such platforms as, first of all, subsurface and surface combat ships and long-range bombers. . . . Any forceful threat to use a high-precision long-range delivery vehicle with a conventional warhead would become the basis of the pre-nuclear deterrence system that amplifies the nuclear deterrence system. . . . Such weapons should be used primarily for hitting high-cost assets and complex national security systems that are located far away from densely populated areas. . . . At higher stages of escalation—still at the pre-nuclear stage, we could be talking about the destruction of similar civilian targets, such as infrastructural assets. . . . The adversary should realize that pre-nuclear deterrence is not a

bluff, but a real political-military tool in the hands of Russia's leadership that is secured by all the necessary components.[119]

In support of this element of Russian military doctrine, Russian planners have explored large-scale strikes by advanced conventional deep-strike systems and have considered the operational and strategic benefits of such attacks on the economy and infrastructure of NATO members.[120] Also, as noted earlier, they have developed concepts for "no-contact warfare" that would rely on nonkinetic means to attack economic and other targets in the West.

The theory of victory described in Chapter 2 encompasses also the threat of strategic nuclear attacks on the American homeland as a way to decouple the United States from the defense of its allies in time of war. In comparison to North Korea, Russia's assets for this purpose are of course extremely robust. Some reports even suggest that the long-range cruise missiles associated with the employment of nonstrategic nuclear weapons may have a role as a step in the escalation ladder with limited strikes on targets in the American homeland.[121] Unlike North Korea, however, there is evidence that Russian military planners define a quantitative threshold in terms of the number of warheads delivered on the United States to impose costs that would be sufficiently unacceptable to deter the United States from taking escalatory action. Kokoshin among others has written about a "safety margin"—a quantity of weapons surviving any U.S. strikes on them and capable of penetrating U.S. ballistic missile defenses sufficient to ensure "a sound retaliatory strike."[122] Sufficiency, he argues, is also a function of the adversary country's political and military decision-making processes in time of war. He cites one Russian analyst's calculations and the assertion that the credible threat of 300 warheads delivered on the United States would be sufficient for deterrence of the United States in time of war.[123]

The theory of victory described in Chapter 2 is a theory of nuclear brinksmanship, not nuclear warfighting. In this regard, the degree of integration of Russian nuclear forces at the substrategic level is deeply troubling. On the basis of available evidence, there is no reason to believe that Russian leaders would cross the nuclear threshold easily. But having once crossed it, they would have options for diverse and continuous nuclear operations at the substrategic level that are truly unique.

The theory of victory described in Chapter 2 is a theory about victory in both war and in peacetime. Russia too hopes to subdue its enemies without fighting them. The Russian foreign policy concept and military strategy discussed in previous pages amply attest to President Putin's ambition to use soft power tools to create political and economic incentives to accede to his preferences in regions neighboring Russia. The energy tool has been wielded explicitly toward this end. Propaganda and disinformation obviously have rising salience in this strategy. These various tools underpin an on-going campaign of coercion of Russian neighbors—coercion backed by military threats. As Russia has become more militarily assertive in the region, it has proven to be more purposeful in utilizing military threats and political promises to try to sow division among the NATO allies and to create the conditions for a re-making of the European security order. NATO's newest members are already subject to such Russian coercion.

This theory of victory is much more than a theory—it is instantiated in doctrine and capabilities. The rapidly deployable conventional forces for the quick suppression of color revolutions were vividly on display in Crimea in spring 2014. (It is important to note, however, that Russian military means to seize and hold enemy territory are not currently robust against a militarily well-armed adversary and a hostile population.[124]) The means to conduct non-strategic nuclear weapons operations are, as already noted, fully integrated into Russian military forces. And the means to conduct long-range nonnuclear precision strikes have improved significantly in recent years with the deployment of new weapons to both naval and long-range aviation delivery systems.[125] According to an analysis by the Swedish government, as of 2013:

> The assets for stand-off warfare in the western strategic direction are estimated to allow for a conventional strike, within 24 hours, with up to 117 medium-range missiles and some 50 long-range ALCMs [air-launched cruise missiles], provided that so many can be set aside. The majority of the medium-range missiles are primarily ASMs [antiship missiles], but at least 50 can be used for land-attack purposes. Alternatively, up to 82 medium-range missiles and 28 long-range SLCMs [submarine-launched cruise missiles] are assessed to be available within 24 hours for sub-strategic nuclear standoff warfare. . . . Allowing some time for preparation, almost double the number of missiles could be available for a stand-off strike in the western strategic direction.[126]

These numbers include the twenty-four new Iskander short-range ballistic missiles deployed by Russia near Saint Petersburg. Although understood to be armed with conventional warheads, Iskander missiles are deemed capable of delivering nuclear weapons, and one analysis attributes between twelve and eighteen substrategic nuclear warheads to this brigade.[127]

Russia is also well launched on a program to modernize its nuclear and other strategic forces. In September 2014, President Putin described a modernization program for 2016–2025 focused on new offensive weapons, rearming strategic and long-range aviation, creating an aerospace defense sector, and developing high-precision conventional weapons, at a cost of $540 billion.[128]

Moreover, standing forces are regularly exercised. Exercises with substrategic nuclear forces, including release of warheads to delivery units, have become more frequent in recent years.[129] Exercises of the prenuclear posture have also become frequent, including for example medium-range bombers operating in the Baltic Sea area with fighter aircraft top cover.[130] Exercises of Russia's strategic nuclear forces resumed in June 1999 with simulated cruise missiles strikes against targets in Europe and North America[131] and in 2012 conducted what was then the largest exercise in Russia's history.[132]

These exercises reportedly serve purposes other than keeping the forces ready. As Andrei Kokoshin has argued, tests and exercises are "strategic gestures" to be used in crisis to achieve "a certain political result—either to prevent the crisis or to put an end to it on mutually acceptable terms. . . . One should not lose sight of the fact that quite often, such actions were (and are) taken not just to catch the opponent's fancy (and thus influence its behavior), but for domestic consumption too."[133] At the height of its military operations in Crimea, Russia conducted one such strategic gesture, in the form of the largest-ever exercise of its nuclear forces.[134]

New allegations about Russia's violation of the Treaty on Intermediate-range Nuclear Forces (INF) add a troubling dimension to this analysis.[135] Russia has long complained that the treaty dangerously constrains its ability to respond to the development and deployment of missiles by countries around its periphery and has periodically sought to widen membership of the treaty or withdraw from it. The preceding analysis suggests that Russia has abundant strategic and substrategic means to support its current military strategy. Thus Russian leaders may perceive a military need not so far articulated or a political value in standing at the brink of breakout. They may see value in weapons that can sit back deeper in Russian territory while threatening NATO, where they would be less vulnerable to attack. They may simply see a value in deploying new nuclear weapons as a signal of confidence in their offensive capabilities (with President Putin hinting at new nuclear offensive capabilities that "we do not yet talk about").[136] If Russia does not proceed to deploy a new INF system, some means must be found to redress its noncompliance to date. If it does proceed to deploy weapons, where and how they are deployed will be a critical determinant of the needed response (as discussed further in Chapter 6).

The New Sources of Strategic Instability

This line of analysis highlights the fact that significant new sources of instability have emerged in the strategic military relationship between the United States and Russia.

From a Russian perspective, as already articulated, the new challenges to strategic stability come from the end of bipolarity, the rise of an assertive United States, and its success in imposing a security order in Europe detrimental to Russian interests. This points also to an additional but unstated Russian concern: regime stability. If the government of Vladimir Putin were more confident of its legitimacy, it might be less preoccupied with neighboring color revolutions.

From a U.S. perspective, the new challenge to strategic stability is at the theater-strategic level, where Russia's progress in conceiving a theory of victory in war with NATO, and in putting into place the associated doctrine and capabilities, is at profound odds with the laissez-faire attitude toward Russia taken by U.S. and NATO military planners over the last twenty-five years. This mismatch brings with it two fundamental problems. The first is that Russian intentions and capabilities might now align in a manner that persuade its leaders to become more risk-taking in their behavior toward the West and to use military threats and, in the North Korean sense of the word, "provocations" to demonstrate resolve and sow division and fear in the West. The second challenge is the potential for miscalculation by Russia of Western resolve. Nuclear deescalation strikes, like missiles strikes on Western infrastructure targets, would be just as likely to generate anger as fear among Western publics.

This line of argument implies that the Blue theory of victory set out in Chapter 3 requires adaptation if it is to be effective in dealing with challenges posed by Russia. In an armed confrontation, the United States would have the ability to match any level of escalation chosen by Russia. But Russia has the ability to counter at any level and an ability to dominate the theater by nuclear means. The United States would have the advantage of strong allies. But Russia might well see those allies as potential sources of restraint on Washington if they could be reminded of their own vulnerability. Russia would have the advantage of being able to operate from its homeland (and can be expected to make clear to Washington that attacks on its homeland in a regional war with the United States would open up the American homeland to retaliation). Both countries would have the assets, vulnerabilities, and risks of advanced competition in the cyber domain.

Implications for the United States

After twenty-five years of working to create the conditions that would allow the United States and Russia to further reduce the role and number of their nuclear weapons by improving their political relationship (and vice versa), the effort came to a turning point in 2014. President Putin sees the adversarial aspects of Russia's relations with the West as vastly outweighing the cooperative ones. He has embraced nuclear weapons as part of the solution. But a fundamental uncertainty remains: whether the "snap back hard" strategy will result in additional military action by Moscow, including action that would call into question the Article V commitment of NATO allies to each other. The West would ignore the developments of 2014 at its peril. So what should it do?

Simply falling back on Cold War approaches would be unpromising. Although some of the problems now present in the Euro-Atlantic security environment are analogous to Cold War problems, the strategic landscape is different in very many respects. There is no Iron Curtain or Fulda Gap with 100-plus divisions of Soviet and Warsaw Pact armored forces waiting to spill across Western Europe. Moreover, the possibility remains that President Putin's grip on the Kremlin will not prove long lived and that his successor will seek a return to more cooperative approaches with the West.

In the basic political strategy toward Russia, the United States and its allies must now accept as prominent the adversarial aspect that Putin has long perceived and the West has long resisted. This does not mean setting aside all efforts to cooperate on areas of mutual interest; it does mean that we should recognize those areas as limited and not likely to grow any time soon. To address the adversarial aspects implies greater assertiveness in defending Western interests where they differ from Russia's while also rebuilding some of the mechanisms for mediating crises if and as they develop.[137]

In the basic nuclear strategy toward Russia, the United States (and its allies) must now acknowledge that the time is not ripe for making further progress in reducing the role and number of nuclear weapons in partnership with Russia. This is not to imply that the time will not ripen again in the future—it well may, as New START expiration in 2021 draws closer. New START reductions can and should continue so long as Russia remains compliant with the treaty. The United States should continue to explore conceptually options to accomplish further reductions in the nuclear arsenals of the two countries.[138] It is possible that Russia's progress in repairing the weaknesses in its conventional forces and adapting its deterrent to new concepts of warfare may, over time, reduce its reliance on nuclear weapons, thus reopening the door to some form of negotiated reductions, especially in Europe.

But the time may not ripen. Whatever Russia's progress in repairing and adapting its military, it may retain a central role for nuclear weapons for the long term. From an arms control perspective, the United States may find itself relying on multilateral mechanisms and informal bargains to try to elicit Russian restraint, predictability, and transparency. These will be weaker by far than bilateral mechanisms.

This implies that the only plausible options for further U.S. reductions at this time are unilateral. As discussed more in a later chapter, such unilateral measures should be rejected at this time. Dialogue with Russia on strategic stability should continue as circumstances permit, but the United States should understand that accommodation on many key points is unlikely, and thus there would be value of a narrowing of focus to a short list of issues where progress might be possible. Missile defense cooperation does not belong on that list.

At this turning point, a central question for the United States is what it can do, together with its allies, to preserve strategic stability on a unilateral as opposed to bilateral basis. This chapter points to an urgent priority: addressing the new theater-strategic instability in Europe following from Russia's preparations for war with NATO and the associated theory of victory. This effort does not follow from a simple assessment that Russia will bring war to the West, and we must be prepared to fight and win. Rather, it follows from the premise that the failure to prepare will contribute to both risk taking and miscalculation by Moscow in ways that will make conflict, including nuclear conflict, more likely. This is a focus of Chapter 6.

5   The Evolving Relationship with China

I F THE U.S.–RUSSIA NUCLEAR STORY IS LARGELY ABOUT THE failure to move nuclear weapons from the foreground into the background of the political relationship, the U.S.–China story is largely about the so far partial success in keeping nuclear weapons from coming from the background into the foreground of the political relationship. Nuclear weapons have never played the role in the U.S.–China relationship that they have in the U.S.–Russia one. But this is changing, not least because the political and security relationship between the United States and China is changing. The nuclear relationship is a key variable in this period of change and seems likely to become increasingly corrosive of the political relationship unless some new steps are taken.

To better understand the unique dynamics of the China–U.S. nuclear relationship, this chapter proceeds as follows. It begins with a review of efforts to improve the political relationship from 1989 to the present. This is a story that shows continuity of purpose in both Washington and Beijing as well as continued frustration in both capitals with the stubborn nature of difficulties in that relationship. It then reviews the way each of the two countries has developed nuclear policy toward the other to support political objectives. The chapter then turns to a review of lessons learned about the nuclear relationship and strategic stability in the unofficial dialogues that have run for ten years in the absence of official dialogue. These dialogues have been substantive and productive, illuminating important areas of agreement and disagreement. The chapter then explores alternative futures. The chapter next turns to the problems of war and deterrence in the bilateral relationship. It then characterizes and assesses China's own version of a theory of victory (as broadly defined here) in a regional conflict with the United States before setting out conclusions.

Promoting Improved Relations from 1989 to 2014

Although democratic change swept most of the rest of the communist world in 1989, the Chinese Communist Party managed to survive the global transition, not least through brutal repression that year of China's own democracy movement at Tiananmen Square. Thus the United States faced the prospect of continued Communist Party rule of the People's Republic of China (PRC) and the difficulties of building relations with a modernizing authoritarian state, guided by values it does not share and relying on nationalism to address challenges to its legitimacy.

The George H. W. Bush administration adopted a cautious, pragmatic attitude to China, largely as a result of its focus on dramatic events unfolding in Europe and the Soviet Union and then later in the Middle East (with Iraq's invasion of Kuwait). Its national security strategy highlighted China as a place where democratic reform needed to be encouraged and argued that "we must carefully watch the emergence of China onto the world stage and support, contain, or balance this emergence as necessary to protect U.S. interests."[1] In a widely criticized move, President Bush sent National Security Advisor Brent Scowcroft and Deputy Secretary of State Larry Eagleburger to Beijing shortly after the Tiananmen crackdown to signal his commitment to sustaining some dialogue and cooperation.[2]

The Clinton administration expressed a commitment to comprehensive engagement with China. It described engagement as a policy "designed to integrate China into the international community as a responsible member and to foster bilateral cooperation in areas of common interest."[3] The administration also expressed a commitment to "a stable, open, prosperous and strong China" and argued that "we have a profound stake in helping to ensure that China pursues its modernization in ways that contribute to the overall security and prosperity of the Asia Pacific region."[4] The administration also emphasized areas of concern to the United States, such as China's practices on human rights, proliferation, and trade.[5] Late in its term, the Clinton administration seemed to adopt an even more cautious tone, arguing that "we must be mindful of threats to the peace" even as we build "principled, constructive, clear-eyed relations" with China.[6]

The George W. Bush administration reflected the dual tendencies to engage China as a "responsible stakeholder" in meeting 21st-century security challenges and to hedge against the possibility that China's economic and military rise might not turn out well. Its national security strategy echoed many of the themes of the Clinton administration, stating that "we welcome the emergence of a strong, peaceful, and prosperous China."[7] But administration leaders also struck a cautious tone, asserting that "China is not a status quo power. . . . Cooperation should be pursued, but we should never be afraid to confront Beijing when our interests collide."[8] The administration's thinking also reflected the radical shift driven by 9/11 and its enthusiasm, reported in a prior chapter, for a concert of power among the major powers, including China, on the basis of "a truly global consensus about basic principles."[9]

The administration attempted to knit together these various strands in an effort to engage China as a "responsible stakeholder":

> We need now to encourage China to become a responsible stakeholder in the international system. As a responsible stakeholder, China would be more than just a member—it would work with us to sustain the international system that has enabled its success. Cooperation as stakeholders will not mean the absence differences—we will have disputes that we need to manage. But that management can take place within a larger framework where parties recognize a shared interest in sustaining political, economic, and security systems that provide common benefits.[10]

The Obama administration echoed these themes in its own national security strategy, emphasizing its commitment to pursue "a positive, constructive, and comprehensive relationship with China." But it stated also that it would "monitor China's military modernization program and prepare accordingly."[11]

There has been similar continuity of purpose in China's general approach to relations with the United States and also similar efforts to balance the positive and the negative. China's defense white papers have conveyed a consistent set of perceptions and commitments since they first appeared in the mid-1990s. China sees itself as a rising power returning to its proper place in the international landscape following a century of humiliation at the hands of capricious imperialist powers. China's leaders also express a commitment to rise peacefully:

> It is China's unshakable national commitment and strategic choice to take the road of peaceful development. China unswervingly pursues an independent foreign policy of peace and a national defense policy that is defensive in nature. China opposes any form of hegemonism or power politics, and does not interfere in the internal affairs of other countries. China will never seek hegemony or behave in a hegemonic manner, nor will it engage in military expansion. China advocates a new security concept featuring mutual trust, mutual benefit, equality and coordination, and pursues comprehensive security, common security, and cooperative security.[12]

China also perceives a security environment that is "complex and volatile":

> Peace and development remain the underlying trends of our times. The global trends toward economic globalization and multi-polarity are intensifying . . . and on the whole the international situation remains peaceful and stable. Meanwhile, however, the world is far from tranquil. There are signs of increasing hegemonism, power politics, and neo-interventionism. . . . Hot spots keep creeping up . . . Competition is intensifying in the military field. . . . Some country has strengthened its Asia-Pacific military alliances, expanded its military presence in the region, and frequently makes the situation tenser there. On issues concerning China's territorial sovereignty and maritime rights and interests, some neighboring countries are taking actions that complicate or exacerbate the situation. . . . Major powers are vigorously developing new and more sophisticated military technologies so as to ensure that they can maintain strategic superiorities in international competition in such areas as outer space and cyber space.[13]

In setting an agenda for improvements in relations with the United States, President Xi Jinping set out a new conceptual approach in a speech in Washington, D.C., on February 15, 2012. He proposed "a new type of relationship between major countries in the 21st century," characterized by mutual understanding and strategic trust, respect for each other's "core interests,'" mutually beneficial cooperation, and enhanced cooperation and coordination in international affairs and on global issues.[14] A subsequent elaboration was provided by Premier Li Keqiang, who argued that "I don't believe conflicts between big powers are inevitable. . . . Shared interests often override their disputes. . . .

We're willing to construct, together with the Obama Administration, a new type of relationship between big powers."[15]

China seeks a "new type" relationship in part because it perceives the United States as seeking to block its rise. Many officials, military leaders, and experts in Beijing believe that the United States is a hegemonic power committed to the containment of China and even to the overthrow of its current system of government. They believe that the United States will not gracefully acquiesce to China's rise and that its need to protect its position of power and influence in the region will inevitably lead to conflict. They also believe that Japan is provoking China militarily with U.S. backing and protection. Such thinking appears to be especially deeply engrained in the People's Liberation Army (PLA). As a symptom of the apparent depth of division in Beijing on these matters, shortly after President Xi set out his proposal for a "new type" relationship, China's national television network broadcast a documentary produced by the PLA titled "Silent Contest," which described alleged plans of the U.S. military to overthrow the government in Beijing and otherwise demonized the United States.[16]

The Obama administration responded positively to the "new type" concept, with then National Security Advisor Tom Donilon embracing a positive vision in China–U.S. relations that avoids war and containment and strengthens cooperation.[17] Some conditional support for this project was also provided by Donilon's predecessor in the George W. Bush administration, Steve Hadley, who argued that there is a "real possibility" that a positive vision can be fulfilled.[18]

The effort to build a "new type" relationship has paid some important political dividends. For example, China now plays a more constructive role in nuclear nonproliferation, especially vis-à-vis North Korea and Iran. But the effort has not fundamentally shifted key elements of the relationship. President Xi has pushed back against a regional order in Asia that he sees as inconsistent with China's interests, in a manner evocative of President Putin's pushback against a regional order in Europe that he considers not consistent with Russia's interests. In May 2014, President Xi proposed setting up a new regional security cooperation architecture that would include Russia and Iran but essentially exclude the United States. Arguing that "no one should seek absolute security for itself at the expense of others . . . we cannot just have security for one or a few countries while leaving the rest insecure," he went on to challenge U.S. alliance relations in the region: "A military alliance which is targeted at a third party is not conducive to common regional security."[19] Note the similarity to concerns articulated by Russian President Putin.

This rising opposition to the U.S.-backed regional order closely aligns with other Chinese efforts to contest American-led approaches to international order, whether locally or globally. These include, for example, the Shanghai Cooperation Organization aimed at countering U.S. influence in Central Asia, the Changmai Initiative to develop an East Asian currency exchange not dependent on the U.S. dollar, and cooperation with other medium-sized powers in building new international financial institutions to counter the roles of the World Bank and International Monetary Fund.

On the other hand, China cannot expect to fully exclude the United States from the region. A key challenge for policy makers in both Washington and Beijing is to turn the separate national agendas for regional order into a common approach to developing a more open and inclusive regional security order, one that integrates both China and the United States while maintaining U.S. security guarantees to regional allies.

In sum, over the last twenty-five years, both the United States and China have tried to strengthen areas of cooperation while trying to manage the sources of competition and conflict between them. Unlike the U.S.–Russia relationship, there has been no regular cycle of rising expectations followed by disappointment and resets. Instead, there has been a steady process of work in both capitals to move the relationship in directions each deems positive while managing the sources of competition and conflict amid dynamic economic and political factors.

There is, however, a rising debate in the United States (as elsewhere) about whether China's external relations are at a fundamental turning point, akin to but not as immediately dangerous as the turning point in Russia's relations with the West. On the one hand, cooperation has improved in many areas. Shared interests have grown. This is reflected in deepening economic integration, improved political cooperation on nuclear nonproliferation, strengthened counter-terror cooperation, and more frequent engagement on a broad set of issues, all suggesting that good progress has been made in improving relations.

On the other hand, divergent economic and political interests tend to dominate the bilateral agenda, as do competitive security interests in the Asia-Pacific region. One recent study probes deeply into continuing U.S.–PRC dialogues on ten key issues and concludes that the differences between the two are not narrowing and indeed continue to harden.[20] David Lampton has argued that the United States and China are "sliding from engagement to coercive diplomacy."[21] James Steinberg and Michael O'Hanlon have argued that "trust in both capitals—and in the countries at large—remains scarce, and the possibility of an accidental or even intentional conflict between the United States and China seems to be growing."[22] These assessments are consistent with rising concern in the United States about the more assertive character of China's foreign policy, especially but not exclusively in its maritime environment. They are consistent also with China's now clearly stated opposition to the U.S.-led regional security order. They are consistent also with China's continued pursuit of military modernization and its buildup of forces, now two decades underway.

But an opportunity seems to remain to build on the substantial shared interests of China and the United States. And the commitment of China's current leadership to seek a "new type" relationship with the United States, one that avoids armed conflict, holds out the possibility of continued leadership commitment in Beijing to partner with the United States in pursuit of common interests. This stands in contrast to Russia's relationship with the West, where no such opportunity or commitment exists today.

The Nuclear Dimension of the Broader Relationship

Efforts to remake the nuclear relationship in some positive new way have not had a central role in efforts to strengthen the U.S.–China relationship in the way they have in the U.S.–Russia one. After all, in the U.S.–Russia relationship, the Cold War nuclear legacy was prominent, given decades of competition and concern about the nuclear balance, whereas in the U.S.–China relationship the Cold War nuclear legacy was essentially a footnote, given the absence of nuclear competition and of significant concern about nuclear war between the two. China deployed its first delivery system capable of reaching the United States with nuclear weapons in 1981 and over the next fifteen years placed only approximately twenty nuclear-armed ICBMs into silos—where they were vulnerable to preemptive attack.

In the development of U.S. nuclear policy over the last twenty-five years, China has been a secondary concern, though its salience has risen steadily, especially as its force modernization has proceeded. The 1994 NPR seems to have taken little note of China. The George W. Bush administration's "new strategic framework," although mostly about Russia and so-called rogue states, took note of China's "substantial effort to modernize its strategic nuclear forces," arguing that this "could provide a credible, survivable deterrent and counterstrike capability."[23] The administration also set out some ideas about how to dissuade China from "sprinting" to nuclear parity with the United States and Russia as they reduced their forces. The case was made most explicitly by Secretary Rumsfeld, when called on in Senate testimony to defend the size of the U.S. nuclear arsenal reflected in the SORT Treaty with Moscow: "To the extent you lower down so low that it looks like some country can, in fact, sprint and get up to a level, then the deterrent effect of having your capability is probably less . . . There is no question in my mind that weakness is provocative."[24] The Bush administration considered various approaches to dissuasion, drawing largely on the "competitive strategies" approach toward the Soviet Union set out by the Reagan administration. Such strategies seek to persuade an adversary or potential adversary not to compete with the United States for strategic advantage by channeling the competition into areas where the adversary or potential adversary cannot afford not to compete but cannot prevail against the United States in a long-term competition.[25]

The Obama administration's NPR emphasized the commitment to a "positive, constructive, and comprehensive relationship" with China. But it also highlighted concern about China's military modernization, including the qualitative and quantitative modernization of its nuclear arsenal. Noting that China's nuclear arsenal remains much smaller than the arsenals of the United States and Russia, it went on to argue that "the lack of transparency surrounding its nuclear programs—their pace and scope, as well as the strategy and doctrine that guides them—raises questions about China's future strategic intentions."[26]

The 2010 NPR report repeatedly emphasizes the commitment of the Obama administration to strategic stability with China, as with Russia, with the hope that this would highlight shared interests in stability, facilitate official dialogue on challenges to stability, and help to create the conditions for China's future participation in the process of negotiating nuclear reductions. The June 2013 report on the updated presidential nuclear employment guidance repeated the commitment to strategic stability with China.

But the administration did not spell out in detail its thinking about the requirements of strategic stability with China, in part with the hope of incentivizing the desired official dialogue with Beijing. Although the invitation to a dialogue on strategic stability was made at the presidential level, six years later there is very little to show for the effort. China also declined an invitation in 2009 to express its views to the incoming Obama administration about its equities in decisions that would be taken in the Nuclear Posture Review. This failure to engage follows a false start on dialogue after a presidential summit commitment in April 2006 and unsuccessful efforts in the 1990s by the United States to elicit PRC interest in nuclear dialogue.

Recognizing an abiding Chinese concern about the impact of U.S. ballistic missile defenses on the credibility of its deterrent, the Obama administration also provided specific assurances in the report of its Ballistic Missile Defense Review:

> Both Russia and China have repeatedly expressed concerns that U.S. missile de-
> fenses adversely affect their own strategic capabilities and interests. The United
> States will continue to engage them on this issue to help them better understand
> the stabilizing benefits of missile defense. . . . As the United States has stated in
> the past, the homeland missile defense capabilities are focused on regional ac-
> tors such as Iran and North Korea. While the GMD [Ground-based Midcourse
> Defense] system would be employed to defend the United States against limited
> missile launches from any source, it does not have the capacity to cope with
> large scale Russian or Chinese missile attacks, and is not intended to affect the
> strategic balance with those countries.[27]

Of note, the Bush administration was also sensitive to possible Chinese reactions to U.S. withdrawal from the ABM Treaty in 2001. As Secretary of State Colin Powell argued subsequently, "The country that I was concerned about the most with respect to a reaction [to ABM withdrawal] was China . . . we gave them the most in-depth briefings we could on what we were think-ing. . . . [and they] have taken it all on board."[28] As the White House argued at the time, "We do not view China as an enemy and our limited missiles de-fenses are not directed at it."[29]

In short, multiple U.S. administrations have promoted strategic stabil-ity in the nuclear relationship with China while avoiding actions that would give increased political prominence to the challenges in that relationship. The overall U.S. approach of recent decades has been to downplay the potential for nuclear conflict with China and to emphasize that developments in the U.S. strategic military posture, such as the introduction of ballistic missile defenses, are focused on other problems. But the United States has not had success in opening up what it considers to be a more normal nuclear relationship with China (that is, one in which the two sides talk to each other) and to put it on a more substantive foundation with a sustained exploration of the requirements of strategic stability on a mutual basis.

Over this period, and as argued further in the following pages, the United States has not so far made significant adjustment to its deterrence posture in Asia to account for changes in China's nuclear capabilities. It has continued to implement the comprehensive strategy for strengthening regional deterrence architectures with an eye primarily on the North Korean threat. The important caveat here is with regard to the U.S. regional ballistic missile defense posture, which, as already noted, seeks to provide protection from any missile attack, whatever its source.

Whether this will remain so in the future is an open question. China's nuclear modernization efforts are resulting in a significant increase in the number of nuclear weapons deliverable by China on the United States and its allies. That number seems likely to grow further as China moves to deploy multiple warheads atop its long-range delivery systems. From a U.S. perspective, the move to MIRVd warheads is a major concern, as it introduces significant new instability to the military balance.

Similarly, over the last twenty-five years, China has endeavored to keep nuclear weapons in the background. Indeed, some Chinese analysts have argued that it has resisted U.S. pressure for more transparency and dialogue largely out of a concern that this would amplify threat perceptions in Washington and bring nuclear weapons more into the forefront of the political relationship.[30]

China's "self-defensive nuclear strategy" was set out publicly and officially in the 2006 defense white paper:

China's nuclear strategy is subject to the state's nuclear policy and military strategy. Its fundamental goal is to deter other countries from using or threatening to use nuclear weapons against China. China remains firmly committed to the policy of no first use of nuclear weapons at any time and under any circumstances. It unconditionally undertakes not to use or threaten to use nuclear weapons against non-nuclear-weapon states or nuclear-weapon-free zones, and stands for the comprehensive prohibition and complete elimination of nuclear weapons. China upholds the principles of counterattack in self-defense and limited development of nuclear weapons, and aims at building a lean and effective nuclear force capable of meeting national security needs. It endeavors to ensure the security and reliability of its nuclear weapons and maintains a credible nuclear deterrent force. China's nuclear force is under the direct command of the Central Military Commission (CMC). China exercises great restraint in developing its nuclear force. It has never entered into and will never enter into a nuclear arms race with any other country.[31]

The 2013 defense white paper sets out the main elements of China's nuclear deterrent, including the commitments to a "lean and effective" force, to a modernization process to ensure continued effectiveness, and to an "elevated" role for the deterrent.[32]

These statements build on and amplify themes previously set out at the national leadership level. Jiang Zemin argued in 2000 as follows:

> We must own strategic nuclear weapons of a definite quality and quantity in order to ensure national security. We must guarantee the safety of strategic nuclear bases and prevent against the loss of combat effectiveness from attacks and destruction by hostile powers. We must ensure that our strategic nuclear weapons are at a high degree of war preparedness. When an aggressor launches a nuclear attack against us, we must be able to launch nuclear counter attack and nuclear re-attack against the aggressor. We must pay attention to the global situation of strategic balance and stability and, when there are changes in the situation, adjust our strategic nuclear weapon development strategy in a timely manor.[33]

China does not conduct or issue NPRs or QDRs, so these annual defense white papers and occasional leadership statements are the best available official source for insights into China's military policy and posture.

China also expresses a commitment to the global disarmament agenda and in recent years has joined with the four other permanent members of the UN Security Council to enhance cooperation in implementing the Nuclear Non-Proliferation Treaty. It is also a party to the Comprehensive Test Ban Treaty, the Limited Test Ban Treaty, and the Chemical Weapons Convention.

But China has not so far joined any other nuclear arms control treaty and shows no signs of doing so any time soon. It has regularly restated its willingness to join the process of nuclear reductions—but only at some future time.[34] It has conditioned its willingness to do so on deep cuts in the arsenals of the "nuclear superpowers." Alas, the goalposts seem to keep moving.[35] In 1982,

China said that it would join nuclear arms control talks only after the United States and Soviet Union halted the testing, manufacture, and deployment of nuclear weapons and also reduced their arsenals by 50 percent. In 1988, as the Strategic Arms Reduction Treaty (START I) was being implemented, China modified its position, promising to join the disarmament process not at the 50 percent mark but only after further "drastic reductions" in the superpower arsenals. In 1995, China stated that it would not join in additional formal nuclear arms control restraints unless the United States and Russia reduced their arsenals far beyond START II numbers, abandoned tactical nuclear weapons, abandoned ballistic missile defenses, and agreed to a joint no-first-use pledge.

Interim progress by the United States and Russia in reducing their nuclear arsenals has not led to a Chinese decision to join the process. Nor has China adopted transparency measures about capabilities of a kind adopted by the other nuclear weapon states (though it has become more transparent in recent years about nuclear policy). It continues to press the United States to embrace no first use (just as it continues to press Russia to return to its prior no-first-use pledge). In short, China's position remains unchanged.

This record implies that Washington and Beijing have shared interests in "keeping nuclear weapons in the background"—that is, in not allowing new forms of competition at the strategic military level to interfere with efforts to improve the political relationship and deepen cooperation in areas of shared interest. This record also implies different preferences in the two capitals about how best to accomplish this. For China, nuclear weapons are best kept in the background by providing transparency about policy and strategy but not about capabilities and by resisting U.S. efforts to feature nuclear dialogue more prominently in ongoing military-to-military and political–military leadership dialogue. For the United States, nuclear weapons are best kept in the background by normalizing them in the relationship and sharing information, perspectives, and concerns, just as we do in so many other areas.

Insights from Unofficial Nuclear Dialogue

In the absence of sustained, substantive, high-level nuclear dialogue between the United States and China, the two sides have supported various unofficial dialogues. These operate somewhat as the Pugwash process did early in the Cold War, bringing together expert communities for informal discussions. For approximately a decade, think tank experts, academics, retired officials, and military and diplomatic personnel from both countries have come together to discuss nuclear topics of mutual interest. Periodically they have been joined by government officials in their private capacities. These dialogues have been helpful for generating an understanding of the nuclear policies of each country and the thinking behind them, as well as of debates within the countries. They have also been helpful for building a common view of the dimensions of the "problem space" and of the essential vocabulary and concepts that each side would bring to an official dialogue when and if it commences. From the perspective of possible future U.S. nuclear policy development, the key insights gained so far touch on many subjects. This summary highlights ten such insights.

First, China has become more transparent over time about its nuclear policy and strategy, about the political assessments that inform its policy, and about the key points of debate in China. This follows a serious and systematic review of its policy and strategy from approximately the mid-1990s to a decade later. To be sure, China has not become more transparent about capabilities. It sees opacity in this respect as necessary and appropriate because it preserves China's deterrent by creating uncertainty in the minds of American military planners about China's points of weakness and strength.

It is important to note that the United States is not as transparent to China as China would wish. China's experts often ask America's experts for predictions of future U.S. behavior, which America's experts are reluctant to provide. They seek clarifications of U.S. strategic intentions, which do not always lend themselves to simple explanations. China's experts also ask whether the Obama administration's commitment to strategic stability with China means that the United States accepts mutual vulnerability and mutual deterrence as the basis of the strategic relationship, as it does with Russia; to this question, the administration has answered only that it has set out its answers in its NPR and BMDR. For the Chinese, this is a key point: If the United States cannot answer so simple a question as "do you accept mutual vulnerability or not?" then something must be seriously wrong in the relationship. They press repeatedly on this.

Second, China too is having a significant debate about the trajectory of relations with the United States and its allies—is that trajectory positive or negative? The concern about power politics and hegemonism reflected in high-level Chinese policy statements is a concern about perceived American assertiveness and encirclement and containment of China. This debate has proven resilient, as it has spanned much of the period since 1989. China too must deal with uncertainty as a defining aspect of the bilateral relationship.

Third, China's experts are careful students of the strategic documents of U.S. administrations. They put very significant stock in official statements of intent and want to understand fully the context and implications of any statements bearing on China. China's experts criticized the 1993 NPR, concluding that "the real war role of nuclear weapons has declined but the political role is on the rise."[36] They stiffly criticized the 2001 NPR, arguing that it cast China as an enemy, foreshadowed nuclear coercion in the Taiwan Strait, and lowered the nuclear threshold.[37] China's experts were less critical of the 2010 NPR Report, concluding that it was less threatening to China, while also repeating familiar laments about continued U.S. rejection of China's no-first-use version of declaratory policy.[38] China's small community of missile defense experts questions how the 2010 BMDR offers any meaningful assurance to China at all. After all, they argue, the credibility of China's deterrent posture depends on absorbing the first blow and retaliating with whatever small number of forces that might remain; the statement that the U.S. does not seek protection against the larger scale strikes of which China is capable misses the point, they argue.[39]

Fourth, China's experts are troubled by developments in the U.S. strategic military posture. They were troubled by the 2001 NPR's call for new nuclear weapons, believing that this would trigger a renewal of arms racing—but this time in a more complex multipolar context. They are troubled by missile defense protection of the American homeland, which they see as weakening China's deterrent posture and requiring additional weapons, deployment of which will fuel new perceptions of the rising threat from a rising China. They are troubled by U.S. missile defense cooperation with Japan, South Korea, and Taiwan, arguing that an inevitable result is the encirclement of China and the deepening of alliance relationships that have little logic in the 21st century unless they are "pointed at" China. They are troubled also by the prospect of improved nonnuclear strike capabilities. Like Russia, China worries about existing U.S. conventional strike capabilities in terms of their potential effectiveness in a first strike; this concern is magnified with promised U.S. development of a "niche capability" for long-range conventional systems capable of promptly striking their targets.[40] And China's experts are troubled by the "rebalance" of U.S. security strategy and military posture toward Asia, as promised in 2014.[41]

All of these capabilities fuel the perception of an America in search of the means to strike preemptively at major, nuclear-armed powers and to protect itself from whatever retaliation they might be capable of mustering. To the Chinese, this foreshadows future coercion by Washington. Accordingly, the Chinese tend to believe that the United States is seeking "absolute security," defined as a situation in which it is free to use force against any other country and free from the effects of attempted use of force against it. This is their version of the Russian complaint that the United States is seeking to escape the nuclear revolution. From a Chinese perspective, this situation is unacceptable both normatively and practically, as they impute absolute insecurity for all others. This view is reflected in a Chinese critique of the national security strategy of the George W. Bush administration:

> The fundamental aim of the US national security strategy is to use the war against terrorism as the means to make full use of the current "period of strategic opportunity" of having no major country whose combined national strength can rival that of the US, and the balance of military forces in the world being seriously unbalanced, to seek the long-lasting and comprehensive political, economic, and military superiority in the new century and ensure and maintain the unipolar world under US hegemony. Actually, the US is seeking absolute superiority rather than absolute security in an effort to establish a balance of the strategic forces throughout the entire world with the US being the axis.[42]

A corollary of this concern is that China rejects the significance for U.S. military planning of the new strategic problem described in Chapter 2. China's experts cannot accept that the United States would adapt its strategic posture as it has merely for the purpose of dealing with a minor irritant like North Korea; instead, they believe that the United States is using North Korea as an excuse to do what it would do anyway to adapt its posture to make it more effective against China. In this respect, Chinese and Russian assessments are strikingly similar.

Fifth, China's experts believe that China's ongoing nuclear modernization is in defense of the status quo ante—that is to say, it is an obligation imposed on China by U.S. deployments of preemptive strike capabilities and missile defenses, which call into question the credibility of China's nuclear strategy in both Chinese and American eyes. They reject any suggestion that China's modernization might somehow affect the fundamentals of China's nuclear policy and strategy. Indeed, they argue that such modernization is essential to maintaining no-first-use because of the pressures put on China's posture by developments in U.S. capabilities.[43] As one senior Chinese expert argued in a Track 1.5 meeting in 2008, "Chinese analysts widely share the belief that, with the end of the Cold War, China's position in America's grand strategy and its nuclear strategy has changed fundamentally, and China cannot afford to neglect this fact when it plans its nuclear development goals."[44]

Similarly, they reject any possible sprint to parity by China. Essentially, this is because they see a situation of parity as already existing—in qualitative terms (which makes quantitative aspects irrelevant in their assessment). As China's Military Encyclopedia defines it,

> [Strategic parity] is a condition wherein the strategic strength of the two sides is equal. It is a condition wherein the overall strength of the various sides in the politics, military affairs, economics, and science and technology appears to be equally matched. However, this does not exclude differences among the various sides in their strengths and weaknesses, their superiority and inferiority, in specific realms.[45]

It is important to note that there are advocates in China for a significant build-up of nuclear forces. Writing in June 2014, one influential academic argued: "Now that Japan and the U.S. choose provocation and confrontation, China can only do to them as they did to us. . . . we should maximally increase the strategic deterrent capability of our missile and nuclear weapons, in order to defend against the U.S. threats and blackmail on a larger scale."[46] This echoes similar remarks made a decade ago by a still serving PLA general arguing that China should have the means to destroy hundreds of American cities with nuclear weapons.[47]

Sixth, China's commitment to no first use is deeply engrained. Chinese experts see proof of the doctrine in a force structure that is not capable of extended nuclear war fighting (that is, they see China as not having enough weapons to engage in protracted nuclear warfare). They see value in no first use as sending a clear deterrence message. They also see virtue in reinforcing the message of China's peaceful rise, on the argument that a no-first-use policy cannot be used coercively against others.[48]

Seventh, China's experts have a very difficult time envisioning any near-term circumstance in which China would join in the nuclear reductions process. They are proud of China's commitment to nuclear disarmament and see

China as having gone far less into the nuclear age and nuclear mind-set than the other nuclear weapon states and thus having a shorter distance to go to disarmament when the time comes. But they believe that the United States and Russia will have to accomplish significantly deeper reductions before China could possibly contemplate joining the process. And they see this taking years, if not decades, if it is possible at all.[49]

But China's experts are not uninterested in confidence-building measures that might be implemented in the shorter term that would be consistent with their disarmament objective and with President Xi's commitment to aggressively support the nuclear security summit process. In recent years, China has strengthened its internal capacity to analyze such measures and has considered the implications of increasing nuclear transparency. If it makes a decision to proceed in this area, this may help to lay the foundations for further and more substantial collaborations at a later time.

Eighth, China is not motivated by traditional U.S. concerns about crisis stability and arms race stability. On crisis stability, the traditional American objective is to ensure that in crisis or war neither enemy sees advantage in making first use of nuclear weapons; the Chinese instead simply argue that nuclear crises will not unfold because China's deterrent posture is credible (and, if they are wrong, then China's counter-attacks will simply continue until the United States stops attacking China).[50] On arms race stability, the traditional American objective is to ensure that neither competing nation believes it can gain a decisive advantage; the Chinese instead reject the possibility of being tricked into an arms race by the United States ("the way the Soviets were" goes their argument). However, they are concerned about action–reaction cycles in the military modernization of two or more countries that have a corrosive impact on political relations. And they are concerned that the United States may be racing to advantages with missile defense and conventional strike that jeopardize the nuclear balance.

Like Russia, China's experts have two basic concepts of strategic stability, one broad and the other narrow. The broad concept has been summarized by one senior Chinese military official:

> Strategic stability can be defined as an enduring situation in which all of the strategic forces of the world are able to establish and sustain a strategic framework in which they can make stable their basic relations among themselves and have an adequate sense of security.[51]

This is a classic Chinese answer, with its emphasis on harmony, aligned trust, and a lack of opposing interests. The narrow concept is the one reflected in Chinese concerns about being able to survive an American first strike and retaliate effectively through U.S. BMD—what is classically called first-strike stability.[52]

Ninth, China's experts are fundamentally ambivalent about the extended deterrence provided by the United States in defense of its allies in Northeast Asia. On the one hand, they prize the stability that this has helped to secure—and the nonnuclear status of Japan. On the other hand, they see these alliances as vestiges of the Cold War, with little plausible purpose in the 21st century other than the containment of China. In fact, over the last few years ambivalence has receded while opposition has grown. Many Chinese experts now believe American allies to be emboldened under the U.S. security umbrella to contest China's interests. As recently argued by two Chinese analysts,

> Extended deterrence has been central to US security and alliance strategy in Northeast Asia since the start of the Cold War. During the Cold War it was rooted in the deep-seated suspicion and resentment between the Eastern and Western blocs, but it did not fade into history upon the collapse of the Soviet Union. On the contrary, the concept, with much broader content today, has moved to the centre of discussions about security in Northeast Asia as the United States and its allies set out to strengthen their existing relationships. For China, this is not a happy prospect. China has been one of the "imagined enemies" of US extended deterrence in this region from the beginning.[53]

Tenth and finally, they anticipate future continuity in China's nuclear policy and strategy. As one influential Chinese analyst has argued,

> It is unlikely for the Chinese government to give up its current defensive nuclear deterrent policy in the foreseeable future. . . . China's nuclear strategy is guided by the following three principles: (1) no first use, (2) maintaining a limited nuclear force, and (3) supporting global nuclear disarmament. These basic tenets are based on a sober understanding of nuclear weapons unique characteristics and roles, which remain unchanged. Despite substantial threat to its nuclear security, including nuclear threats and blackmail, China has maintained these guiding principles, thus proving its resolve to keep its nuclear policy unchanged. Of course, China will also continue with its nuclear weapons modernization, but its main purpose will continue to be to improve the

general survivability of its nuclear weapon force so as to ensure the effectiveness of nuclear deterrence into the future.[54]

Alternative Nuclear Futures

These insights illuminate the inherent complexity of the China–U.S. strategic military relationship. On the one hand, there are reasons to be encouraged. The relationship is not competitive, as each side has avoided an arms race. Political leaders have not so far found nuclear issues to be obstacles to their efforts to improve cooperation in other areas. China has become more transparent. Understanding on both sides of core issues and key challenges has improved. At the unofficial level, each side has demonstrated the intention and capacity to listen, reflect, and respond thoughtfully and, usually, constructively.

On the other hand, there are reasons to be discouraged. The strategic military relationship is entering a new phase, as the incipient sources of competition become more pronounced. The aspiration of political leaders to build a "new type major power relationship" has not so far translated into meaningful efforts to address the deep mistrust and profound misperceptions cluttering the bilateral nuclear agenda. China's transparency has major limits, especially as it bears on the future requirements of "lean and effective." The accomplishments of unofficial dialogue have not led to willingness in Beijing to launch into official dialogue, which means that neither side has the means to express its concerns and seek official reassurances.

Looking to the future, it is possible to imagine three alternative trajectories for the China–U.S. strategic military relationship. The least likely of the three is steady-as-she-goes that keeps nuclear weapons "in the background" without some new mode of political cooperation. The incipient sources of strategic military competition are too pronounced. Nuclear weapons will not remain "in the background" as China begins to deploy multiple warheads atop its long-range delivery systems and as the United States begins its cycle of force modernization (and accordingly debates the requirements of effective deterrence). China's deployments of multiple warheads atop its long-range delivery systems will be seen as particularly destabilizing by the United States (which has always seen MIRVed missiles as destabilizing because of the pressure to use them early in a conflict).

Accordingly, a second alternative trajectory is toward an intensification of strategic military competition. Down this pathway are a potential buildup by China of its long-range nuclear strike forces beyond that already envisioned and a potential response by the United States of some kind. This action–reaction cycle would necessarily have political repercussions and would be interpreted in one or both capitals as signaling a rising concern about potential strategic military conflict.

A third alternative trajectory is toward a "new type major power" nuclear relationship. Down this pathway is a less intense action/reaction cycle as the two sides modernize and adjust to each other without "racing" or "sprinting." More importantly, down this pathway is a sustained political effort to address misperceptions about each other's policies, capabilities, and intentions; to better understand areas of mutual concern; and to develop cooperative means to manage differences of interest. Confidence-building measures tailored to the unique requirements of the U.S.–China strategic military relationship could be helpful in generating the need habits of cooperation and mutual reassurance. But this would take time, persistence, and a political will so far missing in Beijing. It would also require a shared positive vision of the future bilateral strategic military relationship, so far missing in both capitals.

To the Problems of War and Deterrence

Over the last couple of decades, military planners in both countries have recognized the potential for armed conflict between the two. But China appears to have been centrally focused on this problem in a way that the United States has not. After all, China's military modernization of the last twenty-five years has been driven to a significant degree by its sense of what is required to secure its interests in a regional conflict against a conventionally superior, nuclear-armed adversary (a term with a direct parallel in the Russian literature). In contrast, U.S. military modernization for much of that period has been driven by the requirements of counter-terrorism and counter-insurgency. This section begins with a review of U.S. thinking about the problem of war with China and then turns to Chinese thinking.

In U.S. military planning, China has had an important but not central place. The Quadrennial Defense Review of 1997 highlighted China's potential to become a major military power and peer adversary by 2015 and hinted at the possibility of confrontation with China in a major theater war. But it put the emphasis on capabilities for a broad spectrum of contingencies and the global responsibilities of the United States.[55] The 2001 QDR struck many of the same themes about China. But it too put the emphasis on capabilities for a broad spectrum of future contingencies in a global construct and in particular set out the vision of gaining full-spectrum dominance in each potential domain of combat and developing a broad suite of capabilities that might be needed in an unpredictable security environment.

The 2010 QDR also noted China's rise in the context of a changed and changing global security environment, arguing that "whether or how such rising powers fully integrate into the global system will be among the century's defining questions, and are thus central to America's interests."[56] This QDR highlighted the challenges of an adversary armed with technically sophisticated antiaccess, area-denial (A2/AD) capabilities and the need to be capable of deterring and defeating such an adversary and discussed priority investments for ensuring effective and credible capabilities to project power globally. The 2014 QDR clearly associated China with the A2/AD threat and elaborated on aspects of the threat in the cyber and space domains and set out various approaches for rebalancing U.S. capabilities and investments to enhance the security and stability of East Asia.[57] The Department of Defense has also begun to explore operational concepts for ensuring power projection in the face of China's A2/AD capabilities.[58] But the core themes of the 2014 QDR were about fiscal austerity and the need to do more with less.

China's own views about the potential for conflict with the United States are similarly embedded in larger planning constructs—and similarly evolutionary. China worries about the potential for conflict in many different directions, given its long borders and complex relations with its neighbors. In January 1993, Chinese President Jiang Zemin issued "military strategic guidelines for the new period" that directed the PLA to focus on planning for local wars under modern high-tech conditions. These guidelines emphasized the need to prepare for regional wars against adversaries made capable by the revolution in military affairs (RMA) of the kind vividly demonstrated by the United States in the Persian Gulf War of 1991.[59] In 1999, the Central Military Commission revised this formulation to "winning local wars under conditions of informatization and nuclear deterrence."[60] These guidelines have not reportedly been replaced with subsequent guidelines so apparently continue to guide military planning.

China's military then proceeded to develop operational concepts for conflict against a high-tech adversary, including conventionally superior nuclear-armed adversaries, identify the needed capabilities, put in place procurement programs to acquire those capabilities, and train and exercise as these development programs resulted in new forces, while also continuing to innovate at the doctrinal level.[61] The Taiwan missile crisis of 1995 and 1996 brought home to China's political and military leadership the potential for a future military confrontation with the United States over Taiwan, and in follow-up primary focus shifted to this contingency.[62] In more recent years, China's expectations for potential conflict with the United States appear to have broadened to other conflict situations, including those involving Japan.[63]

Like Russia, China pursues a military strategy that it conceives as defensive in nature but that has offensive attributes as well. The term of art in China is *active defense*. It regularly asserts that it will not attack, but it will counterattack if attacked.[64] A primary objective of this strategy is to protect China's sovereignty. But it does so in a situation in which China's sovereignty is incomplete, given the legacy of "the century of humiliation." As China's leaders have declared, "China will resolutely take all necessary measures to safeguard national sovereignty and territorial integrity."[65] Thus the strategy calls for the use of military means to support efforts to recover full sovereignty. To those many neighbors of China with contested territorial issues with China, an active defense strategy is perceived as threatening. This concern is amplified by references in China's military documents to a statement attributed to Deng Xiaoping that "active defense is not simply only defense, there is offense within defense."[66]

At least three potential flashpoints could lead to armed conflict between the United States and China. One is in the maritime environment in the Western Pacific. China's new assertiveness in recent years in pressuring its neighbors to accede to its territorial claims brings with it various "gray zone" conflicts. These have the potential to escalate into armed exchanges and broader confrontation.

The Korean peninsula is also a potential military flashpoint. China is North Korea's only ally (and vice versa). If there were to be a replay of the war of the 1950s, in the form of a large invasion of the South by the North and a large push back into the North by the South and the United States, China might well again intervene. But this type of war seems implausible today given

North Korean conventional military weakness and its new military strategy. If war were to occur of the kind envisioned in Chapter 2, a war of nuclear brinksmanship and escalation through miscalculation, China's role would be far from clear. It would face the dilemmas of two conflicting roles: the ally of a nuclear-armed aggressor and a member of the UN Security Council with the responsibility to prevent threats to the peace. At this time, it seems highly unlikely that China would choose to engage itself in a conflict in a way that might lead to nuclear confrontation with the United States over North Korea.

The final potential military flashpoint is of course Taiwan. In the 1990s and early 2000s, the prospects for armed confrontation over Taiwan seemed to be rising, as an independence movement gained political force on Taiwan and China responded with new political and military pressure and as the United States expressed renewed commitment to the defense of Taiwan and to Taiwanese democracy. As of 2014, there is little immediate concern about a PLA military operation to blockade or invade and conquer Taiwan. But there is also rising concern that shifting domestic politics in Taiwan and in the PRC may lead to a renewal of military tension following elections on Taiwan in 2016.[67] It is important to understand that China's military modernization is guided fundamentally by the desire to defend and restore Chinese sovereignty, which is in dispute over Taiwan. As the U.S. Department of Defense argued in 2014:

> Dealing with a potential contingency in the Taiwan Strait remains the PLA's primary mission despite an overall reduction of cross-Strait tensions. . . . China does not appear to have fundamentally altered its approach to Taiwan. Both sides continue to explore ways to make progress on historically contentious issues. . . . Despite occasional signs of impatience, China appears content to respect Taiwan's current approach to cross-Strait relations.[68]

The report also argues that "should conditions change, the PLA could be called upon to compel Taiwan to abandon possible moves toward independence or to re-unify Taiwan with the mainland by force of arms while deterring or defeating any third-party intervention on Taiwan's behalf."[69]

It is also important to note that the United States is not allied with Taiwan in the way it is allied with Japan or South Korea. Its commitments to Taiwan became unofficial in nature when the United States extended diplomatic recognition to the People's Republic of China. Under the terms of the Taiwan

Relations Act of 1979, the United States maintains relations "with the people on Taiwan" and assists Taiwan in maintaining its defensive capabilities. It is committed to the defense of Taiwan only in the case of aggression against it by the People's Republic of China.[70] This has stimulated discussion of a dual deterrence strategy—deterring the PRC from committing aggression against Taiwan while also deterring Taiwan from undertaking actions that might provoke the PRC into military action.[71]

China's Theory of Victory

As China has faced the challenge of military planning for a possible conflict with a conventionally superior nuclear-armed state, it too has developed concepts for securing its interests. Much of this thinking is available through publications of the People's Liberation Army. China's thinking naturally begins with Sun Tzu and the conviction that it is better to subdue an enemy than to win by fighting. China hopes to be able to create the conditions that lead its potential enemies ultimately to cede to China's preferences in the settlement of territorial and other disputes through a credible active defense strategy.[72] Like Russia, it has a comprehensive approach for using hard and soft power tools, including economic and informational tools of leverage, to induce the political will in regional capitals to accede to Chinese preferences on regional security and other issues. Two Chinese scholars have described this as the art of the stratagem, rather than a deterrence strategy, that draws on all of the instruments of national power to shape the intentions of potential adversaries, and explicitly including actions to shape the perceptions of those actors with both information and misinformation.[73]

If war involving the United States comes to be seen by China as unavoidable, then China's first objective would be to achieve a decisive outcome very quickly, before U.S. forces can begin to engage. It has focused on seizing and holding the military initiative by rapidly massing effects to win capitulation by Taiwan or Japan in a short, sharp war, thus presenting the United States with a fait accompli.[74]

But Beijing would presumably take many actions in order not to be cast as the aggressor in such a contingency. China's military planners attach considerable importance to establishing the moral and political basis of China's position in the world community and indeed expect to have a significant body of political opinion on their side in a conflict ultimately about China's sovereignty.[75] Their theory thus includes the idea that the United States might be constrained from acting by international opinion.

China's military planners are also prepared to take steps to deter U.S. intervention and to limit the ability of the United States to intervene effectively if it chooses to do so. China has fielded large and sophisticated strike systems for attacking enemy assets in the maritime environment. It would showcase its capabilities for imposing costs on U.S. power projection forces and the vulnerability of the United States in all domains—including especially maritime, cyber, and space. It would array its forces so that arriving U.S. naval assets would have to operate remotely and over the horizon rather than to establish a presence immediately reassuring to U.S. allies and/or partners.

China's war concept also includes putting at risk U.S. allies in the region, with the hope that they will deny the United States access to bases and ports and choose not to participate in activities the United States might seek to cast as collective security operations. If these allies choose to support U.S. military operations, China has the means to attack them and the facilities they host by both conventional and nuclear means (as well as cyber).

China's theory of victory builds on the particular escalation challenges for the United States given the asymmetry of geography. By deploying significant land-based strike capabilities, China presents the United States with a choice between fighting largely in a defensive mode from sea and striking at military forces on the Chinese mainland. U.S. strikes on the Chinese mainland would be a significant escalatory step and would open up questions about possible Chinese retaliation on U.S. allies and the U.S. homeland, including not least on the headquarters in Hawaii of those U.S. forces engaged in combat. The escalatory risks of striking the Chinese mainland put U.S. forces in a largely defensive posture, which would make victory more difficult, as much of the military initiative would be in China's hands.

In managing the risks of escalation by the United States, China's ability to conduct attacks in cyberspace plays an important role, as it does in the Russian theory. This includes a preemptive aspect:

> When seizing electromagnetic dominance in local campaigns, adopt the two means of "soft" and "hard," engage in electromagnetic jamming before the enemy, sabotage the enemy's advanced warning capability, paralyze the enemy's command system, then employ missile firepower to implement destruction.[76]

Combined with attacks on U.S. assets in space, this could have a significant operational impact on U.S. forces as well as on broader economic and political interests.

China also prepares for the possibility that the United States might escalate to nuclear weapons if faced with a losing conventional situation.[77] The 2000 edition of China's *Science of Military Campaigns* describes the contributions of nuclear deterrence to China's military strategy:

> The main task of the nuclear retaliation campaign of the Second Artillery is to launch a nuclear attack on key enemy strategic and campaign targets, paralyzing its command system, reducing its war potential, sabotaging its strategic intention, wavering its war will, and stopping the escalation of nuclear war.[78]

The Second Artillery is directed to apply the following principles to its preparations for nuclear conflict:

- Oppose nuclear blackmail: deter the enemy from starting a nuclear war and thwart and neutralize the enemy's nuclear deterrent and blackmail.

- Gain mastery by striking only after the enemy has struck first: at no time be the first to use nuclear weapons, and, if the enemy strikes, authorize only limited nuclear retaliation.

- Centralize command: the Central Military Commission alone has the power to decide on and direct the employment of nuclear missiles.

- Strictly protect the missile units: ensure the survivability of the missiles needed for counter-attack.

- Strike only key targets: choose only strategic targets in the enemy's homeland for effective nuclear retaliation.[79]

The Second Artillery's own campaign theory states that "the goal of campaign deterrence is to force an enemy to accept our will or to contain an enemy's hostile acts. . . . Once deterrence has lost its effectiveness, the campaign large formation can quickly transit to actual combat."[80] That document characterizes the responsibilities of the Second Artillery in carrying out nuclear deterrence, counter–nuclear deterrence, and nuclear-counterstrike duties with the expectation that "this will shock and fear the enemy [sic] to the greatest extent, and effectively contain hostilities and keep them from spreading and escalating."[81]

On the basis of available materials, there is no evidence that China's nuclear war planners have calculated a number of weapons sufficient to ensure the deterrence of the United States by nuclear means, akin to the alleged Russian calculations. Instead, Chinese documents envision nuclear counterattacks to the point where the costs to America and its allies are deemed unbearable:

> In essence, nuclear deterrence is a bargaining chip. When using it, we need to consider whether or not an enemy will accept deterrence and whether or not we can realize the nuclear deterrence when the deterrence fails . . . The better the preparations [for nuclear counterstrike], the more believable the strength of nuclear deterrence is. The better the nuclear deterrence goals are achieved, the less likely that nuclear missile forces will be used in actual combat.[82]

In fact, it is unclear just how important assured retaliation is to China's perceptions of the credibility of its nuclear deterrent. On the one hand, China has invested significantly in assured retaliation.[83] On the other hand, some argue that in a "nuclear strategy with Chinese characteristics," China's deterrence purposes are served adequately by a force that creates uncertainty in the minds of American decision makers about the risks and costs of acting in ways that would cross red lines in China's nuclear declaratory policy, even if Chinese retaliation is not 100 percent assured in American eyes.[84]

Is this a nuclear war-fighting strategy, in the manner in which Russia may conceive one, involving the diverse and sustained employment of nuclear forces? It certainly appears not to be. China apparently does not envision multiple rounds of strikes and counter-strikes in a protracted nuclear war. It does not have tactical nuclear weapons. Nor are its long-range weapons capable of being delivered with sufficient precision to kill hardened targets (where U.S. weapons would be located, and as opposed to "soft" targets such as cities).[85]

But there is a parallel to Russia in the "strategic gestures" described by Andrei Kokoshin. China's theory of victory includes the use of displays, exercises, tests, and other means to demonstrate strength, including political resolve. "We can disseminate information to the enemy about our side's power, decisiveness, and braveness [sic] to attack."[86] Further, "One should also utilize fake launch sites and already-exposed launch silos as deterrence locations, while at the same time arrange various types of missiles and nuclear weapons, as well as relevant coordinating facilities, combining the true and the false."[87]

Like Russia, China has introduced a significant conventional component into its deterrence posture and accordingly has elaborated some concepts analogous to Russia's "prenuclear deterrence." By the early 1990s, China's military leaders had concluded that conventionally armed ballistic missiles could have a dramatic psychological impact on an enemy and could "deter the outbreak of a conventional local war . . . and contain the expansion and escalation of a conventional local war after it had broken out."[88] China has subsequently deployed large numbers of such weapons and continually improved them. As of 2011, China's force of conventionally armed ballistic missiles was seven times as large as China's force of nuclear-armed missiles.[89] Their primary role is to support the Second Artillery's campaign for strategic deterrence, though they are also envisioned for use in selective strikes in support of ongoing military operations and for purposes of delivering strategic warning.[90] A significant role is envisioned in the maritime environment; as one U.S. study concludes, "Two-thirds of the overall Second Artillery Force unit structure is focused on missions associated with the near seas."[91]

China has integrated conventional strike capabilities into the Second Artillery campaigns to a significant degree. It has set out a theory of "double deterrence, double operations, and double command and control" built on the sequential and possibly combined employment of conventional and nuclear missile brigades and a role for nuclear weapons as "a backstop to support conventional operations":[92]

> The most important type of future regional wars will be conventional conflicts under conditions of nuclear deterrence, deterrence and actual war-fighting will exist at the same time, and their function and effectiveness will be mutually complementary.[93]

John Lewis and Xue Litae of Stanford University argue that this approach is deemed by China to be "a fundamental source of political and military strength. It is, however, also the troubling source of critical uncertainties."[94] American attacks on bases launching conventionally armed ballistic missiles at U.S. forces or allies (or the associated command and control systems) may be interpreted by China as attacks on its nuclear deterrent, potentially triggering Chinese nuclear responses. From China's perspective, this may reinforce deterrence, but from an American perspective it introduces a significant new source of instability.

Of note, China's doctrinal writings also suggest the potential need for China to "lower the nuclear deterrence threshold" and "adjust nuclear policy" in response to nonnuclear strategic strikes:

> Lowering the nuclear deterrence threshold refers to a time in which a stronger military power with nuclear missiles relies on its absolute superiority in high-tech conventional weapons to conduct a series of medium-level or high-level air strikes and our side has no good methods to ward this off; the nuclear missiles corps should, according to the orders of the supreme command, adjust our nuclear deterrence policy without delay, taking the initiative to implement a powerful nuclear threat, thereby blocking through coercion the stronger enemy's sustained conventional air strikes against our side's important strategic targets.[95]

This could be read to imply that China's no-first-use policy is conditional. This would align with discussion in PLA doctrine of the use of nuclear weapons "for the purpose of deescalation and, perhaps, war termination."[96]

China's confidence in its ability to manage the risks of escalation seems to be high. It has set out a body of theory for "war control" and catalogued the measures that China might have to take to control the scale, pace, scope, and intensity of conflict so that it maintains the initiative and keeps military actions in line with political objectives.[97] The topic of inadvertent escalation has so far received little attention among China's deterrence experts.[98]

As in the theories of victory of North Korea and Russia, perceptions of stake play a significant role in China's theory of victory. In any confrontation over China's sovereignty, China would likely perceive its stake to be superior to that of the United States and its allies, as their sovereignty would not be in question. In the assessment of China's experts, this lends credibility to its threats and erodes the credibility of U.S. red lines.

As with both North Korea and Russia, this theory of victory is much more than a theory. China has made twenty-five years of investment in developing the doctrine and capabilities and personnel to make good on this theory. Each year it continues to invest significant new resources in this modernization and transformation process. It has deployed missiles of various ranges (short-, medium-, and intermediate-range) to put at risk Taiwan, targets in the neighboring maritime environments, and the first and second island chains. It has well over 1,000 missiles capable of reaching Taiwan and a growing number of missiles capable of reaching more distant targets. It is also modernizing these forces to give them improved accuracy and ensure their effectiveness in penetrating ballistic missile defenses. The part of the force intended to put the U.S. homeland at risk also continues to grow in number and improve (albeit from a small base).[99]

The New Sources of Strategic Instability

This review of the potential for conflict between China and the United States illuminates some new sources of strategic instability for both countries. For China, consider first some parallels from the preceding chapter. Russia has concerns about the destabilizing implications of the end of bipolarity, the rise of an assertive United States, and the emergence of a security order in Europe that it sees as detrimental to its interests. Regime stability in Moscow is itself a topic of rising salience. Each of these has analogues in the case of China. China perceives instability in an international order transitioning from uni-polarity to multipolarity. It perceives the United States as pursuing a strategy of encirclement and containment of its rise. And, increasingly, it perceives the U.S.-backed East Asian security order as outdated and unaccommodating to China's new status. Concerns about domestic political stability also factor into Chinese leadership perspectives in a way few Americans appreciate.

For the United States, two new sources of instability stand out. One is the risk that China's rising confidence in the credibility of its strategic deterrent will embolden it to become more risk taking at the conventional level. Thomas Christensen has highlighted this risk, arguing that "China with a newly estab-lished second strike capability might prove more aggressive."[100]

The other significant new risk is the risk of inadvertent escalation. This has many potential sources. One already highlighted follows from the new role of Chinese attacks in cyberspace and the potential for unexpected responses by the United States and its allies. Another stems from China's dual deterrence doctrine and the potential that U.S. attacks on China's conventional forces might result in a nuclear response. A third source of potential inadvertent escalation stems from lack of clarity about red lines. China has articulated a commitment to defend its "core interests" at all costs, but it has not defined what they are. Similarly, the United States has articulated a commitment to employ nuclear weapons when its "vital interests" or those of its allies are at risk, but it has not defined what they are.[101]

Informal dialogues among American and Chinese analysts suggest a real potential for miscalculation and inadvertent escalation, especially in a confrontation over Taiwan.[102] That potential stems from different perceptions about whether the burden of escalation would fall on China or the United States (with analysts in each country generally believing it would fall on the other) and whether nuclear use would be seen as decisive in halting the conflict (with analysts in each country believing use by their country would be decisive). Analysts also express confidence in the abilities of their country's leaders to manage the risks of escalation and achieve termination of a war gone nuclear on politically acceptable terms. These confident assessments point to the potential for miscalculation. A key issue for American analysts is whether the leaders of a one-party state who have relied on nationalism to maintain political legitimacy can afford to back down in a war with the United States over Taiwan. But there is also historical evidence pointing to the willingness of China's leaders to accept military losses so long as political points have been won.[103]

Thus, from a U.S. perspective, there is a significant new source of instability—as with Russia, at the regional level. The United States and its allies and partners cannot fully rely on conventional superiority and nuclear superiority to deter and defeat challenges from China. China has developed a strategy for negating America's power projection strategy. If deterrence is to be preserved, the United States needs a strategy for negating China's strategy.

The Blue theory of victory set out in Chapter 3 provides a starting point for such a strategy, though with various adaptations. As the stronger military power, the United States would have the advantage in conflict of being able to match or exceed any level of escalation chosen by China. But China now has the capabilities to impress on the United States its vulnerabilities in each and every domain where it operates (land, sea, air, outer space, cyberspace). The United States would have the advantage of strong allies. But China would likely see those allies—and especially Japan—as potential sources of restraint on Washington if they could be reminded of their own vulnerability. The United States would have the advantage of a strong maritime presence, both above and below the surface, but China would have the advantage of being able to operate from its homeland (and can be expected to make clear to Washington that attacks on its homeland in a regional war with the United States would open up the American homeland to retaliation). Both countries would have the assets, vulnerabilities, and risks of advanced competition in the cyber domain.

Conclusions

In comparison to the U.S. relationship with Russia, the U.S. relationship with China has more promise. Washington and Beijing have common interests that Washington and Moscow do not. Many of these interests are in the economic domain, but some are in the security domain—including nuclear nonproliferation in Asia. Moreover, President Xi has oriented his government to work toward a positive image of the relationship with the United States, whereas President Putin has oriented his government to confront an America and a NATO gone bad in his eyes.

But in comparison to the bilateral U.S.–China relationship of twenty years ago, the relationship of today appears to be under increasing pressure. Common economic interests are no longer the driver of political cooperation that they once were. Potential military flashpoints have not gone away; on the contrary, they appear to have multiplied (in the maritime environment). China's opposition to the U.S.-led regional order, and to other aspects of international U.S. leadership, is now clearly articulated at the highest levels of government.

Nuclear weapons have not come into the foreground in the relationship. But the different strategies of the two countries for keeping them there have not converged. China's reluctance to talk at the official level about nuclear weapons and strategic stability, coming at a time of the modernization, diversification, and buildup of its nuclear forces, inflames American concerns and adds to mistrust in the relationship. America's adaptations to its strategic posture to strengthen regional deterrence architectures and its reluctance to answer some of China's most fundamental questions inflame Chinese concerns. In the meantime, unofficial dialogue adds some value but with some clear limits.

What does this imply for U.S. efforts to create the conditions for additional steps to reduce the number and role of nuclear weapons? Quite obviously, the conditions do not today exist for China to join the nuclear arms control process. Given its deep sense of grievance at the damage done to it historically by other states not respectful of its interests, its return to the world stage and rising power, and its efforts to develop a military and deterrence posture that can meet contemporary security challenges, it is difficult to imagine China deciding to relinquish its nuclear weapons or even to reduce their roles in its security strategies. Moreover, China is not prepared to alter its transparency practices out of deference to the desires of the United States and others for new forms of reassurance from China. It is not even prepared to explain the logic by which the commitment to "lean and effective" translates into actual force structure decisions.

As China and the United States appear unlikely to make much progress any time soon in arriving at shared ideas about strategic stability and its requirements, the onus is now on the United States to address more directly and unilaterally the requirements of strategic stability as it now sees them. What then should the United States be doing unilaterally (meaning not in cooperation with China but perhaps in cooperation with U.S. friends and allies)? The answer comes at two levels, political and military.

At the political level, a central question for the United States is whether to address China's fundamental question about strategic stability (that is, does the United States accept mutual deterrence as the basis of the strategic relationship?). A clear "no" in answer to this question would add significant new instability to the bilateral military and political relationship. It would be seen in Beijing as confirming its worst fears that America seeks to escape the nuclear revolution in world politics and envisions a future time when it is free to use force even against major powers armed with nuclear weapons.

But a clear "yes" has not been forthcoming from the Clinton, Bush, or Obama administration—despite all three affirming that they do not seek missile defense protection against China's strategic deterrent. Their reluctance stems from doubts about how that message would be received in Beijing. Would such an affirmation be received as a message of reassurance, leading to a more modest pace and scope of nuclear modernization? Or would it be received as a message of appeasement, leading to tests of American resolve to defend its interests and those of its allies? As China has modernized its military forces, significantly increased the number of nuclear weapons capable of striking the American homeland, become more assertive militarily in its region, confronted Japan in various ways, and otherwise signaled that it is not a status quo power, it has become increasingly risky for Washington to send a message that might come across as appeasement.

The simple truth of the matter is that, as a matter of policy, the United States neither accepts nor rejects mutual deterrence with China. It is divided and has seen no need to address the division, especially while China rejects dialogue. Some future administration might adopt as a matter of policy one view or another, but this would only mask this division. This matter requires a longer-term perspective. How the United States responds to China's rise will be dependent on China's future choices and actions. If the rise is peaceful—as promised—then our shared interests will continue to multiply, and our cooperation will strengthen. In that circumstance, future American leaders should be able to make such a promise. But our relationship remains in transition, and questions about China's future international role remain unanswered.

What unilateral measures are needed in the military domain to support the U.S. commitment to strategic stability?

First, the United States should continue to exercise the restraint in the development of its strategic capabilities that it considers necessary and appropriate vis-à-vis China. It has promised restraint on missile defense and conventional prompt global strike (seeking only a "niche" capability) and has so far promised only to hedge against future growth in China's nuclear arsenal. It should also be prepared to provide credible evidence to China that the promised restraint is being exercised.

But the United States should insist on reciprocal restraint and reciprocal transparency. This could involve bilateral discussions in areas of shared concern (each would benefit from better insight into how the other thinks about and plans for conventional strike in the strategic deterrence portfolio) or in areas of asymmetric concern (with each side introducing discussion of a topic or capability of concern to the other).

Second, the United States should retain a credible capability to respond to a rapid growth in China's deployed nuclear forces with a rapid growth in its own. China's commitment to a "lean and effective" force comes without any clear metrics for establishing how much is enough for "lean." As already noted, there are various voices in China for a more robust nuclear deterrent posture, though they do not appear to have much official influence today. Moreover, analysts in both the United States and Russia have concluded that China may already have a larger arsenal of nuclear weapons that could be deployed in crisis with covertly produced delivery systems.[104] The U.S. need to hedge against a geopolitical surprise from China remains.

Third and most urgently, the United States must have a credible counter to China's strategy to defeat U.S. strategy for power projection and allied defense. China's theory of victory is carefully crafted and clearly expressed for all to understand. Its capabilities to enable the theory are steadily improving.

The United States has a theory of victory for regional conflict, as set out in Chapter 3, but has not done a great deal to apply that theory to the particular new problems generated by China's changing policy and posture. In taking on this task, the United States will face two particular challenges. One is developing operational concepts to defeat Chinese forces that do not involve escalatory attacks against the Chinese mainland (the president should have military options to both escalate and not escalate).[105] The other is reassuring Japan that U.S. responses will be effective and are credible in China's eyes.

Ironically, as it grows stronger, China perceives its security as eroding. This is the classic security dilemma, as reinforced by a country that struggles to modernize its political strategies while modernizing its military capacities. If there is a pathway out of this dilemma, it requires a willingness and a capacity in both Beijing and Washington to begin to articulate a vision for regional order that is inclusive and involves shared responsibilities for defending among other things the shared sea lanes of communication. But this in itself will require China to be willing to assume some of the costs and risks of leadership in defense of common interests—something it seems wholly unprepared to do.[106]

6 Extended Deterrence and Strategic Stability in Europe

ONE OF THE MOST STRIKING RESULTS OF THE END OF THE Cold War was the sudden disinterest in extended deterrence among American security specialists and among many allies as well. With the Presidential Nuclear Initiatives of 1991 and 1992, most of the U.S. nuclear weapons deployed abroad to protect and reassure allies were suddenly brought home and retired. The American strategic community went to work on other problems.

And one of the most striking results of nearly three decades of change since then is that extended deterrence has come back to center stage in American nuclear policy. In Northeast Asia, North Korea's emergence as a nuclear-armed power, along with China's ongoing military modernization, has raised fundamental new questions about the means and ends of U.S. extended deterrence policy. In Europe, Russia's new belligerence, along with instability in the Middle East, has renewed high-level interest in strengthening NATO's deterrence and defense posture. Difficult choices lie ahead for the United States and its allies in these two regions. Some of them will involve highly sensitive questions of nuclear policy and posture.

This chapter and the following take up the new challenges of extended deterrence in these two regions, starting here with Europe. This chapter begins with a review of the key developments in the Euro-Atlantic security environment bearing on questions of extended deterrence. The NATO alliance has existed in a changed and changing security environment ever since the end of the Cold War, and in recent years there has been a rising debate about the impact of those changes on the alliance's overall strategy and supporting deterrence and defense posture. Developments in both Russian policy and posture and the Middle East have driven this debate and in recent years have reinforced the allies' desire to strengthen deterrence.

The chapter then reviews recent efforts by the alliance to align its strategy with the new security environment and to update its deterrence and defense posture. In this process, both NATO and the Obama administration made a number of choices that surprised many outside commentators. This is especially true of the decision to maintain NATO's unique nuclear sharing arrangements, which is described in detail here.

The chapter then considers the impacts of developments in Russia's policy and posture in 2014 on the implementation of NATO's deterrence and defense review, including on the nuclear component. It concludes with an assessment of progress in strengthening deterrence in Europe and of implications for U.S. nuclear policy and posture and of challenges ahead.

But before turning to these tasks, this chapter begins with a definition of extended deterrence and a review of key associated policy issues.

Defining Extended Deterrence

Extended deterrence is a form of protection provided to an ally. Although deterrence can be extended to an ally by various means, the primary historical association has been with nuclear weapons—hence the long-standing reference to the nuclear umbrella for U.S. allies. As Paul Huth has defined it, the purpose of extended deterrence is "to protect other countries and territories from attack, as distinct from preventing a direct attack on one's own national territory."[1] It has two different audiences: the adversary state posing the threat and the allied state under threat. Extended deterrence is intended to prevent aggression and coercion by adversaries and to assure allies that their vital interests will not be jeopardized.[2]

Extended deterrence is provided in the form of both declaratory policy and technical means. The United States reserves the right to use nuclear weapons in defense of its allies as a matter of policy, though the specific formulations of the U.S. threat to adversaries (whether implicit or explicit) and promise to individual allies or alliances are dependent on context. The technical means have been tailored over time to the unique circumstances of individual regions, in terms of geography, history, and political requirements—with U.S. nuclear weapons deployed into some allied countries, but not in others, in a posture that has regularly evolved over time in response to changing circumstances.

A core problem in extending deterrence is making credible the threat to employ nuclear weapons on behalf of another state if retaliation can reasonably be expected. This issue crystallized in the late 1950s, when the American homeland first became vulnerable to Soviet nuclear attack, raising questions about whether the United States was in fact willing to put at risk its own cities in defense of its European allies. In the vernacular of the time, would Washington trade Chicago for Berlin? (More precisely, could it credibly threaten to do so?) Some allies feared that the vulnerability of the United States would result in a strategic decoupling of the United States from their defense in time of crisis and war—essentially, that Washington would be coerced into abandoning their defense. This put high stress on U.S. credibility. As Thomas Schelling argued in 1966:

> The difference between national homeland and everything "abroad" is the difference between threats that are inherently credible, even if unspoken, and the threats that have to be made credible. To project the shadow of one's military force over other countries and territories is an act of diplomacy. To *fight* abroad is a military act, but to *persuade* enemies or allies that one would fight abroad, under circumstances of great cost and risk, requires more than a military capability. It requires projecting intentions. It requires *having* those intentions, even deliberately acquiring them, and communicating them persuasively to make other countries behave.[3]

In the Cold War, this issue of credibility came into sharp focus as the risks grew of an Armageddon-like war beginning in Europe. Debate emerged about what standards of credibility needed to be met to ensure that deterrence and assurance would be effective. A conventional wisdom emerged that the standards for deterrence and assurance are very different. For deterrence of an enemy to be credible requires a relatively low standard, goes the argument, because the risks and costs of war are so high for the potential aggressor. For assurance of allies to be credible, however, requires a very high degree of credibility, goes the argument, because they would bear a significant cost if deterrence were to fail. In what has become known as the Healey theorem, British Defence Minister Denis Healey argued in the late 1960s that "it takes only five percent credibility of American retaliation to deter the Russians, but ninety-five percent credibility to reassure the Europeans."[4]

The end of the Cold War brought with it a sharp reduction in the risks of Armageddon-like nuclear war. But it did not bring with it the end of problems for which extended deterrence is relevant or thus the practice of extended deterrence by the United States, the challenges of credibility in the face of threats to the U.S. homeland, or the need to assure allies that deterrence will be effective. As Chapter 2 argued, the new combination of nuclear proliferation and long-range missiles has empowered regional challengers to U.S. interests. Their strategies seek to split the United States from its allies and their threats to the American homeland are intended to achieve a decoupling effect. Moreover, even as both Russia and China worry less about the problem of global nuclear war, they worry more about the problem of regional war against a conventionally superior nuclear-armed major power, a.k.a. the United States, and they too are pursuing strategies to split and decouple the United States from its allies. These developments have major implications for the practice of extended deterrence.

Furthermore, issues of American credibility have sharpened in a world where actions anywhere have implications everywhere, reinforcing anxiety about U.S. consistency and magnifying the challenges of assurance. Especially prominent among those anxieties is the concern that U.S. efforts to reduce reliance on nuclear weapons (in the formulation of the Clinton and Bush administrations) or to reduce their role and number as steps toward their ultimate elimination (in the formulation of the Obama administration) might result in a closing of the nuclear umbrella—thus stranding and leaving vulnerable the allies that are today assured by its presence.

In U.S. nuclear policy, after a long period of disinterest, extended deterrence has had rapidly rising salience over the last decade. The 2010 NPR gave extended deterrence and the assurance of allies a central place, in contrast to its two predecessors, reflecting the fact that U.S. allies are on the new front line in meeting the challenges of regional deterrence and strategic stability in a changing security environment. Moreover, it expressed the president's commitment to strengthen extended deterrence and assurance. It also expressed a commitment to "tailor" the nuclear component of the regional deterrence architecture to the particular requirements of each region where the U.S. offers security guarantees. This helped to crystallize a focus within the administration on the roles of nuclear weapons in safeguarding the interests of

U.S. allies in the 21st century and the associated requirements of U.S. policy and posture.

With this background in mind, this chapter turns now to examine the efforts to adapt extended deterrence in Europe since the end of the Cold War. Chapter 7 will examine efforts in Northeast Asia. In both cases, analysis focuses on efforts to strengthen and adapt extended deterrence and not on the assurance aspect highlighted in the Healey theorem. Chapter 8 will address that topic with some insights that cut across the two regions.

NATO Nuclear Policy 1991 to 2009

On three occasions since 1991, the NATO alliance has reviewed the security environment, its role and purpose, and its strategy for securing its members and issued updated Strategic Concepts (1991, 1999, 2010). As these Concepts are issued by heads of state and government, they constitute the highest-level political and military guidance to the alliance and serve as the basis for the implementation of alliance policy as a whole.

The Strategic Concept of 1999 was the first to come to terms with the major changes in Euro-Atlantic security that flowed from the end of the Cold War (the previous Strategic Concept was issued in 1991 on the cusp of change). It struck a hopeful but cautious tone: "The Alliance operates in an environment of continuing change. Developments in recent years have generally been positive, but uncertainties and risks remain which can develop into acute crises."[5] It characterized a threat environment including "powerful nuclear forces outside the alliance" and the proliferation of WMD and their means of delivery.[6] It went on to describe the fundamental purposes of NATO's nuclear forces as "political: to preserve peace and prevent coercion and any kind of war. They will continue to fulfill an essential role by ensuring uncertainty in the mind of any aggressor about the nature of the Allies' response to military aggression. They demonstrate that aggression of any kind is not a rational option."[7]

NATO's nuclear forces consist of strategic forces committed to the alliance by the United States and the United Kingdom and of U.S. nuclear weapons deployed in Europe in sharing arrangements unique to NATO. Although these "forward-deployed" weapons remain in the possession of the United States (as is required by Article I of the Nuclear Non-Proliferation Treaty, forbidding the transfer of nuclear weapons to other states), they are dispersed along with the U.S. and allied aircraft to deliver them to a small set of NATO members who would employ them under NATO command (but U.S. presidential authority) in time of war. Nations not hosting U.S. nuclear forces and not equipped with aircraft capable of delivering nuclear weapons are able to share in associated roles, such as providing conventional air cover support for nuclear operations. These sharing arrangements began in the late 1950s and are supported by the NATO Nuclear Planning Group (a body composed of defense ministers) established in 1966–1967.

The aircraft are fighters-bombers and are referred to as dual-capable aircraft (DCA) because they are designed to carry both conventional and nuclear weapons. The weapons have had various labels. The 1999 Strategic Concept, for example, referred to them as "substrategic." This label derives from the association of the weapon with a delivery system not defined as "strategic" by an arms control treaty (which encompasses restraints on long-range bombers and missiles capable of delivering nuclear weapons at global distances). The term was somewhat misleading, as the employment of any nuclear weapon would be a strategic act, whatever its target and whatever its means of delivery. Another label is sometimes used: tactical weapons. This follows from the time when the United States had thousands of nuclear weapons in Europe to support battlefield operations by NATO forces against invading Soviet forces.

It is useful to bear in mind the distinctions between different potential uses of nuclear weapons, whether to influence enemy leadership intent (strategic uses), to influence the key elements of an enemy's war plan (operational uses), or to influence specific outcomes on the battlefield (tactical uses). Some weapons can have multiple purposes; the U.S. weapons deployed to Europe during the Cold War had both the tactical purpose of blunting a Soviet attack and the strategic purpose of coupling the defense of Europe to U.S. strategic nuclear forces. U.S. policy today characterizes weapons deployed with dual-capable fighter-bombers as nonstrategic nuclear weapons (NSNW).

The alliance's reaffirmation in 1999 of the continuing security relevance of U.S. nuclear weapons deployed in Europe a decade after the end of the Cold War reflected assessments that credible extended nuclear deterrence in Europe remained important as a hedge against Russian recidivism and for deterring regional powers armed with WMD.[8] The weapons were also seen as having continuing value as a testament to the transatlantic link at the core of the alliance.[9]

These decisions notwithstanding, after 1999 NATO continued to reduce the number of U.S. nuclear weapons deployed in Europe. This process actually began in the late 1970s, but it accelerated with the Presidential Nuclear Initiatives of 1991.[10] In 2008, the United States revealed that U.S. nuclear weapons deployed in Europe had been reduced by 97 percent since their peak.[11]

In the decade after the 1999 Strategic Concept, debate shifted increasingly to whether to retain any U.S. nuclear weapons in Europe at all.[12] This policy question was joined with increasing intensity as the drawdown continued, often behind closed doors in NATO member capitals. This debate became only more intense after President Obama's speech in Prague in April 2009 and its vision of steps toward the long-term disarmament goal.

Through this period, there was also a significant further differentiation of views within the alliance about the continued role of NATO's nuclear sharing arrangements. As David Yost has observed:

> Certain political leaders in allied nations in western Europe with long standing [nuclear] host and delivery responsibilities appear to place less emphasis on the imperative of maintaining NATO's established nuclear deterrence posture, including U.S. nuclear weapons in Europe, than political leaders in some of the new allied nations in East and Central Europe. The new allies are, however, politically barred from hosting allied nuclear weapons by the "three no's" commitment of the alliance, first articulated in 1996 and repeated in the 1997 NATO–Russia Founding Act.[13]

In that political declaration, NATO allies stated that they have "enlarging the Alliance will not require a change in NATO's nuclear posture. . . . therefore NATO has no intention, no plan and no reason to deploy nuclear weapons on the territory of new members, nor any need to change any aspect of NATO's nuclear posture or nuclear policy—and we do not foresee any future need to do so."[14]

Aspects of this debate broke into public view with the publication in 2008 of the second report of the Secretary of Defense Task Force on Nuclear Weapons Management, which made a forceful case for the retention of NATO's unique sharing arrangements as a tool of deterrence and assurance.[15] It concluded that the drive to reduce nonstrategic nuclear weapons to the minimum necessary had crippled efforts within the alliance to maintain a nuclear force posture with "the necessary characteristics and appropriate flexibility and survivability, to be perceived as a credible and effective element of the Allies' strategy in preventing war."[16] It also criticized NATO's failure to make good on the 1999 commitment to ensure "widespread participation by European

Allies involved in collective defense planning in nuclear roles, in peacetime basing of nuclear forces on their territory and in command, control and consultation arrangements."[17]

In sum, the Obama administration inherited a major political question about whether to remove the remaining 3 percent of the U.S. nuclear weapons historically deployed in Europe and, if not, how to meet the requirements of credibility and effectiveness in the 21st-century security environment, restore leadership focus and institutional excellence after a period of significant erosion, and ensure viable sharing arrangements.

From the 2010 Strategic Concept to the Deterrence and Defense Posture Review

The Obama administration clearly stated its intent to address the future of NATO's nuclear posture together with its allies rather than unilaterally. In the words of the 2010 NPR Report: "Any changes in NATO's nuclear posture should only be taken after a thorough review within—and decision by—the Alliance.[18] For months it collaborated with allies to develop a new Strategic Concept and associated decisions about nuclear policy and posture. The result was released in November 2010 and set out the following key ideas and guidance on the alliance's nuclear strategy:

- "Deterrence, based on an appropriate mix of nuclear and conventional capabilities, remains a core element of our overall strategy. The circumstances in which any use of nuclear weapons might have to be contemplated are extremely remote. As long as nuclear weapons exist, NATO will remain a nuclear alliance."

- "The supreme guarantee of the security of the Allies is provided by the strategic nuclear forces of the Alliance, particularly those of the United States; the independent strategic nuclear forces of the United Kingdom and France, which have a deterrent role of their own, contribute to the overall deterrence and security of the Allies."

- "We will ensure that NATO has the full range of capabilities to deter and defend against any threat to the safety and security of our populations. . . . We will maintain an appropriate mix of nuclear and conventional forces. . . . [and] ensure the broadest possible participation of Allies in collective defence planning on nuclear roles, in peacetime basing of nuclear forces, and in command, control, and consultation arrangements."

- "We will . . . develop the capability to defend our populations and territories against ballistic missile attack as a core element of our collective defence."

- "NATO seeks its security at the lowest possible level of forces. Arms control, disarmament, and non-proliferation contribute to peace, security, and stability, and should ensure undiminished security for all Alliance members. . . . With the changes in the security environment since the end of the Cold War, we have dramatically reduced the number of nuclear weapons stationed in Europe and our reliance on nuclear weapons in NATO strategy. We will seek to create the conditions for further reductions in the future. In any such reductions, our aim should be to seek Russian agreement to increase transparency on its nuclear weapons in Europe and relocate these weapons away from the territory of NATO members. Any further steps must take into account the disparity with the greater Russian stockpiles of short-range weapons."[19]

A reading of the full document reveals that it aligns well with the comprehensive approach to strengthening regional deterrence architectures set out in Chapter 3. It calls for the alliance to maintain a "full range of capabilities" for deterrence and defense, including "robust, mobile, and deployable conventional forces," missile defense, counter-cyber capabilities, counter-CBRN (chemical, biological, radiological, and nuclear) capabilities, and nuclear weapons, in addition to improved counter-terror capabilities and improved energy infrastructure security. The alliance's embrace of territorial missile defense as a NATO mission was a major advance, following years of concern in some NATO capitals about being drawn into an American project they worried might be destabilizing and costly.[20] Perhaps most important, it expressed the commitment of the alliance's political leadership "to continue renewal of our Alliance so that it is fit for purpose in addressing the 21st Century security challenges."[21]

In its nuclear aspects, the 2010 Strategic Concept aligned well with the balanced approach set out in President Obama's April 2009 Prague speech. On the one hand, it expressed a commitment to work to create the conditions through an arms control process with Russia to eliminate the remaining nuclear weapons in Europe. On the other hand, it expressed a commitment to preserve an "appropriate mix" of conventional and nuclear capabilities until those conditions are met. This result followed the recommendation of a Group of Experts chaired by Madeleine Albright that had offered advice to allied leaders while preparing the Strategic Concept, along the following lines:

> As long as nuclear weapons exist, NATO should continue to maintain secure and reliable nuclear forces, with widely shared responsibility for deployment and operational support, at the minimum level required by the prevailing security environment. . . . Any change in this policy, including in the geographic distribution of NATO nuclear deployments in Europe, should be made, as with other major decisions, by the Alliance as a whole.[22]

NATO's decision to retain nuclear weapons in Europe was nonetheless surprising to many experts and government officials, who interpreted the Prague speech to imply that the Obama administration would withdraw the remaining U.S. nuclear weapons in Europe at an early moment. But the administration's choice to make the nuclear decision in concert with its allies rather than unilaterally was consistent with the administration's broader vision of leadership (by renewing alliances) and its rejection of the unilateralism of the preceding administration. The decision reflected also deliberations during the NPR on the requirements of tailoring the nuclear deterrent to meet the twin requirements of extended deterrence and assurance.[23]

But the 2010 Strategic Concept did not settle all of the major issues. Although it stated clearly leadership commitment to an "appropriate mix" of conventional and nuclear forces, it did not specify what that mix should be. The introduction of missile defenses into the mix invited a debate about their contributions to deterrence and also about whether they could be a substitute for, and not just a complement to, the nuclear deterrent. The amplification of the alliance's strategy for arms control, disarmament, and nonproliferation also invited a debate about the mix of political and military tools in shaping the security environment. As Simon Lunn has characterized it, the 2010 Strategic Concept was "enigmatic" on the desired appropriate mix.[24]

Accordingly, the alliance subsequently undertook a Deterrence and Defense Posture Review (DDPR). Following a year of analysis and debate, the DDPR report was released in May 2012. The review began with an exploratory phase, as food-for-thought papers were developed by multiple stakeholders inside and outside the alliance, examining a broad range of issues. Formal inputs to the review were made by the nuclear High Level Group among many others.[25] Informal inputs came from many nongovernmental organizations (NGOs), as discussed in the following paragraphs.[26] This was followed by a deliberative phase to frame key issues and make decisions, which involved over a dozen meetings of the North Atlantic Council (NAC). The review was a "top-down process," directed by the alliance's political leadership, with deep involvement by capitals, and ultimately decided by it, and not a "bottom-up process" driven by the stakeholders in specific capabilities. It was analytically rigorous, politically vigorous, and ultimately revealed the breadth and depth of leadership commitment, across much of the alliance, to retain the nuclear sharing arrangements.

A key backdrop for NAC debates during the DDPR was the January 2012 release of updated defense planning guidance for the United States. This guidance stated the administration's intention to "rebalance toward the Asia-Pacific region," in part because "most European countries are now producers of security rather than consumers of it."[27] This significantly sharpened questions in Europe about the continued commitment of the United States to European security and about the future viability of the alliance in the absence of strong U.S. engagement in Europe. These factors reinforced the salience for some of traditional arguments about the unique role of nuclear weapons in signaling an enduring transatlantic link.

Not surprisingly, a central point of DDPR debate was the continued deterrence value of NATO's nuclear sharing arrangements and the associated forward-deployed U.S. nuclear weapons. On this topic, many NGOs advocated energetically for NATO leadership on disarmament. The European Leadership Network, for example, weighed in with calls for "significant changes to NATO nuclear policy," including, for example, further reductions, consolidation, and eventual elimination of nuclear weapons in Europe in the context of a mutual and verifiable agreement with Russia.[28] The Global Zero Movement issued a report calling for the elimination of U.S. nuclear weapons in Europe on the argument that their military utility in Europe is "practically nil" and that the assurance requirements of U.S. allies can be met "amply" with U.S. strategic forces.[29] A publication by the Nuclear Threat Initiative in Washington argued that "maintaining the status quo, with its attendant costs and risks, can undermine, not strengthen NATO security," concluding that the rationale for maintaining U.S. nuclear weapons in Europe "is dangerously out of date," and recommending changes to NATO's nuclear policy and posture on the premise that in Europe there is "a race between cooperation and catastrophe."[30] A joint project of the U.S. Arms Control Association, the British American Security Information Council, and the Institute for Peace Research and Security Policy at the University of Hamburg called on NATO to reject DCA modernization and allow the deterrent forces to age out.[31]

Such advocacy had a sympathetic hearing in certain NATO quarters. But others were less receptive. At the start of the DDPR process, four informal camps had emerged within the NATO community. One camp viewed U.S. NSNW as militarily obsolete[32] Cold War relics[33] and sought their removal as a contribution to nuclear disarmament.[34] A second camp viewed these weapons as having military and political utility in negating coercive threats from Russia and valued the sharing arrangements for their continuing deterrence and assurance values. Within this group were some who worried that Moscow's current leadership would interpret further reductions to NATO's nuclear posture as a sign of weakness and appeasement.[35] A third camp subscribed to the view that the NATO's nuclear posture needs to remain credible in the long term vis-à-vis emerging threats from the Middle East and saw a further weakening of NATO's nuclear deterrent posture as unhelpful.[36] A fourth camp seemed to believe that the NATO nuclear debate had largely lost its salience in a changing world and could accept any result that proved acceptable to those in the alliance with more at stake.

Resistance to the final abandonment of NATO's sharing arrangements was reflected in frequent discussion of what is sometimes called "the Elaine Bunn wedding ring analogy":

> Nuclear weapons are kind of like the wedding ring of the marriage—there are those in cultures that don't wear wedding rings who are perfectly committed to their spouses, and others who wear them who don't really have much of a commitment at all. But once you start wearing one, it means something entirely different to be seen without it than it does for someone who never wore one.[37]

By this analogy, withdrawal of U.S. nuclear weapons would be widely interpreted as signaling a major weakening of the transatlantic link.

By 2012, there were additional incentives to sustain the nuclear sharing arrangements in "the mix." One incentive was the continued failure of most European members of NATO to make good on their 2010 commitments to invest in improvements to conventional forces. Another incentive was moral in nature and flowed from a private discussion about whose interests should govern fundamental decisions about the alliance's nuclear posture: the interests of its strongest and most secure members (some of which are ready to cease hosting U.S. nuclear weapons) or of its weakest and most vulnerable members (which are not ready to endorse the removal of these weapons and to relinquish all they imply for the credibility of the NATO guarantee)? There was also pragmatic advice from influential voices to "avoid abstract debates over complete disarmament or the need to keep nuclear weapons indefinitely."[38]

Over time, these various camps converged on an answer that was politically acceptable in all capitals. As previously argued, this had something to do with the concerns generated by the U.S. rebalance to the Asia-Pacific region. It also had something to do with a widespread perception in NATO that the security environment after the 2010 Lisbon summit was eroding, as Moscow's approach to the alliance became more combative (with for example threats to target NATO with nuclear means if it proceeded with missile defense deployments) and as the Arab spring gave way to an Arab autumn of mounting instability in the Middle East. Continued erosion in the security environment after 2010 reinforced a shared perception of the need to strengthen deterrence rather than take more risks with it. Many of the recommendations from the NGO community were built on rather different assumptions about the world. Accordingly, the fourth camp largely disappeared, and the first camp was much reduced in size and ultimately accepted the need for a consensus solution.

The key findings of the DDPR of May 2012 were as follows:

- "Allies' goal is to bolster deterrence as a core element of our collective defence."

- "Nuclear weapons are a core component of NATO's overall capabilities for deterrence and defense alongside conventional and missile defence forces. The review has shown that the Alliance's nuclear force posture currently meets the criteria for an effective deterrence and defence posture."

- "While seeking to create the conditions and considering options for further reductions of non-strategic nuclear weapons assigned to NATO, Allies concerned will ensure that all components of NATO's nuclear deterrent remain safe, secure, and effective for as long as NATO remains a nuclear alliance. That requires sustained leadership focus and institutional excellence for the nuclear deterrence mission and planning guidance aligned with 21st century requirements."

- "Missile defence will become an integral part of the Alliance's overall defence posture. . . . Missile defence can complement the role of nuclear weapons in deterrence; it cannot substitute for them. This capability is purely defensive and is being established in the light of threats from outside the Euro-Atlantic security area."

- "Arms control, disarmament, and non-proliferation play an important role in the achievement of the Alliance's security objectives. Both the success and failure of these efforts can have a direct impact on the threat environment of NATO."

- "Allies look forward to continuing to develop and exchange transparency and confidence building ideas with the Russian Federation in the NATO–Russia Council, with the goal of developing detailed proposals on and increasing mutual understanding of NATO's and Russia's non-strategic nuclear force postures in Europe."

- "NATO has determined that, in the current circumstances, the existing mix of capabilities and plans for their development are sound. . . . NATO will continue to adjust its strategy, including with respect to the capabilities and other measures required for deterrence and defence, in line with the trends in the security environment."[39]

These results are less "enigmatic" than the Strategic Concept. They provide a road map for maintaining a mix of nuclear and other capabilities and enabling the needed leadership focus and commitment to deterrence excellence, while at the same time using political tools to try to create the more positive political conditions that would allow further changes to NATO's nuclear posture. They also reflect the assessment of the NATO allies that the strategic forces of the alliance's three nuclear-armed members are not sufficient for purposes of deterrence and assurance because they do not provide the message of alliance solidarity and the essential transatlantic link uniquely provided by NATO's nuclear sharing arrangements.

DDPR Implementation and the Crimea Shock

The DDPR committed the allies, and the alliance as such, to dozens of implementation actions. But implementation has proved challenging. As Polish analyst Jacek Durkalec put it in 2013, the DDPR resulted in "advantageous words but uncertain deeds."[40] Continued financial difficulties in Europe have had a significant impact on the ability of the allies to sustain the commitment to conventional force modernization.[41] The spring 2013 U.S. decision to cancel Phase IV of the European Phased Adaptive Approach (EPAA) to missile defense in favor of accelerated purchases of U.S.-based interceptors has cast some doubt in Europe on the U.S. commitment to EPAA, which has raised questions about the future missile defense contributions of NATO allies. The public and political discussion of NATO's nuclear posture has continued, with continued advocacy in some quarters for the withdrawal of U.S. nuclear weapons—but only after "additional consultations" (as if they might produce an outcome different from the DDPR).[42] There was also continued advocacy for retaining them.[43]

More fundamentally, DDPR implementation has run up against the shock to NATO delivered by President Putin's military-backed annexation of Crimea, his continued interference in Ukrainian domestic affairs, his promise to "snap back hard" against the post–Cold War political order in Europe, and his commitment to defend Russian-speaking people wherever they live. Some of the most basic premises reflected in the 2010 Strategic Concept have been called into question and with them the results of the DDPR. Today, the Euro-Atlantic security area is not at peace. Russia no longer sees a basis for strategic partnership with NATO; indeed, it sees NATO as a threat. There appears to be no political basis for cooperation on missile defense in the Euro-Atlantic security area. The conditions under which Russia might relinquish its nuclear weapons in the Euro-Atlantic security area (and elsewhere) seem more remote than ever. Additionally, Russia is deploying new capabilities that target NATO members (as discussed in Chapter 4) and, if it proceeds with a breakout from the INF Treaty, may deploy an entire new set of nuclear weapons threatening to the West.[44]

At its September 2014 NATO summit in Wales, the alliance began the process of adaptation. The summit addressed changing Western views of Russia and the need to respond credibly to newly adversarial relations without foreclosing future cooperation. It called on Russia to ensure its compliance with the INF treaty but sought no change to NATO's nuclear posture in response, in part to keep the spotlight for now where it belongs—on Russia's treaty violation. It began to strengthen the conventional defense of the Baltic states while also setting in motion processes that will lead to other adaptations to the alliance's deterrence and defense posture over time.[45]

Looking to the future, NATO faces the challenge of again adapting its Strategic Concept and further adapting its deterrence and defense posture to a changed and changing world, to ensure that the alliance remains "fit for purpose." Adaptations to the Strategic Concept must reflect the more adversarial quality in the relationship with Russia. This does not require embracing Russia as an enemy; it does require setting aside the West's long-held positive vision of cooperation and community with Russia as not viable for the foreseeable future. It does not require closing the door on future cooperation, but it does require taking steps to defend the interests of the alliance that Russia will find uncongenial. The alliance's vision must include a remaking of the political relationship with Russia with an eye to reducing the risks of conflict through calculation or miscalculation and increasing mutual confidence in the avoidance of war.

Adaptations to the Strategic Concept will also require a remaking of the alliance's arms control strategy. The DDPR set out a pathway toward the ultimate elimination of nuclear weapons in the Euro-Atlantic security area, on the basis of reciprocal steps by Russia to reduce, relocate, and eliminate its nuclear weapons in the region and taking due account for the disparity in the size of Russia and NATO nonstrategic nuclear forces. These efforts are, for the foreseeable future, at a dead end. As argued earlier, it is too early to argue that Russia is no longer interested in nuclear arms control. Accordingly, NATO should not abandon its arms control strategy. But it should have no expectation that it will pay any dividends in the short term.[46]

If in fact arms control with Russia as it has been practiced since the late 1960s proves no longer viable, major new questions emerge about whether and how to lend stability and predictability to the European security environment. The deep continuing appeal of arms control in the West may make it vulnerable to bad deals promulgated by Moscow that are blatantly beneficial to Russia and not materially beneficial to the West. It is possible also that there may be new approaches, not yet conceived, that are mutually beneficial to the interests of Russia as Mr. Putin understands them and to the West. It is important, therefore, to retain a body of expertise and focus on arms control in the West so that opportunities can be defined, tested, negotiated, and implemented if successfully concluded and ratified. In follow-up to one of the DDPR taskings, Poland has taken the lead in convening an international process to think through options for nuclear transparency and confidence building as the first steps on the pathway to agreement with Russia on arms control on nonstrategic nuclear weapons (NSNW). In a reflection of current times, this work takes a pessimistic view of short-term opportunities.[47] But this topic deserves continued attention as a needed investment in a future renewal of cooperation with Russia.[48]

Emerging Challenges:
Deterrence in the New NATO–Russia Context

Adaptations to the alliance's deterrence and defense posture are also needed in light of changes in Russia's policy and posture. NATO must reopen the "appropriate mix" question in a different context. But before deciding whether and how to "remix the mix," NATO needs clarity about that context. In the language of Chapters 2 and 3, it needs to understand Russia's theory of victory—that is, Moscow's thinking about how to prevail in war and peace through nuclear blackmail and brinksmanship—and to have a theory of victory of its own that promises to negate the coercive value of Russian hard and soft power and to manage effectively the challenges of escalation if Moscow chooses war. Without a Blue theory of victory of its own, NATO is left with the unpromising task of strengthening individual tools in the toolkit without knowing how to rebalance them or achieve a comprehensive effect. NATO's preparation of a theory of victory against Russia's theory of victory, and of the needed military means, can help to send a message of deterrence to Russia that its own theory of victory is not credible and a message of reassurance to NATO members that NATO's defense strategy is in fact viable and thus credible.

Toward this end, NATO must closely study developments in Russian military strategy and doctrine so that it understands the potential routes to escalation and deescalation of a conflict with Russia and the means of influencing Moscow's decision making at each threshold. NATO needs, in the words of Forrest Morgan, "a clear and realistic understanding of where all the important thresholds reside."[49] This is essential to understanding what makes a particular mix of capabilities appropriate.

Moreover, such an understanding may help to lay the foundations for a renewal of cooperative efforts to preserve strategic stability. To cite Morgan further, "every party to a conflict" must have such an understanding of where thresholds reside, "its own as well as those of the other belligerents,"[50] if they are to be successful in avoiding escalation and indeed conflict. The effort to arrive at such a mutual understanding should become possible over time and ought to be pursued once NATO has done its homework. Such a joint exploration could also reinforce NATO's main message that its intention is to blunt coercion and aggression and not to attack and defeat Russia or to intervene militarily inside Russia.

As NATO puts its intellectual house in order, in a manner that aligns its military strategy with the potential dynamics of a conflict that Russia brings to it, how should it think about rebalancing the mix of deterrence and defense capabilities so that it is appropriate to a new strategy?[51]

With the Wales summit, NATO is already well launched on the project of adapting its conventional force posture to the risk of Russian military grab of some part of the Baltics. The adoption of rotational deployments of forces and the prepositioning of military equipment strengthen the needed conventional defense of these allies. Deeper and broader cooperation with non-NATO partners in the region (for example, Sweden) is also important. Over time, this conventional aspect of "the mix" must become more effective in meeting the challenges of Russia's hybrid warfare concept. Especially important will be measures that expose credibly Russian efforts to infiltrate special forces and employ disinformation.[52]

Russian ballistic and cruise missile threats to the West necessarily reopen the discussion of whether NATO's territorial missile defense is oriented solely at potential threats from the Middle East, as agreed in 2010, or also has a role in addressing Russian threats. Russia knows that this will be a contentious debate in NATO and has done everything possible to fuel that debate so that the alliance is divided on the question. NATO's desire to reduce the coercive value of those Russian capabilities suggests that NATO will move, over time, to define a role for BMD in the deterrence architecture vis-à-vis Russia and to seek the stabilizing benefits of limited BMD set out in Chapter 3 rather than defense dominance.

Russia's deployment of conventionally armed ballistic missiles targeting Western countries also promises to open a debate within NATO about whether to counter such deployments with deployments of their own. Prompt conventional strike capabilities play an important role in the Blue theory of victory set out in Chapter 3 but have so far played no role in NATO's deterrence and defense posture. This is in part because the INF treaty prohibits both nuclear and conventionally armed ballistic missiles. If and as Russia deploys INF-range missiles, NATO would be well served by deployment of a small arsenal of conventionally armed ballistic missiles with a range sufficient to strike Russian bases from which strike operations against NATO would be conducted. This would be a preferable alternative to sole reliance on nuclear strike systems as a counter to Russian dual capable strike systems and as a necessary component of a mixed offense-defense strategy.

This brings us to the nuclear tool in "the mix." The central question for NATO must be whether a symmetric response to Russia's new nuclear posture in Europe is necessary. A symmetric response would match Russian forces in numbers and types of deployed nuclear weapons. The case that it is necessary derives from the history of nuclear deterrence in Europe and the past need to maintain a credible posture aligned with the NATO doctrine of flexible response in a context of massive Soviet conventional supremacy. In the Cold War, a symmetric NATO posture was necessary to make the case clear to the Soviets that any nuclear conflict at any level would likely escalate to major nuclear exchanges. If Russia is replicating the Soviet nuclear force structure of old, goes the argument, then NATO must replicate its old posture to restore balance and strategic stability.

The case against a symmetric response is more compelling. Whatever the Russian threat to the Baltic states, there is no prospect of a massive Russian conventional intervention deep into Europe promising prolonged armored ground combat. Flexible response is gone. NATO nuclear strategy needs to be able to demonstrate to Moscow that its deescalation strikes, and other actions that jeopardize the vital interests of U.S. allies, can and will be met with a Western nuclear response that will lead Moscow to choose to deescalate rather than expand a conflict. It must be able to demonstrate in time of military crisis that an attack on one will, indeed, be treated by NATO as an attack on all. And in peacetime, Western allies must be able to do what they consider necessary to safeguard their interests without concern for Russian nuclear-backed threats and coercion. For these purposes, NATO does not need a symmetric nuclear posture. It needs a capacity for limited retaliation. It needs the sharing arrangements. And it needs the strategic deterrents of its three nuclear-armed allies to be prepared to act in support of their allies if Russia's response to a limited exchange of nuclear weapons is to broaden and increase the intensity of its nuclear attacks.

Lastly in the nuclear domain, NATO needs to be prepared, and to be seen to be prepared, to take future additional steps to strengthen its nuclear posture if the relationship with Russia continues to worse. Such possible future steps must include setting aside the assurances about NATO's nuclear posture made to Moscow in the NATO–Russia Council Founding Act and opening the door to the participation of NATO's newer members in the nuclear sharing ar-rangements.[53] NATO should signal to Moscow that the security environment has been changed by Russia's behaviors in some fundamental respects since 1997 and that it can and will take significant steps to adapt and strengthen its nuclear deterrent if the nuclear threat to NATO continues to grow.

This line of argument illuminates how sharply contentious NATO's rising debate about how to "remix the mix" is likely to be. The advocates of rapid ad-justments to NATO's deterrence and defense posture must be mindful of the need to not pursue so divisive an agenda as to cripple the alliance's ability to act and thus to hand Russia a major political prize. The advocates of a go-slow approach must be mindful of the fact that Russia is very far along in adapt-ing its own deterrence and defense strategy and posture to enable its "snap back hard" strategy. Division within the alliance will be sharpened by Russia's keen objections to any of the adaptations to "the mix" discussed here. Moscow sees the deployment of strong conventional forces on NATO's northern flank as dangerously provocative. It keenly objects to a missile defense that might offer some protection of Europe as negating its deterrent. It sees prompt con-ventional strike systems as part of a strategy for a decapitation strike against Moscow. And it sees NATO's modest force of nonstrategic nuclear weapons as requiring the deployment of thousands of its own such weapons. Its shrill rhetoric attests to the fact that it would much rather that NATO not strengthen and adapt its deterrence and defense posture.

The choice for NATO is simple but politically fraught. It will have to decide how much deference to continue to show Russian interests as it understands them. While seeking a political settlement in Ukraine, NATO must be mind-ful of the fine line between compromise and appeasement, recognizing that Moscow itself apparently sees no mutual accommodation as possible so long as the existing security order in Europe is preserved.[54] Accordingly, NATO's military strategy vis-à-vis Russia cannot be separated from its political strat-egy, which continues to evolve as the Ukraine crisis drags on. NATO will also have to become the master of the public narrative about what Russia is doing and why NATO's responses will reinforce stability and peace in Europe rather than erode them. That narrative must include clear messages to Moscow—in what we say and what we do—about the escalation thresholds in a potential conflict in Europe and the strengths of NATO's response in enabling actions by NATO that are consistent with its interests. With this as a starting point, a new dialogue with Russia may yet prove possible that reduces the risks of conflict and puts the strategic landscape on a more stable footing.

Conclusions

Developments in the security environment have put extended deterrence back at the center of transatlantic security. In the last few years, NATO has passed through a period of significant debate about how to adapt its deterrence posture to 21st-century purposes. This debate will continue and intensify if and as President Putin continues to "snap back hard" against the post–Cold War European security order (and if nuclear and missile proliferation continue in the Middle East). Three lessons stand out.

First, the comprehensive approach to strengthening regional deterrence architectures is well advanced in Europe. NATO has explicitly introduced missile defense and other nonnuclear means into its deterrence and defense posture. But its effective implementation is a long-term project and one severely constrained by economic factors. The future resilience of NATO's deterrence and defense posture cannot be taken for granted.

Second, Russia now calls NATO an enemy, even as NATO tries to avoid accepting Russia as an enemy. Russia's direct threat to NATO remains unclear, and the uncertainty here is part of the challenge for NATO. But the deterrence and defense posture agreed in 2012 was based on a different premise. Even as NATO takes urgent steps to bolster the conventional defense of its Baltic members, it must tackle more difficult questions. These include assessing which scenarios of Russian aggression plausibly threaten NATO and the implications of Russia's noncompliance with the INF treaty. More fundamentally, NATO must come to terms with the theory of victory that Russia seems to have constructed for itself for confrontation with NATO. All of this will require re-creating expertise on these topics that has been allowed to decay for two decades.

Third, NATO's commitment to remaining a nuclear alliance is deep and abiding. For all of the continuing debate outside government about whether U.S. nuclear weapons should remain deployed in Europe, along with the associated debate about the continued deterrence and assurance values of NATO's nuclear sharing arrangements, there is essentially no debate at the leadership level about the alliance's commitment to remain a nuclear alliance so long as nuclear weapons remain. The modalities of that commitment will remain under debate but the commitment to the role of nuclear weapons in the alliance's deterrence strategy in the new security environment is essentially uncontested.

7   Extended Deterrence and
       Strategic Stability in Northeast Asia

IN EUROPE, COLD WAR HISTORY HAS CAST A LONG SHADOW over efforts to adapt and strengthen extended deterrence for new purposes in the new century. The situation in Northeast Asia is quite different, as the Presidential Nuclear Initiatives of the early 1990s essentially wiped the slate clean.

The Northeast Asian Cold War nuclear slate was in any case different from the European one. There were no nuclear sharing arrangements and no elaborate consultations on how and when U.S. nuclear weapons might be employed. U.S. nuclear weapons were deployed to South Korea beginning in the late 1950s; by the mid-1960s there were almost 1,000 U.S. nuclear weapons there (a fact not acknowledged officially until 1975).[1] Nuclear weapons were not deployed to Japan, consistent with its long-standing "three no's" policy (Japan shall neither possess nor manufacture nuclear weapons, nor shall it permit their introduction into Japanese territory),[2] though there was a political understanding by which U.S. naval vessels carried nuclear weapons in Japanese waters.[3] With the U.S. decision in 1991 to eliminate all land-based nuclear weapons from East Asia and all nuclear weapons from naval surface vessels, this Cold War history largely receded from memory. For the next two decades, the United States maintained a declaratory policy of providing a nuclear umbrella to Japan and South Korea and also the capability to redeploy in time of crisis nuclear-armed cruise missiles on attack submarines (the nuclear armed Tomahawk, or TLAM/N). Some East Asians interpreted the promise to redeploy weapons in a future crisis as a promise to reextend deterrence rather than to maintain the nuclear umbrella on an ongoing basis.

The long interregnum in policy concern about nuclear deterrence in Northeast Asia helped to keep the slate clean. In the first two post–Cold War decades, there were few major decisions for allies in Northeast Asia to make on extended deterrence and no major alliance management challenges on nuclear deterrence policy, unlike in Europe.

But all this has begun to change in recent years, and the process of change is accelerating. The stories of adapting and strengthening extended deterrence in Europe and Northeast Asia are similar but not identical. On the one hand, the underlying challenges are the same: to establish the credibility of U.S. nuclear guarantees in the face of new threats, while also diversifying the extended deterrence toolkit through the comprehensive strengthening approach. On the other hand, given the specific geographic, historical, and political contexts, the effort in Northeast Asia has proceeded in different ways and with different results from the effort in Europe.[4]

This chapter illuminates these similarities and differences. It begins with a review of those developments in the regional security environment driving new interest in the U.S. nuclear umbrella. It turns then to a review of efforts since 2009 to adapt and strengthen extended deterrence, including the process of institution building within the two bilateral alliances in Northeast Asia (U.S.–Japan and U.S.–Republic of Korea, or RoK). It then reviews key issues posing long-term challenges for the strengthening process. The chapter concludes with an assessment of progress in strengthening deterrence and of implications for U.S. nuclear policy and posture.[5]

The Changing Security Environment and the New Demands on Extended Deterrence

Four key factors in the security environment are driving this agenda.

North Korea's progress in developing long-range missiles and nuclear weapons is the first key factor, along with its growing strategic reach and its apparent ambitions to exploit a theory of victory that depends fundamentally on blackmail and decoupling the United States from the defense of South Korea and Japan. In case there were any doubt that Japan might be vulnerable in a conflict on the Korean peninsula, Kim Jong Un made the danger clear: "Japan is always in the cross-hairs of our revolutionary army and if Japan makes a slightest move, the spark of war will touch Japan first."[6]

China's progress in military modernization is the second key factor, along with its increasingly prominent regional military role, its rising confidence in its strategic deterrent, and its assertiveness in pursuing territorial disputes in the neighboring maritime environment. This factor brings with it a fundamental question about whether the United States might now "choose to defend a narrower set of vital interests," as some in Asia have feared.[7]

Provocations in the gray zone are the third key factor. Both North Korea and China are militarily assertive at the conventional level but while also avoiding overt hostilities. North Korea conducts "provocations" while China engages in what Japan refers to as "creeping international expansionism."

The final factor is continued concern in both Japan and South Korea about American abandonment. This is not a new phenomenon, as allies in Northeast Asia as elsewhere have sometimes worried about potential American disengagement from their defense at times of strategic retrenchment following, for example, the Korean and Vietnamese wars.[8] But it is given a qualitatively different character as the U.S. homeland comes under threat and America is expected to fight regional wars with its own homeland at risk of nuclear attack. The 2012 promise to "rebalance" helped address these concerns. But mounting subsequent doubts about how much rebalancing will prove possible at a time of declining U.S. defense spending and continuing conflict in the Middle East and Europe have again inflamed them.

Just as in Europe, U.S. allies in Northeast Asia do not have identical views of these developments. Japan feels threatened by China in a way that South Korea does not (though South Korea is concerned about whether a rising China will respect its core interests, not least in eventual denuclearization of the North and reunification on peaceful terms on a political model largely set by Seoul). But, as in Europe, these differences of view have not been so stark as to make it impossible for the United States to work with its allies on a common agenda for adapting and strengthening extended deterrence.

Cumulatively, these developments in the security environment have resulted in what one study has called a "security deficit" for Japan: "In the 21st century, Japan's security surplus is slowly shifting toward a deficit. . . . The United States and Japan could lose their nearly exclusive dominance over the conflict escalation ladder in the region."[9] An analogous argument can be made for South Korea: despite the clear superiority of its political and economic models over those of North Korea, and the relative decline of the North Korean military in terms of conventional war-fighting capabilities, it is increasingly subject to provocations by a nuclear-armed North Korea.

Note the adverb *slowly* and the future conditional tense ("could lose") in the citation in the preceding paragraph. The shift has not yet been completed, and the loss has not been realized. Despite their progress, North Korea and China have not yet completed their projects or come to dominate potential future escalation. Whether they are successful in shifting the U.S.–Japan and U.S.–RoK alliances into "deficit" depends not just on what they do but on what the United States and Japan and South Korea do to preserve deterrence and stability.

On Adapting and Strengthening Extended Deterrence

What should they do? The answer flows in part from the deterrence spectrum set out in Chapter 2. To strengthen deterrence in the gray zone, the United States and its allies must become more effective at deterring conventional provocations, where nuclear threats may not be seen as credible or helpful. To strengthen deterrence in the red zone, the United States and its allies must be capable of protecting themselves, of responding forcefully if attacked, and of credibly demonstrating their combined and collective resolve to stand together in defense of their interests. In short, they must have a theory of victory of their own and the means to defeat the theories of victory of potential adversaries. Additionally, they must strengthen deterrence of North Korea and China while working to maintain a stable balance with China and to avoid an arms race of a kind that would further damage the political relationship with Beijing.

Where should they start? A first priority has been to institutionalize cooperation on extended deterrence. In Europe, mechanisms have long been in place for such cooperation; in Northeast Asia, they did not exist until recently. Improved cooperation on extended deterrence between the United States and its two allies in Northeast Asia began in 2009. In the course of conducting the Nuclear Posture Review, the Obama administration encouraged any potential stakeholder, including especially allied governments, to express its views about the necessary and appropriate results of the review. Japan and South Korea were among the many countries that took up this opportunity.[10]

It is important to acknowledge that the new initiatives to cooperate in this area in 2009 built on solid foundations. In the prior decade, Japan and the United States had broken significant new ground in developing cooperative approaches to missile defense, while also taking some initial steps to discuss nuclear deterrence in the new strategic environment. Similarly, the Republic of Korea and the United States had renewed the two-plus-two framework (a process of alliance coordination involving ministries of defense and foreign affairs and their U.S. counterparts) with an eye to strengthening deterrence of North Korea.

The consultations in 2009 focused heavily on U.S. declaratory policy and on U.S. capabilities for extended nuclear deterrence. On declaratory policy, the Obama administration carefully considered the views of its allies in Northeast Asia (and elsewhere) before rejecting the "sole purpose formulation" and modifying the negative security assurance. The "sole purpose formulation" would have reduced the role of nuclear weapons in U.S. deterrence strategy to the sole purpose of deterring nuclear attack on the United States or its allies, thereby eliminating their role in deterring attacks on vital interests by other means, including chemical and biological weapons and large-scale conventional wars. The result is a U.S. policy that specifies a continued role for U.S. nuclear weapons in deterring attacks on allies by nonnuclear means that threaten their vital interests. The modified negative security assurance also clarifies that states such as North Korea that cheat and leave the NPT and threaten the United States and its allies are objects of U.S. deterrence planning.

The bilateral dialogue with Japan about whether to maintain or modify U.S. declaratory policy was complicated in part by a language translation issue. As Yukio Satoh has noted,

> Discussions about the term "first use" in Japan are somewhat distorted because of the Japanese translation of the term. The widely used Japanese term for "first use"—"*sensei-shiyo*"—literally means "preemptive use" in Japanese, while "first use" does not always imply "preemptive use," particularly in contrast to preemptive "first strike." It is understandable that a notion of "preemptive use" is repugnant to many, and the Japanese are no exception . . . However it would be counterproductive for the sake of the country's security if the Japanese people

would become critical of the U.S. policy of calculated ambiguity about "first use," believing that "first use" is always preemptive.[11]

On capabilities, the Obama administration carefully considered the views of its allies in Northeast Asia and elsewhere before retiring the nuclear-armed Tomahawk cruise missile and committing to modernize dual-capable aircraft (DCA) that are globally deployable in support of a commitment to an ally anywhere, not just in Europe. The two capabilities to forward-deploy nuclear weapons with a nonstrategic delivery system were essentially redundant from a U.S. perspective. From an alliance perspective, the DCA had benefits for deterrence that the Tomahawk did not. Deployment of DCA is a way to signal the shared and collective resolve of the United States and its allies to stand together in the face of nuclear coercion and aggression and efforts to split them from one another with nuclear threats. These decisions reflected a view shared by allies in Northeast Asia and Europe: that the strategic systems of the United States alone are not sufficient for purposes of deterrence and assurance.[12]

One of the most important results of the NPR-era consultations was the personal engagement of the U.S. president and his clear commitment to preserve the nuclear umbrella even while reducing the role and number of U.S. nuclear weapons. As President Obama declared in Tokyo in November 2009: "So long as these [nuclear] weapons remain, the United States will maintain a strong and effective nuclear deterrent that guarantees the defense of our allies—including South Korea and Japan."[13] He followed this with written guidance to the U.S. military "reaffirming the role of nuclear weapons in extending deterrence to U.S. Allies and partners and the U.S. commitment to strengthen regional deterrence architectures" and directing the military to ensure "a wide range of effective response options" drawing on both a strong strategic deterrent and the capability to deploy nuclear weapons in the region.[14]

On conclusion of the NPR in 2010, the United States, Japan, and South Korea were all interested in sustaining the high-level substantive dialogue that had been built during the NPR. Accordingly, the United States and Japan founded the Extended Deterrence Dialogue (EDD), and the United States and the Republic of Korea founded the Extended Deterrence Policy Committee (EDPC).

The mechanisms serve multiple purposes: to institutionalize sustained leadership focus on these issues, to enable active policy discussion and development where needed, and to ensure sustained progress on practical agendas of cooperation in support of the comprehensive strategy for strengthening regional deterrence architectures. The EDD and EDPC have helped to ensure coordinated policy development in the subsequent strategic documents and leadership statements of all three countries, as for example in the development of South Korea's "proactive deterrence strategy" and Japan's "dynamic deterrence." The EDD process had an impact on Japan's 2010 National Defense Program Guidelines, where Japan clarified its intention to play a role in countering nuclear threats rather than simply "relying on" U.S. extended deterrence.[15] The EDPC has produced a tailored deterrence strategy that helps the two countries to "work together more seamlessly to maximize the effects of our deterrence."[16] These processes have also provided both allies the opportunities that European allies have had for decades to have firsthand experience of the capabilities the United States provides in support of its extended deterrence commitments through visits to U.S. nuclear bases and facilities.[17] Cumulatively, these various new forms of interaction have helped to build common understanding of emerging deterrence challenges, the nature of potential conflicts, and the means to address the risks of escalation.

These processes have also helped to meet rising demand in Japan and South Korea for a deeper understanding of extended deterrence and of what they can do to increase its credibility. As one observer has argued, officials in Northeast Asia "want more than verbal reassurances; they want to know how deterrence *works*."[18] Yukio Satoh summarized the issue cogently in 2009:

> If the credibility of the U.S. commitment is the question at issue, it is Japanese perceptions that matter. The U.S. commitment to provide extended deterrence to Japan has been repeatedly affirmed by presidents, including President Obama, and other senior officials in agreed documents. Nevertheless, Japanese misgivings and doubts about American commitment persist . . . it is important for Tokyo to be officially engaged in consultations with Washington on deterrence strategy, including nuclear deterrence. Without such consultations, the Japanese government, let alone the public, will have to be speculative about the credibility of U.S. commitment. That U.S. strategic thinking is undergoing epoch-making changes makes such consultations more important.[19]

All three capitals have wanted to ensure that efforts to adapt and strengthen extended deterrence do not come at the expense of efforts to use political tools to reduce and ultimately eliminate nuclear dangers. Without strong agendas to try to denuclearize North Korea, to try to engage China on strategic stability, to combat proliferation networks in the region, and to strengthen nuclear materials security, it is not clear that the political commitment would have been found or sustained for these new deterrence-focused processes.

In fact, the three capitals have largely converged on a common view of a balanced approach to reducing nuclear dangers with a mix of military and political tools and of the fundamentally complementary roles of these tools. With an effective extended deterrent in place, the nonproliferation and disarmament effort may yet be advanced with denuclearization of the Korean peninsula—if and as leaders in Pyongyang come to understand that new nuclear and missile capabilities bring no enduring advantages for the North and indeed bring significant new risks. And with a stable strategic balance, that effort may also yet be advanced by China's participation in the nuclear transparency and reductions process—if and as leaders in Beijing come to believe that China's interest in a stable security environment is best served by the practice of strategic restraint in a manner that meets the transparency and other requirements of other stakeholders in stability.

Implementation Challenges

As this work has proceeded, a number of challenges have come into focus. This analysis highlights three.

Challenge #1: Deepening Trilateral Cooperation

As noted previously, the political relationship between Japan and South Korea is troubled by many factors and constrains the security relationship. This is more than an inconvenience from the perspective of deterrence and assurance. In a war on the Korean peninsula, the successful defense of the Republic of Korea would not be possible without the support of Japan. Japan is host to eight bases that fly the flag of the UN Command in support of the RoK, and the flow of forces from those bases would require prior consultation with Japan's prime minister. Japan would also be expected to provide logistical support to U.S. forces in time of war. In the 1950s, Japan was a safe rear area and could provide such support without risk to itself; this has now changed fundamentally. The incentive for North Korea to drive a wedge between Tokyo and Seoul in time of war would thus be high, and political friction between the two would make for a ready target of opportunity.

Improved trilateral cooperation needs a firmer foundation than divergent threat perceptions and cajoling by Washington. It could be encouraged by a better mutual understanding of the potential dynamics of North Korea's implementation of its apparent theory of victory, which would trigger better understanding of the shared interests and separate stakes that would be in play in such a conflict for all three countries.[20] This work can be facilitated by improved cooperation among the relevant policy and intelligence analysts in all three countries.

As in the dialogues with Russia, China, and NATO allies, the unofficial Track 1.5 process has added useful value and context in the absence of an official trilateral dialogue in Northeast Asia. One such effort organized by Pacific Forum CSIS in Honolulu brought together experts from the three—the United States, Japan, and South Korea—in the summer of 2014 to explore the potential dynamics of a conflict on the Korean peninsula initiated by the North and involving first nuclear threats and then a small-scale nuclear attack generating low casualties but backed by the threat of more to come, in the form of attacks on Japan, unless the United States and its allies sued for peace on terms dictated by Pyongyang. The simulation highlighted the dependence of the conventional defense of South Korea on forces stationed in Japan, whose use would have to be authorized by the Japanese prime minister—whose decision would reflect in part his concern about potential retaliation on Japan. These interdependencies are little understood among the separate national expert communities in Northeast Asia. They generate new political demands for forms of consultation in crisis not so far clearly envisioned.[21]

Challenge #2: Maintaining Consensus on the Nuclear Component

The nuclear component of the regional deterrence architecture has been tailored, as already argued, to the unique circumstances of Northeast Asia. Consultations in 2009 and 2010 helped to generate consensus among the U.S., Japanese, and South Korean governments on the tailoring of policy and posture reflected in the 2010 NPR Report. But given the rising salience of nuclear deterrence in the Northeast Asian security debate, continued evaluation of this approach to nuclear deterrence and exploration of alternatives can be expected. A number of issues are likely to be in debate.

One is declaratory policy. The "sole purpose formulation" (by which the United States would declare that the sole purpose of U.S. nuclear weapons is to deter nuclear attack on itself and its allies) remains in discussion in Tokyo and Seoul, with some advocates in the expert community continuing to call for such a policy.[22] Moreover, the 2010 NPR committed the United States to work with its allies to establish the conditions under which a "sole purpose formulation" in declaratory policy could be adopted sometime in the future. The United States, Japan, and South Korea could work together to clarify what those conditions might be and whether or how it might be possible to bring them into being.

A second issue of continuing debate among policy makers and experts is the validity of the logic that leads to different approaches in Europe and Northeast Asia to extended nuclear deterrence. In Northeast Asia, there is a strong continuing demand for NATO-like extended deterrence arrangements, generally without a clear appreciation of what specifically is meant by "NATO-like." The NATO model has multiple attributes. The nuclear forces of NATO's three nuclear-armed members (the United States, the United Kingdom, and France) provide the "supreme guarantee" of the security of NATO allies, while a subgroup of other NATO allies participates in the alliance's nuclear sharing arrangements. Moreover, nuclear roles and responsibilities within the alliance are coordinated by defense ministers (absent the French minister, as France did not join NATO's Nuclear Planning Group when it returned to the alliance's integrated military structure in 2009). This political consultation on nuclear policy and strategy is aligned with military coordination on potential nuclear deterrence and crisis management operations within the relevant command structures.

In contrast, in East Asia there are no nuclear-armed allies and no nuclear sharing arrangements; thus, there is no military coordination on potential nuclear deterrence operations. The U.S. commitment to the nuclear defense of its allies in East Asia is met first and foremost with the strategic triad. The capability to deploy nuclear weapons in time of crisis into the region with nonstrategic delivery systems implies some possible future political and military coordination requirements, however. This is a strong model, well suited to the current strategic environment. The triad is highly capable of any needed nuclear employment. For the signaling of U.S. resolve in crisis, alert levels can be changed and bombers can be visibly used, as for example in March 2013, when they were flown into South Korean airspace. But for the signaling of the shared resolve of the United States and its allies, the possible deployment of nonstrategic delivery systems is of potential high value (depending on the particular characteristics of a regional military crisis).

An alternative model is the Cold War East Asian model. In this model, the triad and DCA were supplemented by the deployment of tactical nuclear weapons in South Korea and aboard U.S. naval surface combatants and attack submarines (as noted, these weapons were withdrawn in 1991, and most were then retired and eliminated). Some experts and politicians in the Republic of Korea have called for the redeployment of these weapons.[23] But this would be unhelpful today. It would significantly erode the political pressure on North Korea to denuclearize, increase nuclear targeting of South Korea by the North, and add little to either the deterrence of the North or the assurance of the South. Additionally, the reintroduction of nuclear weapons to U.S. surface naval combatants or attack submarines is politically unrealistic at this time.

Moreover, NATO's unique nuclear sharing arrangements reflect NATO's unique strategic challenge—convincing potential adversaries (as well as individual allies) that an attack on one ally will be treated as an attack on all twenty-eight. In the absence of such sharing arrangements in the U.S.–Japan and U.S.–RoK contexts, there is no need for an operational planning mechanism such as that implemented in NATO's military command. There is, however, a need for ministerial dialogue and guidance—and this can readily occur in the existing ministerial meetings. To the extent that improved coordination for extended deterrence was needed between the United States and its two allies in Northeast Asia, the new mechanisms agreed in 2010 have made a substantial start.

A final model is sometimes proposed by politicians and pundits in Japan and South Korea: acquiring nuclear deterrents of their own. Of course, this is not a model of extended U.S. deterrence. Moreover, for reasons discussed elsewhere in this volume, barring dramatic changes in the security environment, such acquisitions would trigger reactions harmful to the interests of these two states while also undermining U.S. extended deterrence more generally.[24]

One further factor may come into broader discussion—the technical attributes of the U.S. nuclear arsenal. Australian analyst Rod Lyon has set out the case forcefully:

> While they might not be obsessive about the need for large numbers of nuclear weapons, America's allies in particular do have a continuing interest in the size of the U.S. arsenal and, more importantly, in its shape. . . . No one in Asia wants

a U.S. nuclear force presence so large that it appears to be principally about swaggering rather than about deterrence and assurance. Indeed, the question tends to be one of where the acceptable minimum is rather than the tolerable maximum . . . The contraction of the U.S. theatre- and tactical-range nuclear arsenal suggests a U.S. less interested in forward-deployed nuclear weapons. And that in turn suggests a U.S. less interested in extended nuclear assurance. . . . Allies are looking for some concrete evidence that U.S. warheads appropriate to their needs exist within the U.S. arsenal.[25]

This way of thinking is alien to many U.S. nuclear deterrence experts, but it is symptomatic of the different ways of thinking among U.S. allies that must be accounted for in any assurance strategy. Some allies are troubled by the aging character of U.S. nuclear forces and continued doubts about American political will to modernize them.

Challenge #3: Aligning Extended Deterrence and Strategic Stability

The third key challenge is aligning efforts to strengthen the regional deterrence architecture with efforts to preserve strategic stability with China. The challenge is complicated by the problem, discussed in Chapter 5, that China has so far refused to engage in dialogue on this topic, putting itself in a position of reacting adversely to the thinking of others it has not tried to shape constructively. Additionally, China is deeply opposed to stronger trilateral cooperation (on the argument that it is a form of containment), especially if it were to be extended in operationally meaningful ways to encompass the defense of Taiwan (for example, through a regional missile defense architecture incorporating also Taiwanese sensors and interceptors). It is also deeply opposed to any developments in the U.S. strategic military posture in the region that would enhance U.S. capabilities against China. These factors highlight the challenges of finding a strategy that is acceptable to all and illustrate the kinds of trade-offs that might have to be faced in the absence of some degree of policy convergence among the main actors in the region.

The challenge begins with finding a common understanding of strategic stability and its requirements. The United States, China, and Japan have not converged on a common view. The United States perceives strategic stability as potentially threatened by the expansion of both the size and role of China's nuclear force, China's development of robust anti–access area–denial capabilities in the conventional realm, and the emerging competition in the cyber and space domains—all in the context of a more assertively nationalist regime that sometimes pushes diplomatic crises to the brink of military confrontation. In contrast, China perceives strategic stability as threatened by the combination of U.S. prompt conventional strike and ballistic missile defense capabilities and by possible threats to its interests, including vital ones in Taiwan, from the increased freedom of maneuver that the United States and its allies will enjoy with a strengthened regional deterrence architecture. Chinese analysts have sought assurances that the United States accepts mutual vulnerability as the basis of the strategic relationship, on the U.S.–Russian model. In contrast, Japan perceives strategic stability as threatened by China's success in consolidating a modern nuclear retaliatory capability and by its rising willingness to contest the regional order. Some in Japan are concerned that the United States will accept mutual vulnerability as the basis of the strategic relationship and worry that this would encourage Chinese assertiveness at the conventional level. Japanese experts seek credible assurances that the United States is not committed to a vision of strategic stability that comes at the expense of the U.S.–Japan alliance.[26] As Yukio Satoh has argued, "The nuclear force balance between the U.S. on one side and Russia and China on the other that Washington would find acceptable for the sake of strategic stability would not necessarily be reassuring particularly to Tokyo and Seoul."[27]

At the very least, sustained engagement between Washington and Tokyo on the next steps on strategic nuclear arms control is needed. The U.S. commitments to maintain the strategic nuclear triad and to pursue further reductions in the context of negotiated cuts together with Russia have had a reassuring effect in Tokyo.[28] But NATO's commitment to seek a negotiated solution to the NSNW problem in Europe has not, as it leaves open the possible relocation of Russian nuclear weapons in a manner that could be threatening to Japan.[29]

As the United States, Japan, and China discuss and debate the requirements of strategic stability, the United States and its allies face two key capability decisions as they implement the comprehensive strengthening approach that will touch directly on questions of strategic stability. The first set of decisions is about regional missile defense. The second set of decisions is about regional conventional strike systems.

Over the last decade, the United States and Japan have made significant progress in developing, deploying, and operating ballistic missile defenses, both separately and together.[30] The RoK has made important progress in deploying lower-tier defenses for the protection of key bases, ports, and urban centers but has not so far fielded capabilities against medium-range missiles. As we now look ahead to the next decade and beyond, it will be important to ensure that U.S., Japanese, and South Korean missile defense planning is well aligned. Planning for the further development and deployment of additional capabilities must be informed by an understanding of how missile defense supports the deterrence and stability strategies of the three allies.

Japan's current plans focus on increasing the number of interceptors and launch vessels while also developing an advanced interceptor in partnership with the United States. Tokyo currently has the ability to provide full missile defense coverage of the Japanese archipelago, though the capacity to conduct multiple intercepts remains modest (hence the decision to increase forces). Its capabilities contribute significantly to American homeland defense, with the x-band radar at Shariki providing early tracking information for U.S. interceptors (the new second radar provides needed new coverage for both the United States and Japan). At some future time Japan may also be in a position to conduct intercepts of attacks from North Korea on the U.S. homeland under the collective defense principle, if political agreement is achieved to interpret the constitution accordingly.[31]

Japanese experts have also set out comprehensively the arguments for the varied contributions of missile defense to deterrence, including to the credibility of U.S. extended deterrence.[32] Some Japanese commentators have recognized the powerful deterrence signal that comes from U.S.–Japanese cooperation in this area.[33]

As the Japanese government determines what kind of future missile defense protection it requires, it will have to address difficult questions about what kind of protection it might want vis-à-vis China. Until now, its focus has been entirely on the missile threat from North Korea. It will also face difficult decisions about whether and how to integrate with RoK missile defenses.

The RoK will face analogous questions. If and as it integrates improved interceptors and sensors into its existing missile defense posture, it will face decisions about how much is enough and whether it can find a balanced approach that provides improved protection against North Korea without generating antagonistic responses from China. Chinese analysts have already expressed concerns about possible RoK acquisition of the THAAD system, on the flawed argument that it will have a negative impact on China's strategic deterrent.[34] In comparison to the Japanese analytic community, the RoK analytic community has generated relatively little new thinking on BMD and its deterrence values.

The second set of pending decisions is about what nonnuclear strike capabilities should be acquired by the three allies.

The United States has significant strike capabilities. It possesses and deploys a large number of conventional weapons that can be delivered at various ranges by different means. But the only means the United States has to strike at long range very promptly is with missiles tipped with nuclear weapons. A prompt but nonnuclear attack capability is of increasing deterrence value as North Korea and others deploy road-mobile missile launchers aimed at the United States and/or its allies, as the threat to employ it preemptively would likely be seen as credible. Having recognized this gap in the U.S. deterrence posture, both the Bush and Obama administrations have sought to develop acquisition strategies for a Conventional Prompt Global Strike (CPGS) system, but so far without success.

Of note, the United States has foresworn the right to deploy intermediate-range land-based missiles in the context of the Treaty on Intermediate-range Nuclear Forces (INF), so this rules out potentially valuable parts of the "solution space." Russia's violation of the INF treaty may lead to the end of this regime and thus open up technical opportunities to solve address this part of the deterrence spectrum.

A key emerging question is whether and how U.S. allies might contribute conventional strike capabilities to regional deterrence architectures. Of the more than forty U.S. allies globally, only approximately ten currently possess long-range ballistic or cruise missiles; this reflects the fact that the United States treats the strike capabilities of individual allies on a case-by-case basis. The United Kingdom is the only country to have received exports of the Tomahawk cruise missile (the nonnuclear variant).[35] In 2012, the United States agreed with the Republic of Korea to support an increase of the range of its domestically produced ballistic missiles as a way to increase the robustness of its overall deterrence posture, which followed prolonged discussion within alliance processes about how to ensure an alliance solution to an alliance problem that would reinforce the comprehensive alliance deterrence architecture.[36]

This raises a logical question about Japan's possible development of a strike capability of its own. This question has been in discussion in Japan episodically since the 1950s and with renewed focus following the Taepodong launches over Japanese territory in 1998.[37] In 2013 the governing Liberal Democratic Party recommended that a future strike system be studied as part of the next National Defense Program Guidelines.[38] A decision to proceed in this direction is possible only after a careful review within the alliance of the benefits, costs, and risks. The benefits to deterrence could be significant. But the costs may be high, especially if strike systems are paid for by decreased missile defense investments. And the risks are difficult to characterize, though negative reactions from Japan's neighbors are quite likely.

Conclusions

In Northeast Asia, as in Europe, extended deterrence has become more important as the security environment has evolved over the last two decades, not less so as might have been expected. New problems have emerged for which these particular U.S. guarantees and capabilities are relevant. In this region, as in Europe, recent years have seen a renewal of high-level focus on extended deterrence and nuclear policy and some significant decisions about how to proceed in adapting and strengthening regional deterrence architectures. Four lessons stand out from this experience.

First, in Northeast Asia as in Europe, the views of U.S. allies are overlapping but not identical. Both Japan and South Korea want to partner with the United States to adapt and strengthen regional deterrence, but they are focused on different challenges. This complicates the pursuit of an integrated approach. But it does not cripple it.

Second, the problem posed by China in Northeast Asia is analogous to but not identical to the problem posed by Russia in Europe. Both oppose the regional security order promoted by the United States and its allies, but Russia has moved to contest that order by military means in a way that China has not. But China is also employing military means—in this case, strong naval and air presence—to bolster its territorial claims in the maritime environment. The fact that China has common economic interests with its neighbors and the United States of a kind that Russia does not have is a positive factor that helps to mitigate the risks of armed conflict. The continued commitment of China's political leadership to a positive relationship with the United States is another important difference.

Third, the commitment of allies in Northeast Asia to a continued role for the U.S. nuclear umbrella has proven to be as strong as the commitment of

NATO allies as reflected in the DDPR result. Moreover, Northeast Asian experts keep a close eye on developments in NATO's nuclear policy and posture for signs of a weakening U.S. commitment to the capability to deploy globally nuclear weapons with nonstrategic delivery systems.[39]

Fourth and finally, there is no reason to think that these issues will become less salient politically in Northeast Asia in the years ahead. Barring some major change in the regional security environment to alleviate nuclear pressures, such as a decision by North Korea to abandon its nuclear weapons or by China to agree to join the nuclear reductions process, the United States can expect a sustained, substantive, high-level discussion of the kind that has become the norm in recent years.

8   The Broader Nuclear Assurance Agenda

AS THE LAST TWO CHAPTERS FOCUSED ON EFFORTS TO strengthen deterrence of regional adversaries, this chapter turns now to the directly related topic of strengthening the assurance of allies. It begins with some conclusions from the prior two chapters about the particular challenges of assuring U.S. allies under the U.S. nuclear umbrella.

But the chapter goes further in exploring the nuclear assurance agenda, because the assurance of allies with an explicit nuclear guarantee from the United States is only one form of assurance required in U.S. nuclear strategy. To better understand the full scope of the assurance agenda, this chapter explores additional assurance requirements—those of U.S. allies and partners not explicitly under the U.S. nuclear umbrella, of other non–nuclear weapon states party to the NPT, of adversaries in time of war, and of Russia and China. The chapter concludes with some observations about the role of U.S. nuclear forces in providing assurance to the United States itself.

On Assuring Allies under the U.S. Nuclear Umbrella

The efforts catalogued in the prior two chapters to strengthen and adapt extended deterrence do not translate automatically into the needed assurance of allies. Recall the high threshold set in the so-called Healey theorem—that successful assurance of U.S. allies facing nuclear threats requires as much as

95 percent confidence that U.S. security guarantees are credible. What lessons can be drawn from the prior two chapters about the assurance of such allies?

A key crosscutting lesson is that some allies are in need of new assurance in the new security environment. To be sure, of the more than forty countries allied with the United States globally, many perceive themselves to be as secure as ever, if not more than before. But approximately a quarter do not; in fact, they are anxious—about emerging threats to their security and about the reliability of U.S. security guarantees in the new security environment.

A second crosscutting lesson is that anxious U.S. allies under the nuclear umbrella are deeply wedded to the balanced approach recommended by the 2009 Strategic Posture Commission and reflected in the 2010 NPR. They are committed to the proposition that the U.S. nuclear deterrent should remain safe, secure, and effective—especially when it may be put to the test on their behalf. They are equally committed to the proposition that the United States should make every reasonable effort to use political and economic tools to try to reduce nuclear dangers—especially when threat reduction may pay local dividends in their regions. Any sign of the United States veering too much in one direction or the other prompts diplomatic and military concern among these anxious allies.

A third crosscutting lesson is that assurance can be strengthened by various means. Assurance flows from continued efforts to ensure that views of the security environment, of its particular deterrence challenges, and of the "right answer" are shared. If the United States and its allies do not see the local context in the same way, assurance is weakened. Assurance also flows from consultations. Allies deserve a seat at the table and full participation when the United States is making decisions potentially affecting their vital interests. When the United States acts unilaterally in making and implementing extended deterrence policies, assurance is weakened. Assurance also flows from the understanding that the commitment expressed in extended deterrence is more than the words of politicians and officials who come and go and of photos on PowerPoint slides. Having firsthand experience of the capabilities the United States contributes to their defense uniquely conveys to allies the depth of investment the United States has made in these capabilities and its own confidence in the credibility of its nuclear deterrent.

A fourth crosscutting lesson is that further reductions in the role and number of U.S. nuclear weapons are troubling to allies who count on credible extended deterrence and on strategic stability between the United States and their major power neighbors. Further bilateral U.S.–Russian reductions are welcomed by nearly all U.S. allies, but uncertainty about how large those reductions might be raises questions for allies in Northeast Asia about strategic stability with China (on the argument that China might seek quantitative parity with Russia and the United States if the reductions are too deep or precipitous). Such reductions also raise questions for some allies about whether a substantially reduced U.S. nuclear force would be capable of deterring both Russia and China at the same time. Further reductions in the U.S. capability to deploy nuclear weapons with nonstrategic delivery systems in support of commitments to allies would raise questions about the effectiveness of regional nuclear deterrence and U.S. resolve to support its allies. Not all allies share these concerns. But those allies anxious about their security are genuinely apprehensive. The Obama administration has built agreement with these allies, and others, about the conditions that would need to be created to take additional steps, especially in Europe, to reduce U.S. nuclear weapons. Washington must remain attentive to these views even as it tries to shape them in a manner consistent with its own.

A final crosscutting lesson is that the assurance of U.S. allies hinges on both dimensions of the Blue theory of victory set out in Chapter 3. Allies seek assurance that deterrence will be effective in crisis and war. Allies also seek assurance that U.S. and allied security strategies will be effective in convincing regional challengers to abandon confrontation and seek cooperation.

In characterizing the progress made in recent years in strengthening the assurance of U.S. allies, a key question emerges: By what metrics can we assess their assurance? Part of the problem is that the assurance of allies is not well studied as a topic separate and apart from its relation to extended deterrence.[1]

One indicator of allied assurance is public opinion polling data. In fact, direct indicators of assurance are rarely tracked among U.S. allies. South Korea is perhaps the most persistent U.S. ally in tracking public confidence in the United States as a security partner and guarantor; the results consistently show high public confidence.[2] Support for the alliance with the United States remains high in both Japan and Europe, especially among NATO's newer members.[3]

The existence of a public debate in one or more countries about acquiring national nuclear deterrents of their own is sometimes taken in the United States as a sign of the failure of assurance. Individual advocates of such a policy may indeed not be assured in the way the United States would wish. But the existence of a debate as such is healthy. After all, the process of adjusting extended deterrence and strengthening it for new purposes is as much a political as a technical endeavor and involves significant political commitments. If the United States and its allies are confident that their policies are well crafted and their posture strong, they should welcome debate about both.

Public opinion is an important indicator of the success of assurance but also an imprecise one, not least because perceptions of the desirability of a security relationship with the United States and of its benefits are colored by many factors, not just or even primarily the credibility of extended deterrence. Accordingly, a narrower body of opinion is also important: that of policy makers and decision makers in allied governments, up to and including the top leadership levels. This is the second important metric. Of course, this opinion is not regularly sampled in a thorough and effective way. But some useful analysis has been done that highlights the positive impact of recent efforts to strengthen assurance in Northeast Asia.[4]

The impact of credibility on the effectiveness of deterrence is much studied, but the impact of credibility on the effectiveness of assurance has received much less attention.[5] The study of the impact of credibility on the effectiveness of deterrence has illuminated the fact that most allied leaders distinguish between the credibility of individuals and the credibility of the United States as such and form judgments about U.S. credibility in particular contexts that are to a significant extent impervious to the ebb and flow of criticism of specific American presidents. This logic may well apply in the assurance domain as well. This may help to explain the relative continuity of allied views on the credibility of the United States even as the domestic U.S. political popularity of presidents rises and falls.

The debate about credibility is at its core a debate about the choices that might be made or avoided in a future conflict.[6] Thus, it is a debate that ebbs and flows with new evidence and new political factors but that cannot be settled definitively except in the case of a test in war.

A third and final metric of successful assurance is the way a nation postures itself for a possible future decision to rely on its own means for deterrence. In other words, how it hedges is a signal of how assured it is. A hedge is a measure to protect oneself against a future loss with compensating measures. In the security domain, states sometimes hedge against negative developments in their security environment that are unlikely but plausible and consequential for their security. They identify risks and take steps to reduce them. There is a long history of hedging behavior among states that joined the Nuclear Non-Proliferation Treaty as non–nuclear weapon states, that see as plausible even if unlikely that the regime might collapse in the future and put in place some of the capabilities and capacities they would need to develop deterrents of their own in that circumstance. Some have been content with a modest level of scientific know-how. Others have sought more robust industrial capacity. Still others have positioned themselves near a higher threshold from which they could move into the nuclear weapons domain without significant additional effort extending over many years and decades.[7]

Over the decades, these hedges have been adjusted in response to changing circumstances, with some states adopting more relaxed hedges as their security environment improved, while others have made the hedge more robust as their security environment grew more troubled. For example, after the U.S. withdrawal from Southeast Asia in the mid-1970s, some U.S. allies took steps to strengthen their nuclear hedge.[8] Today, some U.S. allies seek to develop nuclear power industries in what might be a move to improve future capacity for nuclear weapon development—Turkey, for example.[9] Some maintain a robust hedge posture. Japan, for example, has many of the technical capacities in place for potential future nuclear requirements, and its debate about whether to maintain a nuclear power industry after the Fukushima accident is in part a debate about whether to maintain that national security hedge.[10] For many countries, the latent military potential is merely a by-product of investments in nuclear technology made solely for purposes of power generation and other civilian applications. Alas, no systematic analysis has been done of hedge capabilities as an indicator of assurance.[11]

Is it possible to achieve 100 percent assurance of those U.S. allies who are anxious about their security and the effectiveness of U.S. guarantees? Probably not. Strategic dependence must sit uncomfortably with any country, especially one facing a plausible threat to its vital interests. Allies must always concern themselves with the effectiveness and credibility of their partners and cannot take either for granted.

Is 100 percent assurance necessary? It may be preferable, but it is not necessary. As a practical matter, reliance on the United States for extended deterrence must simply seem preferable to the plausible alternatives. One alternative is acquiescence to, and appeasement of, the political demands of a local challenger. This is anathema to countries with any plausible alternative. In practice, however, a modified form may be pursued, as allies depart more frequently from U.S. policy preferences and bandwagon increasingly with neighboring major powers in a bid to avoid pressure from them. The other alternative is to move away from reliance on the United States by acquiring an independent nuclear deterrent.

On the face of it, this second alternative is appealing as a solution to the problems of strategic dependence on another country. A state with its own nuclear weapons need not overly concern itself with the credibility of the United States or the capacities of U.S. deterrent forces or the quality of its consultations with it. Moreover, there is an argument (inherited from the Cold War) about the deterrence values of "second centers of decision," to the effect that deterrence is strengthened if an enemy has to deter not one but multiple nuclear-armed states, any one of which might opt not to be deterred. This was an argument used to defend the strategic value of the then-new British deterrent in the 1960s.[12] It was a way of thinking long advanced by Kenneth Waltz with his argument that "more nuclear proliferation may be better" because nuclear deterrents are proven sources of international stability.[13] More recently, some analysts have argued that American interests in effective deterrence in the 21st century would be better served by facilitating rather than resisting nuclear weapon acquisition by U.S. allies.[14]

On closer examination, this second alternative has many deficiencies. Unless there were to be a complete breakdown first of the nuclear nonproliferation regime, such a step would require withdrawal by a U.S. ally from the NPT and, potentially, a long list of associated penalties and consequences, including especially in terms of access to the global trade in nuclear-related materials and technologies. In the absence of such a breakdown, any U.S. or other assistance to any ally to acquire nuclear weapons would itself be a violation of the NPT. Moreover, any decision by an ally today to acquire nuclear weapons would be widely interpreted as a loss of confidence in the United States; indeed, it would likely put into question the very premise of the alliance relationship with the United States (which is that the two countries have sufficiently convergent national security interests to join as allies). Additionally, even if a U.S. ally might be able to replace or perhaps even improve its level of deterrence protection by acquiring nuclear weapons of its own, it could not replace the power and influence of the United States in shaping the security environment in other ways that reinforce deterrence and also that may reduce or eliminate threats through cooperative political and other measures.

On balance, this analysis suggests that the benefits of remaining a non-nuclear ally of the United States are high relative to the benefits of the available options, while the costs are relatively low. Thus it is hardly surprising that no U.S. ally has determined to have nuclear weapons of its own since the very earliest days of the Cold War, when Britain and France chose to do so (and at a time when the U.S. commitment to Europe's security was not as clear as it became later). This points to the conclusion that even imperfect but relatively high assurance is sufficient for the basic political requirement.

This line of argument could be read incorrectly to imply that the purpose of U.S. security guarantees to its allies is to keep them from going nuclear. The United States does not have allies to keep them from doing things they think are needed for their security. It has allies because it has shared interests with them of a kind that warrant cooperative defense. A benefit of these alliance relationships is evident in the nonproliferation domain—but this is not the purpose as such.

On Assuring Allies and Partners Not Explicitly under the Nuclear Umbrella

The cases so far examined address the unique assurance requirements of U.S. allies that are the beneficiaries of some form of explicit nuclear guarantee from the United States. In fact, such explicit guarantees are not provided universally to U.S. allies. Although all U.S. allies and partners are covered by the general declaratory policies issued by U.S. presidents (and as reflected in the 2010 NPR Report), no treaty establishing a security relationship with another state explicitly extends U.S. nuclear protection to others. The United States has elaborated specific nuclear roles in its security relations with other states only in response to specific requirements and circumstances.

The assurance of allies and partners not explicitly under the U.S. nuclear umbrella is also a U.S. policy objective and raises some important and challenging nuclear policy questions. This is a diverse group and includes U.S. allies and partner states around the globe. The following analysis focuses on one subset: U.S. security partners in the Persian Gulf.[15]

The possibility that Iran might emerge as a nuclear-armed state has raised many difficult questions for U.S. policy makers about how to adapt and strengthen the regional deterrence architecture there and what a tailored nuclear component might require in the future. Failure of U.S. assurance in this region could reinforce the possibility that an Iranian decision to cross the nuclear threshold would cause a nuclear tipping point and the active, competitive pursuit of nuclear weapons and the means to deliver them by multiple states in the region.[16] Iran's ongoing development and deployment of ballistic and cruise missiles of ever-longer ranges, in combination with an assertive and sometimes coercive regional political posture, have already catalyzed an effort in the region to adapt and strengthen regional deterrence, with strong U.S. engagement. This work echoes the July 2009 statement by then Secretary of State Hillary Clinton:

> We want Iran to calculate what I think is a fair assessment, that if the U.S. extends a defense umbrella over the region, if we do even more to support the military capacity of those in the gulf, it's unlikely that Iran will be any stronger or safer, because they won't be able to intimidate and dominate, as they apparently believe they can, once they have a nuclear weapon.[17]

The U.S. approach to adapting and strengthening regional deterrence reflects the unique historical, geographic, and political features of the Middle East and of the U.S. role in it. Unlike Europe but like Northeast Asia, there is no multilateral security architecture to build on. The United States has bilateral alliance relations with a number of states. Its security relationship with Israel is anathema to many of its other security partners, who reject any cooperative effort to strengthen regional deterrence in a manner that could be seen to be to Israel's benefit. Unlike both Europe and Northeast Asia, there is no neighboring major power with interests of a kind to cast a shadow over efforts to strengthen regional deterrence (Russia's security interests here being of a different character from its interests in Europe). Unlike both Europe and Northeast Asia, there is no history in this region of the forward stationing of U.S. nuclear weapons—or of nuclear consultations and sharing arrangements. Also unlike Europe and Northeast Asia, the long-term presence ashore of American military forces is widely seen as unacceptable. Moreover, the Middle East is passing through a period of intense and far-reaching political change, with an impact on future stability and political alignments that cannot yet be ascertained, and which raises important questions about the future U.S. role in the region.

To the extent there is a regional approach to adapting and strengthening the regional deterrence architecture, it is built on collaborations within the Gulf Cooperation Council (GCC). The participating states began a formal dialogue on Persian Gulf security in 2006. In March 2012, the United States and the GCC partners established a Strategic Cooperation Forum with the objective of enhancing cooperation on a broad set of political, economic, and military issues.[18] In the military domain, key objectives are to integrate defense planning and procurement, to integrate air defenses, and to enhance cooperation on regional missile defense.[19]

Looking to the future of U.S.-led efforts to adapt and strengthen regional deterrence, there are at least three key challenges.

First, within the region there is broad agreement about the deterrence and protection values of ballistic missile defense, and thus a desire to strengthen cooperation and integration. But while the United States cooperates and integrates with Israel, other U.S. allies and partners in the region will not do so. This points to a continuing challenge of integrating sensors and data communications in a way that aligns with political preferences.

Second, within the region there is rising interest in conventional strike capabilities, including missiles. How to meet the demand from allies for such systems without intensifying arms competitions in the region, and creating new threats to those outside the region, is a key emerging challenge.

Third, there is evidence of a rising discussion in the region about the needed nuclear response if and as Iran crosses the nuclear threshold. That discussion appears to be at its most advanced in Saudi Arabia. According to one recent study, the key concerns driving the Saudi discussion are the need to defend the holy sites by Muslim means, Iran's aggressive behavior and hegemonic ambitions, and the loss of strategic balance in the relationship with Israel.[20] The author, Norman Cigar, argues that Saudi leaders believe in nuclear deterrence and have considered carefully the options available to them.[21] The option of relying on the United States for extended deterrence has been thoroughly vetted, he maintains, and deemed unacceptable for various reasons, including the argument that it is "the job of Arabs to defend Arabs."[22] He argues further that the Saudi leadership assesses U.S. credibility to be low, given policy failures in Syria and in managing the transition through the Arab Spring and its aftermath.[23] Accordingly, Cigar provides evidence that the Saudis expect a transfer of nuclear weapons from Pakistan, and with that transfer Riyadh anticipates extending a nuclear umbrella to others.[24] His central conclusion is as follows:

> The regime's need to retain its legitimacy, embodied in a requirement to defend the country and the region from an Iranian threat, has provided a key impulse to addressing the nuclear issue, and Riyadh has been building a number of blocks with a view toward preparing the domestic and regional publics if and when the time comes to exercise its nuclear option. . . . There is a strong likelihood that Saudi Arabia will seek to acquire nuclear weapons when and if Iran does so.[25]

In a meeting with U.S. Middle East expert Dennis Ross in 2009, King Abdullah reportedly stated twice that "if they get nuclear weapons, we will get nuclear weapons."[26]

These assessments are not universally shared within the U.S. analytic community. Surveying the available evidence, other analysts are skeptical that the Saudis would see nuclear weapons as necessary or useful even if Iran were to acquire and field them and would focus instead on strengthening its conventional defenses and developing a robust hedge against a future decision to build nuclear weapons.[27]

The Saudi case is taken here as a single case study. The introduction of nuclear competition into the Middle East could have a cascading nuclear proliferation effect, causing additional states to seek to acquire nuclear weapons and perhaps also to establish new relationships of extended deterrence. The policy tools available to the United States to address the ensuing pressures are not as promising as the tools available in Europe and Northeast Asia. Striking a long-term deal with Iran that secures its nuclear capabilities on a peaceful and transparent basis would contribute very significantly to avoiding a set of future policy challenges that would be even more daunting.

As already noted, the nuclear component of the comprehensive strengthening approach is tailored in a quite specific way in this region. U.S. nuclear weapons are not deployed in the region; nor are there explicit, treaty-based nuclear guarantees to individual allies. But the United States retains the means to employ nuclear weapons any time its vital interests, or those of its allies and partners, are at risk. And it maintains the means to do so with both the strategic assets in the triad and dual-capable, forward-deployable fighter-bombers.

Any future variation on this approach will have to be tailored to address new security and political factors. The conditions under which the United States would formalize nuclear deterrence arrangements with allies in the Middle East are difficult to imagine. Even more difficult to imagine are the circumstances that would permit the deployment there of U.S. nuclear weapons and the stationing of dual-capable aircraft in sharing arrangements with regional allies. This suggests that any future expression of the U.S. nuclear umbrella to the region will be done indirectly with assets from outside the region and with political statements of strategic intent. Of course, strategic surprises of various kinds have regularly led to policy choices in Washington and elsewhere that were difficult to imagine ahead of time.

What conclusions follow about the assurance requirements of U.S. allies and partners not explicitly under the nuclear umbrella? In certain cases, the requirements may not be difficult to meet—but accordingly are easily overlooked. Australia is an example of a U.S. ally not highly concerned about the credibility of U.S. extended deterrence but seeking engagement and sustained participation in efforts to adapt and strengthen the deterrence architecture in the Western Pacific. In other cases, the requirements may be impossible to meet. If the line of analysis given in the preceding pages about Saudi Arabia proves valid, then the United States must conclude that it cannot provide a measure of assurance to at least one key Middle Eastern ally sufficient to induce it to increase its reliance on U.S. extended deterrence as a substitute for proceeding with a nuclear deterrent of its own. This conclusion will be tested if and as Iran crosses the nuclear threshold.

On Assuring Non–Nuclear Weapon States Party to the NPT

An additional form of assurance is needed by states that opted to join the NPT as non–nuclear weapon states. Having made a political decision some decades ago (the treaty entered into force in 1970) to forswear the right to nuclear weapons, these states need regular assurance that the bargain they made is sound. Of course this category of states includes the states in the first two categories already discussed; but it also includes a much larger number of states not allied or aligned with any state and not interested in promises from the United States to use nuclear weapons in their defense (though potentially quite interested in the effective functioning of the United Nations Security Council in dealing with threats to international peace and security).

Non–nuclear weapon states party to the NPT are beneficiaries of two types of security assurances by the five nuclear weapon states recognized by the treaty. Positive assurances are promises to come to the aid of such states if they are the victim of nuclear threats or attack. Negative assurances are promises not to threaten or use nuclear weapons against them.[28] The nuclear weapon states attach certain conditions to these assurances; the Obama administration's adjustments to the U.S. negative security assurance were discussed in Chapter 1. The credibility and effectiveness of such assurances has been a topic of continuing debate and analysis.[29]

A central question is the impact of Ukraine crisis on positive security assurances. This question arises because of the failure to uphold the Budapest memorandum. This is the 1994 agreement whereby Ukraine agreed to transfer to Russia the nuclear weapons it inherited with the collapse of the Soviet Union in exchange for promises by the United States, Russia, and the United Kingdom to "respect the independence and sovereignty and the existing borders of Ukraine" and "refrain from the threat or use of force against the territorial integrity or political independence of Ukraine."[30] These promises were built directly on the foundations of analogous assurances by the nuclear weapon states in the context of the NPT. Non–nuclear weapon states party to the NPT have long demanded legally binding assurances from the nuclear weapon states as opposed to unilateral statements of political intent. They are likely to interpret the Ukraine crisis as confirming the near irrelevance of assurances that are not legally binding. Russia showed itself willing to infringe the independence and sovereignty of Ukraine, and the United States and the United Kingdom showed themselves unwilling to employ force to ensure that the terms of the agreement were honored. This cannot help but have a corrosive impact on the nonproliferation regime.

While this debate unfolds, we should be looking more broadly into what is required to assure these states. It is useful to think of both a minimum and maximum assurance requirement of non–nuclear weapon states party to the NPT. The minimum assurance requirement of these states is that the NPT and associated regime of monitoring and compliance mechanisms not be at serious and imminent risk of collapse. This has been a rising challenge since the decision of states party to the NPT to extend the treaty indefinitely in

1995.[31] In a legal sense, that decision was taken without conditions. But practically and politically, the conditions were expressed in the form of a program of work to advance implementation of the treaty's objectives. That program of work has proven difficult to implement, and many non–nuclear weapon states believe that the commitments of 1995 on disarmament, entry into force of the Comprehensive Test Ban Treaty, and the Middle East (with a program of worked aimed at addressing the problem of nuclear weapons there) simply have not been fulfilled. Moreover, continued concern about the potential for nuclear tipping points in both Northeast Asia and the Middle East has fueled expectations of future regime collapse.

The maximum assurance requirement of these states is that the NPT and associated regime be effective at delivering the objectives of the treaty—and in a timely fashion. This too has been a rising challenge in recent years, given revelations about the limited effectiveness of the regime in dealing with willful challengers such as Iraq and North Korea. The emergence of informal supplier networks of technology, materials, and expertise and the associated proliferation pathways outside the state system have only worsened the picture. The failure of the nuclear weapon states to live up to expectations that they would cut their nuclear arsenals and eliminate them after the Cold War has magnified the perception of the regime as ineffective.

It is not up to the United States alone to determine the success or failure of the NPT regime. But, as the regime's most powerful adherent, it is in a position to help it succeed—or, alternatively, to do it grievous damage. The damage would be done if the United States were to reject dialogue with the non–nuclear weapon states or were to cease making its case for squaring its twin commitments to deterrence and disarmament. The help must be provided in many ways. These include direct engagement at all levels of the nonproliferation regime as well as policies and a deterrence posture aligned with NPT commitments. This requires that they be consistent with national leadership promises to reduce reliance on nuclear weapons to the extent possible, to reduce their number in a safe manner and to constrain their potential future use.

Looking to the future, a central question is whether the United States and other advocates of practical steps toward long-term goals can effectively engage the non–nuclear weapon states in a frank discussion about what is possible in today's world as opposed to the world as envisioned at prior review conferences. The Obama administration has made a good-faith effort to create the conditions that would allow the other nuclear weapon states to join it in taking additional steps to reduce the role and number of nuclear weapons in a manner consistent with NPT obligations and the results, as reflected in this volume, are both disappointing and corrosive for the treaty regime. Concrete steps to advance the nonproliferation and disarmament objectives of the NPT must reflect this experience and the lessons that can be learned from it.

On Assuring Adversaries in Time of War

Assurance strategies must address also an entirely different category of states: adversaries. The effective functioning of deterrence requires an element of assurance. The adversary must believe that the restraint asked of it by the United States and its allies will be reciprocated by restraint of their own.

According to the standard model of deterrence, as the United States and its allies try to influence the decision calculus of an enemy about initiating, escalating, or terminating a war, the adversary will be calculating the benefits, costs, and risks of the action we seek to deter while at the same time calculating the benefits, costs, and risks of inaction. For deterrence to function, the adversary must conclude that inaction will be rewarded with a result that is better than the result that might have come with action. As Thomas Schelling put it five decades ago, "To say, 'One more step and I shoot,' can be a deterrent threat only if accompanied by the implicit assurance, 'And if you stop, I won't.'"[32] In a war in which the enemy stops short of unleashing all the means available to it to avoid the risk or likely penalty of regime removal, it must also believe that the United States will not seek regime removal even if its deterrence is successful in inducing the enemy's restraint.

This is a difficult form of assurance for the United States to deliver. It may forswear regime removal as a goal or promise not to impose other penalties on the aggressor regime and stop short, as it did in the Persian Gulf War of 1990–1991. But it may not have the means—or desire—to take an active role in preserving the regime as a conflict winds down and new political factors come into play domestically and/or regionally that put the regime in jeopardy. The George H. W. Bush administration forswore regime removal in the war to expel Iraq from Kuwait in 1990–1991, but the ensuring peace was sufficiently unacceptable to the George W. Bush administration that it pursued regime removal.

The difficulty of delivering this form of assurance is magnified by the deep grievance that leaders like Kim Jong Un, Ayatollah Khamenei, or Mullah

Omar hold against the United States and the regional orders it helps to secure at their expense. As pragmatic as they may be in any given instance, they seem strongly disinclined to accept an American promise that the United States will not do their regime, their interests, and their long-term vision harm again, sooner or later. After all, regime change remains the long-term U.S. goal, even if its preference is to accomplish that goal by peaceful means. Such assurance may also falter on a problem identified by Lawrence Freedman in 2004: "Compliance [with a U.S. demand] may be a form of humiliation and an acknowledgment of submission."[33]

Looking to the future, the United States should be analyzing how to send signals to specific adversaries in specific crises, with the expectation that this will enhance the effectiveness of U.S. strategic messages if crisis comes. But it should also be realistic in appreciating the limits of its ability to effectively communicate assurance messages in crisis, leading to behaviors from adversaries that the United States would likely perceive as irrational in terms of the interests of those adversaries as the United States might understand them.

On Assuring Russia and China

If ever there were a major war between the United States and Russia or China, the assurance requirements set out in the previous section would also be relevant. They would want assurance that the United States would avoid escalatory steps if they were to also avoid them. But the focus here is on the assurance demands of strategic stability in peacetime as opposed to crisis stability in time of war.[34]

At the most basic level, Russia and China seek three forms of strategic assurance from the United States in peacetime as opposed to war. The first is that the United States will not use its power to their disadvantage in their regions at a time when they perceive themselves as militarily and economically weak. The second is that the United States is not seeking to escape the nuclear revolution in world politics by putting itself in a position to use its conventional and perhaps even nuclear weapons against them even at a future time when they have redressed their military and economic weakness. The third is that the United States will not actively seek to destabilize their regimes and foment internal opposition. The former is a short-term challenge, while the latter two are longer term.

Each post–Cold War U.S. president has sought to provide such assurances, as Chapter 1 attests. Administrations have tried to calibrate the needed level of assurance: sufficient to make worst-case military planning by Moscow or Beijing seem unnecessary but not so restrained as to be taken as a message of appeasement and unwittingly invite new tests of American resolve.[35] Yet the assurance requirements have to date been poorly met, as leaders in both Moscow and Beijing remain highly motivated by the specter of American coercion. Indeed, it may be that these requirements are impossible to meet, if minds have closed in both capitals and/or there has so far been insufficient effort and creativity in finding ways to build the needed transparency, confidence, and trust in all three capitals.[36] The failure of various U.S. reassurance efforts to actually reassure Moscow and Beijing is telling and implies that their reassurance requires more than promises of American strategic restraint.

Moreover, it is possible that the United States will become less willing to try to meet these assurance requirements in the future. In the immediate aftermath of the annexation of Crimea, there is no appetite in Washington for assuring Moscow's current leaders on any point—except on American resolve to defend its allies. More important, the ease with which American military experts have readily expressed support for mutual vulnerability in the U.S.-Russian strategic relationship is firmly rooted in the logic and experiences of the Cold War. If one has in mind the experience of the 1961 Berlin crisis or the 1962 Cuban missile crisis, the logic of a mutual interest in avoiding nuclear Armageddon is clear. If one has in mind the experience of 2014 and Russia's new military assertiveness and new theory of victory vis-à-vis the West, the logic of mutual interest in avoiding nuclear first use is less clear.

Analogous arguments may be made vis-à-vis China. As noted in a preceding chapter, the United States has never accepted mutual vulnerability as the basis of the strategic relationship with China; doing so in the future may become more politically difficult if it is seen to reinforce attempts by China to challenge the regional security order and jeopardize strategic stability.

In short, the demands of Russia and China for strategic assurance of various kinds may well go unmet. There may also be a more fundamental problem at work here. The governments in Moscow and Beijing may be of a type that cannot be assured. The Russian government is threatened by color revolutions and has had to use force to suppress popular opposition to its rule. It imputes to the United States a nefarious role in shaping or leading prodemocracy movements in Russia and in former Soviet republics as a way to misdirect attention from the genuinely local character of the prodemocracy spirit. To be sure, Western values, and the success of the West more generally as a community governed by those values, helped to inspire those revolutions. Moreover, the Russian government is a kleptocracy that serves both the private interests of its leading members as well as the public interests of Russia as it understands them—a fact that may reinforce perceptions of vulnerability.[37]

The Chinese government is similarly haunted by the prospect of domestic instability arising from political opposition to the continued dominance of the Chinese Communist Party. It too is fearful of the consequences of a stronger U.S. commitment to human rights and the rule of law.

In short, it is unreasonable to expect to be able to fully address the concerns and anxieties of these regimes of U.S. strategic intentions so long as they lack political legitimacy and enduring popular support and foment suspicion of the United States in part in a bid to bolster domestic political legitimacy.

On Assuring the United States

Lastly and finally in this catalogue of assurance requirements, we come to the United States. It may seem odd that the most powerful state in the world requires assurance of its own. But in fact, the United States seeks many forms of assurance in the current security environment.

The United States seeks assurance that the proliferation of nuclear weapons and long-range delivery systems will not fundamentally alter the global order or paralyze the functioning of common and collective defense arrangements.

It seeks assurance from Russia and China that its restraint in the development of its strategic military posture, in the form of limited ballistic missile defenses and limited conventional strike capabilities and additional nuclear reductions, will be reciprocated. The United States must be concerned that Russia and China might themselves contest the existing vision of stability at the strategic nuclear level and, as they modernize their forces, deploy new capabilities that pose new threats and new challenges to deterrence. More specifically, the United States must be concerned that they will exploit its restraint at the theater nuclear level to gain military advantage and political influence. As a general matter, Russia and China have scoffed at such U.S. requirements, as they lead the charge in arguing that the United States is seeking "absolute security" for itself.

The United States seeks various forms of assurance from its allies. It seeks assurance that they will share the burdens and costs of strengthening regional deterrence architectures even as they share the benefits and that they will stand up with the United States in confronting dangerous adversaries.[38] As Secretary of State Hillary Clinton argued in 2011, "As a nuclear alliance, sharing [NATO's] nuclear risks and responsibilities widely is fundamental."[39] There continues to be debate in the United States about how equitably these burdens and risks are shared in the alliance. Franklin C. Miller, for example, has argued as follows about the European advocates of the withdrawal of U.S. nuclear weapons:

> By shirking the responsibility for nuclear risk sharing and burden sharing—but not the need for nuclear deterrence—they are asking the American people to put the U.S. homeland at risk while they get a free ride. There can be no more cynical expression of this than the statement attributed to [German] Foreign Minister Westerwelle last year that NATO needed a nuclear umbrella but that that umbrella should be based in the United States . . . This attitude assumes that America's willingness to defend NATO is a constant; it ignores the fact that American internationalism is an historical aberration: isolation, rather than engagement, has been the dominant theme throughout most of our history. Try explaining to a freshman Congressman why the U.S. homeland should be subject to nuclear attacks to deter aggression against NATO while NATO allies are unwilling even to share the risk and burden of basing a very small part of the deterrent on their soil. And good luck in doing so.[40]

Washington also seeks assurance that its allies will not act precipitously in a crisis such that the United States is drawn into a war it views as having been avoidable and in a manner that requires it to use military means it might have otherwise sought to withhold or keep in reserve.[41] From its nuclear allies in particular (Britain and France), the United States seeks assurances that the three will act in concert rather than at cross purposes in any conflict invoking questions of nuclear employment by one or all.

The United States also seeks to assure itself that geopolitical surprise will not jeopardize its vital interests, including the regional orders it seeks to defend and its continued role as a security guarantor. In an effort to review nearly five decades of nuclear history, James Schlesinger argued in 1993 that the primary impact of nuclear weapons to that point in history was not deterrence of conflict in Europe but empowering American leadership after World

War II by making its price seem bearable.[42] In short, America's nuclear deterrent had an assurance value: that, even after a long depression and world war, the United States had the means to run the risks of engagement and leadership in a changing and dangerous world.

In recent decades, the classic formulation of this requirement to anticipate geopolitical surprise has been for the United States to be ready for the possibility that the Soviet Union, then Russia, might not comply with an existing strategic arms control treaty obligation and might seek to break out by recreating forces that it had eliminated under that treaty. Accordingly, the United States has sought to hedge against this form of geopolitical surprise by maintaining the ability to reconstitute its strategic nuclear forces to the level in place before implementation of each new treaty began.

Given the changing international security environment, it is increasingly useful to think about additional dimensions of the needed geopolitical hedge. Two potential requirements can be identified at this time. The first relates to China. The requirement is to be able to reconstitute some strategic forces in case China were ever to conclude that it should increase its strategic forces to establish quantitative parity with the United States and Russia. Given uncertainties about the true size of China's strategic forces, there may also be a case for hedging against the possibility that China maintains hidden forces that could be deployed in time of crisis.

The second relates to adversarial multipolarity. A significant geopolitical surprise would result from the breakdown of existing regional nuclear orders in the Middle East and/or East Asia and the potential emergence of new nuclear-armed actors, new extenders of nuclear deterrence protection, and new coalitions hostile to the United States. The hedge requirement is to be able to create in a timely fashion the future desired mix of defensive and offensive forces and to work with our allies toward those ends as well.

These are potential geopolitical surprises; they are not predictions. But they are sufficiently plausible to require some tailoring of the U.S. military posture to ensure an effective hedge. That tailoring must be in the nuclear domain, where reconstitution, upload, and flexible infrastructure remain important hedge capabilities. But tailoring must encompass also the nonnuclear elements of the comprehensive approach to strengthening regional deterrence architectures, so that, for example, BMD and strike systems can be rapidly adapted to new circumstances if the need emerges. The hedge posture of the

United States must be sufficient to enable timely changes to these nonnuclear elements as well as the nuclear elements of the standing force.

In short, assurance of the United States requires in part a hedge tailored to potential future requirements created by geopolitical surprises.

Competing Agendas

It is not possible to meet the assurance requirements of all of these actors at all times. There are trade-offs among competing priorities to consider. Three stand out.

There is an obvious trade-off between assuring allies and assuring major powers. U.S. allies seek assurances that regional deterrence architectures will remain effective against evolving threats, while major powers seek assurances that those architectures will not be turned against them. Conversely, Russia and China seek assurances on future U.S. missile defense and strike capabilities will remain limited, while allies seek assurances that these capabilities will continue to grow to address local threats. The premise of U.S. policy is that there is a fine line that allows the needed assurance of both—a fine line that has been difficult to find.

A second trade-off is between assuring non–nuclear weapon states and U.S. allies anxious about the credibility of extended U.S. deterrence guarantees. Non–nuclear weapon states seek assurance that the United States remains committed to the disarmament goal and is willing to take continued steps in that direction, while anxious U.S. allies worry that the capabilities most valued for extended deterrence will be the next sacrifices to the disarmament goal. Ironically, as many U.S. allies both support disarmament and depend on extended deterrence, both forms of assurance are sometimes required for individual allies. This challenge is compounded in the NATO context, as among the twenty-eight allies are states with different views about which priority should dominate.

A third trade-off is between assuring adversaries in time of war and assuring the United States. Adversaries would seek assurance from the United States that their regimes would survive intact in exchange for a promise to de-escalate, while the United States would seek assurance that any such conflict under the nuclear shadow would teach the right lessons about its power and about the utility of nuclear weapons.

Conclusion

The nuclear assurance agenda of the United States begins with the assurance of U.S. allies under the U.S. nuclear umbrella. But it does not stop there. This chapter has explored five additional assurance challenges for U.S. nuclear policy. Some put particular demands on the U.S. nuclear umbrella. Others require broader military solutions. Still others are amenable only to diplomatic and other political strategies. Accordingly, these assurance requirements put multiple and sometimes competing demands on U.S. nuclear policy and posture.

Assurance, like beauty, is in the eye of the beholder. There is much that the United States can say and do to influence the assessments of others, whether friend, foe, or potential foe. Especially with friends, its views are influential. But they are not decisive. So long as assurance remains an important objective of American policy, then the United States must sometimes take steps it would not otherwise take for the sole purpose of deterrence. This chapter has highlighted the many ways that U.S. nuclear weapons and strategy have assurance values in the 21st-century security environment that are sometimes overlooked in the debate about their deterrence values. When it comes to the assurance of the United States, it is important to remember that the U.S. nuclear posture has a continuing role in making bearable the burdens of leadership in dangerous times.

9 Conclusions

CHAPTERS 2 THROUGH 8 HAVE REVIEWED THE EXPERIENCE OF the United States over the last twenty-five years in adapting deterrence to a changed and changing world and in creating the conditions to further reduce the number and role of nuclear weapons. With this experience in mind, we can now return to the questions posed at the end of Chapter 1: Do the conditions now exist that would allow the United States to take additional substantial steps to safely reduce the role of nuclear weapons in its security strategies and the number of nuclear weapons in its arsenal (recalling the catalogue at the end of Chapter 1)? If they do not exist today, can they reasonably be expected to be brought into being soon enough to avoid the modernization of some or all U.S. nuclear forces? What lessons follow from this experience about the case against nuclear weapons and for nuclear disarmament? What lessons follow for the case for U.S. nuclear weapons? What does this case imply about the needed U.S. nuclear posture?

Do the Conditions Exist Now for Further Steps? Are they Proximate?

In a positive and pragmatic way, the United States has worked to seize the opportunities presented by the end of the Cold War, to transform political relationships with Russia and China in a way that would make the nuclear factor ever less relevant, to prevent the emergence of new threats for which nuclear weapons would be relevant, to adapt extended deterrence to new purposes, and to assure allies in a changing security environment. Within the tradition of policy as pursued over four administrations since the end of the Cold War, the Obama administration pursued a more specific set of goals. How far have we gotten?

The proliferation risks posed by North Korea and Iran have been a priority for the Obama administration, as for its predecessors. It sought dialogue with each with an eye to eliciting their nuclear restraint and avoiding a nuclear standoff. This policy has gotten nowhere with North Korea. The leadership in Pyongyang perceives itself as vulnerable to hostile American policies and in need of a nuclear deterrent to ensure the security of the regime and state. The circumstances that would lead Pyongyang to conclude that it can safely relinquish its nuclear arsenal are not conceivable today. It may be that only regime change will make this possible. This is plausible only with wide-reaching economic, social, and political reform.

The policy of dialogue and negotiation with Tehran has paid a dividend in 2015 but leaves an open long-term question. Even if Iran stops short of developing and deploying nuclear weapons at this time, its latent potential to do so, along with its arsenal of long-range ballistic missiles, poses a deterrence challenge. Tehran too perceives itself as vulnerable to hostile American policies and in need of a robust deterrent to ensure the security of the regime and state.

Accordingly, rather than welcoming Pyongyang and Tehran to "a solid international consensus against nuclear weapons," U.S. policy makers must instead be concerned with the requirements of effective deterrence of them, and of effective assurance of U.S. allies neighboring them.

With Russia, the objective of the incoming Obama administration was to try to put past difficulties behind us and to use arms control as a means to help accelerate positive changes in the security and political relationships. This effort has come to an apparent dead end. The pathway forward has been blocked by Moscow as it "snaps back hard" against a security order perceived by President Putin as damaging to Russian interests. He has rejected an additional bilateral arms control step with the United States. Efforts to promote cooperation with Russia on missile defense, on both U.S.–Russia and NATO–Russia tracks, have come to a dead end over differences that can only be understood as historically entrenched. The West must now address in a serious and sustained way difficult questions about how its deterrence and defense posture toward Russia must be adapted, and so too its political strategies. As discussed in Chapter 6, in the absence of a cooperative approach with Russia to strategic stability, unilateral action by NATO is needed to preserve strategic stability.

Accordingly, nuclear deterrence continues to play a role in the West's relations with Russia, a point Mr. Putin pointedly and frequently makes. The question of future nuclear reductions and an additional arms control measure may not ultimately be settled until expiration of the New START Treaty in 2021 (or 2026, if it is extended once for five years by mutual consent, as permitted). By that time, much more will have changed in Russia's relations with the West, in directions impossible to predict.

With China, the Obama administration's objective in 2009 was to begin a substantive dialogue on nuclear policy and posture in the context of a broader dialogue on strategic stability. A closely related objective was to bring China's transparency practices into better alignment with the practices of the other nuclear weapon states and thus to begin to mitigate some of the mounting pressures on strategic stability. As of late 2014, there is nothing to show for the administration's efforts in this regard. For nearly twenty years now, China has refused to move forward on nuclear dialogue with the United States. Its transparency practices have improved on nuclear policy and strategy but not at all on capabilities and plans for future forces. Moreover, the buildup of China's nuclear forces continues. There is no prospect at this time of China joining the nuclear reductions process or even clarity about the conditions that would allow it to do so at some future time.

With allies, the Obama administration's objective has been to develop and implement in partnership with them comprehensive strategies for strengthening regional deterrence architectures. The changes between Cold War–vintage approaches to extended deterrence and 21st-century approaches are profound. As a general matter, the role of nuclear weapons has been reduced relative to the roles of other capabilities in the extended deterrence toolkit. But it has not been possible to eliminate the requirement for those U.S. nuclear capabilities uniquely associated with extended deterrence—nuclear weapons that can be deployed in support of U.S. allies with nonstrategic delivery systems. America's most secure allies might be willing to accept that their requirements for nuclear protection from the United States can readily be met by its strategic forces alone. But its less secure and more anxious allies believe otherwise. Abandoning these capabilities now would be interpreted by such allies as signaling that the United States puts its interest in taking next steps on disarmament ahead of its interests in protecting them. This could have a significant negative impact on nonproliferation if these allies come to the point of concluding that they need nuclear weapons of their own. This was once a taboo topic but is no more.

In terms of the grand disarmament project, these objectives of the Obama administration are relatively modest. These next steps on the pathway to zero, as it has envisioned them, are a very long way from the last steps. Yet even these modest steps have proven unattainable.

So the conclusions are obvious. The conditions do not now exist to allow other nuclear-armed states to join with the United States in taking additional steps to reduce the role and number of nuclear weapons. Russia and China are not moving away from reliance on nuclear weapons. Extended deterrence cannot be changed in ways that eliminate the requirement for the capability to deploy nuclear weapons with nonstrategic delivery systems in support of U.S. allies. The "fundamental transformation" of the international political system deemed necessary by the Strategic Posture Commission remains out of our reach today.

Put differently, the desired "solid international consensus against nuclear weapons" is not plausible in current international circumstances. As an abstract notion, political leaders may be willing to accept that the world would be a better place without nuclear weapons. But in the here and now, the leaders of North Korea, Russia, China, and anxious U.S. allies do not accept that they would be better off without nuclear weapons absent quite fundamental changes to their security environments. Many other countries, perhaps yet to include Iran, have concluded that their interests require them to have some latent capabilities as a hedge against a potential future need to acquire nuclear weapons, but not the weapons themselves. And of course there are yet others beyond the scope of the analysis here who appear wedded to their own nuclear weapons for reasons of national security and national prestige (the two being directly related). The United States is apparently alone among the states with nuclear weapons to believe that it has more nuclear weapons than it needs.

Even if these conditions do not exist today, might it be possible to bring them into being sufficiently soon so as to avoid the modernization of U.S. nuclear forces? It is plausible that there may be an unexpected turn for the better in one or more of the factors reviewed earlier, leading to a reduced nuclear requirement of one kind or another. But this seems unlikely, and increasingly so. As argued further below, it is not plausible that the coming few years will see a radical reversal of fortunate on all fronts, putting us onto a trajectory of rapid disarmament. Disarmament remains a long-term project.

Lessons for the Case against Nuclear Weapons and for Disarmament

This sharp contrast between the premises of disarmament advocacy and the world as experienced by the Obama administration points to a number of lessons for the case against nuclear weapons and for disarmament.

A first lesson is that more substantive work needs to be done on how to create the conditions that do not now exist. This work could usefully focus more on political than nuclear questions. The United States is still looking for better answers about how to move the political relationships with Russia, China, and regional challengers in a positive direction. The advocates of disarmament would be well served to set aside the argument that the world is on "a glide path to disarmament," as some have contended (the image implying an approach to a destination that might somehow be fulfilled on the basis of its own momentum).[1] Further progress will be driven by major political developments bringing a relaxation of tensions in key relationships and not by agreeing to grand but impractical schemes for disarmament.

A second lesson is that the security environment is not nearly as benign as many disarmament advocates appear to believe. They have been so worried by the prospect of terrorist use of nuclear weapons (something to be seriously worried about) as to have neglected new problems in the security environment and the need to ensure that U.S. nuclear deterrence remains effective for the problems for which it is relevant in the 21st century. The alternative global deterrence construct envisioned by some (to recall, moving from a construct based on bilateral confrontation to one based on multilateral cooperation) simply isn't plausible in today's circumstances.

A third lesson is that the U.S. nuclear posture isn't simply a barrier to more effective international cooperation in the NPT framework, where many states complain about the slow pace of the nuclear weapon states in reducing and eliminating their nuclear arsenals. The U.S. nuclear posture is also a tool of nonproliferation, in that the guarantees the United States has provided to others have played a critical role in leading them to conclude that they do not need nuclear deterrents of their own. Reducing the effectiveness of extended U.S. nuclear deterrence by eliminating key capabilities in the name of disarmament could actually unleash a new wave of proliferation—but among U.S. friends and allies rather than among its foes.

This is not an argument that the needed conditions to allow substantial further reductions in the role and number of U.S. nuclear weapons will never come into being. They might. In a changed and changing world, there is always the possibility of dramatic change of a kind that makes possible new things. The end of the Cold War is powerful testament to this fact. Russia may yet find accommodation with the existing European security order. But this positive turn seems unlikely so long as President Putin remains in charge (and it seems certain that he will ensure his successor is of like mind). China may yet accept the existing regional order as conductive to its interests and may yet come to see its assertive nationalism as too risky and deeper partnership with the United States as beneficial. But its wariness of the United States is deeply engrained, and its rise is destined to deeply unsettle its neighbors. Korea may yet reunify in a way that eliminates the nuclear threat. But the North Korean regime and state have long surpassed predictions of their demise. One or more major positive change could have a significant impact on U.S. nuclear policy and posture. But major positive change on all of them seems especially unlikely.

For now, we must cope with the reality we face. Negative developments in the changed and changing security environment are both disappointing and dangerous. They imply that the timeline to abolition will not be measured in a decade or two, as members of the Global Zero Movement and others might have believed. And they also imply that the pathway to zero, if and as it is taken, will be shaped as much by choices made in foreign capitals as by those made in Washington. Disarmament remains a long-term project.

Lessons for the Case for U.S. Nuclear Weapons

The conclusion that the conditions do not now exist to allow the United States to safely take substantial additional steps to reduce the role and number of nuclear weapons makes an obvious and simple case for U.S. nuclear weapons in that they are a form of insurance in a dangerous and unpredictable world. But in and of itself, this is an inadequate case, as it conveys nothing about what is required for the U.S. nuclear deterrent to be effective for the problems for which it is relevant in the 21st century. Thus a better case is needed.

That case begins not with nuclear strategy, deterrence strategy, or military strategy, but with national strategy. Consistently since World War II, including explicitly since the end of the Cold War, the United States has chosen to play a role in the world that has fundamental implications for its military strategy and posture. It has sought to engage and lead. It has aspired to defend its values globally. It has chosen to ally with others with shared security interests and, more durably, those with shared values also. In accepting a role as a permanent member of the UN Security Council, it has accepted a responsibility to serve as a guarantor of the peace and security of others, including explicitly from the threat posed by the proliferation of weapons of mass destruction. It has played a special role since it led the way into the nuclear age in 1945 in trying to bring order to that age, with political and military means. It has aspired to do the right thing, however defined, when circumstances compel action and not just when narrowly defined national security interests might require it. All of these aspirations bring with them responsibilities and risks.

One such responsibility is to compose a military that aligns with these aspirations, responsibilities, and risks. Accordingly, and especially since the end of the Cold War, U.S. leaders have consistently chosen an approach to defense planning enabling power projection, military supremacy at the conventional level of war, strong regional deterrence, and reliable strategic stability.

U.S. national security strategies generally reflect the optimism that is a core attribute of American strategic culture and a public expectation of our leaders. They also reflect the pragmatism of American culture and leaders' desires to make a practical difference on their watch. Thus, in characterizing the challenges to U.S. security in changed and changing international circumstances, these strategies commonly depict a mix of positive and negative trends. And they express a commitment to employ U.S. power to reinforce the positive trends and protect against and try to reverse the negative ones.

Both the positive and negative trends now present are consequential for the questions posed at the beginning of this chapter. Salient positive trends include the following. The Cold War has receded into history and with it the plausibility of an Armageddon-like nuclear war between East and West. U.S. alliances have proven durable and adaptable. The proliferation of nuclear weapons, though it has continued, has not crossed a tipping point to the feared cascade. Most fundamentally, much of the world still seeks U.S. leadership or at least partnership; Russia and China each have one ally, while the United States has more than forty.

Salient negative trends include the following. Old ideological contests have given way to new ones, and U.S. values are not shared by many of the most influential actors on the world stage. In the third decade after the Cold War, there has been a surge of conflict that puts major new stress on stability and security in many of the worlds regions. Major power relations have not transformed as desired. Both Russia and China overtly contest U.S.-backed regional orders. They reject U.S. arguments about why and how it is adapting its military to 21st-century requirements. Proliferation has put nuclear weapons (and the long-range missiles to deliver them) into the hands of one regional adversary and potentially more in the future. Some U.S. allies are back on the front lines, though in confrontations entirely different from those of the Cold War. There is a potential for major changes to the interstate system in the Middle East and with it the potential for the emergence of new states with revolutionary ambitions. There is also a widely shared perception of American decline (whether merely on a relative scale, in comparison to rising powers, or on an absolute scale is of course much debated), as it fails to come to terms with deep political and economic problems.

It is useful to put this argument into a larger historical framework. As the Cold War ended, pundits wrote about the end of history, politicians spoke about a new world order, and historians described an era of unprecedented order.[2] Americans were infused with a sense of hope about all that might be possible with the end of the Cold War.

Twenty-five years later, we cling to optimism in a world that hasn't met our expectations. Moscow and Beijing have not embraced partnership with Washington; to varying degrees, they are both aggrieved and vulnerable, suspicious of U.S. intentions, and opposed to many aspects of the liberal international order promoted by the United States. Regional challengers have emerged more prominently, similarly aggrieved, vulnerable, and suspicious, while also opposing U.S. regional roles. Revolutionary actors who would rewrite the state system have appeared in the Middle East. Our hope for a more orderly, peaceful, and just world has been challenged by interim developments. As Henry Kissinger has argued, "A quarter century of political and economic crises . . . has thrown into question the optimistic assumptions of the immediate post-

Cold War era: that the spread of democracy and free markets would automatically create a just, peaceful, and inclusive world."[3] In 2011, Thérèse Delpech put a finer point on this shift: the 21st century, she argued, is marked by a growing disrespect for international law and accepted rules of behavior—a new form of piracy has taken hold as a rising number of actors, both state and nonstate, contest the liberal international order backed by the United States and its allies.[4]

Of course these developments raise fundamental questions about the role of nuclear weapons in a security environment undergoing ever more profound change. Will they be a source of order, security, and safety? Or will they be a source of disorder, insecurity, and damage to our societies? As nuclear weapons played so central a role in the main international conflicts of the second half of the 20th century (the Cold War), it is difficult to imagine that they will not play some role in the main conflicts of the 21st century.

These positive and negative factors have had a mixed impact on U.S. nuclear policy and posture. On the one hand, the positive factors have combined to allow major steps away from Cold War–vintage approaches to nuclear deterrence, to adapt arms control to new purposes, and to strengthen the nonproliferation regime. On the other hand, the negative factors have combined to require steps to adapt deterrence to new purposes and to recognize the shortcomings of arms control and nonproliferation in delivering the kind of results that would enable more dramatic departures from past deterrence approaches.

Red Theories of Victory and Their Risks

In this new security environment, there is a small set of countries whose leaders prepare for war with the United States and its allies. This volume has looked at three such countries—North Korea, Russia, and China.

The differences among them are of course substantial and the conditions that could lead them to conflict with the United States are varied. But there are some key similarities among these cases. There is mixed evidence that, to varying degrees, each of these states has developed a set of ideas for deterring and defeating a "conventionally superior nuclear-armed major power and its allies." These theories of victory are not theories of nuclear war fighting as it was understood in the Cold War, which presumed the employment of nuclear weapons in large numbers and in diverse ways to fight and win mixed conventional–nuclear wars. Instead, they appear to be built on conventional faits accomplis, nuclear blackmail, and, if necessary, brinksmanship. Whether the leaders of these three states actually envision recourse to nuclear employment in time of war cannot be known. But they must ensure that their threats to employ nuclear means to defend their core interests are credible in the eyes of the United States and its allies.

These nuclear theories of victory appear to include elements of both Clausewitz and Sun Tzu. To recall, Clausewitz focused on war as a continuation of politics by other means and thus described victory as a "culminating point" when an enemy not fully subdued on the battlefield accedes to the preferences of the victor in establishing the conditions of peace, conditions aligned with the victor's original political objectives.[5] Sun Tzu argued that "the supreme art of war is to subdue the enemy without fighting."[6] Based on the available evidence, it appears that North Korea, Russia, and China have developed a body of ideas about how to employ nuclear threats in support of their political objectives in crisis and war and about how to exploit their postures to attain political objectives in peacetime.

From a U.S. perspective, how troubling are the theories of victory of North Korea, Russia, and China? On the one hand, they proceed from the premise that the United States will be the aggressor. They are aligned with national security strategies that are defined as self-defensive in character. The disincentives to go to war with the United States are many. This suggests that these theories of victory will be more troubling to the United States in peacetime than in crisis and war, as the conditions that would lead to war are unlikely.

On the other hand, though pursuing self-defensive strategies, each of these regimes is inherently revisionist in character. Putin's slogan "new rules or no rules" illustrates the point. Their propensity for risk taking seems to have increased along with confidence in their theories of victory. There is a significant potential that their efforts to shape their regional security environments through coercion and provocation will precipitate the very confrontation with the United States that they seek to avoid.

Moreover, these theories of victory are rife with the potential for miscalculation and inadvertent and accidental escalation. This follows in part from dangerous assumptions they make about likely American strategic behavior in time of war and perhaps also about their ability to escalate regional conflicts without serious risk of U.S. nuclear retaliation.[7] Although the leaders of these states appear to not understand America well, because of their ideological predispositions, they appear to think they do. The risk of miscalculation and unwanted escalation follows also in part from the fact that much of their strategic analysis appears to be informed by a sense of anger, vulnerability, and even humiliation in the face of American power.

Accordingly, it is plausible that these states would act in crisis and war in ways that would invoke questions of U.S. nuclear employment. To recall, U.S. nuclear declaratory policy states that the United States will consider the use of nuclear weapons in extreme circumstances to defend its vital interests or those of its allies and partners, whether those extreme circumstances are created by nuclear attack or other means. In short, their theories of victory invoke questions for the United States about the possible employment of its nuclear weapons.

This is not to imply that armed conflict with these states is inevitable. It is certainly not to imply that U.S. strategy should be driven by the worst-case thinking sometimes evident in Pyongyang, Moscow, or Beijing. Nor is it to imply that their theories of victory are sound and would be proven successful in war. But the United States cannot simply ignore these developments. It must understand the plausible military and political choices of its potential adversaries, as well as their strategies for nuclear blackmail and brinksmanship at the heart of their theories of victory.

The Blue Theory of Victory and U.S. Nuclear Weapons

This line of argument is consistent with the hypothesis that U.S. nuclear forces are a form of insurance against uncertainty. They are the most powerful tools available for preventing challenges to the vital interests of the United States and its allies. The shadow they cast over adversaries contemplating challenges to U.S. interests is not inconsequential, even if it cannot be quantified. U.S. nuclear forces are also a general inducement to restraint by others and an important form of assurance for the United States and its allies and partners.

But this line of argument points to a conclusion that U.S. nuclear forces are more than just a form of insurance against unpredictable dangers. If the United States faces an adversary that believes that limited nuclear war against the United States can be won and thus can be fought, then the United States had better have a theory of victory of its own, one consistent with its interests and those of its allies and embedded in intellectually and politically defensible assumptions. It must be able to act as its declaratory policy states that it will.

As argued in previous chapters, such a theory must guide U.S. choices in peacetime, crisis, and war and its attempts to orchestrate military, political, economic, and other actions to achieve U.S. objectives. In peacetime, that theory seeks to persuade potential challengers that their interests are better served through cooperation than confrontation with the United States and its allies, while also negating their attempts to coerce U.S. allies. In crisis, that theory seeks to achieve a favorable outcome without fighting by making it clear that actual hostilities will not result in an adversary's success in meeting his objectives and will leave it worse off than choosing restraint, while also negating attempts to use nuclear threats to blackmail the United States and its allies. In war, the theory seeks to restore deterrence rapidly once it has broken down, while also enabling an early termination of the conflict on political terms consistent with U.S. and allied objectives. This is not a theory for fighting and winning a nuclear war. But it is necessary to be prepared to actually employ nuclear weapons if the red lines in U.S. nuclear declaratory policy are crossed in ways consistent with U.S. political objectives.

During the Cold War, the United States had a theory of victory. Widely debated, it was accordingly widely known. Today, a successor theory of victory for the kind of regional conflicts the United States might have to face under the nuclear shadow is beginning to take shape. Its existence is implied in the QDR 2014 statement that the United States will not allow adversaries to escalate their way out of failed aggression at the conventional level of war. As argued in Chapter 3, this emerging theory is derived from principles set out in the strategic reviews of conventional, nuclear, missile defense, cyber, and space postures conducted in 2009 and 2010; from the spectrum of deterrence challenges in regional wars; and from the strategy to strengthen the regional deterrence architectures comprehensively. This theory seeks the synergistic integration of the deterrence benefits of multiple tools of deterrence, both nuclear and nonnuclear.

The primary objective of the Blue theory of victory is to strip Red's blackmail strategy of its credibility and thereby dilute its effectiveness in brinksmanship. If this objective can be achieved, Red leaders ought to perceive aggression as too risky and coercion as futile. Accordingly, they ought to become more risk averse and less confident that they can change the course of history in their favor, and therefore more amenable to U.S.-preferred solutions to regional political problems. In short, the Blue theory also has elements of both Clausewitz and Sun Tzu.

In this Blue theory of victory, nuclear weapons have unique and so-far irreplaceable functions in meeting the new challenges of a new spectrum of deterrence requirements. These are:

1. To cast a shadow of unacceptable cost and/or incalculable risk over an adversary's decision about whether to put in jeopardy a vital interest of the United States and/or an ally or partner;

2. To signal the resolve of the United States, and the collective resolve of its allies when these are being tested by an adversary, whether through displays of capability or through employment of nuclear weapons to shock an enemy leadership into understanding the depth of its miscalculation;

3. To demonstrate U.S. capacity to respond to any level of nuclear escalation by an adversary, whether horizontal or vertical, and to remain resilient in the face of attack;

4. To assure U.S. allies that U.S. commitments to them are credible;

5. To ensure a balance of power with both Russia and China sufficient to the requirements of strategic stability; and

6. To assure the United States that the risks associated with its national strategy of international engagement and power projection are manageable.

The first three functions are obviously directly relevant to negating Red theories of victory and to denying regional aggressors confidence in their strategies to escalate their way out of a failed act of conventional aggression.

In arguing that these functions are unique and so-far irreplaceable, I am not implying that the other capabilities in the comprehensive strategy for strengthening regional deterrence architectures do not contribute usefully. On the contrary, the other tools in the regional deterrence toolkit have reinforcing values, as argued in Chapter 3. Missile defense and conventional strike systems, among other means, contribute meaningfully to deterrence and assurance. Their deployment helps to reduce U.S. reliance on nuclear weapons. But these capabilities are not substitutes for nuclear weapons when adversaries are at the brink of jeopardizing the vital interests of the United States or an ally (and crossing the red lines in U.S. nuclear declaratory policy). To an extent, this is case dependent; that is, some of these complementary capabilities may be more effective in achieving U.S. objectives against some adversaries than others.

Three conclusions follow from this elaboration of the case for U.S. nuclear weapons in the 21st century. First, U.S. nuclear weapons today are not, as some would argue, simply relics of a time past, without utility, and thus ready for the dustbin of history along with the Soviet Union and the Cold War. As argued previously, three decades after the end of the Cold War they have unique and so far irreplaceable roles in U.S. military strategy and in support of U.S. national strategy. From the larger perspective of U.S. defense strategy and national security strategy more generally, nuclear weapons are relevant to very few problems. But they are relevant to a few key problems—and powerfully so.

Second, the effectiveness of nuclear weapons in delivering the desired deterrence and assurance benefits cannot be taken for granted. They are tools for achieving U.S. objectives, but they are not guarantees. Nuclear deterrence may yet prove to be unreliable; after all, there is no promise that the Blue theory of victory will be successful in preventing war or escalation. But without such a theory, success is impossible.

Third, the moral argument has been touched only in part by the international humanitarian movement. Recall their argument as set out in Chapter 1: The employment of nuclear weapons would necessarily violate international humanitarian law, and thus nuclear weapons are immoral and should be banned. Without doubt, the employment of nuclear weapons on a large scale would be a catastrophe without precedent. But this does not exhaust the moral discussion. The potential consequences of use must be measured also against the damage avoided to vital national interests, including the survival and independence of the United States or an ally or partner. They must also be measured against the damage avoided in general conventional war which, as World War II proved, can be massively devastating for states and societies. If the employment of one or more U.S. nuclear weapons can be successful in stopping the escalation of nuclear conflict from small scale to large, that is a strategic value of some moral consequence. Moreover, from a U.S. perspective, its employment of nuclear weapons in war might be accepted in retrospect as necessary and just under certain conditions—if (1) it is seen to have used all of its power to avoid the circumstances that led to its use of nuclear weapons and (2) it is seen to have employed nuclear weapons in a manner consistent with the principles of international law. Additionally, in a world in which potential U.S. enemies are not prepared to disarm themselves in this respect, to do so unilaterally is to invite the costs that would follow in terms of coercion and aggression.[8]

Implications for the U.S. Nuclear Posture

What sort of posture is required to support the functions set out in the preceding discussion? This is not simply a question of "how many nuclear weapons are enough?" It is a question of what capabilities, capacities, and competencies are required of the United States to underwrite these functions.

Function number one (to cast a shadow . . .) from the preceding section imposes a general requirement for the preservation of nuclear forces that are seen as being effective if ever required in war. But it's not that simple. As the analysis of the Red theories of victory suggests, Red perceptions are informed as much by assessments of intention as capability. This attests to the continued deterrence value of leadership focus and visible institutional excellence for nuclear deterrence in the United States. It attests also to the utility of "strategic gestures" (to borrow the Russian term for sending deterrence messages through the display of force) in regularly sending messages of deterrence.

Function number two (to signal U.S. and collective resolve) imposes multiple requirements. One is the ability to employ a very few nuclear weapons with a very high degree of confidence in their success. This calls for weapons and delivery systems with a high degree of reliability and also intelligence, surveillance, and reconnaissance systems sufficient to identify and monitor especially high-value targets. Another is the ability to deploy weapons into regions in time of crisis or to move them within a region to points of operational relevance. Yet another is the ability to share the risks and burdens of deterrence operations with U.S. allies, primarily with forward-deployable weapons and delivery systems. A triad alone without the dual-capable aircraft (DCA) component would fall short in this regard. Capacity must be sufficient to underwrite global U.S. commitments and not just the currently forward-deployed component in Europe. After all, U.S. DCA may sometime be deployed in support of commitments to U.S. allies in Northeast Asia and elsewhere.

Function number three (to demonstrate escalation capability and resilience) imposes variable demands depending on the strategic reach and depth of the adversary. For demonstrating U.S. escalation capacity to regional adversaries without much depth or reach, the key requirement of U.S. nuclear forces is the ability to flow more forces into the region, a function for which nuclear-armed bombers are well suited. For demonstrating U.S. escalation capacity to near-peer powers, the key requirement is to have a force that is large, secure, redundant, and sufficiently alert not to be vulnerable to preemption. In both cases, the forces must themselves be able to operate in an environment where the effects of nuclear employment are present through some appropriate combination of radiation hardening, redundancy, stand-off, and other technical fixes and operational concepts. A key associated requirement is for a nuclear command and control system that is resilient under attack and capable of supporting the president as he or she deliberates among different courses of action with multiple actors, including U.S. allies.

Function number four (to assure U.S. allies) requires forward-deployable capabilities that are visible and would be effective if ever called on to deliver nuclear weapons. This requirement also has an associated command and control requirement to ensure presidential deliberation and control and military effectiveness in employment. And the capacity must be sufficient to meet global commitments, not just those in Europe.

Function number five (to ensure strategic stability) requires that there be no large disparities in the different strategic forces of the United States and Russia and that the United States not abandon the "second to none" criterion in sizing the force. It requires also some redress of the imbalance in nonstrategic forces in the Euro-Atlantic security area, preferably through Russian reductions. In the U.S.–China dimension, it requires a force sufficiently large that China remains unmotivated to seek numerical parity with the United States (and Russia).

Function number six (to assure the United States) requires nuclear forces that are safe, secure, and effective, as well as a hedge against geopolitical surprise that is shaped and sized appropriately for the types of surprises that can reasonably be anticipated.

In addition to these capabilities and capacities, the U.S. nuclear deterrent requires certain core competencies. The armed services performing the deterrence missions (the Navy and Air Force) must sustain for decades the highest degree of competence in those missions. The organizations that develop and implement policy must have the requisite expertise and focus. The standing forces must be supported by a technical enterprise that is capable of ensuring the safety, security, and effectiveness of U.S. nuclear forces and of meeting the hedge requirements set out by national policies.

Perhaps most important, national leadership must have political ownership of nuclear deterrence policy and strategy and must exhibit the necessary focus on a sustained basis. This is first and foremost the president's responsibility. But it also a responsibility of key committee chairs in the Congress as of senior congressional leadership as a whole, preferably on a bipartisan and bicameral basis. This must be reflected in a forthright dialogue with the American public that explains U.S. policy and puts it in a meaningful context.

A key additional enabler of effective nuclear deterrence (and assurance) is a community of interested analysts, inside government and out, to work on better understanding the potential dynamics of regional wars under the nuclear shadow and on testing the Red and Blue theories of victory. In the Cold War, this analysis required collaboration between experts on the Soviet Union and experts on nuclear deterrence; in the current era, this analysis requires new forms of interaction between experts on particular regions, countries, and leaders and experts on the multiple tools of deterrence. This analytic work requires in turn a flow of resources sufficient to sustain investigation and focused debate from key stakeholders in the nuclear deterrence enterprise, including the Office of the Secretary of Defense, the armed services, the Joint Staff, the Combatant Commands, relevant defense support agencies, the Departments of State and Energy, and the intelligence community.

A Closing Note of Historical Perspective

Writing in 2005, Thérèse Delpech posed a simple question: Would the 21st century be more or less savage than the 20th?[9] She recalled the 20th century as the most savage in human history, with approximately 150 million people perishing in war and another approximately 80 million perishing in one way or another at the hands of their state.[10] This tragedy unfolded, she argued, despite the best efforts of statesmen, diplomats, military strategists, scientists, and scholars. Will we do better or worse, in the 21st century, she asked. And will nuclear weapons be part of the solution or part of the problem? In other words, will they reinforce peace and enable just settlement of disputes? Or will they be used to their full potential for havoc?

A decade later, the answers to these questions have become no clearer. In relations among the major powers, deep peace remains elusive, and incipient sources of conflict are more numerous. Regional orders are under challenge by increasing and violent means. Savagery itself has been embraced by the Islamic State as a key tactic. In the hands of revolutionaries, nuclear weapons could produce great tragedy. In regional conflicts, they may yet generate catastrophe and chaos. The fundamental transformation of international relations that might make abolition possible seems a remote possibility. The continued presence of nuclear weapons will shape the century in significant ways. The problems they pose cannot be wished away, just as the weapons cannot be wished away. From a U.S. perspective, this obliges us to ensure that U.S. nuclear deterrence is effective for the problems for which it is relevant, even as we work to address the underlying sources of conflict. This will help us avoid a dark answer to the "simple question" above.

Epilogue

Implications for Future Strategy Policy, and Posture Reviews

ITH THESE LESSONS IN MIND FROM THE TWIN U.S. PROJECTS to adapt U.S. nuclear deterrence to 21st-century purposes and to create the conditions for the United States and other nuclear weapon states to take additional steps to reduce the role and number of nuclear weapons, what implications follow? To frame an answer to this question, this epilogue returns to where the book began: with the cycle of reviews of nuclear policy and posture that each new administration has undertaken since the end of the Cold War. With a Nuclear Posture Review (or something like it) likely in 2017, and subsequent ones every four or eight years later, future administrations will put their imprint on the nation's nuclear policy and posture. Each will attempt to start with the proverbial clean sheet of paper and then find itself testing the validity of instincts honed on the campaign trail, ideas carried by a core national security team, and approaches embedded in standing presidential guidance (that remains in place until replaced by something new).

This epilogue highlights a small set of key questions that will be central to future reviews and that merit deeper discussion and debate in the interim. It uses these questions to organize discussion of the implications of the analysis and arguments in the preceding chapters. It does so from the perspective of experience gained by 2014, recognizing that future experience will shed new light on these questions and thus shape U.S. policy in additional ways.

The First Question: Is the Balanced Approach Still Necessary?

Recall the essence of the recommendation of the 2009 report of the Strategic Posture Commission: that the United States pursue a nuclear strategy that balances the use of political and legal tools such as arms control and non-proliferation to reduce and eliminate threats with the use of military tools to ensure that nuclear deterrence remains effective so long as nuclear weapons remain.

A case against the balanced approach can be made. The optimism of 2009 about reducing the role and number of nuclear weapons has given way to an appreciation of the difficulty of achieving U.S. nonproliferation and arms control objectives. North Korea is proceeding to develop and deploy a nuclear force despite major efforts to stop it from doing so. Relations with Russia have taken a radical turn for the worse, including in the nuclear domain. Nuclear relations with China have not improved as they might have done, and political tensions are rising, not least because of difficulties in the military domain. The assurance requirements of some allies are rising. All this would seem to imply that the United States should do substantially less with political and legal tools and should do substantially more to ensure the effectiveness of nuclear deterrence.

But the case for the balanced approach remains stronger than this case against. It is both a strategic virtue and a political expedient.

The case for the balanced approach as a strategic virtue follows from the fact that the security we seek and the stability we prize require the combined benefits of the two approaches. The deterrence of North Korea requires the full and effective implementation of the comprehensive approach to strengthening regional deterrence, but containing the pressures on further proliferation in Northeast Asia and elsewhere requires a viable nonproliferation regime. Predictability in the strategic relationship with Russia is a high and rising value and requires an arms control framework or something like it. Strategic stability with Russia is also not possible without a credible deterrence strategy in Europe. The assurance of allies requires credible U.S. strategies for both deterring threats to them and working over time to mitigate the circumstances that give rise to those threats. In short, these are interconnected problems requiring a balanced approach.

Moreover, the United States should not abandon its commitment to work toward the ultimate goal of eliminating nuclear weapons. To do so would damage the nonproliferation regime significantly. It would alarm allies and encourage challengers. It would be widely interpreted as confirmation of American retreat from international leadership. In addition, the experience of the Obama administration has not proven that the conditions needed to allow substantial further reductions in the role and number of U.S. nuclear weapons will never come into being. Rather, it has proven that those conditions do not now exist and do not appear proximate. As argued further in the last chapter, in a changed and changing world, there is always the possibility of dramatic change of a kind that makes possible new things. Leading international efforts to create the conditions of peace and justice that would make nuclear abolition possible is a project for which the United States is well suited.

The case for the balanced approach as a political expedient is even more straightforward. As a decade or more of gridlock before 2009 amply demonstrated, without a modicum of agreement between the two camps in the U.S. nuclear policy debate, neither can accomplish its goals. And as the period since then has shown, a balanced approach can produce in the Congress a measure of agreement sufficient to sustain both the deterrent (with decisions to fund two warhead life extension programs and to begin replacement of the fleet of ballistic missile submarines) and arms control (with the decision to support ratification of the New START Treaty).

This line of argument about the continued value of the balanced approach draws on an important assumption: that there will be no changes to American national security strategy at a higher level that would have implications for the approach to nuclear deterrence. But two such changes have been in debate. One is to move from engagement to isolation, on the argument that the leadership role of the United States suited to the period following World War II is not necessary and appropriate in the 21st century, when others should be stepping up to do more to look after their own security.[1] The other possible change is to accept the decision by additional allies and partners to acquire nuclear deterrents of their own.[2] Either choice could be seen as providing an escape from the burdens of extended nuclear deterrence and of maintaining strategic stability with Russia and China, pushing America in a direction of distinct nuclear autonomy.

But it is difficult to imagine either change as proving advantageous to the United States, barring radical changes in the international context. The United States might relinquish leadership and alliances, but it cannot disengage and thereby become invulnerable. The two wide oceans that enabled isolation early in the country's history have been rendered irrelevant by long-range missiles, cyberspace, and nonstate actors. The choice for disengagement would likely also inflame resentment toward the United States, deepening its isolation even from those with whom it might expect partnership. In times of crisis, the United States might well be left to act alone—or not act at all. It should be added that regional challengers would take such a U.S. choice as a demonstration of the credibility of their theories of victory, potentially encouraging their aggression.

Similarly, the choice to welcome additional allies to the nuclear club would come at a dramatic cost—to the nuclear nonproliferation regime. Britain and France joined the nuclear club before the club itself was formalized in the NPT in 1970, and other U.S. allies have joined the NPT as nonnuclear states. The path for them to nuclearization would be through withdrawal from the treaty, likely leading to penalties of various kinds, both political and economic. These would include penalties the United States is legally bound to impose under the 1978 Nuclear Nonproliferation Act. The NPT itself might not long survive. If the NPT were to collapse for other reasons, then such a step might be possible. But even in that circumstance, the choice by an ally to seek nuclear weapons of its own would be widely interpreted—especially by other U.S. allies—as a powerful sign of lack of confidence in the U.S. umbrella, which could push other allies over the tipping point and unleash the feared cascade of proliferation. This might well result in a more isolated United States.

Barring changes at the grand strategy level, the balanced approach is here to stay. Having made the case for the balanced approach, it is necessary also to acknowledge that the precise balance struck in the 2010 NPR is unlikely to be replicated in future reviews. Some lessons have been learned in implementing the review that bear on considerations of future balance. In addition, in a security environment that remains "changed and changing," policy must be dynamic. How this balance needs to be adjusted, in the light of interim lessons and circumstances as they have changed so far, is discussed in the next two sections.

What More Can Be Achieved with Political and Legal Tools?

As argued by the Strategic Posture Commission, the purpose of such tools is to shape the security environment in ways that help to reduce nuclear dangers and thus also the demands on the U.S. nuclear deterrent, in part to enable further reductions by the United States and other nuclear weapon states. As we look to the future, three key questions stand out: Are further reductions in the role and/or number of U.S. nuclear weapons possible or desirable? Can and should more be done to signal U.S. support for nonproliferation? Is strategic stability still the right organizing concept for the nuclear relationships with Russia and China?

On Further Reductions

Three reviews have resulted in twenty-five years of pruning of the U.S. nuclear arsenal. The low-hanging fruit was harvested unilaterally by the George H. W. Bush administration with major changes to the U.S. posture, including the retirement of capabilities rendered irrelevant by the end of the Cold War and the collapse of the Soviet Union. Following on those so-called Presidential Nuclear Initiatives, presidential interest in reductions has been sustained. The Clinton administration focused on leading toward deeper arms control reductions. The George W. Bush administration focused on unilateral measures to cut the arsenal and on deemphasizing nuclear weapons in deterrence strategy. The Obama administration has focused on reducing the role and number of nuclear weapons where it could do so safely, while working to create the conditions for future steps by the United States and others to further reduce roles and numbers. Accordingly, fruit higher in the tree (meaning weapons that can be eliminated only in the context of verifiable, reciprocal, legally binding measures) has been harvested in parallel with Russia, allowing a significant shrinkage of the strategic posture by reducing the number of weapons in light of reciprocal Russian steps. Can this continue?

The Obama administration has argued that future reductions in the U.S. nuclear arsenal must be made in partnership with Russia and that these should include not just additional reductions in weapons deployed with strategic delivery systems but also nonstrategic and nondeployed weapons. With regard to potential future reductions of nonstrategic nuclear weapons in Europe, it has lined up with its NATO allies on the principle that future NATO reductions require reductions in Russia's arsenal of weapons in the Euro-Atlantic security area, taking due account of the disproportionately much larger Russian force.

Whether Russia is still willing to join in additional nuclear reductions is a question that may not be answered definitively for a long time. After all, the New START Treaty does not expire until 2021 and may be extended once for five years on the basis of mutual agreement. This may effectively defer for more than a decade an answer to this question. Moreover, given disagreement in Europe about the continued value of forward-deployed U.S. nonstrategic nuclear weapons and the expense of replacing dual-capable aircraft in Europe, Russia has every incentive to wait and see whether NATO disarms unilaterally.

Given these political realities, the only potential pathway to additional reductions in the U.S. nuclear arsenal in the next few years is unilateral action. This equates with concluding that, because the conditions so far identified to enable further reductions do not now exist, we will simply set them aside. At least four unilateral measures can be imagined.

One is to withdraw the remaining U.S. nuclear weapons from Europe and retire the capabilities associated with the promise to be able to deploy globally nuclear weapons with nonstrategic delivery systems. This would satisfy the demands of those who see such weapons as irrelevant in the new security landscape. It would also be politically appealing to some constituencies in Europe.

But, as argued elsewhere in this volume, this step would come with significant costs. It would weaken extended deterrence, by taking out a key step in the escalation ladder and undermining the ability to signal collective resolve. It would weaken strategic stability, by ceding to Russia complete dominance at the nuclear level in Europe. Both of these factors would weaken the assurance of allies in both Europe and Northeast Asia—not all of them, just those that are already anxious about their security environment and the credibility of U.S. commitments to them. It would also pass through the filter of their debate about American decline and be interpreted more broadly not as principled commitment to the goal of abolition but as a budgetary expedient signaling American retreat and retrenchment.

Thus a possible alternative would be to withdraw U.S. nuclear weapons and DCA from Europe but not retire them. Instead, they could be kept in ready reserve to support a future decision to deploy them in time of crisis. But it is doubtful that this approach would prove viable over the long term, as the armed services have a difficult time sustaining such hedge options when military spending is declining. Moreover, in time of crisis, redeployment to Europe might be rejected by some allies as unhelpfully provocative, thus stalling the action and unhelpfully signaling division among the allies. Such redeployment to Europe in time of crisis could also unhelpfully accelerate the momentum of a crisis in the way that military mobilization accelerated the pathway to war in August 1914. Additionally, the deterrence and assurance values of these capabilities most prized by anxious U.S. allies would now be thousands of miles away.

A second potential unilateral measure would be to take the one-third reduction (from 1,550) in deployed strategic nuclear forces that the Obama administration has indicated it is prepared to take in parallel with Russia. This would be helpful for demonstrating to the non–nuclear weapon states the commitment of the United States to continue the reductions process despite obstacles in Moscow and Beijing.

But such a step would constitute formal abandonment of the second-to-none criterion, raising new questions about the U.S. commitment to strategic stability with the major powers. This would have a corrosive effect on the assurance of anxious allies neighboring Russia and China.[3] In addition, advocacy for this second unilateral initiative hinges on the dubious argument that additional reductions involve nothing more than shedding excess Cold War forces. After all, the political relationship between the United States and Russia is no longer improving; thus it cannot any longer be argued that arms reductions contribute to the improvement of the political relationship on the transition away from the Cold War. Additionally, Russia is now well along in fielding a fully modern nuclear force sized and scaled to meet its 21st-century requirements. Moreover, an ever smaller nuclear force is ever less resilient in meeting potential future demands, as it sheds reserve capacities and cross-leg flexibility. So long as such resilience remains a leadership priority, this potential constraint deserves careful attention.

A third potential unilateral measure would be to prune one or more legs from the U.S. force structure (for example, by deactivating the ICBM force) while also taking additional reductions below the level of 1,000 deployed strategic weapons. In advocating for such steps, the Global Zero Movement has argued explicitly that although such steps would best be taken in partnership with Russia, they should be done unilaterally if necessary.[4]

This would allow continued reductions in the total number of U.S. nuclear weapons and delivery systems. It would avoid some significant costs of force modernization. But its other values are dubious. The case for such unilateral reductions in U.S. nuclear forces includes the following hypotheses: that strategic stability with Russia no longer requires parity; that China won't exploit U.S. reductions to move to parity with it (or surpass it quantitatively); that U.S. allies will tolerate this change and Russian and Chinese reactions to it, albeit perhaps grudgingly; that further reductions are needed by the United States to keep the NPT viable; and that substantially reduced forces can meet the assurance requirements of the United States and its allies. These hypotheses are not supported by the analysis found elsewhere in this book.

A key additional hypothesis is that unilateral action would be understood as leadership by example, such that others would want to follow, or at least would feel unbearable pressure to do so. Recent history is unkind to this hypothesis. NATO's effort to lead by example by reducing its arsenal of U.S. nuclear weapons by more than 95 percent has been met on the Russian side with no comparable reductions, a complete unwillingness to discuss tactical and theater weapons, and continued deployment of modernized strategic forces, as well as the integration of nuclear weapons at the tactical, theater, and strategic level of forces in its Western "strategic direction." The George W. Bush administration's unilateral reduction of U.S. strategic forces to the number it considered necessary and appropriate for the security environment and without regard for reciprocal Russian reductions has been met on the Russian side with a full program of nuclear modernization and the additional development of prenuclear and nuclear deescalation options. The Obama administration took a more modest step to lead by example, with a first-ever declaration of the total size of the U.S. nuclear stockpile. Neither Russia nor China has found it possible to put so simple a fact onto the table.

A fourth potential unilateral measure would be to move to a posture of minimum deterrence. The premise of such a posture is that deterrence can be effective with the credible threat that only a few weapons might get through to an enemy country, given the profound damage to an enemy society that is possible with even a single nuclear weapon. The supporting hypothesis is that no country today would risk the dire results of attack on even a single city. Essentially, goes the argument, the United States could adopt China's policy and posture and thus move rapidly to a force equivalent to China's (with one-tenth the number of current U.S. land-based missiles, one-half the number of submarines, and a small fraction of the number of nuclear warheads), thereby making a dramatic move away from Cold War approaches and sharply reducing costs.

But minimum deterrence is a strategy ill suited to the current moment for the United States. Of the six functions of U.S. nuclear weapons catalogued in the prior chapter, only the first two would be effectively supported. Retaliation might be ensured, but strategic stability and extended deterrence and assurance of allies—and of the United States itself—would not be. It is of course possible that deterrence might be effective with only a small number of weapons, but, given what we know about Red theories of victory and the leaders who subscribe to them, it is possible also that it might not be. To move to a minimum deterrence posture would require that this risk be accepted. It would require also that the United States abandon its commitment that its employment of nuclear weapons would be consistent with the principles of discrimination and proportionality and other requirements of the international laws of war.[5] Moreover, a minimum deterrence posture would deprive the United States of a key capacity identified in the prior chapter: the capacity to adapt to changing circumstances and changing requirements.[6]

In sum, none of these unilateral actions is consistent with the interests of the United States and its allies at this time. Until and if Russia is willing to continue the arms reductions process, and until and if the United States no longer cares about strategic stability, extended deterrence, or assurance, the prospects for further U.S. nuclear reductions beyond the New START Treaty appear to be nearly zero.

Thus, a strong dose of strategic patience among advocates of arms control is required. Both American political leadership and the relevant nongovernment communities would be well served to adjust their aspirations accordingly and to focus their thinking on how best to seize future opportunities and how to sustain our interest in strategic stability if those opportunities do not appear. More work could usefully be done exploring the problems that Washington and Moscow each perceives in the strategic posture of the other and identifying elements of a potential agreement that might be seen in both capitals as serving national interests.

On Support for Nonproliferation

Shifting from arms control to nonproliferation in the "balanced approach," what lessons can be learned from recent experience? One is that the United States needs to engage the non–nuclear weapon states in a sustained and substantive discussion about the lessons of recent efforts to implement NPT obligations. It could advance this discussion with a clearer case about the conditions that would need to be created to take the next steps and the follow-on steps and about the timeline needed to determine if these conditions can be created. The United States also could do more to highlight the barriers to further steps at this time—barriers largely having to do with choices in capitals other than Washington. Finally, the United States would be well served by joining the moral debate about nuclear deterrence in the 21st century and making its case that its policies are both legal and just.

Can and should the United States take additional steps to support nuclear nonproliferation, in the form of further steps to reduce the role of nuclear weapons in its national security and military strategies? For example, is it time to embrace "sole purpose" (the version of declaratory policy that would state that the sole purpose of U.S. nuclear weapons is to deter nuclear attack, thereby further circumscribing their role by ruling out a role for them in deterring attacks on the vital interests of the United States or its allies by other means)?

Recall that three policy and posture reviews over twenty-five years have already resulted in many reductions of the nuclear role in U.S. security strategies. Recall also that the "sole purpose" formulation was considered and rejected by the Obama administration, on the assessment that the vital interests of the United States and its allies could be jeopardized by nonnuclear means, including with chemical and biological weapons. So far, at least, those threats have not disappeared.

But the demand from the nonproliferation movement for additional steps by the United States has not slackened. Indeed, it appears to be insatiable. To be sure, the United States has a responsibility to work purposefully toward the objectives to which it committed in signing the NPT, including the Article VI obligation to pursue "negotiations in good faith on effective measures relating to cessation of the nuclear arms race at an early date and to nuclear disarmament" and toward a "treaty on general and complete disarmament under strict and effective international control." In fact, the United States has much to show for this responsibility, including the track record of "pruning" of excess capabilities and roles over four presidential administrations. It has helped to end the arms race. It has steadily reduced reliance on nuclear weapons to a point where they are significantly marginalized in U.S. national security strategy and military policy and where they are relied on for a narrow range of circumstances and only in the absence of any available substitute. Moreover, for the last three decades, and especially in the Obama administration, national leadership has been focused on taking next steps and creating the conditions that would allow further steps at a future time by the United States and also by other nuclear-armed nations.

As argued elsewhere in this volume, the United States should not abandon the nonproliferation regime and disarmament objective. The costs would well outweigh the benefits. The costs would come in many forms, including domestic division frustrating modernization plans and allied division and resentment. Sooner or later, they would likely also include additional nuclear-armed regional challengers and the related increased risk of nuclear terrorism. Such a move would also open up to other states opportunities to set global nuclear agendas detrimental to U.S. interests. Potential benefits are difficult to conceive.

Rather than abandon the regime or serve up additional palliatives, the United States should draw lessons from recent experience to remake its leading role. First, it should talk directly and seriously about both its efforts to create the conditions for additional steps and the lessons learned. The United States has a better story than anyone to tell about the practicalities of moving toward a world free of nuclear weapons. Its experience points to the need for strategic patience here as in the arms control domain. Second, it should try to seize the moral high ground on nuclear deterrence from the international humanitarian movement. This is a project best undertaken with the other nuclear weapon states; if that's not possible, then a reasonable fallback would be a concerted effort of the United States and its two nuclear allies, Britain and France. Third, it should argue against the proposition that its choices of policy and posture are determinative of the choices of others to adhere to the nonproliferation regime. U.S. choices are important to some states but not determinative to any but our allies who count on the U.S. nuclear umbrella. This line of argument fits well with the continued argument that "general and complete disarmament," as called for in Article VI of the NPT, and the policing of the world order to follow, is everyone's business.

On Strategic Stability with Russia and China

The American strategic community keeps gravitating back to strategic stability as an organizing concept in relations with Russia. It does so in part because the concept is familiar, in part because it is seen as a shared interest with Russia and China, and in part because American experts tend to see strategic stability as a virtue. With Russia, the United States has talked about moving away from mutual assured destruction and toward mutual assured stability.

With China, it has simply advocated for better mutual understanding of the requirements of strategic stability.

But this focus on strategic stability has not proven useful for generating agreement or actions in either bilateral relationship. Moscow has burdened the agenda by adding every possible grievance to its list of complaints about the U.S. approach to strategic stability. Beijing has been unwilling to embrace dialogue on the nuclear relationship between the two countries or the principles that should govern its management.

Moreover, both Moscow and Beijing react to developments in the U.S. strategic postures as deeply unsettling. One simple means of alleviating their concern would be to abandon ballistic missile defense and prompt conventional strike capabilities and along with it the strategy to comprehensively strengthen regional deterrence architectures. This has a superficial appeal if one takes a one-dimensional view of the problem of strategic stability—that is, as it exists in the context of relations with Russia and China. But the world would become a more dangerous place if the United States were to abandon its project to negate the nuclear deterrents of regional challengers. Moreover, it is not clear that such dramatic action would have the desired dramatic effect on perceptions in Moscow and Beijing, where the complaints about developments about the U.S. strategic posture mask deeper concerns about Washington's respect for their core interests and acceptance of their political legitimacy.

Is there a useful alternative organizing concept? A return to Cold War–vintage approaches seems unnecessary and unhelpful. The United States should not try to put nuclear weapons back in a central, dominant place in relations with either Russia or China. It is in the interest of all three countries to avoid a renewal of competition among the major powers for qualitative and perhaps quantitative advantage.

For now at least, the U.S. effort to push forward to a new model based on Mutual Assured Stability (MAS) appears to have come to a dead end. It was premised on continued progress away from adversarial relations with Russia and on the successful avoidance of conflict with China. It was premised also on a perception of shared risks to strategic stability equally valued by all. These premises have proven unsound in current international circumstances.

One viable alternative to strategic stability as an organizing concept for the bilateral dialogues is to have no organizing concept at all. In fact, this may be possible and useful in the U.S.–China relationship, where a dialogue between the two about nuclear deterrence might constructively begin with a dialogue about what the dialogue should be about. Strategic stability objectives and concerns might well inform the thinking of both Washington and Beijing about what issues to discuss, but strategic stability as such need not be the focus of discussion.

But, in the U.S.–Russia relationship, there is no escaping the long history of strategic stability as a central organizing concept. And there is no alternative to coming to some agreements, both formal and informal, about the main elements of the stability framework as a precondition to further nuclear arms reductions—when and if that becomes possible again politically.

Toward these ends, the expert community in the United States could usefully be engaged in a more focused analysis of the issues and concepts the United States should try to bring into discussion with both Russia and China when the opportunity is ripe. The United States needs both a broad and a narrow definition of strategic stability, akin to those of Russia and China. It needs to do more to understand the requirements of stability in the unfolding competitions at the regional or "theater strategic" level. And it needs to better understand what it can be doing unilaterally (and with its allies), as opposed to bilaterally with Russia or China, to protect its own vision of strategic stability.[7]

What More Should Be Done with Military Means?

The purpose of military means is to ensure that deterrence is effective for the problems for which it is relevant. In recent years we have learned a good deal about what needs to be done to ensure this effectiveness. From a high-level policy perspective, three key questions stand out. Is sufficient progress being made in strengthening regional deterrence architectures? Does the United States have the right nuclear forces? Does U.S. nuclear deterrence strategy need to be revised?

On Progress in Strengthening Regional Deterrence Architectures

The United States and its allies have put together a solid approach to adapting and strengthening regional deterrence architectures for 21st-century challenges. The political foundations of continued consultation and cooperation have been put in place. The assurance of anxious allies has been strengthened. But some problems have come into focus.

One problem is the fact that momentum is uneven in the different regions. In Northeast Asia, the progress in adapting and strengthening the regional deterrence architectures has been rapid and substantial. To be sure, significant challenges lie ahead, including the challenge of ensuring a robust architecture vis-à-vis China that does not also inflame worst-case planning in Beijing. In Europe, the progress has been less rapid. The accomplishments of the Deterrence and Defense Posture Review are significant, especially on missile defense and nuclear sharing arrangements, but capabilities have not grown at anything like the desired rate. Moreover, a significant challenge lies ahead in adapting a NATO posture tailored for deterrence of potential aggressors from the Middle East to the new Russian threat to NATO's newest members. In the Middle East, the foundations are being set for future capability growth, but, in comparison to missile proliferation and other developments in the region, the progress is modest at best.

A second problem is that progress in developing the nonnuclear components of the comprehensive strengthening approach has been slow. Regional ballistic missile defenses, for example, still exist only in small numbers. Long-range U.S. conventional prompt strike systems do not exist at all after nearly three decades of discussion. Cyber and space defenses are not yet sufficiently resilient.

This slow progress has been aggravated by problems in the economic domain. Very few of America's allies have the financial means to grow the deterrence architecture at the rate desired. NATO countries continue to fall well short of political pledges to increase defense spending to 2 percent of gross domestic product (GDP). Japan and South Korea have both increased defense spending in recent years but at small marginal rates. U.S. economic difficulties only magnify this problem. The preservation of conventional forces sufficient to ensure favorable local balances has been undermined by the continued contraction of the U.S. military.

All of this implies that the comprehensive strengthening approach remains heavily reliant on the nuclear component of the approach. In fact, if the catalogue of adversary decision points in the spectrum of deterrence challenges is valid, the United States remains reliant on nuclear means to deter certain types of decisions by an adversary for which U.S. nuclear threats may not be credible and effective. This is inconsistent with U.S. interests and with U.S. policy objectives and should motivate urgency in making the needed investments.

In 2017 and beyond, a key issue will be what metric to use in assessing progress in strengthening and adapting regional deterrence architectures. A simple measure is suggested in the preceding paragraphs: financial. A better measure would be to assess progress in each of the capability areas. The best measure would be to assess progress comprehensively in a net assessment relative to the progress of adversaries, real and potential, in fielding capabilities supporting their own theories of victory. Is Red likely to assess the Blue theory of victory as plausible, or will its confidence in its own theory only have grown?

On U.S. Nuclear Deterrence Strategy

U.S. nuclear deterrence strategy was revised in 2013 following a lengthy period of study and deliberation by the Obama administration. As discussed in Chapter 1, the administration reviewed the standing guidance from 2002, assessed changes in the security environment in terms of their impact on U.S. nuclear deterrence, and considered alternative approaches. This was done with some interagency participation and direct presidential engagement. The administration then produced a result with elements of continuity in terms of the strategy of deterrence but elements of change in terms of the nature of potential conflicts. It put a special focus on what it deems "more likely 21st century contingencies" than a major bolt-out-of-the-blue attack by a major power. The subsequent 2014 QDR added that enemy states would not be allowed to escalate their way out of failed conventional aggression.

Experts outside government continue to argue that further changes are warranted. As catalogued in Chapter 1, some groups have argued that existing operational plans are outdated and need to be discarded, while others have argued that planning is "driven largely by inertia and vested Cold War interests." Their advocacy in this area bleeds over into their advocacy for further de-alerting of the ICBM force and for minimum deterrence. Observing that the triad remains, they appear to assume that the American way of thinking about nuclear war hasn't changed since the triad came together in the 1960s. This is simply wrong.

Future reviews will again consider what kinds of contingencies the president and his or her national security team see as plausible and want to prepare for and how such preparations should be done. Leaders will have to form their own judgments about whether and how existing plans are outdated.

On U.S. Nuclear Forces

One way of looking at the U.S. nuclear posture is that it is an artifact of a different time, ill-suited to current purposes, oversized, and excessively expensive to maintain. Another way of looking at it is that it is the natural result of twenty-five years of pruning of excess capabilities and tailoring to newly defined objectives, strategies, and requirements. By this way of thinking, its outward appearance as a Cold War vestige masks substantial transformation in its roles, purposes, and functions in a manner consistent with U.S. interests in a changed and changing world.

I subscribe to this latter view. The current U.S. nuclear posture is, more or less, what we should want in the sense that the basic scale and structure of the force, and the associated capabilities, support the primary functions identified in Chapter 9. This force posture has been modified repeatedly over the three decades since the end of the Cold War to align with the conditions that now exist, as opposed to the conditions we might wish could be brought into existence. The current policy and posture supports all of the six functions set out previously. The posture underwrites a deterrence strategy tailored to the requirements of deterrence, assurance, and strategic stability in the 21st century. It is focused on potential pathways to U.S. nuclear employment in the conditions created by regional actors that might cross the red lines in U.S. declaratory policy. It affords full presidential control but also affords the president the needed decision time to deliberate in crisis. It is robust against further erosion of the security environment—and also easy to tailor in responses to positive changes in that environment.

The one key attribute that is out of sync with requirements is in the aged character of the force. It's running out of shelf life and needs to be replaced. The United States needs to get on with the delayed replacement of aging delivery systems, warheads and bombs, and the associated command and control system. It can do so in a manner that avoids arms races with other major powers. It can do so at a level affordable to the nation and to the Departments of Defense and Energy. Will it be expensive? Yes. Will it be controversial, especially among those not invested in the strategic patience called for above? Of course. Is it essential to underwrite the objectives of U.S. national security strategy? Yes. Perhaps most fundamentally, modernization of these U.S. capabilities would affirm to potential adversaries and allies alike that the United States remains committed to its role as a security guarantor despite new nuclear challenges. This would send a powerful message at a time of widespread debate about American decline and disengagement.

Two key questions will shape the future modernization program. Is the entire current force structure still needed? Are new warheads needed as opposed to extending the life of existing warheads (the current practice)?

This book has made a strong case for modernization of the dual-capable aircraft (and associated bomb) as essential for both extended deterrence and assurance. It has not so far made a case for the triad, except insofar as it underwrites U.S. commitments to its allies and to strategic stability with Russia and China. It has also argued that U.S. nuclear forces must remain resilient in the face of attack on them.

All of these factors imply a continued value for the triad. A decision to retire the submarine leg would strip away the most secure of America's retaliatory capabilities. A decision to retire the bomber leg would weaken the ability of the United States to signal its resolve in crisis and its support of its allies and to track and attack mobile missiles, precisely the kind of targets it is likely to want to be able destroy in an escalating regional conflict. A decision to retire the land-based ICBMs, in the absence of a similar Russian commitment, would undermine strategic stability (by moving the United States from a second-to-none position to a second-to-one) and eliminate the leg of the triad most capable of prompt and highly accurate attack in limited numbers. It would also be placing a major bet on the long-term survivability of the sea-based deterrent—a bet that the revolution in sensors and computing that have made fully transparent the surface of the earth and the air and space above it will not, over the multidecade life of the submarine force, have some similar impact there as well. Moreover, elimination of such a large set of targets (that is, ICBM silos) that an enemy would need to strike preemptively could also have unanticipated consequences in a future major military confrontation with a peer or near-peer military power; if not faced with the need to strike at hundreds of missiles in the American heartland, an enemy leader might conclude that a preemptive attack on the United States could so reduce American retaliatory forces as to make American retaliation either implausible or bearable.

Vladimir Putin has boasted that Russia has kept its strategic powder dry. The United States would run unneeded risk if it were not to do the same. Retiring one leg of the triad as the next contribution to arms control and disarmament, or as a bow to fiscal austerity, is just the form of unilateral action the United States should resist. The benefits to the United States in the absence of reciprocal steps by Russia and China are not obvious, except on the specific basis of costs avoided by retiring rather than modernizing the force.

The second key question associated with modernizing the military means is whether new nuclear warheads are needed, as opposed to the current practice of extending the life of existing warheads. These warheads would be new in the sense that their performance characteristics in terms of yield and other effects on target are not available in the current arsenal.

The central question is whether an arsenal originally built for major nuclear war with a major power has the right suite of capabilities for deterrence in a limited regional war. The case has been made that deterrence would be more effective if the president were to be able to threaten to employ quickly a weapon with low yield.[8] Right now the only nuclear weapons a U.S. president can employ promptly at long range are high-yield weapons with potentially significant collateral effects, such as downwind radiation, that may weigh heavily on neighboring states. The only weapons with lower collateral effects are delivered by bombers or cruise missiles, which may take hours or days to strike their target—assuming they are capable of penetrating air defenses.

The case for the addition of these weapons to the U.S. arsenal hinges on an assessment of whether they add credibility to U.S. threats in the eyes of the adversary. An enemy leader may believe that the U.S. president is more likely to employ weapons with low collateral damage than with high collateral damage if there is some risk that collateral damage will be harmful to neighboring states. This seems plausible but is not testable.

The usual case against the addition of these weapons is that the effort to fund them would derail the balanced approach and rule out sustainment of existing capabilities through life extension of the warhead. In short, the perfect might prove to be the enemy of the good enough. This is a testable proposition, and the message from the Bush years is clear—its efforts to fund a new earth-penetrating weapon and then a new, more generic replacement warhead were both rejected by Congress, and the only modernization agreed was for a life extension program for an existing warhead. Of course, changes in the domestic political context, including perhaps changes of threat perception emanating from changes in the security environment, may yet cause a shift in the ability of the U.S. Congress to support modernization of a kind that permits some new capabilities.

The case can also be made that the existing nuclear arsenal has all of the tools needed to support national deterrence strategy and gives the president all of the options he might want in war. The perception that lower-yield weapons are more usable and thus more credible as threats somewhat misses the point about why the United States has nuclear weapons in the first place. It has them not to signal continuity of war from the conventional level but to signal the dramatic new front opened in a war by an enemy's actions that put our vital interests (or those of an ally or partner) at risk. Nuclear weapons are inherently brutish. Lower-yield weapons with reduced collateral effects may offer some deterrence and assurance benefits but would not fundamentally erase the usefully large gap between conventional and nuclear war.

This review of key issues in modernizing the deterrent has focused on core U.S. capabilities. As argued in Chapter 9, the U.S. nuclear posture consists of not just capabilities but also capacities and competencies. These too require investment and modernization after a long period of stagnation and decay. The United States must have the technical capacity to respond to geopolitical and technical surprises with the production of additional nuclear weapons (or with refurbishment at an accelerated rate). The United States must also reinvest in the intellectual infrastructure in a manner sufficient to 21st-century purposes. This work should include exploration and testing of the Red theories of victory that have or are taking shape and the corresponding Blue theory.

Conclusion

The balanced approach to U.S. nuclear strategy has an enduring value to the United States and its allies, though it must be periodically realigned to lessons learned and new circumstances. It is a political expedient, in that it is necessary to get anything accomplished in a divided system of government. But it is much more than that, in that the two elements of the balanced approach provide strategic benefits of many kinds and are mutually reinforcing.

With regard to the political and legal aspects of the approach, some hard lessons have been learned in recent years. The door to additional negotiated nuclear arms reductions with Russia appears firmly closed until the New START Treaty expires in 2021 (or 2026). Russia will then face a choice about whether its interests are better served by legal restraints on American strategic forces. Strategic patience is in order. The only option for additional reductions in U.S. deployed forces for the next few years are unilateral, and these should be avoided as not consistent with the interests of the United States or its allies. In political efforts to advance cooperation with Russia and China, strategic stability remains the right organizing concept—but the United States should have at best modest expectations for any transformational effect in terms of enhanced appreciation of shared interests and shared approaches.

With regard to the military aspects of the approach, some other hard lessons have been learned. One is the need for unilateral steps to ensure strategic stability, in addition to whatever bilateral steps may yet prove possible with Russia and China. This means continued pursuit of the comprehensive approach to strengthening regional deterrence architectures. In the absence of better headway in the future, the United States and its allies will remain uncomfortably reliant on U.S. nuclear threats to deal with deterrence challenges for which they may not be fully reliable or effective. To inform and guide this effort, the United States must more fully elaborate its own theory of victory in regional wars under the nuclear shadow, with an eye on the thinking of both Clausewitz and Sun Tzu.

Additionally, the United States is entering a phase when it can no longer avoid modernization of U.S. nuclear forces. It must modernize capabilities, capacities, and core competencies. All three have been left to decline and decay at a time of shifting U.S. priorities. The United States should modernize the triad along with the dual-capable aircraft and associated warheads, bombs, and command and control system. This will not be inexpensive, but it is affordable.

The closing message of this book must be about leadership focus. In the absence of the needed leadership focus in the 1990s and 2000s, the case for deterrence and the deterrent began to come apart. The main message came through loudly enough: presidents wanted to shift away from Cold War thinking and approaches and to deemphasize nuclear weapons. President Obama embraced this shift but also laid the foundation for a push to meet the requirements of safe, secure, and effective nuclear deterrence so long as nuclear weapons remain. The next president, and his or her successors, needs to see nuclear weapons as an enduring challenge for American security policy and not merely a Cold War legacy. This message too must come through loudly, in a forthright presidential dialogue with the American people (and allied publics) about the content and context of U.S. nuclear policy and strategy.

Future presidents must understand that nuclear weapons are uniquely the president's weapons: they are his or her most powerful tool for preventing threats to the vital interests of the United States and its allies, and the president alone has the authority to employ them in what would be a highly momentous act. He or she must be willing to clearly set out the current roles of nuclear weapons and their relationship to high-level political objectives. He or she must be the steward of the balanced approach, compelling the executive departments to proceed in close coordination and resisting the temptation to align solely with one camp or the other in the sharply divided debate about U.S. nuclear policy. Future presidents must also be mindful of the need to be successful with the Congress and to temper partisan agendas with a view to ensuring the long-term viability of the balanced approach. And they must be mindful of the need to safeguard the interests of U.S. allies and partners, by signaling continued U.S. commitment to a form of extended deterrence suited to the 21st century and to their assurance. Finally, future presidents would be well advised to look to the future rather than the past, to spend less energy moving away from the Cold War and more energy ensuring that policy, posture, and strategy are well aligned with the world in which we now live.

REFERENCE MATTER

Notes

Introduction

1. Michael May, "The Trouble with Disarmament," *Bulletin of the Atomic Scientists*, Vol. 64, No. 5 (November/December 2008), pp. 20–21.

Chapter 1

1. *Nuclear Weapons Employment Policy*, National Security Decision Directive No. 13, October 1981, originally top secret but partially declassified on December 9, 1998.

2. David Kunsman and Douglas B. Lawson, *A Primer on U.S. Strategic Nuclear Policy* (Albuquerque, NM: Sandia National Laboratory, 1991); and Henry D. Sokolski, ed., *Getting MAD: Mutual Assured Destruction, Its Origins and Practice* (Carlisle Barracks, PA: Strategic Studies Institute of the U.S. Army War College, 2004).

3. Ronald Reagan, "State of the Union" address, January 1984.

4. Joe Holley, referencing a 1997 letter to the editor of the *Washington Post*, in Obituary, "Leon Sloss, 80; Expert on U.S. Nuclear Policy," *Washington Post*, November 10, 2006.

5. Bernard Brodie, *Strategy in the Missile Age* (Princeton, NJ: Princeton University Press, 1959), p. 278.

6. Colin S. Gray, "Nuclear Strategy: The Case for a Theory of Victory," *International Security*, Vol. 4, No. 1 (Summer 1979), p. 62. See also Colin S. Gray and Keith Payne, "Victory is Possible," *Foreign Policy*, No. 39 (1980), pp. 14–27; and Michael E. Howard, "On Fighting a Nuclear War," *International Security*, Vol. 5, No. 4 (1981), pp. 2–17.

7. John Hines, Ellis M. Mishulovich, and John F. Shulk, *Soviet Intentions 1965–1985, Vol. I: An Analytical Assessment of U.S.–Soviet Assessments during the Cold War* (Arlington, VA: BDM Federal Inc., 1995).

8. See Sokolski, *Getting MAD.*

9. President George H. W. Bush, "Address to the Nation on Reducing United States and Soviet Nuclear Weapons," September 27, 1991.

10. "The Presidential Nuclear Initiatives (PNIs) on Tactical Nuclear Weapons at a Glance" (Washington, DC: Arms Control Association, August 2012).

11. Richard B. Cheney, *Annual Report of the Secretary of Defense to the President and Congress* (Washington, DC: Department of Defense, February 1992).

12. *A National Security Strategy of Engagement and Enlargement,* The White House, July 1994, p. i.

13. Ibid., p. ii.

14. John Lancaster, "Aspin Pledges New Military Efforts to Counter Weapons Proliferation," *Washington Post,* December 8, 1993, p. 7.

15. The results of the review were not published as a self-standing report. Rather, they were included as a chapter in the secretary of defense's annual report to Congress. See "Nuclear Posture Review," in *1995 Annual Defense Report, Department of Defense.* See also Janne E. Nolan, *An Elusive Consensus: Nuclear Weapons and American Security after the Cold War* (Washington, DC: Brookings Institution, 1999).

16. William A. Perry, from transcript of Defense Department Briefing, *Nuclear Posture Review,* September 22, 1994, p. 1, cited in Michael R. Boldrick, "The Nuclear Posture Review: Liabilities and Risks," *Parameters* (Winter 1995–1996), pp. 80–91.

17. "Senate Rejects Comprehensive Test Ban Treaty; Clinton Vows to Continue Moratorium," *Arms Control Today* on-line, September 10, 1999, available at www.armscontrol.org.

18. Ibid.

19. Greg Thielman, "The National Missile Defense Act of 1999," *Arms Control Today,* July 8, 2009.

20. Robert G. Bell, senior director for defense policy at the National Security Council, cited in R. Jeffrey Smith, "Clinton Directive Changes Strategy on Nuclear Arms," *Washington Post,* December 7, 1997, p. 10.

21. Ibid.

22. See, for example, the *1995 Secretary of Defense Annual Report to Congress.*

23. For examples of this work, see Kenneth Watman et al., *U.S. Regional Deterrence Strategies* (Santa Monica, CA: RAND, 1995); Dean Wilkening and Kenneth Watman, *Nuclear Deterrence in a Regional Context* (Santa Monica, CA: RAND, 1995); and Victor Utgoff, ed., *The Coming Crisis: Nuclear Proliferation, U.S. Interests, and World Order* (Cambridge, MA: MIT Press, 2000).

24. See, for example, *Toward a Nuclear Peace: The Future of Nuclear Weapons in U.S. Foreign and Defense Policy,* Report of the CSIS Nuclear Strategy Study Group (Washington, DC: Center for Strategic and International Studies, 1994).

25. Randy Rydell, "Looking Back: The 1995 NPT Review and Extension Conference," *Arms Control Today*, April 1, 2005. Available at www.armscontrol.org/act/2005_4/LookingBack

26. The broader mandate addressed cooperative threat reduction activities with the states of the former Soviet Union. *Defense Nuclear Agency, 1947–1997* (Washington, DC: Office of the Historian of the Defense Threat Reduction Agency, 2000).

27. Statement by Vice President Al Gore, White House, April 18, 1997.

28. Matthew Rojansky and Andrew Semmel, *Congress Needs Bigger Role in Arms Control* (Washington, DC: Carnegie Endowment for International Peace, 2010).

29. Fred Ikle, "The Second Coming of the Nuclear Age," *Foreign Affairs*, Vol. 75, No. 1 (January/February 1996).

30. See also Richard K. Betts, "The New Threat of Mass Destruction," *Foreign Affairs*, Vol. 77, No. 1 (January/February 1998).

31. Keith B. Payne, *Deterrence in the Second Nuclear Age* (Lexington: University Press of Kentucky, 1996), p. 116.

32. Ibid., pp. 158–159.

33. Colin S. Gray, *The Second Nuclear Age* (Boulder, CO: Lynne Rienner, 1999), p. 33.

34. Lawrence Freedman, *Deterrence* (Cambridge, UK: Polity Press, 2004), p. 1.

35. See, for example, McGeorge Bundy, William J. Crowe Jr., and Sidney D. Drell, *Reducing Nuclear Danger: The Road Away from the Brink* (Washington, DC: Council on Foreign Relations, 1993); and Graham Allison et al., eds., *Cooperative Denuclearization: From Pledges to Deeds* (Cambridge, MA: Center for Science and International Affairs, Harvard University, 1993). See also Cathleen Fisher, *Reformation and Resistance: Nongovernmental Organizations and the Future of Nuclear Weapons* (Washington, DC: Henry L. Stimson Center, 1999).

36. Leon Sloss, *The Current Nuclear Dialogue*, Report No. 156 (Washington, DC: Institute for National Strategic Studies of the National Defense University, 1999).

37. *The National Security Strategy of the United States of America*, The White House, September 2002. See also Brad Roberts, *American Primacy and Major Power Concert: A Critique of the 2002 National Security Strategy* (Alexandria, VA: Institute for Defense Analyses, 2002).

38. Jim Garamone, "Rumsfeld Warns of Nexus of Rogue States, Terror Networks," American Forces Press Service, February 3, 2002.

39. *Rationale and Requirements for U.S. Nuclear Forces and Arms Control, Volume I, Executive Summary* (Fairfax, VA: National Institute for Public Policy, 2001).

40. Stephen A. Cambone and Patrick J. Garrity, "The Future of U.S. Nuclear Policy," *Survival*, Vol. 36, No.4 (1994–1995), pp. 73–95.

41. Janne E. Nolan, "Preparing for the 2001 Nuclear Posture Review," *Arms Control Today*, Vol. 30, No. 9 (2000), pp. 10–14.

42. Douglas J. Feith, statement before the Senate Armed Services Committee hearing on the Nuclear Posture Review, February 14, 2002. See also "U.S. Department of Defense Briefing Slides," January 9, 2002; Donald H. Rumsfeld, foreword to *Nuclear*

Posture Review Report, January 2002; and Rumsfeld, *Annual Report to the President and the Congress* (Washington, DC: Office of the Secretary of Defense, 2003).

43. Keith B. Payne, "The Nuclear Posture Review: Setting the Record Straight," *Washington Quarterly*, Vol. 28, No. 3 (Summer 2005), pp. 135–151. See also Payne, "The Nuclear Posture Review and Deterrence for a New Age," *Comparative Strategy*, Vol. 23, No. 4/5 (2004); Kurt Guthe, *The Nuclear Posture Review: How Is the "New Triad" New?* (Washington, DC: Center for Strategic and Budgetary Assessments, 2002); Daryl G. Kimball, Janne E. Nolan, Rose Gottemoeller, and Morton H. Halperin, "Parsing the Nuclear Posture Review," *Arms Control Today*, Vol. 32, No. 2 (2002), pp. 15–21; and Richard Sokolsky, "Demystifying the U.S. Nuclear Posture Review," *Survival*, Vol. 44, No. 3 (2002), pp. 133–148.

44. Speech by President George W. Bush, National Defense University, Washington, DC, May 1, 2001.

45. Paul I. Bernstein, "Post–Cold War US Nuclear Strategy," in Jeffrey A. Larsen and Kerry M. Kartchner, eds., *On Limited Nuclear War in the 21st Century*, p. 89 (Stanford, CA: Stanford University Press, 2014).

46. Secretary of Defense Donald Rumsfeld, "Adapting U.S. Strategic Forces," *Annual Report of the Secretary of Defense to the President and Congress, 2002*, chapter 7, p. 5. See also Payne, "The Nuclear Posture Review: Setting the Record Straight," p. 142.

47. Terence Neilan, "Bush Pulls Out of ABM Treaty; Putin Calls Move a Mistake," *New York Times*, December 13, 2001.

48. See letter of transmittal, President George W. Bush to the U.S. Senate, the Treaty between the United States of America and the Russian Federation on Strategic Offensive Reductions, signed at Moscow on May 24, 2002 (the Moscow Treaty), June 20, 2002.

49. *The Commitment of the United States of America to Article VI of the Treaty on the Nonproliferation of Nuclear Weapons*, White House, 2005. On Ford's work, see, for example, Christopher A. Ford, "Achieving and Sustaining Nuclear Weapons Elimination, delivered at a conference on "Preparing for 2010: Getting the Process Right," Annecy, France, March 17, 2007." The text is available at the on-line archive of the U.S. Department of State at http://2001-2009.state.gov/t/isn/rls/other/81943.htm. Retrieved September 8, 2014.

50. *Report of the Secretary of Defense Task Force on DoD Nuclear Weapons Management, Phase 1, The Air Force's Nuclear Mission*, September 2008, and *Phase 2*, December 2008.

51. *National Security and Nuclear Weapons in the 21st Century*, September 2008. Washington, DC: Departments of Defense and Energy.

52. *A More Secure World: Our Shared Responsibility*, Report of the Secretary General's High-Level Panel on Threats, Challenges, and Change (New York: United Nations, 2004), p. 40, para. 111.

53. Kurt M. Campbell, Robert J. Einhorn, and Mitchell B. Reiss, eds., *The Nuclear Tipping Point: Why States Reconsider Their Nuclear Choices* (Washington, DC: Brookings, 2004).

54. *Report on Discouraging a Cascade of Nuclear Weapon States*, International Security Advisory Board. Washington, DC: Department of State, October 19, 2007.

55. George P. Shultz, William J. Perry, Henry A. Kissinger, and Sam Nunn, "A World Free of Nuclear Weapons," *Wall Street Journal*, January 4, 2007. See also Sidney D. Drell and James E. Goodby, *The Gravest Danger: Nuclear Weapons* (Stanford, CA: Hoover Institution Press, 2008); and Drell and Goodby, *What Are Nuclear Weapons For? Recommendations for Restructuring U.S. Strategic Nuclear Forces* (Washington, DC: Arms Control Association, 2005).

56. Shultz et al., "A World Free of Nuclear Weapons."

57. George P. Shultz, William J. Perry, Henry A. Kissinger, and Sam Nunn, "Toward a Nuclear-Free World," *Wall Street Journal*, January 15, 2008.

58. Stephen I. Schwartz, *Barack Obama and John McCain on Nuclear Security Issues* (Monterey, CA: James Martin Center for Nonproliferation Studies, September 2008).

59. See *A World without Nuclear Weapons* (Global Zero). Retrieved on February 15, 2014, from www.globalzero.org/our-movement.

60. Thérèse Delpech, "Nuclear Weapons and the New World Order: Early Warning from Asia?" *Survival*, Vol. 4, No. 4 (Winter 1998–1999), p. 57. See also Delpech, *Nuclear Deterrence in the 21st Century: Lessons from the Cold War for a New Era of Strategic Piracy* (Santa Monica, CA: RAND, 2012).

61. Paul Bracken, *Fire in the East: The Rise of Asian Military Power and the Second Nuclear Age* (New York: Harper Collins, 1999), p. 96.

62. Muthiah Alagappa, ed., *The Long Shadow: Nuclear Weapons and Security in 21st Century Asia* (Stanford, CA: Stanford University Press, 2008), p. 89.

63. Stephen Peter Rosen, "After Proliferation: What to Do If More States Go Nuclear," *Foreign Affairs*, Vol. 85, No. 5 (September/October 2006). See also T. V. Paul, Patrick M. Morgan, and James J. Wirtz, *Complex Deterrence: Strategy in the Global Age* (Chicago: University of Chicago Press, 2009).

64. Ibid.

65. Mark Fitzpatrick, *The World After: Proliferation, Deterrence, and Disarmament if the Nuclear Taboo Is Broken*, Proliferation Paper (Paris: IFRI, 2009).

66. Remarks of President Barack Obama, Hradčany Square, Prague, Czech Republic, April 5, 2009.

67. *America's Strategic Posture: The Final Report of the Congressional Commission on the U.S. Strategic Posture* (Washington, DC: United States Institute of Peace, 2009), p. xvi. See also background papers published as Taylor Bolz, ed., *In the Eyes of the Experts: Analysis and Comments on America's Strategic Posture* (Washington, DC: U.S. Institute of Peace, 2009).

68. *National Security Strategy*, May 2010.

69. *Nuclear Posture Review Report, 2010*, pp. vii–viii.

70. William J. Perry and James R. Schlesinger, "Nuclear Review Shows Bipartisanship," *Politico*, April 14, 2010.

71. Daryl G. Kimball and Greg Thielman, "Obama's NPR Transitional, Not Transformational," *Arms Control Today* (May 2010).

72. *Report on Nuclear Employment Strategy of the United States, Specified in Section 491 of 10 U.S.C.*, White House, June 12, 2013.

73. Ibid., pp. 4–5.

74. Bruce Blair et al., "Smaller and Safer: A New Plan for Nuclear Postures," *Foreign Affairs*, Vol. 89, No. 5 (September/October 2010), p. 10.

75. *Report on Nuclear Employment Strategy of the United States*, p. 5.

76. White House Fact Sheet, *New Nuclear Employment Guidance*, June 12, 2013.

77. Ibid.

78. *Quadrennial Defense Review 2014*, p. v.

79. See Hans M. Kristensen, "Falling Short on Prague: Obama's Nuclear Weapons Employment Policy," *Arms Control Today*, September 2013.

80. Clark Murdock, "Little Content, Even Less Satisfaction in Obama's Nuclear Weapons Policy," *Arms Control Today*, September 2013.

81. See, for example, Steven Pifer and Michael O'Hanlon, *The Opportunity: Next Steps in Reducing Nuclear Arms* (Washington, DC: Brookings Institution, 2012); and CSIS Next Generation Working Group on U.S.–Russian Arms Control, *Beyond New START: Advancing U.S. National Security through Arms Control with Russia* (Washington, DC: Center for Strategic and International Studies, 2011).

82. See, for example, Elbridge Colby and Michael Gerson, *Strategic Stability: Contending Interpretations* (Carlisle Barracks, PA: U.S. Army War College Strategic Studies Institute, 2013); James Clay Moltz, *Assessing the Impact of Low Nuclear Numbers on Strategic Stability: A Regional Analysis*, Report No. 2013-003 (Monterey, CA: Naval Postgraduate School, 2013); and Jeffrey A. Larsen et al., *Qualitative Considerations of Nuclear Forces at Lower Numbers and Implications for Future Arms Control Negotiations*, INSS Occasional Paper 68 (Colorado Springs, CO: U.S. Air Force Academy, July 2012).

83. See, for example, *Global Zero Nuclear Policy Commission Report: Modernizing U.S. Nuclear Policy, Force Structure, and Posture* (Web: Global Zero, 2012). Available at www.globalzero.org/files/gz_us_nuclear_policy_commission_report.pdf. See also Catherine Kelleher and Judith Reppy, eds., *Getting to Zero: The Path to Nuclear Disarmament* (Stanford, CA: Stanford University Press, 2011); and Sidney D. Drell and James E. Goodby, *A World without Nuclear Weapons: End-State Issues* (Stanford, CA: Hoover Institution Press, 2009).

84. George P. Shultz, William J. Perry, Henry A. Kissinger, and Sam Nunn, "Deterrence in the Age of Nuclear Proliferation," *Wall Street Journal*, March 7, 2011.

85. George P. Shultz, William J. Perry, Henry A. Kissinger, and Sam Nunn, "Next Steps in Reducing Nuclear Risks: The Pace of Nonproliferation Work Today Doesn't Match the Urgency of the Threat," *Wall Street Journal*, March 6, 2013.

86. Henry A. Kissinger and Brent Scowcroft, "Nuclear Weapon Reductions Must Be Part of Strategic Analysis," *Washington Post*, April 22, 2012.

87. See, for example, George Perkovich and James M. Acton, eds., *Abolishing Nuclear Weapons: A Debate* (Washington, DC: Carnegie Endowment for International Peace, 2009).

88. Bruce Blair et al., "Smaller and Safer: A New Plan for Nuclear Postures," *Foreign Affairs*, Vol. 89, No. 5 (September/October 2010); and James Wood Forsyth Jr., B. Chance Saltzman, and Gary Schaub Jr., "Remembrance of Things Past: The Enduring Value of Nuclear Weapons," *Strategic Studies Quarterly* (Spring 2010), pp. 74–89. See also James M. Acton, *Low Numbers: A Practical Path to Deep Nuclear Reductions* (Washington, DC: Carnegie Endowment for International Peace, 2011); Malcolm Chalmers, *Less Is Better: Nuclear Restraint at Low Numbers*, Whitehall Paper 78 (London: Royal United Services Institute, 2012); and Forsyth et al., "Minimum Deterrence and Its Critics," *Strategic Studies Quarterly* (Winter 2010), pp. 3–12.

89. See, for example, George Perkovich and James Acton, *Abolishing Nuclear Weapons* (Oxford, UK: Routledge for the International Institute for Strategic Studies, 2008).

90. Ward Wilson, *Five Myths about Nuclear Weapons* (New York: Houghton Mifflin Harcourt, 2013).

91. From the Chair's Summary, Second Conference on the Humanitarian Impact of Nuclear Weapons, Mexico City, February 14, 2014.

92. Gareth Evans and Yoriko Kawaguchi, cochairs, *Eliminating Nuclear Threats: A Practical Agenda for Global Policymakers*, Report of the International Commission on Nuclear Non-Proliferation and Disarmament (Canberra: Paragon, 2009).

93. *Global Zero Action Plan.*

94. Ibid.

95. *Global Zero U.S. Nuclear Policy Commission Report*, p. 3.

96. Ibid., pp. 9, 14, 9.

97. Ibid., p. 2.

98. Ibid., p. 18.

99. Ibid., p. 1.

100. Franklin C. Miller, *The Need for a Strong U.S. Nuclear Deterrent in the 21st Century* (Washington, DC: Submarine Industrial Base Council, 2012), p. 9.

101. Richard Mies, "Strategic Deterrence in the 21st Century," *Undersea Warfare* (Spring 2012), pp. 12–19. See also Michael Quinlan, *Thinking about Nuclear Weapons: Principles, Problems, and Prospects* (Oxford, UK: Oxford University Press, 2009); and Elbridge A. Colby, "Why Nuclear Deterrence Is Still Relevant," in Adam B. Lowther, ed., *Deterrence: Rising Powers, Rogue Regimes, and Terrorism in the 21st Century*, pp. 51–74 (New York: Palgrave Macmillan, 2012).

102. Forsyth et al., "Remembrance of Things Past," p. 74.

103. Jeff Schogol, "Are Purple Hearts from 1945 Still Being Awarded?" *Stars and Stripes*, September 1, 2010.

104. Marco J. Lyons, "U.S. Nuclear Policy, Strategy, and Force Structure: Insights and Issues from the 1994, 2001, and 2010 Nuclear Posture Reviews," Thesis, Naval Postgraduate School, Monterey, CA, September 2014.

105. Kurt Guthe, *Ten Continuities in U.S. Nuclear Weapons Policy, Strategy, Plans, and Forces* (Fairfax, VA: National Institute for Public Policy, 2008).

106. From remarks by Stephen Hadley, National Security Advisor, to the Center for International Security and Cooperation, Stanford University, February 11, 2008.

107. Supplemental materials provided in conjunction with testimony by Elaine Bunn, Deputy Assistant Secretary of Defense for Nuclear and Missile Defense Policy, Senate Committee on Armed Services Committee, Subcommittee on Strategic Forces, March 16, 2014. See also Karen Parrish, "DOD Officials Update Congress on Nuclear Weapons Program," American Forces Press Service, April 9, 2014.

108. Ibid. See also William J. Perry and John P. Abizaid, cochairs, *Ensuring a Strong U.S. Defense for the Future*, Report of the National Defense Panel Review of the 2014 Quadrennial Defense Review, August 2014, p. 51.

109. Madelyn Creedon, "Ash Carter Got It Right," *Defense One* on-line service, July 30, 2013. Retrieved on June 3, 2014, from www.defenseone.com/voices/madelyn-creedon/7349/.

110. Figures from *Projected Costs of U.S. Nuclear Forces, 2014 to 2023* (Washington, DC: Congressional Budget Office, 2013). The U.S. government does not provide a single annual statement of spending on nuclear deterrence, and there is considerable debate about how it should be calculated and the final total. See "U.S. Nuclear Weapons Budget: An Overview," Nuclear Threat Initiative (Washington, DC) on-line. Retrieved on August 11, 2014, from www.nti.org/analysis/articles/us-nuclear-weapons-budget-overview/.

111. For an important exception, see Clark A. Murdock, Stephanie Spies, and John Warden, *Forging a Consensus for a Sustainable Nuclear Posture*, A Report of the CSIS Nuclear Consensus Working Group (Washington, DC: Center for Strategic and International Studies, 2013).

112. *America's Strategic Posture*, p. 66.

113. "U.S. Military Leaders and Bipartisan National Security Officials Overwhelmingly Support New START," Arms Control Association on-line Issue Brief, Vol. 1, No. 44 (December 16, 2010). Retrieved on November 13, 2013, from www.armscontrol.org/issuebriefs/bipartisanNewSTARTSupport.

114. For a representative sample of the caustic tone of the ratification debate, see Mark Schneider, *New START: The Anatomy of a Failed Negotiation* (Fairfax, VA: National Institute for Public Policy, July 2012).

115. Tom Z. Colina and the Arms Control Association Research Staff, *The Unaffordable Arsenal: Reducing the Costs of the U.S. Nuclear Stockpile* (Washington, DC: Arms Control Association, October 2014).

116. Citations in William J. Broad, "Which President Cut the Most Nukes," *New York Times*, November 1, 2014.

117. George P. Shultz, William J. Perry, Henry A. Kissinger, and Sam Nunn, "How to Protect Our Nuclear Deterrent," *Wall Street Journal*, January 19, 2010.

118. William J. Perry and John P. Abizaid, cochairmen, *Ensuring a Strong U.S. Defense for the Future*, the National Defense Panel Review of the 2014 Quadrennial Defense Review, July 2014, pp. 50–51.

119. *Nuclear Posture Review Report, 2012*, pp. 48–49.

120. John Kyl, "Kyl Remarks at Carnegie Nuclear Conference," Kyl Press Release, March 29, 2011; and Douglas J. Feith, Frank J. Gaffney, James A. Lyons, and R. James Woolsey, "Obama's Harmful Nuclear Illusions," *Washington Post*, March 31, 2013, p. 15. See also Harold Brown and John Deutch, "The Nuclear Disarmament Fantasy," *Wall Street Journal*, November 19, 2007, p. 19.

Chapter 2

1. The view was expressed to a conference of the Defense Nuclear Agency in June 1993. See *Proceedings*, Defense Nuclear Agency Second Annual Conference on Controlling Arms, June 1993.

2. Paul Nitze, "Atoms, Strategy and Policy," *Foreign Affairs*, Vol. 35, No. 1 (January 1956).

3. See the *Report to the President of the United States, Commission on the Intelligence Capabilities of the United States Regarding Weapons of Mass Destruction*, March 31, 2005.

4. Patrick Garrity, "Implications of the Persian Gulf War for Regional Powers," *Washington Quarterly*, Vol. 16, No. 3 (Summer 1992), pp. 171–184.

5. Thomas H. Henriksen, *America and the Rogue States* (New York: Palgrave, 2012).

6. This chapter and the following draw in part on arguments first appearing in Brad Roberts, *The Strategic Values of Ballistic Missile Defense*, Proliferation Paper No. 50 (Paris: Institut Français des Relations Internationale, 2014).

7. This chronology is taken from the Libya country profile of the Nuclear Threat Initiative. See also Joshua Sinai, "Libya's Pursuit of Weapons of Mass Destruction," *Nonproliferation Review*, Vol. 4, No. 2 (Spring–Summer 1997); and Sharon Squassoni and Andrew Feickert, *Disarming Libya: Weapons of Mass Destruction* (Washington, DC: Congressional Research Service, April 2004).

8. This chronology is taken from the Syria country profile of the Nuclear Threat Initiative. See also Thérèse Delpech, "Un An Après: Nouvelles Questions sur le Raid du 6 Septembre 2007," *Politique Étrangère*, No. 3 (2008), pp. 643–652.

9. See *Comprehensive Report of the Special Adviser to the DCI on Iraqi WMD*, September 30, 2004.

10. Norman Cigar, *Iraq's Nascent Nuclear Doctrine: Insights from a Captured Document*, Policy Watch No. 723 (Washington, DC: Washington Institute for Near East Policy, March 2003). See also Hal Brands and David Palkki, *Why Did Saddam Want the Bomb? The Israel Factor and the Iraqi Nuclear Program*, Foreign Policy Research Institute E-Notes, August 2011. Retrieved on February 11, 2014, from www.fpri.org.

11. Charles A. Duelfer, "Weapons of Mass Destruction Programs in Iraq: Testimony of Charles A. Duelfer to the Subcommittee on Emerging Threats and Capabilities Armed Services Committee of the United States Senate," February 27, 2002. See also Graham S. Pearson, *The Search for Saddam's Weapons of Mass Destruction: Inspection, Verification, and Nonproliferation* (New York: Palgrave MacMillan, 2005).

12. See *Comprehensive Report of the Special Adviser to the DCI on Iraqi WMD.*

13. Ibid.

14. Kenneth M. Pollack, *Unthinkable: Iran, the Bomb, and American Strategy* (New York: Simon and Schuster, 2013), p. 33.

15. As cited in ibid., p. 14. See also Akbar Ganji, "Who Is Ali Khamenei? The Worldview of Iran's Supreme Leader," *Foreign Affairs*, Vol. 92, No. 5 (September/October 2013), pp. 24–48.

16. Pollack, *Unthinkable*, p. xviii.

17. Alireza Nader, *Iran after the Bomb: How Would a Nuclear-Armed Tehran Behave?* (Santa Monica, CA: RAND, 2013); and Lynn E. Davis et al., *Iran's Nuclear Future: Critical U.S. Policy Choices* (Santa Monica, CA: RAND, 2011).

18. Nader, *Iran after the Bomb*, p. 3. See also James M. Lindsay and Ray Takeyh, "After Iran Gets the Bomb," *Foreign Affairs*, Vol. 89, No. 2 (March/April 2010), pp. 33–49.

19. Pollack, *Unthinkable*, pp. 66–67.

20. Eric S. Edelman, Andrew F. Krepinevich, and Evan Braden Montgomery, *The Dangers of a Nuclear Iran: The Limits of Containment*, Vol. 90, No. 1 (January/February 2011), p. 74.

21. Henry Kissinger, *World Order* (New York: Penguin Press, 2014), p. 152.

22. Ibid., p. 140.

23. Edelman et al., *The Dangers of a Nuclear Iran*, p. 74.

24. Davis et al., *Iran's Nuclear Future*, pp. xiv–xvi.

25. Michael Eisenstadt, *The Strategic Culture of the Islamic Republic of Iran: Operational and Policy Implications*, Middle East Studies Monograph No. 1 (Quantico, VA: Marine Corps University, 2011).

26. Mark Nicol, "Exposed: Jihadi Kidnap and Murder Handbook," *Daily Mail on-line*, October 11, 2014. Retrieved on November 15, 2014, from www.dailymail.co.uk/news/article-2789482/exposed-jihadi-kidnap-murder-handbook-plan-infiltrate-british-army-police.html.

27. Kissinger, *World Order*, pp. 118–122, 144.

28. Ibid., p. 121.

29. This shifting thinking is reflected in the National Intelligence Estimates done at the time and available in declassified form in the China collection, retrieved on May 12, 2014, from www.foia.cia.gov/collection/china-collection. See especially *Communist China's Strategic Weapons Programs*, NIE 13-8-67, August 3, 1967; *Communist China's ICBM and Submarine-launched Ballistic Missile Programs*, Special NIE 13-10-8, September 19, 1968; and *Communist China's Weapons Programs for Strategic Attack*, NIE 13-8-71, October 28, 1971.

30. Jonathan D. Pollack, *No Exit: North Korea, Nuclear Weapons, and International Security* (London: Routledge for International Institute for Strategic Studies, 2011).

31. Choe Sang-Hun, "1953 Armistice Is Nullified, North Korea Declares," *New York Times*, March 12, 2013, New York edition; Max Fisher, "Here's North Korea's Official Declaration of 'war,'" *Washington Post*, March 30, 2013; and "North Korea States 'Nuclear War Is Unavoidable and Declares First Target Will Be Japan,'" *Express* (Tokyo), April 12, 2013.

32. Marc Santora and Choe Sang-Hun, "North Korean Propaganda Video Imagines a Brighter World, without Manhattan," *The Lede, The New York Times News Blog*, February 5, 2013, retrieved on February 15, 2013, from http://thelede.blogs.nytimes.com/2013/02/05/north-korea-propaganda-video-uses-call-of-duty-and-we-are-the-world-to-imagine-a-brighter-world-without-manhattan/?_r=1.

33. For a review and analysis, see Ken E. Gause, *North Korean Leadership Dynamics and Decision-Making under Kim Jong-un: A Second Year Assessment* (Alexandria, VA: CNA, 2014), pp. 106–109.

34. *North Korean Security Challenges: A Net Assessment*, IISS Strategic Dossier (London: International Institute for Strategic Studies, 2011).

35. See *Military and Security Developments Involving the Democratic People's Republic of Korea, 2012, Annual Report to Congress*, Office of the Secretary of Defense, February 2013. For regularly updated analysis of North Korea's progress in developing, testing, and deploying nuclear weapons and their means of delivery, see 38 North, a program of the U.S.-Korea Institute at the Johns Hopkins School of Advanced International Studies, retrieved on May 12, 2014, from www.38North.org. In October 2014, a senior U.S. defense official stated that North Korea has the capability to produce warheads for ballistic missile delivery. See David E. Sanger, "U.S. Commander Sees Key Nuclear Step by North Korea," *New York Times*, October 24, 2014.

36. Ibid. See also Markus Schiller, *Characterizing the North Korean Nuclear Missile Threat*, Technical Report (Santa Monica, CA: RAND Corporation, 2012).

37. This assessment is from Toshi Yoshihara and James R. Holmes, eds., *Strategy in the Second Nuclear Age: Power, Ambition, and the Ultimate Weapon* (Washington, DC: Georgetown University Press, 2012), p. 228.

38. See *Military and Security Developments Involving the Democratic People's Republic of Korea, Annual Report to Congress, 2013* (Washington, DC: Department of Defense, 2013); and *Annual Report on Military Power of Iran, 2012* (Washington, DC: Department of Defense, 2012).

39. See Pollack, *No Exit*; Andrew Scobell, *North Korea's Strategic Intentions* (Carlisle Barracks, PA: U.S. Army War College Strategic Studies Institute, 2005); Joseph S. Bermudez Jr. and Sharon A. Richardson, "A North Korean View on the Development and Production of Strategic Weapons Systems," in Henry Sokolski, ed., *Planning for a Peaceful Korea* (Washington, DC: Strategic Studies Institute, 2001); and Kongdan Oh and Ralph C. Hassig, *North Korea: Through the Looking Glass* (Washington, DC: Brookings Institution Press, 2000).

40. "DPRK FM on Its Stand to Suspend Its Participation in Six-Party Talks for Indefinite Period," Korean Central News Agency, February 10, 2005.

41. "DPRK Foreign Ministry Clarifies Stand on New Measure to Bolster War Deterrent," Korean Central News Agency, October 3, 2006. These and additional statements appear in Terence Roehrig, "North Korea's Nuclear Weapons Program," in Yoshihara and Holmes, *Strategy in the Second Nuclear Age*, p. 90.

42. Cited in Joseph S. Bermudez, "North Korea's Strategy: Regime Survival and More?," presentation to a workshop on "Toward a 'Red Theory of Victory' in Limited Nuclear War," coorganized by the Center for International Security and Cooperation, Stanford University and Los Alamos National Laboratory and convened in Los Alamos, NM, February 19, 2014.

43. Mira Rapp-Hooper and Kenneth N. Waltz, "What Kim Jong-Il Learned from Qaddaffi's Fall: Never Disarm," *The Atlantic on-line*, October 24, 2011, citing a North Korean spokesperson. Retrieved on January 10, 2014, from www.theatlantic.com/international/archive/2011/10/what-kim-jong-il-learned-from-qaddafis-fall-never-disarm/247192/.

44. "Law on Consolidating Position of Nuclear Weapons State Adopted," Korean Central News Agency, Pyongyang, April 1, 2013. Retrieved on June 14, 2014, from www.kcna.co.jp/item/2013/201304/news01/20130401-25ee.html. For a discussion, see Peter Hayes and Roger Cavazos, "North Korean and U.S. Nuclear Threats: Discerning Signals from Noise," *Asia-Pacific Journal*, Vol. 11, No. 14.2 (April 2013).

45. "Report on Plenary Meeting of WPK Central Committee," Korean Central News Agency, Pyongyang, March 31, 2013. Retrieved on February 15, 2014..

46. As cited in "The Korean Peninsula: 'Nuclear Weapons State' North Korea Aiming to Become an Economic Power, RoK Seeking Active Deterrence Capability," *East Asian Strategic Review 2013* (Tokyo: National Institute for Defense Studies, 2013), p. 147.

47. "N. Korea Revised 'Detailed Operational Guidelines for Wartime,'" *Dong-A Ilbo* (Seoul), August 22, 2013.

48. These potential North Korean theories of victory and the associated pathways to North Korean nuclear employment have been explored in a series of tabletop exercises and workshops in recent years with American experts on North Korea and on deterrence and with counterparts in Northeast Asia. This work was conducted on a not-for-attribution basis.

49. Yoshihara and Holmes, *Strategy in the Second Nuclear Age*, p. 6.

50. Kongdan Oh Hassig and Ralph Hassig, "Military Confrontation on the Korean Peninsula," *Joint Forces Quarterly*, Vol. 64, No. 1 (January 2012), pp. 82–90.

51. For further discussion of these Cold War concepts, see Glenn H. Snyder, "The Security Dilemma in Alliance Politics," *World Politics*, Vol. 36, No. 4 (July 1984), pp. 461–495. See also Snyder, "The Balance of Power and the Balance of Terror," in Paul Seabury, ed., *The Balance of Power* (San Francisco, CA: Chandler, 1965), pp. 196–201; and Robert Jervis, *The Illogic of American Nuclear Strategy* (Ithaca, NY: Cornell University Press, 1986), especially pp. 29–34.

52. Han Ho Suk, "N. Korea Military Tactics in a War with U.S.: A Strategy of Massive Retaliations [sic] against U.S. Attacks (Pyongyang: Center for Korean Affairs, 2003). This is an English abstract of a paper available at www.rense.com. See also Homer T. Hodge, "North Korea's Military Strategy," *Parameters* (Spring 2003), pp. 68–81; and Kongdan Oh Hassig, *North Korean Policy Elites*, Paper No. P-3903 (Alexandria, VA: Institute for Defense Analyses, 2004).

53. As cited in Bermudez, unclassified conference presentation, February 2014.

54. Ibid.

55. Forrest E. Morgan et al., *Dangerous Thresholds: Managing Escalation in the 21st Century* (Santa Monica, CA: RAND, 2011), especially pp. 18–19.

56. Bruce E. Bechtol Jr., "Planning for the Unthinkable: Countering a North Korean Nuclear Attack and Management of Post-Attack Scenarios," *Korean Journal of Defense Analyses*, Vol. 23, No. 1 (March 2011).

57. Keir A. Lieber and Daryl G. Press, "The Next Korean War," *Foreign Affairs*, on-line edition, April 2013, retrieved on September 15, 2013, from www.foreignaffairs.com/articles/north-korea/2013-04-01/next-korean-war.

58. See *Military and Security Developments Involving the Democratic People's Republic of Korea, Annual Report to Congress, 2013.*

59. Carl von Clausewitz, *On War*, Michael Howard and Peter Paret, eds. (Princeton, NJ: Princeton University Press, 1989), especially book 7, chapter 21.

60. Paul Huth and Bruce Russett, "Deterrence Failure and Crisis Escalation," *International Studies Quarterly*, Vol. 32, No. 1 (March 1988), pp. 29–45.

61. Robert W. Rauchhaus, "Evaluating the Nuclear Peace Hypothesis: A Quantitative Approach," *Journal of Conflict Resolution*, Vol. 53, No. 2 (April 2009), pp. 258–277.

62. Joseph S. Bermudez Jr., *North Korea's Strategic Culture*, prepared for the Defense Threat Reduction Agency Advanced Systems and Concepts Office, October 31, 2006, p. 6.

63. Patrick M. Cronin, *If Deterrence Fails: Rethinking Conflict on the Korean Peninsula* (Washington, DC: Center for a New American Security, 2014), p. 7. For a further analysis of this "perceived need," see Gause, *North Korean Leadership Dynamics and Decision-Making under Kim Jong-un.*

64. Ibid.

65. Richard K. Betts, *Nuclear Balance and Nuclear Blackmail* (Washington, DC: Brookings Institution, 1987).

66. McGeorge Bundy, "To Cap the Volcano," *Foreign Affairs*, Vol. 48, No. 1 (October 1969).

67. Roehrig, "North Korea's Nuclear Weapons Program," in Yoshihara and Holmes, *Strategy in the Second Nuclear Age*, p. 95.

68. Stanley Hoffmann, *The State of War: Essays on the Theory and Practice of International Politics* (New York: Praeger, 1965), p. 236.

69. Kroenig, "Nuclear Superiority and the Balance of Resolve," p. 142.

70. In addition to the specific items cited in the following discussion, see Jeffrey A. Larsen and Kerry M. Kartchner, eds., *On Limited Nuclear War in the 21st Century*

(Stanford, CA: Stanford University Press, 2014); Bruce W. Bennett, "Weapons of Mass Destruction: The North Korean Threat," *Korean Journal of Defense Analysis*, Vol. 16, No. 2 (Fall 2004), pp. 79–108; and Bennett, *Uncertainties in the North Korean Nuclear Threat* (Santa Monica, CA: RAND Defense Research Institute, 2010).

71. Keir Lieber and Daryl Press, *Coercive Nuclear Campaigns in the 21st Century: Understanding Adversary Incentives and Options for Nuclear Escalation* (Monterey, CA: U.S. Naval Postgraduate School, March 2013), p. 8. See also Lieber and Press, "The Next Korean War," *Foreign Affairs*, Vol. 92, No. 3 (May/June 2013); and Lieber and Press, "The Nukes We Need: Preserving the American Deterrent," *Foreign Affairs*, Vol. 88, No. 6 (November/December 2009), pp. 40–41. Vipin Narang has also argued that assured nuclear retaliation may fail to deter intense conventional conflicts. See Vipin Narang, "What Does It Take to Deter? Regional Power Nuclear Postures and International Conflict," *Journal of Conflict Resolution*, Vol. 57, No. 3, pp. 478–508.

72. Dennis C. Blair, "Annual Threat Assessment of the Intelligence Community for the Senate Select Committee on Intelligence," report for U.S. Senate, February 12, 2009, pp. 24–25.

73. Robert Powell, *Nuclear Deterrence Theory: The Search for Credibility* (Cambridge, UK: Cambridge University Press, 1990). See also Kevin Chilton and Greg Weaver, "Waging Deterrence in the 21st Century," *Strategic Studies Quarterly* (Spring 2009), pp. 31–35; and Matthew Kroenig, "Nuclear Superiority and the Balance of Resolve: Explaining Nuclear Crisis Outcomes," *International Organization*, Vol. 67 (Winter 2013), pp. 141–171.

74. David Ochmanek and Lowell H. Schwartz, *The Challenge of Nuclear-Armed Regional Adversaries* (Santa Monica, CA: RAND, 2008), p. 42.

75. Victor Utgoff and Michael O. Wheeler, *On Deterring and Defeating Attempts to Exploit a Nuclear Theory of Victory*, Paper No. 4978 (Alexandria, VA: Institute for Defense Analyses, April 2013), p. iii.

76. I am grateful to Victor Utgoff for this set of arguments.

77. Michael Horowitz, "The Spread of Nuclear Weapons and International Conflict: Does Experience Matter?" *Journal of Conflict Resolution*, Vol. 53, No. 2 (April 2009), pp. 234–257.

78. Fred Charles Iklé, *Every War Must End* (New York: Columbia University Press, 1991).

79. Jeffrey A. Larsen, "Preface," in Larsen and Kartchner, *On Limited Nuclear War in the 21st Century*.

80. This case is made in Payne, *Deterrence in the Second Nuclear Age*, pp. 138–139.

81. This point is made in Terence Roehrig, *North Korea's Nuclear Weapons: Future Strategy and Doctrine*, Policy Brief (Cambridge, MA: Belfer Center for International Security, May 2013). See also *Military and Security Developments Involving the Democratic People's Republic of Korea, Annual Report to Congress, 2013*; and Scott Stossel, "North Korea: The War Game," *Atlantic* (July/August 2005).

82. "DOD News Briefing on Missile Defense from the Pentagon," Secretary of Defense Chuck Hagel; James Miller, Undersecretary for Policy, Department Of Defense;

Admiral James Winnefeld, Vice Chairman, Joint Chiefs of Staff, The Pentagon, March 15, 2013.

83. This analytic framework is informed by Cold War–vintage work on limited nuclear war and subsequent work to update that work in light of changing international circumstances. See Robert Osgood, *Limited War: The Challenge to American Strategy* (Chicago, IL: University of Chicago Press, 1957); Kenneth Watman et al., *U.S. Regional Deterrence Strategies* (Santa Monica, CA: RAND, 1995); Dean Wilkening and Kenneth Watman, *Nuclear Deterrence in a Regional Context* (Santa Monica, CA: RAND, 1995); Keir A. Lieber and Darryl G. Press, *Coercive Nuclear Campaigns in the 21st Century*, Report No. 2013-01 (Monterey, CA.: Naval Postgraduate School, 2013); and Jeffrey A. Larsen and Kerry M. Kartchner, eds., *On Limited Nuclear War in the 21st Century* (Stanford, CA: Stanford University Press, 2014).

84. These are what the 2013 Japanese defense white paper defines as "gray zone" conflicts. See *Defense of Japan 2013* (Tokyo: Ministry of Defense, 2013).

85. Victor A. Utgoff and Michael O. Wheeler, *On Deterring and Defeating Attempts to Exploit a Nuclear Theory of Victory* (Alexandria, VA: Institute for Defense Analyses, April 2013).

86. Barry Wolf, *When the Weak Attack the Strong: Failures of Deterrence* (Santa Monica, CA: RAND Corporation, 1991).

87. Morgan et al., *Dangerous Thresholds*.

Chapter 3

1. See the Obama Administration's 2009 *Quadrennial Defense Review* (Washington, DC: Department of Defense, 2009), p. 14; *2010 Nuclear Posture Review Report* (Washington, DC: Department of Defense, 2010), pp. 31–35; and the *2010 Ballistic Missile Defense Review* (Washington, DC: Department of Defense, 2010), pp. 23–27.

2. *National Security Strategy of the United States of 2010* (Washington, DC: White House, 2010), pp. 41–43.

3. For the results of high-level Obama administration policy reviews, see *Cyber Policy Review: Assuring a Trusted and Resilient Information and Communications Infrastructure*, White House, May 29, 2009; and *National Security Space Strategy*, White House, February 2011.

4. M. Elaine Bunn, *Can Deterrence Be Tailored?* INSS Strategic Forum No. 225 (Washington, DC: National Defense University, January 2007).

5. Wade L. Huntley, *Assessing the Impact of Low Nuclear Numbers on Strategic Stability: The Cases of Japan and South Korea* (Monterey, CA: U.S. Naval Postgraduate School, December 2012), p. 21.

6. For more on the deterrence values on Conventional Prompt Global Strike (CPGS) capabilities, see Barry D. Watts, *Long-Range Strike: Imperatives, Urgency, and Options* (Washington, DC: Center for Strategic and Budgetary Assessments, 2005); and *U.S. Conventional Prompt Global Strike: Issues for 2008 and Beyond*, Report of

the Committee on Conventional Prompt Global Strike Capability (Washington, DC: National Research Council of the National Academies, 2008).

7. For a key early marker in this debate, see *Discriminate Deterrence: Report of the Commission on Integrated Long-Term Strategy*, cochaired by Fred C. Iklé and Albert Wohlstetter (Washington, DC: U.S. Government Printing Office, 1988).

8. Amy Woolf, *Conventional Prompt Global Strike and Long-Range Ballistic Missiles: Background and Issues*, CRS Report for Congress (Washington, DC: Congressional Research Service, 2013); and James M. Acton, *Silver Bullet: Asking the Right Questions about Conventional Prompt Global Strike* (Washington, DC: Carnegie Endowment for International Peace, 2013).

9. This argument is set out in David C. Gompert and Philip C. Saunders, *The Paradox of Power: Sino-American Strategic Restraint in an Age of Vulnerability* (Washington, DC: National Defense University, 2011).

10. As of October 2013, there had been eleven successful intercepts by the Terminal High Altitude Area Defense (THAAD) system in eleven attempts since the beginning of the Engineering and Manufacturing Development (EMD) phase, and twenty-eight successful intercepts by the Aegis Ballistic Missile Defense System in thirty-four at-sea attempts. See Missile Defense Agency Fact Sheet, "Ballistic Missile Defense Intercept Flight Test Record," October 4, 2013.

11. As of October 2013, eight of the sixteen attempted intercepts by the Ground-Based Midcourse Defense System had been successful. Ibid. See also Statement by J. Michael Gilmore, Director, Operational Test and Evaluation, Office of the Secretary of Defense, to the House Armed Services Committee, Strategic Forces Subcommittee, March 6, 2012.

12. Dean A. Wilkening, "Does Missile Defence in Europe Threaten Russia?" *Survival*, Vol. 54, No. 1 (Winter 2012), pp. 31–52; L. David Montague and Walter B. Slocombe et al., *Making Sense of Ballistic Missile Defense: An Assessment of Concepts and Systems for U.S. Boost-Phase Missile Defense in Comparison to Other Alternatives* (Washington, DC: The National Academies Press, 2012); and *Science and Technology Issues of Early Intercept Ballistic Missile Defense Feasibility* (Washington, DC: Department of Defense, Defense Science Board, September 2011).

13. See *2010 Ballistic Missile Defense Review*.

14. See *Regional Ballistic Missile Defense*, Report to Congress, Department of Defense, August 23, 2013.

15. See *Missile Defense Protection of the Homeland: Hedge Strategy*, Report to Congress, Department of Defense, March 15, 2013. See also remarks on this topic delivered by Secretary of Defense Chuck Hagel on that date, available at www.defense .gov/speeches/speech.aspx?Speech ID=1759.

16. This catalogue is derived by the author from the approaches of the Obama and predecessor administrations and from the research sources indicated further in the following discussion. These values have not been catalogued in this form in any official document.

17. I am grateful to General Patrick O'Reilly, former director of the Missile Defense Agency, for this important point.

18. See, for example, Jacek Durkalec, "The Role of Missile Defence in NATO Deterrence," in M. Piotrowski, ed., *Regional Approaches to the Role of Missile Defence in Reducing Nuclear Threats* (Warsaw, Poland: Polish Institute of International Affairs, July 2013), pp. 19–28; Lukasz Kulesa, *Poland and Ballistic Missile Defense: The Limits of Atlanticism*, Proliferation Paper No. 48 (Paris, Institut Français des Relations Internationales, 2014); Hideaki Kaneda et al., *Japan's Missile Defense: Diplomatic and Security Policies in a Changing Strategic Environment* (Tokyo: Japan Institute of International Affairs, March 2007), pp. 125–141; Shinichi Ogawa, *Missile Defense and Deterrence*, NIDS Security Reports No. 3 (March 2002), pp. 24–55; Vit Stritecky, "Missile Defence as Reinforcement of Deterrence in the 21st Century," in Piotrowski, *Regional Approaches to the Role of Missile Defence in Reducing Nuclear Threats*; and Sugio Takahashi, *Ballistic Missile Defense in Japan: Deterrence and Military Transformation*, Proliferation Papers No. 44 (Paris: Institut Français des Relations Internationales, 2012).

19. Steven A. Hildreth and Carl Ek, *Long-Range Ballistic Missile Defense in Europe*, CRS Report for Congress (Washington, DC: Congressional Research Service, 2008), updated September 3, 2008, especially pp. 13–19.

20. Bunn, *Can Deterrence Be Tailored?*

21. For example, the 1995 *Secretary of Defense Annual Report to Congress* discussed the need "to continually assess the strategic personalities of countries with these weapons" as it emphasized the new defense planning challenges of major theater wars against WMD-armed adversaries.

22. Kathleen Hicks, "The Case for Deterrence," in Craig Cohen et al., *Global Forecast 2015: Crisis and Opportunity* (Washington, DC: Center for Strategic and International Studies, 2015), pp. 10–11.

23. Harlan K. Ullman and James P. Wade, *Shock and Awe: A Sufficient Condition for Victory?* (Newport, RI: U.S. Naval War College, 2001), p. 17.

24. To be clear, this work draws on but goes beyond the foundational work of the Obama administration of 2009 and 2010 to include the author's own analysis of the key ingredients of such a theory. See also Kevin Chilton and Greg Weaver, "Waging Deterrence in the Twenty-First Century," *Strategic Studies Quarterly* (Spring 2009), pp. 31–42; and Stephen J. Cimbala, *Nuclear Weapons in the Information Age* (New York: Continuum, 2012).

25. For more nuclear coercion and compellence strategies and their effectiveness, see Thomas C. Schelling, *Arms and Influence* (New Haven, CT, and London: Yale University Press, 1966), pp. 69–91; Gary Schaub, "Deterrence, Compellence, and Prospect Theory," *Political Psychology*, Vol. 25, No. 3 (June 2004), pp. 389–411; Maria Sperandei, "Bridging Deterrence and Compellence: An Alternative Approach to the Study of Coercive Diplomacy," *International Studies Review*, Vol. 8, No. 2 (June 2006), pp. 253–280; and Todd S. Secsher and Matthew Fuhrmann, "Crisis Bargaining

and Nuclear Blackmail," *International Organization*, Vol. 67, No. 1 (January 2013), pp. 173–195.

26. Brad Roberts, "Rethinking How Wars Must End: NBC War Termination Issues and Major Regional Contingencies," in Victor Utgoff, ed., *The Coming Crisis: Nuclear Proliferation, U.S. Interests, and World Order* (Cambridge, MA: MIT Press, 2000).

27. This case is made most forcefully in Payne, *Second Nuclear Age*.

28. Forrest E. Morgan, *Dancing with the Bear: Managing Escalation in a Conflict with Russia* (Paris: Institut Français des Relations Internationales, 2012), p. 29, citing Alexander L. George and William E. Simons, "Findings and Conclusions," in George and Simons, *The Limits of Coercive Diplomacy* (Boulder, CO: Westview Press, 1994), pp. 281–282.

29. Chilton and Weaver, "Waging Deterrence in the Twenty-First Century," pp. 32–33.

30. See Van Jackson, "Beyond Tailoring: North Korea and the Promise of Managed Deterrence," *Contemporary Security Policy*, Vol. 33, No. 2 (August 2012), pp. 289–310.

31. Chilton and Weaver, "Waging Deterrence in the Twenty-First Century," pp. 37–40; and James A. Lewis, *Cross Domain Deterrence and Credible Threats* (Washington, DC: Center for Strategic and International Studies, July 2010).

32. Jeffrey A. Larsen and Kerry M. Kartchner, eds., *On Limited Nuclear War in the 21st Century* (Stanford, CA: Stanford University Press, 2014), p. 6.

33. Morgan et al., *Dangerous Thresholds*.

34. Barry R. Posen, "U.S. Security Policy in a Nuclear-Armed World, or: What if Iraq Had Had Nuclear Weapons?" *Security Studies*, Vol. 6, No. 3 (Spring 1997), pp. 1–31.

35. Kerry M. Kartchner and Michael S. Gerson, "Escalation to Limited Nuclear War in the 21st Century," in *On Limited Nuclear War in the 21st Century*, p. 145.

36. Ibid., p. 166.

Chapter 4

1. Secretary of Defense William Perry, remarks on the 1994 Nuclear Posture Review, September 22, 1994.

2. President George W. Bush, remarks to the faculty and students of National Defense University, Fort Lesley J. McNair, Washington, DC, May 1, 2001.

3. See, for example, *Report on Mutual Assured Stability: Essential Components and Near Term Actions*, report of the International Security Advisory Board, Department of State, August 14, 2012. See also *Joint Statement by Ellen Tauscher and Igor Ivanov on Mutual Assured Stability*, Washington, DC, April 18, 2013; this was a private endeavor of two former officials in support of a bilateral nongovernmental effort.

4. Angela E. Stent, *The Limits of Partnership: U.S.–Russian Relations in the Twenty-First Century* (Princeton, NJ: Princeton University Press, 2014), p. 256.

5. Ibid.

6. George Bush and Brent Scowcroft, *A World Transformed* (New York: Vintage Books, 1999).

7. Remarks by President Bill Clinton to the American Society of Newspaper Editors, The White House, April 1, 1993. See also Strobe Talbott, *The Russia Hand: A Memoir of Presidential Diplomacy* (New York: Random House, 2002).

8. Memorandum of Understanding Relating to the Treaty between the United States of America and the Union of Soviet Socialist Republics on the Limitation of Anti-Ballistic Missile Systems on May 26, 1972, Department of State, Washington, DC, available at www.state.gov/s/l/65590.htm.

9. Alexander A. Pikayev, *The Rise and Fall of START II: The Russian View*, Working Paper No. 6 (Washington, DC: Carnegie Endowment for International Peace, 1999).

10. Stent, *The Limits of Partnership*, p. 30.

11. Ibid., p. 44.

12. Ibid., p. 37. See also Mary Elise Sarotte, "A Broken Promise? What the West Really Told Moscow about NATO Expansion," *Foreign Affairs*, Vol. 93, No. 5 (September–October 2014), pp. 90–97.

13. Stent, *The Limits of Partnership*, p. 20.

14. Condoleezza Rice, "Promoting the National Interest," *Foreign Affairs*, Vol. 79, No. 1 (2000), pp. 45–62.

15. President George W. Bush, cover letter, *National Security Strategy of the United States of America, September 17, 2002.*

16. Speech by President George W. Bush, National Defense University, Washington, DC, May 1, 2001. See also White House papers on ballistic missile defense as briefed to the media, July 11, 2001.

17. George Bush, "A Distinctly American Internationalism," speech at Ronald Reagan Presidential Library, November 19, 1999.

18. Stent, *The Limits of Partnership*, pp. 49–75.

19. H. H. Gaffney and Dmitry Gorenburg, *CNA's Russia Program, 1991–2004: A Valedictory* (Alexandria, VA: CNA Corporation, August 2005).

20. Stent, *The Limits of Partnership*, p. 78.

21. This and the immediately following citations all from Remarks by Russian President Vladimir Putin, Munich conference on security policy, February 10, 2007.

22. Thom Shanker, "Gates Counters Putin's Words on US Power," *New York Times*, February 11, 2007.

23. *Bucharest Summit Declaration*, Issued by the Heads of State and Government Participating in the North Atlantic Council meeting in Bucharest, April 3, 2008, paragraph 23.

24. From a working paper prepared for candidate Obama by the Russia and Eurasia Working Group, chaired by Michael McFaul, who went onto become senior director for Russia at the White House and then ambassador to Russia. Cited in Stent, *The Limits of Partnership*, p. 214.

25. David Holloway, "Strategic Stability, Strategic Cooperation, and Missile Defense," unpublished paper prepared for a workshop on Cooperation in Early Warning and Ballistic Missile Defense, Center for International Security and Cooperation, Stanford University, April 25–28, 2011.

26. David C. Gompert and Michael Kofman, *Raising Our Sights: Russian–American Strategic Restraint in an Age of Vulnerability*, INSS Strategic Forum No. 274 (Washington, DC: National Defense University, 2012), p. 8.

27. Stent, *The Limits of Partnership*, pp. 250–251.

28. *Direct Line with Vladimir Putin*, of April 17, 2014.

29. Fyodor Lukyanov, "What Russia Learned from the Iraq War," *Al-Monitor*, March 18, 2013.

30. *Concept of the Foreign Policy of the Russian Federation*, Ministry of Foreign Affairs, Moscow, February 12, 2013.

31. "Putin Orders Defense Ministry to Get House in Order," *RIA Novosti*, February 27, 2013.

32. Cited in Stent, *The Limits of Partnership*, p. x.

33. All immediately subsequent quotations are from President Vladimir Putin's remarks to the Russian Duma, March 18, 2014.

34. See Dmitry Gorenburg, "Tracking Developments in the Russian Military," on-line commentary, May 29, 2014. Retrieved on June 3, 2014, from https://russiamil.wordpress.com/.

35. "Vladimir Putin Meets with Members of the Valdai Discussion Club," transcript of the final plenary session, October 25, 2014, available at www.valdaiclub.com.

36. For one Russian catalogue of Russian interests allegedly ignored or damaged by the United States through this period, see Alexei Arbatov et al., *Strategic Stability after the Cold War* (Moscow: IMEMO, 2010), p. 27.

37. President Putin, newspaper interview, *Politika* (Serbia), October 15, 2014. Available at the website of the President of Russia at http://eng.news.kremlin.ru/transcripts/23099.

38. See, for example, John J. Mearsheimer, "Why the Ukraine Crisis Is the West's Fault: The Liberal Delusions That Provoked Putin," *Foreign Affairs*, Vol. 93, No. 5 (September/October 2014), pp. 77–89.

39. Robert Legvold, "Managing the New Cold War: What Moscow and Washington Can Learn from the Last One," *Foreign Affairs*, Vol. 93, No. 5 (September/October 2014), pp. 74–75.

40. This conclusion is reflected in Keir Giles, Philip Hanson, Roderic Lyne, James Nixey, James Sherr, and Andrew Wood, *The Russia Challenge* (London: Royal Institute for International Affairs, June 2015).

41. "The Russian Economy: The End of the Line," *Economist*, November 22, 2014, pp. 21–24.

42. These insights are drawn from off-the-record exchanges with experts in the United States and Russia, including but not limited to so-called Track 2 meetings that bring together academics or Track 1.5 meetings that bring together academics, retired

government officials or military leaders, and individuals currently in government or military service but participating in their private capacity. Reports on the results of these dialogues are not available at a single access point but are available on a limited basis from separate organizers and sponsors. For one example, see Jerome Conley and Mikhail Tsypkin, "Perceptions and Misperceptions: Exploring the U.S.–Russian Strategic Impasse," *Strategic Insights*, Vol. 7, No. 2 (April 2008).

43. Alexander Lukin, "What the Kremlin Is Thinking: Putin's Vision for Eurasia," *Foreign Affairs*, Vol. 93, No. 4 (July/August 2014), pp. 85–93.

44. From the transcript of his remarks to the Federation Council, Moscow, March 18, 2014.

45. The term *nuclear revolution* is a reference to the historical impact of nuclear weapons in reducing the risks of major war among major powers by making its costs unbearable. See Robert Jervis, *The Meaning of the Nuclear Revolution: Statecraft and the Prospect for Armageddon* (Ithaca, NY: Cornell University Press, 1990). For the Russian line of argument, see for example Sergey Rogov, "The Bush Doctrine and the Prospects for Russo–American Relations: Washington Is Endeavoring to Prevent the Appearance in the 21st Century of an Adversary Equal in Strength to the United States," original in Russian in *Yadernyy Kontrol*, April 3, 2002, FBIS Document ID CEP20020403000075.

46. *National Security Strategy of the Russian Federation to 2020*, May 12, 2009, Para. 30.

47. A leading U.S. defense analyst has made the case on technical grounds that U.S. and NATO BMD does not threaten Russia's deterrent. Writing in 2012, Dean Wilkening argued that to be effective missile defenses must meet four criteria: (1) their "kinetic footprint" must provide full coverage against potential missile attacks; (2) the probability of kill with a single intercept must be sufficiently high, especially in face of counter-measures; (3) the sensors and interceptors must survive direct (or cyber) attack on them; and (4) the force must be large enough to not be exhausted before intercepting all incoming missiles. See Dean A. Wilkening, "Does Missile Defence in Europe Threaten Russia?" *Survival*, Vol. 54, No. 1 (February–March 2012), pp. 31–52.

48. Alexei Arbatov and V. Dworkin, *Missile Defense: Confrontation and Cooperation* (Moscow: Carnegie Center Moscow, 2013).

49. Robert M. Gates, *Duty: Memoirs of a Secretary at War* (New York: Alfred A. Knopf, 2012), p. 405.

50. David Herszenhorn, "As U.S. Seeks Security Pact, Obama Set to Meet Putin," *New York Times*, April 15, 2013; and Kathleen Hennessey and Christi Parsons, "Obama's Moscow Visit Is Called Off, and Not Just Because of Snowden," *Los Angeles Times*, August 7, 2013.

51. Zyga, *NATO-Russia Relations and Missile Defense*. For a late 2014 assessment of that process, see Roberto Zadra, "NATO, Russia and Ballistic Missile Defence," *Survival*, Vol. 56, No.4 (August–September 2014), pp. 51–61, which makes the case that "NATO–Russia missile-defence cooperation . . . has probably reached its end" (p. 51).

52. For a summary of those efforts to 2010, see *Report to Congress on Potential Missile Defense Cooperation with Russia*, U.S. Department of Defense in consultation with Department of State, May 2010. See also Gates, *Duty*, pp. 157–162 and 402–405.

53. Russia is reportedly developing and deploying advance BMD countermeasures and penetration aids, including maneuvering reentry vehicles and hyperglide nonballistic systems, while also modernizing its missile forces in a way that enables additional MIRVing. Russia is also upgrading the missile defense of Moscow while significantly expanding its other defensive means with creation of a new Aerospace Defense Force. See Jakob Hedenskog and Carolina Vendil Pallin, eds., *Russian Military Capability in a Ten-Year Perspective—2013* (Stockholm: Swedish Defence Research Agency, 2013), pp. 31, 151.

54. S. M. Rogov et al., *Ten Years without the ABM Treaty: The Issue of Missile Defense in Russian–US Relations* (Moscow: Institute for U.S. and Canadian Studies, 2012), p. 4.

55. From his annual special live television broadcast, *Direct Line with Vladimir Putin*, on April 17, 2014.

56. From the U.S.–Soviet Joint Statement on the Treaty on Strategic Offensive Arms of 1990.

57. Dean Wilkening, "Strategic Stability between the United States and Russia," in David Ochmanek and Michael Sulmeyer, eds., *Challenges in U.S. National Security Policy* (Santa Monica, CA: RAND, 2014), pp. 123–140.

58. Thomas Schelling, *Strategy of Conflict* (Cambridge, MA: Harvard University Press, 1960), p. 232.

59. Harold Brown, *Annual Report to Congress, 1979.* (Washington, DC: Department of Defense, 1979).

60. Ioanna-Nikoletta Zyga, *NATO–Russia Relations and Missile Defense: "Sticking Point" or "Game Changer"?* (Moscow: Carnegie Center Moscow, 2012).

61. See also Arbatov et al., *Strategic Stability after the Cold War.*

62. Pavel Podvig, "The Myth of Strategic Stability," *The Bulletin Online*, October 31, 2012.

63. Eugene Ivanov, "New START Ratification in Russia: A Symmetric Response," *Russia beyond the Headlines*, February 1, 2011; and Yevgeny Shestakov, "Will Russia Stop New START?" on-line supplement, *Rossiyskaya Gazeta* (Russia), December 4, 2012. Available at www.telegraph.co.uk/sponsored/rbth/opinion/9720883/russia-new-start-arms-reduction.html.

64. Henry A. Kissinger and Brent Scowcroft, "Nuclear Weapon Reductions Must Be Part of Strategic Analysis," *Washington Post*, April 22, 2012.

65. Ibid.

66. *Concept of the Foreign Policy of the Russian Federation.* See also Alexei G. Arbatov, "Multilateral Nuclear Disarmament: Are We Ready to Open the Box of Pandora?" in David Ochmanek and Michael Sulmeyer, *Challenges in U.S. National Security Policy*, pp. 175–186 (Santa Monica, CA: RAND, 2014).

67. As reported in *Rossiskaya Gazeta*, February 20, 2012.

68. Alexei Arbatov, *Gambit or Endgame? The New State of Arms Control* (Washington, DC: Carnegie Endowment for International Peace, Carnegie Moscow Center, 2011).

69. There are advocates in both Washington and Moscow for doing so. See "Some Russian Lawmakers Want to Withdraw from Key Arms Control Pact," *Nuclear Security Newswire*, Washington, DC, July 18, 2014; and Michaela Dodge, *U.S. Nuclear Weapons Policy: After Ukraine, Time to Reassess Strategic Posture* (Washington, DC: Heritage Foundation, March 2014).

70. See, for example, *Report on Mutual Assured Stability*. See also Matthew Bunn et al., *Transcending Mutual Deterrence in the U.S.–Russian Relationship* (Cambridge, MA: Harvard University's Belfer Center in partnership with the Moscow-based Institute for U.S. and Canadian Studies of the Russian Academy of Sciences, 2013); and Celeste Wallander, *Mutual Assured Stability: Establishing US–Russia Security Relations for a New Century* (Washington, DC: Atlantic Council, 2013).

71. *Direct Line with Vladimir Putin*, April 17, 2014.

72. As one indicator of this shift, see Anne Applebaum, "War in Europe Is Not a Hysterical Idea," *Washington Post*, August 29, 2014.

73. *Quadrennial Defense Review Report, 1997,* p. 5.

74. *Quadrennial Defense Review Report*, September 30, 2001, pp. 3, 5.

75. *Quadrennial Defense Review, 2014*, p. 6.

76. *Active Engagement, Modern Defence*, Strategic Concept for the Defence and Security of the Members of the North Atlantic Treaty Organization, adopted by Heads of State and Government in Lisbon, December 2011, paragraphs 7 and 16.

77. Ibid., paragraphs 33 and 24.

78. *Report on Nuclear Employment Strategy of the United States, Specified in Section 491 of 10 U.S.C.*, U.S. Department of Defense, June 12, 2013, p. 2.

79. Ibid., p. 3.

80. Ibid., p. 5.

81. Ibid., p. 3.

82. Ibid., pp. 6–7.

83. Key themes drawn from the *Concept of the Foreign Policy of the Russian Federation, May 12, 2009, National Security Strategy of the Russian Federation to 2020*, and President Putin's March 18, 2014, speech.

84. Stephen J. Blank, *Threats to Russian Security: The View from Moscow* (Carlisle, PA: Strategic Studies Institute of the U.S. Army War College, 2000), pp. 3, 16.

85. Ibid., p. 11.

86. See Oksanna Antonenko, "Russia, NATO, and European Security after Kosovo," *Survival*, Vol. 41, No. 4 (Winter 1999–2000), pp. 124–144; and Celeste A. Wallander, "Russian Views on Kosovo," a synopsis of a panel discussion convened by the Program on New Approaches to Russian Security, Davis Center for Russian Studies, Harvard University, Cambridge, MA, April 1999.

87. See Alexander Golts, "Reform: The End of the First Phase—Will There Be a Second?" *Journal of Slavic Military Studies*, Vol. 27, No. 1 (March 2014), pp. 131–146;

Keir Giles, "A New Phase in Russian Military Transformation," *Journal of Slavic Military Studies*, Vol. 27, No. 1 (March 2014), pp. 147–162; Per Enerud, "Russian Defence Politics," in Hedenskog and Pallin, *Russian Military Capability in a Ten-Year Perspective—2013*, pp. 89–99; and Roger N. McDermott, "Russia's Conventional Armed Forces: Reform and Nuclear Posture to 2020," in Stephen J. Blank, ed., *Russian Nuclear Weapons: Past, Present and Future* (Carlisle, PA: Strategic Studies Institute, U.S. Army War College, November 2011), pp. 33–97.

88. This summary of Russia's thinking about the problem of war with the United States and how to manage its risks of escalation is drawn from two workshops convened in 2014 in preparation of this volume. Presentations and discussion were on a not-for-attribution basis.

89. Daniel Goure, "Moscow's Vision of Future War: So Many Conflict Scenarios So Little Time, Money and Forces," *Journal of Slavic Military Studies*, Vol. 27, No. 1 (March 2014), pp. 63–100; and Stephen J. Blank, ed., *Whither the Russian Military: U.S., European, and Russian Perspectives* (Carlisle Barracks, PA: Strategic Studies Institute, U.S. Army War College, 2013).

90. *Concept of the Foreign Policy of the Russian Federation, 2013*, p. 1.

91. Vladimir Putin, "Strength is the Guarantee of Security for Russia," *Rossiskaya Gazetta*, February 20, 2012.

92. Carolina Vendil Pallin, "Russian Military Capability in a Ten-Year Perspective," in Hedenskog and Pallin, *Russian Military Capability in a Ten-Year Perspective—2013*, pp. 143.

93. Jakob Hedenskog and Fredrik Westerlund, "Introduction," in Hedenskog and Pallin, *Russian Military Capability in a Ten-Year Perspective—2013*, pp. 18–19. For a discussion of China's place in the development of Russian military thinking, see Jacob W. Kipp, "Asian Drivers of Russia's Nuclear Force Posture," unpublished research paper, 2012.

94. Marcel de Haas, "Russia's Military Doctrine Development (2000–2010)," in Stephen J. Blank, ed., *Russia's Military Politics and Russia's 2010 Defense Doctrine*, pp. 1–62 (Carlisle, PA: Strategic Studies Institute of the U.S. Army War College, 2011); and Gudrun Persson, "Security Policy and Military Strategic Thinking," in Hedenskog and Pallin, *Russian Military Capability in a Ten-Year Perspective—2013*, pp. 71–88.

95. Karin Dawisha, *Putin's Kleptocracy: Who Owns Russia?* (New York: Simon and Schuster, 2014).

96. "Russia Takes Complete Advantage of Castrated Armed Forces of the West," *Pravda*, November 13, 2014.

97. Alexander G. Savelyev, "Russian Defense Doctrine," in Blank, *Russia's Military Politics and Russia's 2010 Defense Doctrine*, p. 176.

98. Marta Carlsson, Johan Norberg, and Fredrik Westerlund, "The Military Capability of Russia's Armed Forces in 2013," in Hedenskog and Pallin, *Russian Military Capability in a Ten-Year Perspective—2013*, p. 23.

99. Hedenskog and Westerlund, "Introduction," in Hedenskog and Pallin, *Russian Military Capability in a Ten-Year Perspective—2013*, p. 17.

100. Yury Federov, *New Wine in Old Bottles: The New Salience of Nuclear Weapons* (Paris: Institut Français Relations Internationales, 2007). See also "Russia Prepares Nuclear Surprise for NATO," *Pravda*, November 12, 2014.

101. Dimitry Adamsky, "If War Comes Tomorrow: Russian Thinking about 'Regional Nuclear Deterrence,'" *Journal of Slavic Military Studies*, Vol. 27, No. 1 (March 2014), pp. 163–188.

102. Andrei Kokoshin, *Ensuring Strategic Stability in the Past and Present: Theoretical and Applied Questions* (Cambridge, MA: Belfer Center for Science and International Affairs, Harvard Kennedy School, 2011), pp. 33, 43. Kokoshin is a member of the Russian parliament (Duma) and former secretary of Russia's Security Council.

103. Alexander Golts, "Russia's Nuclear Euphoria Ignores Reality," *Moscow Times*, October 6, 2014.

104. Paul Goble, "Putin Believes He Can Win a War with NATO, Piontkovsky Says," *The Interpreter*, August 10, 2014.

105. Ibid. See also Jeffrey Tayler, "Putin's Nuclear Option: Would Russia's President Really Be Willing to Start World War III?" *Foreign Policy*, September 4, 2014.

106. Forrest E. Morgan, *Dancing with the Bear: Managing Escalation in a Conflict with Russia* (Paris: Institut Français Relations Internationales, 2012), p. 37.

107. Adamsky, "If War Comes Tomorrow," pp. 164, 185.

108. James T. Quinlivan and Olga Oliker, *Nuclear Deterrence in Europe: Russian Approaches to a New Environment and Implications for the United States*, RAND MGF 1075 (Santa Monica, CA: RAND, 2011).

109. Marta Carlsson, Johan Norberg, and Fredrik Westerlund, "The Military Capability of Russia's Armed Forces in 2013," in Hedenskog and Pallin, *Russian Military Capability in a Ten-Year Perspective—2013*, pp. 32, 51.

110. Jacob Kipp, "'Smart' Defense from New Threats: Future War from a Russian Perspective: Back to the Future after the War on Terror," *Journal of Slavic Military Studies*, Vol. 27, No. 1 (March 2014).

111. Timothy Thomas, "Russia's Information Warfare Strategy: Can the Nation Cope in Future Conflicts?" *Journal of Slavic Military Studies*, Vol. 27, No. 1 (March 2014), pp. 105–106.

112. Giles, "A New Phase in Russian Military Transformation," pp. 155–159.

113. Timothy L. Thomas, "Russia's Reflexive Control Theory and the Military," *Journal of Slavic Military Studies*, Vol. 17 (2004), pp. 237, 241.

114. This view is expressed in Julian Lindley-French, *NATO and New Ways of Warfare: Defeating Hybrid Threats*, a NDC Conference Report, Vol. 3, No. 15 (Rome: NATO Defense College, May 2015). See also Kristen Ven Bruusgaard, "Crimea and Russia's Strategic Overhaul," *Parameters*, Vol. 44, No. 3 (Autumn 2014), pp. 81–90.

115. Valery Gerasimov, then chief of the Russian General Staff, "The General Staff and the Country's Defense," published as "Gerasimov on New Regulations, Military Science,", *Moscow VPK Voyenno-Promyshlennyy Kuryer*, February 5, 2014, FBIS CER2014020469632972, as discussed in Roger McDermott, "Gerasimov Unveils Russia's 'Reformed' General Staff," *Eurasia Daily Monitor*, Vol. 11, No. 27,

February 11, 2014, available at www.jamestown.org/single/?tx_ttnews[tt_news]=41951#.VX3B1Kbnd74.

116. Jacob W. Kipp, "Russia as a Nuclear Power in the Eurasian Context," in Ashley J. Tellis, Abraham M. Denmark, and Travis Tanner, eds., *Asia in the Second Nuclear Age*, pp. 43–44 (Seattle, WA: National Bureau of Asian Research, 2013).

117. Nikolai N. Sokov, "Why Russia Calls a Limited Nuclear Strike 'De-escalation,'" *Bulletin of the Atomic Scientists*, on-line service, March 13, 2014, available at http://thebulletin.org/why-russia-calls-limited-nuclear-strike-de-escalation. See also Andrei Zagorski, *Russia's Tactical Nuclear Weapons: Posture, Politics, and Arms Control* (Hamburg: Institut fuer Friedensforschung und Sicherheitpolitik, 2011).

118. Sokov, "Why Russia Calls a Limited Nuclear Strike 'De-escalation.'"

119. Kokoshin, *Ensuring Strategic Stability in the Past and Present: Theoretical and Applied Questions*, pp. 57–58. See also McDermott, "Russia's Conventional Armed Forces: Reform and Nuclear Posture to 2020," pp. 68–70; and V. M. Burenok and O. B. Achasov, "Non-Nuclear Deterrence," *Military Thought*, Vol. 1, No. 17 (2008), pp. 1–6.

120. Goure, "Moscow's Vision of Future War," pp. 81–82, citing Col. S. G. Chekinov and Lt. Gen. S. A. Bogdanov, "Asymmetric Actions to Maintain Russia's Military Security," *Military Thought*, No. 1 (2010), p. 8. For additional discussion and Russian sources, see Adamsky, "If War Comes Tomorrow," pp. 171–172.

121. Sokov, "Why Russia Calls a Limited Nuclear Strike 'De-escalation.'"

122. Kokoshin, *Ensuring Strategic Stability in the Past and Present*, pp. 26–28.

123. Ibid.

124. Johan Norberg and Fredrik Westerlund, *Russia and Ukraine: Military-Strategic Options, and Possible Risks, for Moscow*, RUFS Briefing No. 22 (Stockholm: Swedish Defence Research Agency, March 2014).

125. Marta Carlsson, Johan Norberg, and Fredrik Westerlund, "The Military Capability of Russia's Armed Forces in 2013," in Hedenskog and Pallin, *Russian Military Capability in a Ten-Year Perspective—2013*, p. 61, which notes the deployment of a new conventionally armed ALCM with a range of 5,000 kilometers. See also Sokov, "Why Russia Calls a Limited Nuclear Strike 'De-escalation.'"

126. Ibid., p. 61.

127. Ibid., p. 61.

128. Vladimir Isachenkov, "Putin Promises New Weapons to Fend Western Threats," Associated Press (Moscow), September 10, 2014.

129. Ibid., p. 48.

130. Hedenskog and Westerlund, "Introduction," p. 15.

131. Kipp, "Russia as a Nuclear Power in the Eurasian Context," p. 44.

132. Carlsson et al., "The Military Capability of Russia's Armed Forces in 2013," p. 48.

133. Kokoshin, *Ensuring Strategic Stability in the Past and Present*, pp. 31–32.

134. Zackary Keck, "Russia Begins Massive Nuclear War Drill," *The Diplomat*, March 29, 2014.

135. U.S. Department of State, *Adherence to and Compliance with Arms Control, Nonproliferation, and Disarmament Agreements and Commitments*, July 2014, p. 8. See also Michael R. Gordon, "U.S. Says Russia Tested Missile, Despite Treaty," *New York Times*, January 29, 2014.

136. Pavel Felgenhauer, "Putin to Decide Next Moves in Standoff with West over Ukraine," *Eurasia Daily Monitor*, Vol. 11, No. 150 (August 14, 2014), citing Putin in Yalta August 14 promising that Russia would soon "surprise the West with our new developments in offensive nuclear weapons about which we do not talk yet." See also Vladimir Isachenkov, "Putin Promises New Weapons to Fend Western Threats," Associated Press, September 14, 2014.

137. This theme is developed in *Report on U.S.–Russia Relations*, International Security Advisory Board (Washington, DC: Department of State, December 9, 2014).

138. Some senior Russian experts assert that opportunities remain for arms control so long as it is built on principles set out by President Putin. See A. G. Saveleyev, Z. V. Dvorkin, V. I. Yessin, N. N. Detinov, and A. V. Zagorsky, *Multilateral Approaches to Nuclear Disarmament* (Moscow: Russia International Affairs Council, 2014).

Chapter 5

1. *National Security Strategy, 1993* (Washington, DC: White House, 1993), p. 8.

2. Maureen Dowd, "Two U.S. Officials Went Secretly to Beijing in July," *New York Times*, December 19, 1989.

3. *A National Security Strategy of Engagement and Enlargement, 1996* (Washington, DC: White House, 1996), p. 40.

4. Ibid.

5. Ibid.

6. *A National Security Strategy for a Global Age, December 2000* (Washington, DC: White House, 2000).

7. *National Security Strategy, 2002* (Washington, DC: White House, 2002), p. 27.

8. Condoleeza Rice, "Promoting the National Interest," *Foreign Affairs*, Vol. 75, No. 1 (January–February 2000), pp. 45–62.

9. *National Security Strategy, 2002*, pp. 26–28.

10. Robert Zoellick, "Whither China: From Membership to Responsibility?" Remarks to the National Committee on U.S.–China Relations, 2005, as published in *NBR Analysis*, Vol. 16. No. 4 (December 2005), p. 13.

11. *2010 National Security Strategy* (Washington, DC: White House, 2010), pp. 3, 43.

12. *The Diversified Employment of China's Armed Forces* (Beijing: People's Republic of China, April 2013), p. 1.

13. Ibid.

14. Xi Jinping, speech to the National Committee on U.S.–China Relations and U.S.–China Business Council, Washington, DC, February 15, 2012.

15. "More Opportunities for Sino–U.S. Trade, Investment: Premier," *Xinhua*, March 17, 2013.

16. Jane Perlez, "Strident Video by Chinese Military Casts U.S. as Menace," *New York Times*, October 31, 2013.

17. Remarks by Tom Donilon, "The United States and the Asia Pacific in 2013," Asia Society, New York, March 11, 2013. See also Michael S. Chase, "China's Search for a 'New Type of Great Power Relationship,'" Jamestown Foundation, China Brief, September 7, 2012; and Zhang Tuosheng, "Developing a New Type of Major Power Relationship between China and the U.S.," *China and U.S. Focus*, January 4, 2013.

18. Stephen J. Hadley, "U.S.–China: A New Model of Great Power Relations," remarks delivered to the Carnegie-Tsinghua Center for Global Policy, Beijing, October 10, 2013.

19. "China's Xi Proposes Security Concept for Asia," *Xinhua*, May 22, 2014.

20. Nina Hachigian, ed., *Debating China: The U.S.–China Relationship in Ten Conversations* (New York: Oxford University Press, 2014). See also Chris Twomey, "Chinese–U.S. Strategic Affairs: Dangerous Dynamism," *Arms Control Today* (January 2009).

21. David M. Lampton, *The U.S. and China: Sliding from Engagement to Coercive Diplomacy*, PacNet #63 (Honolulu, HI: Pacific Forum CSIS, August 2014).

22. James Steinberg and Michael O'Hanlon, "Keep Hope Alive: How to Prevent U.S.–Chinese Relations from Blowing Up," *Foreign Affairs*, Vol. 93, No. 4 (July/August 2014), p. 107. See also Steinberg and O'Hanlon, *Strategic Reassurance and Resolve: U.S.–China Relations in the 21st Century* (Princeton, NJ: Princeton University Press, 2014).

23. *2005 Annual Report to the Congress on the Military Power of the PRC* (Washington, DC: Department of Defense, 2005).

24. Remarks, Secretary of Defense Donald Rumsfeld, Hearing on the 2001 Nuclear Posture Review, Senate Armed Services Committee, February 14, 2002.

25. Andrew F. Krepinevich and Robert Martinage, *Dissuasion Strategy* (Washington, DC: Center for Strategic and Budgetary Assessments, 2008); and Brad Roberts, *Operationalizing Dissuasion of China: Practicalities and Pitfalls* (Alexandria, VA: Institute for Defense Analyses, 2005).

26. *Nuclear Posture Review Report, 2010* (Washington, DC: Department of Defense, 2010), p. 5.

27. *Ballistic Missile Defense Review Report, 2010* (Washington, DC: Department of Defense, 2010), pp. 12–13.

28. Remarks of Secretary of State Colin Powell, Hearings on the Ratification of the Strategic Offensive Reductions Treaty, July 17, 2002.

29. "Administration Missile Defense Papers," posted at the White House website, July 11, 2001, and retrieved on July 13, 2001.

30. This characterization of Chinese views, like many of those to follow, is drawn from a decade of informal dialogue with Chinese experts from the military, Party,

think tanks, and universities that have been conducted on a not-for-attribution basis. Where possible, citations are provided to specific references. In the absence of such citations, key views can be found in the record of these dialogues as sometimes available from their various sponsors, hosts, and coorganizers.

31. *China's National Defense in 2006*, section II. The main elements of China's nuclear strategy were set out by Chairman Mao in 1964, with the central place given to no first use. See M. Taylor Fravel and Evan Medeiros, "China's Search for Assured Retaliation: The Evolution of China's Nuclear Strategy and Force Structure," *International Security*, Vol. 35, No. 2 (Fall 2010), pp. 47–87.

32. *The Diversified Employment of China's Armed Forces.*

33. "Jiang Zemin Defines Position of China's Strategic Nuclear Weapons," *Hong Kong Tai Yang Pao*, July 17, 2000, Foreign Broadcast Information Service, CPP20000727000021.

34. See Walter C. Clemens Jr., "China," in Richard Dean Burns, ed., *Encyclopedia of Arms Control and Disarmament*, pp. 59–74 (New York: Charles Scribner's Sons, 1993).

35. For additional discussion, see Brad Roberts, "Arms Control and Sino–U.S. Strategic Stability," in Christopher P. Twomey, ed., *Perspectives on Sino-American Strategic Nuclear Issues* (New York: Palgrave Macmillan, 2008).

36. Zhou Rong, "Can New Strategy Guarantee US Security," *Beijing Shijie Zhishi*, May 1, 2002, pp. 20-21.

37. Tian Jingmei, "The Bush Administration's Nuclear Strategy and its Implications for China," working paper (Stanford, CA: Center for International Security and Cooperation of Stanford University, 2003).

38. Lora Saalman, *China and the U.S. Nuclear Posture Review* (Washington, DC: Carnegie Endowment, 2011); and Thomas Fingar, "Worrying about Washington: China's Views on the U.S. Nuclear Posture Review," *Nonproliferation Review*, Vol. 18, No. 1 (February 2011), pp. 51–68.

39. Wu Riqiang, "China's Anxiety about U.S. Missile Defense: A Solution," *Survival*, Vol. 55, No. 5 (October–November 2013), pp. 29–52. See also Wu, "Global Missile Defense Cooperation and China," *Asian Perspectives*, Vol. 35 (2011), pp. 595–615.

40. Yao Yunzhu, "China's Perspective on Nuclear Deterrence," *Air and Space Power Journal*, Vol. 24, No. 1 (Spring 2010), pp. 27–30.

41. Philip C. Saunders, *The Rebalance to Asia: U.S.–China Relations and Regional Security*, INSS Strategic Forum No. 281 (Washington, DC: National Defense University, 2013).

42. Chen Zhou, "US Security Strategy and East Asia," Foreign Broadcast Information Services, CPP20021210000027, December 10, 2002.

43. Sun Xiangli, "Analysis of China's Nuclear Strategy," *China Security*, Vol. 1, No. 1 (Autumn 2005), pp. 23–27; and Shen Dingli, "Nuclear Deterrence in the 21st Century," *China Security*, Vol. 1, No. 1 (Autumn 2005), pp. 10–14.

44. Not-for-attribution discussion paper.

45. Li Laizhu, "Strategic Parity," in Song Shilun and Xiao Ke, eds., *Chinese Military Encyclopedia, Vol. 3* (Beijing: Military Science Publishing House, 1997), p. 723.

46. Chu Shulong, "Maximally Increase Nuclear Deterrence to Deal with the Threat of U.S. and Japan," *People's Daily*, June 4, 2014.

47. Danny Gittings, "General Zhu Goes Ballistic," *Wall Street Journal*, July 18, 2005.

48. Pan Zhenqiang, "China's Insistence on No-First-Use," *China Security*, Vol. 1, No. 1 (Autumn 2005), pp. 5–9. See also Christopher T. Yeaw, Andrew S. Erickson, and Michael S. Chase, "The Future of Chinese Nuclear Policy and Strategy," in Toshi Yoshihara and James Holmes, eds., *Strategy in the Second Nuclear Age: Power, Ambition, and the Ultimate Weapon*, pp. 53–80 (Washington, DC: Georgetown University Press, 2012).

49. Frank G. Klotz and Oliver Bloom, "China's Nuclear Weapons and the Prospects for Multilateral Arms Control," *Strategic Studies Quarterly*, Vol. 7, No. 4 (Winter 2013), pp. 3–10; and Roberts, "Arms Control and Sino–U.S. Strategic Stability."

50. Michael Swayne with Zhang Tuosheng and Danielle F. S. Cohen, *Managing Sino-American Crises: Case Studies and Analysis* (Washington, DC: Carnegie Endowment, 2006).

51. Discussion paper prepared not for attribution.

52. For a constructive binational effort to explore the elements of strategic stability, see Thomas Finger and Fan Jishe, "Ties That Bind: Strategic Stability in the U.S.–China Relationship," *Washington Quarterly*, Vol. 36, No. 1 (Winter 2013), pp. 125–138.

53. Li Bin and He Yun, "Credible Limitations: U.S. Extended Nuclear Deterrence and Stability in Northeast Asia," in Rory Medcalf and Fiona Cunningham, eds., *Disarming Doubt: The Future of Extended Deterrence in East Asia*, p. 47 (Sydney: Lowy Institute for International Policy, 2012).

54. Sun, "China's Nuclear Strategy," p. 27. See also Yao, "China's Perspective on Nuclear Deterrence."

55. *Report of the Quadrennial Defense Review, 1997* (Washington, DC: Department of Defense, 1997).

56. *Report of the Quadrennial Defense Review, 2010* (Washington, DC: Department of Defense, 2010), p. 7.

57. *Report of the Quadrennial Defense Review, 2014* (Washington, DC: Department of Defense, 2014), pp. 6–7.

58. *AirSea Battle: Service Collaboration to Address Anti-Access and Area Denial Challenges* (Washington, DC: Air-Sea Battle Office, Department of Defense, May 2013). See also Jan Van Tol et al., *AirSea Battle: A Point-of-Departure Operational Concept* (Washington, DC: Center for Strategic and Budgetary Assessments, May 2010); and T. X. Hammes, *Offshore Control: A Proposed Strategy for an Unlikely Conflict*, INSS Strategic Forum No. 278 (Washington, DC: National Defense University, June 2012).

59. David M. Finkelstein, "China's National Military Strategy: An Overview of the 'Military Strategic Guidelines,'" in Roy Kamphausen and Andrew Scobell, eds.,

Right Sizing the People's Liberation Army: Exploring the Contours of China's Military,
pp. 69–140 (Carlisle, PA: Strategic Studies Institute of the U.S. Army War College,
2007).

60. John Lewis and Xue Litae, "Making China's Nuclear War Plan," *Bulletin of the
Atomic Scientists,* Vol. 68, No. 5 (2012), p. 51.

61. James Mulvenon and David Finkelstein, *China's Revolution in Doctrinal Affairs: Emerging Trends in the Operational Art of the People's Liberation Army* (Alexandria, VA: RAND and the Center for Naval Analyses, 2003).

62. Andrew Scobell, *Show of Force: The PLA and the 1995–1996 Taiwan Strait Crisis* (Stanford, CA: Center for International Security and Cooperation, Stanford University, 1999); and M. Taylor Fravel, "The Evolution of China's Military Strategy: Com-
paring the 1987 and 1999 Editions of Zhanluexue," in ibid., pp. 79–100.

63. *The Diversified Employment of China's Armed Forces,* April 2013.

64. Ibid.

65. Ibid.

66. Yu Jixun, ed., *The Science of Second Artillery Campaigns* (Beijing: Press of the
People's Liberation Army, 2004), p. 259.

67. Robert Manning, "Forget the South China Sea: Taiwan Could be Asia's Next
Big Security Nightmare," *National Interest* on-line, December 5, 2014. Available
at www.atlanticcouncil.org/news/in-the-news/manning-taiwan-could-be-asia-s-
next-big-security-nightmare.

68. *Annual Report to Congress: Military and Security Developments Involving the
People's Republic of China 2014* (Washington, DC: Department of Defense, 2014), p. 6.

69. Ibid.

70. See *U.S. Relations with Taiwan,* Fact Sheet (Washington, DC: Bureau of East
Asian and Pacific Affairs, U.S. Department of State, February 12, 2014); Richard C.
Bush, *At Cross Purposes: U.S.–Taiwan Relations since 1942* (New York: M. E. Sharpe,
2004); and Bush, *Uncharted Strait: The Future of China–Taiwan Relations* (Washington, DC: Brookings Institution, 2013).

71. Richard Bush, "The U.S. Policy of Dual Deterrence," in Steve Tsang, ed., *If
China Attacks Taiwan: Military Strategy, Politics, and Economics* (New York: Routledge, 2006), pp. 35–53; and Thomas J. Christensen, "The Contemporary Security Dilemma: Deterring a Taiwan Conflict," *Washington Quarterly,* Vol. 25, No. 4 (Autumn
2002), pp. 7–21.

72. This review of China's thinking about the possibility of war with the United
States and how to manage the risks of escalation draws heavily on two workshops
convened during the preparation of this volume. Discussion was conducted on a not-
for-attribution basis. Without attributing specific views to him, I would like to acknowledge the important intellectual contributions to this topic by Dr. Philip Saunders, director of the Center for the Study of Chinese Military Affairs at the National
Defense University in Washington, D.C.

73. Zhang Junbo and Yao Yunzhu, "Traditional Chinese Military Thinking: A Comparative Perspective," in Suisheng Zhao, ed., *Chinese Foreign Policy: Pragmatism and Strategic Behavior* (White Plains, NY: M. E. Sharpe, 2004), pp. 128–139.

74. On seizing the initiative, see Mark Burles and Abram N. Shulsky, *Patterns in China's Use of Force: Evidence from History and Doctrinal Writings*, MR-1160-AF (Santa Monica, CA: RAND Corporation, 2000), pp. 5–21.

75. Paul H. B. Goodwin and Alice L. Miller, *China's Forbearance Has Limits: Chinese Threat and Retaliation Signaling and Its Implications for Sino–U.S. Confrontation*, China Strategic Perspectives, No. 6 (Washington, DC: National Defense University, 2013).

76. *The Science of Second Artillery Campaigns*, p. 263.

77. For more on how China thinks about the risks of nuclear escalation and how to manage them, see Forrest Morgan et al., *Dangerous Thresholds: Managing Escalation in the 21st Century*, RAND Monograph MG-614-AF (Santa Monica, CA: RAND Corporation, 2008), pp. 47–76; and Evan S. Medeiros, "'Minding the Gap': Assessing the Trajectory of the PLA's Second Artillery," in Scobell and Kamphausen, *Right Sizing the People's Liberation Army*, pp. 143–190.

78. Wang Houqing and Zhang Xingye, eds., *The Science of Military Campaigns* (Beijing: Guofang Daxue, May 2000), p. 369.

79. Lewis and Xue, "Making China's Nuclear War Plan," p. 55.

80. *The Science of Second Artillery Campaigns*, p. 219.

81. Ibid., p. 111.

82. Ibid., p. 238.

83. M. Taylor Fravel and Evan S. Medeiros, "China's Search for Assured Retaliation: The Evolution of Chinese Nuclear Strategy and Force Structure," *International Security*, Vol. 35, No. 2 (Fall 2010), pp. 44–87; and Michael S. Chase, "China's Transition to a More Credible Nuclear Deterrent: Implications and Challenges for the United States," *Asia Policy*, No. 16 (July 2013), pp. 69–101.

84. Wu Riqiang, "Certainty of Uncertainty: Nuclear Strategy with Chinese Characteristics," *Journal of Strategic Studies*, Vol. 36, No.4 (July/August 2013), pp. 579–614.

85. Hans M. Kristensen and Robert S. Norris, "China's Nuclear Forces 2013," *Bulletin of the Atomic Scientists*, Vol. 69, No. 6 (November 2013); and Lyle J. Goldstein, ed., with Andrew S. Erickson, *China's Nuclear Force Modernization* (Newport, RI: Naval War College, 2005).

86. *The Science of Second Artillery Campaigns*, p. 222. See also Andrew Erickson and Phillip Saunders, "Selective Transparency: How the PLA Uses Development, Testing, Deployment, and Exercises as Shaping and Signaling Tools," unpublished paper, December 2013.

87. *The Science of Second Artillery Campaigns*, p. 222.

88. Lewis and Xue, "Making China's Nuclear War Plan," p. 53.

89. Ron Christman, "Conventional Missions for China's Second Artillery Corps," *Comparative Strategy*, Vol. 30 (2011), p. 198.

90. Ibid., p. 207.

91. Ron Christman, "China's Second Artillery Force: Capabilities and Missions for the Near Seas," in Peter Dutton, Andrew S. Erickson, and Ryan Martinson, eds., *China's Near Seas Combat Capabilities*, p. 31 (Newport, RI: U.S. Naval War College, 2014); and Christman, "Conventional Missions for China's Second Artillery Corps," *Comparative Strategy*, Vol. 30 (2011), pp. 198–228.

92. *The Science of Second Artillery Campaigns*, pp. 222, 226. See also Lewis and Xue, "Making China's Nuclear War Plan," pp. 53, 60.

93. *The Science of Second Artillery Campaigns*, p. 275.

94. Lewis and Xue, "Making China's Nuclear War Plan," p. 60.

95. *The Science of Second Artillery Campaigns*, p. 274.

96. As cited in Morgan et al., *Dangerous Thresholds*, pp. 61–62.

97. Lonnie D. Henley, "Evolving Chinese Concepts of War Control and Escalation Management," in Michael D. Swaine, Andrew N. D. Yang, and Evan S. Medeiros, eds., with Oriana Skylar Mastro, *Assessing the Threat: The Chinese Military and Taiwan's Security* (Washington, DC: Carnegie Endowment, 2007), pp. 85–110.

98. Inadvertent escalation results when a combatant acts in a way that it does not perceive to be escalatory but its enemy perceives as escalatory. See Morgan et al., *Dangerous Thresholds*; and Swaine; and Zhang, *Managing Sino-American Crises*.

99. *Annual Report to Congress: Military and Security Developments Involving the People's Republic of China 2014* (and its predecessors); David Shambaugh, "China's Military Modernization: Making Steady and Surprising Progress," in Ashley J. Tellis and Michael Wills, eds., *Strategic Asia 2005–06: Military Modernization in an Era of Uncertainty* (Seattle, WA: National Bureau of Asian Research, 2005); and Mark A. Stokes, *China's Evolving Conventional Strategic Strike Capability* (Washington, DC: Project 2049 Institute, 2009). See also Stokes and Dean Cheng, *China's Evolving Space Capabilities: Implications for U.S. Interests* (Washington, DC: Project 2049 Institute, 2012).

100. Thomas J. Christensen, "The Meaning of the Nuclear Evolution: China's Strategic Modernization and US–China Security Relations," *The Journal of Strategic Studies*, Vol. 35, No. 4 (August 2012), pp. 463, 466.

101. Avery Goldstein, "China's Real and Present Danger: Now Is the Time for Washington to Worry," *Foreign Affairs* (September/October 2013) as adapted from Goldstein, "First Things First: The Pressing Danger of Crisis Instability in U.S.–China Relations, *International Security* (Spring 2013).

102. These insights are summarized in Brad Roberts, "The Nuclear Dimension: How Likely? How Stable?" in Evan Medeiros, Michael D. Swaine, and Andrew Yang, eds., *Assessing the Threat: The Chinese Military and Taiwan Security* (Washington, DC: Carnegie Endowment, 2007). See also Brad Roberts, *China–U.S. Nuclear Relations: What Relationship Best Serves U.S. Interests?* (Alexandria, VA: Institute for Defense Analyses, 2001), pp. 19–20.

103. Alan S. Whiting, *The Chinese Calculus of Deterrence* (Ann Arbor: University of Michigan Press, 1975). See also Abram N. Shulsky, *Deterrence Theory and Chinese Behavior* (Santa Monica, CA: RAND, 2000).

104. Philip A. Karber, *Strategic Implications of China's Underground Great Wall* (Washington, DC: Georgetown University's Asian Arms Control Project, 2011); and Alexei Arbatov and Vladimir Dvorkin, *The Great Strategic Triangle* (Washington, DC: Carnegie Endowment, 2012).

105. David Gompert and Terrence Kelly, "Escalation Cause: How the Pentagon's New Strategy Could Trigger War with China," *Foreign Policy*, August 2, 2013.

106. Robert Sutter, *China's Rise in Asia: Promises and Perils* (Lanham, MD: Rowman and Littlefield, 2005); and Sutter, *Chinese Foreign Relations* (Lanham, MD: Rowman and Littlefield, 2010).

Chapter 6

1. Paul Huth, "Extended Deterrence and the Outbreak of War," *American Political Science Review*, Vol. 82, No. 2 (1988), p. 424. See also Huth, *Extended Deterrence and the Prevention of War* (New Haven, CT: Yale University Press, 1988).

2. Michael Howard set out these twin elements in a seminal article at the height of the Cold War. See Michael Howard, "Reassurance and Deterrence: Western Defense in the 1980s," *Foreign Affairs*, Vol. 61, No. 2 (Winter 1982–1983).

3. Thomas Schelling, *Arms and Influence* (New Haven, CT: Yale University Press, 1966), p. 36. Emphasis in original.

4. Denis Healey, *The Time of My Life* (London: Michael Joseph, 1989), p. 243.

5. *Strategic Concept* issued by the North Atlantic Treaty Organization, April 24, 1999, from para. 12.

6. Ibid., paras. 21 and 22.

7. Ibid., para. 62.

8. Ibid., p. 759. See also Michael Rühle, "NATO and Extended Deterrence in a Multinuclear World," *Comparative Strategy*, Vol. 28 (2009), pp. 10–16.

9. Alois Mertes, cited in David S. Yost, "Assurance and U.S. Extended Deterrence in NATO," *International Affairs*, Vol. 85, No. 4 (2009), p. 764.

10. David Yost, *The U.S. and Nuclear Deterrence in Europe*, Adelphi Paper 326 (London: Oxford University Press for the International Institute for Strategic Studies, March 1999), p. 9.

11. See *NATO's Nuclear Forces in the New Security Environment*, NATO Factsheet, as updated October 22, 2009. For the reference to a 97 percent reduction, see *Report of the Secretary of Defense Task Force on DoD Nuclear Weapons Management, Phase II, Review of the DoD Nuclear Mission* (Arlington, VA: Secretary of Defense Task Force on DoD Nuclear Weapons Management, December 2008), p. 59.

12. Tom Nichols, Douglas Stuart, and Jeffrey D. McCausland, eds., *Tactical Nuclear Weapons and NATO* (Carlisle Barracks, PA: Strategic Studies Institute of the U.S. Army War College, 2012).

13. Yost, "Assurance and U.S. Extended Deterrence in NATO," p. 771.

14. As cited in ibid.

15. James R. Schlesinger, chairman, *Report of the Secretary of Defense Task Force on DoD Nuclear Weapons Management*, Phase II (Washington, DC: Department of Defense, 2008), pp. 14–15, 59–60.

16. Ibid.

17. *NATO Strategic Concept 1999* (Brussels: NATO, 1999), para. 63.

18. *Nuclear Posture Review Report, 2010* (Washington, DC: Department of Defense, 2010), p. 32.

19. *Active Engagement, Modern Defence*, Strategic Concept adopted by heads of state and government at the NATO summit in Lisbon, November 19–20, 2010, paragraphs 8–9, 17–19, 26.

20. Martin Andrzej Piotrowski, ed., *Regional Approaches to the Role of Missile Defence in Reducing Nuclear Threats*, Report of the Polish Institute of International Affairs (Warsaw: PISM, July 2013).

21. *Strategic Concept, 2010*, para. 38.

22. *NATO 2020: Assured Security, Dynamic Engagement*, report of a group of experts chaired by Madeleine K. Albright and convened by the NATO Secretary General, May 17, 2010.

23. This debate encompassed a broad range of views inside the administration. See Ivo Daalder and Jan Lodal, "The Logic of Zero: Toward a World without Nuclear Weapons," *Foreign Affairs*, Vol. 87, No. 6 (November/December 2008), pp. 80–95. See also Clark Murdock et al., *Exploring the Nuclear Posture Implications of Extended Deterrence and Assurance* (Washington, DC: Center for Strategic and International Studies, 2009).

24. Simon Lunn, *NATO Nuclear Policy—Reflections on Lisbon and Looking Ahead*, The NTI Study on Nuclear Weapons and NATO (Washington, DC: Nuclear Threat Initiative, 2011), p. 23.

25. The High Level Group (HLG) is NATO's senior nuclear advisory body tasked with formulating policy recommendations to defense ministers when they convene as the Nuclear Planning Group (NPG). It coordinates with the NPG Staff Group, which consists of members of national delegations, to carry out detailed work on behalf of the alliance's permanent representatives and as tasked by the NPG. All NATO allies except France participate in the NPG, HLG, and NPG Staff Group.

26. See for example Paul Ingram and Oliver Meier, eds., *Reducing the Role of Tactical Nuclear Weapons in Europe: Perspectives and Proposals on the NATO Policy Debate*, An Arms Control Association and British American Security Information Council Report (Washington, DC: Arms Control Association, 2011).

27. *Sustaining U.S. Global Leadership: Priorities for 21st Century Defense* (Washington, DC: U.S. Department of Defense, January 2012), pp. 2–3.

28. David Owen, Des Brown, and Sir Malcolm Rifkind, *NATO Must Lead on Nuclear Disarmament* (London: European Leadership Network, February 16, 2011).

29. *Global Zero U.S. Nuclear Policy Commission Report: Modernizing U.S. Nuclear Strategy, Force Structure, and Posture*, Global Zero on-line, 2012, p. 9, available at www.globalzero.org/files/gz_us_nuclear_policy_commission_report.pdf.

30. Steve Andreasen and Isabelle Williams, eds., *Reducing Nuclear Risks in Europe: A Framework for Action* (Washington, DC: Nuclear Threat Initiative, 2011), pp. 4, 23, 8. See especially Sam Nunn, "The Race Between Cooperation and Catastrophe," pp. 8–23.

31. Oliver Meier, *Revising NATO's Nuclear Posture: The Way Forward*, Nuclear Policy Paper No. 8, jointly published by the Arms Control Association, the British American Security Information Council, and the Institute for Peace Research and Security Policy at the University of Hamburg, August 2011.

32. Former German Foreign Minister Frank-Walter Steinmeier, as cited in Oliver Meier, "Steinmeier Calls for U.S. to Withdraw Nukes," *Arms Control Today* on-line, May 8, 2009, available at www.armscontrol.org/act/2009_5/Steinmeier.

33. Guido Westerwelle, then Federal Minister of Foreign Affairs and Vice Chancellor, Speech at the 46th Munich Security Conference, February 6, 2010.

34. See also Helmut Schmidt, Richard von Weizsäcker, Egon Bahr, and Hans-Dietrich Genscher, "Toward a Nuclear-Free World: A German View," *International Herald Tribune*, January 9, 2009.

35. Lukasz Kulesa, ed., *The Future of NATO's Deterrence and Defence Posture: Views from Central Europe* (Warsaw: Polish Institute of International Affairs, 2012); and Kulesa, "Impact of U.S. Nuclear Reductions on European Security," *Bulletin* [of the Polish Institute of International Affairs], Vol. 26 (479), March 2013.

36. For a useful discussion of the potential implications for NATO of a nuclear Iran, see Jean-Loup Samaan, "The Day after Iran Goes Nuclear: Implications for NATO," Research Paper No. 71 (Rome: NATO Defense College, January 2012).

37. Cited in Chris Jones, "Process over Politics: NATO's TNW Decision," *CSIS On-line*, Washington, DC, May 7, 2010, available at http://csis.org/blog/process-over-politics-nato%E2%80%99s-tnw-decision.

38. Detlef Waechter, *Thinking beyond Theories: Concrete Proposals to Make NATO's Future Nuclear Policy Work*, Carnegie Policy Outlook (Washington, DC: Carnegie Endowment for International Peace, 2011), p. 1.

39. *Deterrence and Defence Posture Review*, NATO, May 20, 2013, paragraphs 2, 4, 8, 11, 18, 20, 22, 25, 34.

40. Jacek Durkalec, "The Future of NATO's Defence and Deterrence Posture: V4 Perspectives," in Kulesa, ed., *The Future of NATO's Deterrence and Defence Posture*, p. 10.

41. Leo G. Michel and James J. Przystup, *The U.S. "Rebalance" and Europe: Convergent Strategies Open Doors to Improved Cooperation*, INSS Strategic Perspectives No. 16 (Washington, DC: National Defense University Press, 2014).

42. *Strategic Agility: Strong National Defense for Today's Global and Fiscal Realities*, A Summary of the Findings of the Defense Advisory Committee (Washington,

DC: Stimson Center, 2013); and Barry Blechman and Russell Rumbaugh, "Bombs Away: The Case for Phasing out U.S. Tactical Nukes in Europe," *Foreign Affairs*, Vol. 93, No.4 (July/August 2014), pp. 163–175.

43. Brent Scowcroft, Stephen J. Hadley, Franklin Miller, "A Dangerous Proposition," *Washington Post*, August 18, 2014, p. A15.

44. Jacek Durkalec, *Russia's Violation of the INF Treaty: Consequences for NATO*, Bulletin No. 107 (702) (Warsaw: Polish Institute of International Affairs, August 13, 2014).

45. *Wales Summit Declaration, Issued by the Heads of State and Government Participating in the meeting of the North Atlantic Council in Wales*, September 5, 2014. As context for the discussion of future NATO policy and posture vis-à-vis Russia, see Martin Smith, *Russia and NATO since 1991: From Cold War to Cold Peace to Partnership* (London: Routledge, 2006).

46. Zdzislaw Lachowski, "Back to the Future? Euro-Atlantic Arms Control in a 'Post-Ukraine' Era: A Polish View," in Lukasz Kulesa, ed., *Is a New Cold War Inevitable? Central European Views on Rebuilding Trust in the Euro-Atlantic Region* (Warsaw: Polish Institute of International Affairs, October 2014). Citation is from p. 11.

47. Jacek Durkalek and Andrei Zagorski, *Options for Transparency and Confidence Building Measures Related to Non-Strategic Nuclear Weapons in Europe: Cost–Benefit Matrix*, PISM-IMEMO RAN Workshop Report (Warsaw: Polish Institute of International Affairs, July 2014).

48. Paul Schulte et al., *The Warsaw Workshop: Prospects for Information Sharing and Confidence-Building on Non-Strategic Nuclear Weapons in Europe*, Post-Conference Report (Warsaw: Polish Institute of International Affairs, 2013).

49. Forrest E. Morgan, *Dancing with the Bear: Managing Escalation in a Conflict with Russia*, Proliferation Papers (Paris: Institut Français Relations Internationale, 2012), p. 41.

50. Ibid.

51. James T. Quinlivan and Olga Oliker, *Nuclear Deterrence in Europe: Russian Approaches to a New Environment and Implications for the United States* (Santa Monica, CA: RAND, 2011); and Dave Johnson, *Russia's Approach to Conflict: Implications for NATO's Deterrence and Defence*, Research Paper No. 111 (Rome: NATO Defense College, April 2015).

52. Julian Lindley-French, *NATO and New Ways of Warfare: Defeating Hybrid Threats* (Rome, NATO Defense College, April 2015).

53. For the case that nuclear weapons "are likely to remain a central, enduring, and often controversial element of NATO policy," see Matthew Kroenig and Walter B. Slocombe, *Why Nuclear Deterrence Still Matters to NATO*, Issue Brief (Washington, DC: Atlantic Council, August 2014), p. 6.

54. Justyna Gotkowska, *A Weak Link? Germany in the Euro-Atlantic Security System* (Warsaw: Center for Eastern Studies, January 2015).

Chapter 7

1. Andrew O'Neil, *Asia, the US, and Extended Nuclear Deterrence* (New York: Routledge, 2013), pp. 60–61.

2. These principles were outlined by Prime Minister Eisaku Satō in a speech to the House of Representatives in 1967 amid negotiations over the return of Okinawa from U.S. control. The Diet formally adopted the principles in 1971. See Kurt M. Campbell and Tsuyoshi Sunohara, "Japan: Thinking the Unthinkable," in Campbell, Robert Einhorn, and Mitchell Reiss, eds., *The Nuclear Tipping Point: Why States Reconsider Their Nuclear Choices* (Washington, DC: Brookings Institution, 2004), pp. 218–253.

3. Ibid., p. 85.

4. Richard C. Bush, *The U.S. Policy of Extended Deterrence in East Asia: History, Current Views, and Implications*, Arms Control Series Paper No. 5 (Washington, DC: Brookings Institution, 2011); Seongwhun Cheon, "Changing Dynamics of US Extended Nuclear Deterrence in the Korean Peninsula," *Pacific Focus*, Vol. 26, No. 1 (April 2011), pp. 37–64; Rod Lyon, "The Challenges Confronting U.S. Extended Nuclear Assurance in Asia," *International Affairs*, Vol. 89, No. 4 (2013), pp. 929–941; Rory Medcalf and Fiona Cunningham, *Disarming Doubt: The Future of Extended Nuclear Deterrence in East Asia* (Sydney: Lowy Institute for International Policy, 2012); O'Neil, *Asia, the US, and Extended Nuclear Deterrence*; and Keith Payne et al., *U.S. Extended Deterrence and Assurance for Allies in Northeast Asia* (Fairfax, VA: National Institute Press, 2010).

5. This chapter draws selectively from Brad Roberts, *Extended Deterrence and Strategic Stability in Northeast Asia* (Tokyo: National Institute for Defense Studies, 2013).

6. "North Korea states 'nuclear war is unavoidable and declares first target will be Japan,'" *Express* (Tokyo), April 12, 2013. See also Max Fisher, "Here's North Korea's Official Declaration of 'War,'" *Washington Post*, March 30, 2013.

7. Raoul E. Heinrichs, "Australia's Nuclear Dilemma: Dependence, Deterrence or Denial?" *Security Challenges*, Vol. 4 (Autumn 2008), p. 61.

8. Victor D. Cha, "Abandonment, Entrapment, and Neoclassical Realism in East Asia: The United States, Japan, and Korea," *International Studies Quarterly*, Vol. 44 (2000), pp. 261–291.

9. James L. Schoff, *Realigning Priorities: The U.S.–Japan Alliance and the Future of Extended Deterrence* (Cambridge, MA: Institute for Foreign Policy Analysis, 2009).

10. For Japanese analyses of the 2010 Nuclear Posture Review, see Jimbo, "Japanese Perceptions of Obama's Nuclear Twin Commitments"; James L. Schoff, *Does the Nonproliferation Tail Wag the Deterrence Dog?* PacNet 9 (Honolulu, HI: Pacific Forum CSIS, February 2009); Yukio Satoh, "Agenda for Japan–US Strategic Consultations," in *Major Powers' Nuclear Policies and International Order in the 21st Century*, Report of the NIDS International Symposium on Security Affairs 2009 (Tokyo: National Institute for Defense Studies, 2010), pp. 21–34; and Satoh, "On Rethinking Extended

Deterrence," in *Shared Responsibilities for Nuclear Disarmament: A Global Debate* (Washington, DC: American Academy of Arts and Sciences, 2011), pp. 32–35.

11. See Satoh, "Agenda for Japan–US Strategic Consultations," pp. 27–28.

12. Clark Murdock et al., *Exploring the Nuclear Posture Implications of Extended Deterrence and Assurance* (Washington, DC: Center for Strategic and International Studies, 2009).

13. Remarks by President Barack Obama at Suntory Hall, Tokyo, on November 14, 2009; available at www.whitehouse.gov. This commitment followed on prior assurances of the United States, including most recently following the North Korean nuclear test in 2006, when Secretary of State Condoleeza Rice stated in Tokyo that "the United States has the will and the capability to meet the full range, and I underscore full range, of its deterrence and security commitments to Japan" ("U.S. Is Japan's Nuclear Shield, Rice Says," *Los Angeles Times*, October 19, 2006).

14. *Report on Nuclear Employment Strategy of the United States*, June 19, 2013, p. 8.

15. As discussed in Takahashi, *Ballistic Missile Defense in Japan*, p. 23.

16. Karen Parrish, "U.S., South Korea Announce 'Tailored Deterrence' Strategy," American Forces Press Service, October 2, 2013.

17. The role and value of these mechanisms are discussed further in Richard L. Armitage and Kurt M. Campbell, *Strengthening Deterrence in Asia, Chairman's Statement for the Atlantic Council Task Force on Extended Deterrence in Asia* (Washington, DC: Atlantic Council, October 2014). See also Robert A. Manning, *The Future of US Extended Deterrence in Asia to 2025* (Washington, DC: Atlantic Council, October 2014).

18. Tim Sullivan, "Deter and Assure: Charting a Course for America's Asian Alliances in a New Nuclear Age" (Washington, DC: AEI Center for Defense Studies, November 2010); emphasis in original.

19. Yukio Satoh, "Agenda for Japan–US Strategic Consultations," in *Major Powers' Nuclear Policies and International Order in the 21st Century*, Report of the NIDS International Symposium on Security Affairs 2009 (Tokyo: National Institute for Defense Studies, 2010), p. 25.

20. James Schoff, *Realigning Priorities*, p. xiv.

21 *U.S.–RoK–Japan Trilateral Extended Deterrence Dialogue*, Maui, July 23–24, 2014, report prepared by Pacific Forum CSIS, November 2014.

22. Views expressed to the author on a not-for-attribution basis in summer 2013.

23. For more on South Korea's nuclear debate, see Toby Dalton and Yoon Ho Jin, "Reading into South Korea's Nuclear Debate," *PACNet* #20 (Honolulu, HI: Pacific Forum CSIS, March 2013); and Jinho Park, "Response to PacNet #20 'Reading into South Korea's Nuclear Debate,'" *PACNet* #21 (Honolulu, HI: Pacific Forum CSIS, April 2013). See also Seongwhun Cheon, "A Tactical Step That Makes Sense for South Korea," *Global Asia*, Vol. 7, No. 2 (Summer 2012), pp. 74–76.

24. The technical possibilities for Japan are explored in Richard J. Samuels and James L. Schoff, "Japan's Nuclear Hedge: Beyond 'Allergy' and Breakout," in Ashley J.

Tellis, Abraham M. Denmark, and Travis Tanner, *Asia in the Second Nuclear Age*; *Strategic Asia 2013–2024* (Seattle: National Bureau of Asian Research, 2013), pp. 233–264; and in Toshi Yoshihara and James R. Holmes, "Thinking about the Unthinkable: Tokyo's Nuclear Option," *Naval War College Review*, Vol. 62, No. 3 (Summer 2009), pp. 59–78. For a discussion of Japan's own exploration of nuclear identity, see Kurt Campbell and Tsuyoshi Sunohara, "Japan: Thinking the Unthinkable," in Campbell et al., *The Nuclear Tipping Point: Why States Reconsider Their Nuclear Choices* (Washington, DC: Brookings Institution, 1994), pp. 218–253; Selig Harrison, ed., *Japan's Nuclear Future: The Plutonium Debate and East Asian Security* (Washington, DC: Carnegie Endowment for International Peace, 1996); and Emma Chanlett-Avery and Mary Beth Nikitin, *Japan's Nuclear Future: Policy Debate, Prospects, and U.S. Interests* (Washington, DC: Congressional Research Service, February 2009).

25. Lyon, "The Challenges Confronting U.S. Extended Nuclear Assurance in Asia," pp. 935–936, 941.

26. These views were gathered during informal consultations in Tokyo in spring and summer 2013 on a not-for-attribution basis.

27. Satoh, "Agenda for Japan–U.S. Strategic Consultations," pp. 32–33.

28. *Report on Nuclear Employment Strategy of the United States*, pp. 5–6.

29. Yukio Satoh has argued: "The Strategic Concept adopted at NATO's Lisbon Summit in 2010 . . . fell short of what Japan had expected of NATO: a global perspective from which to address the issue of nuclear weapons." See Satoh, *The Emerging Security Nexus between Japan and Europe*, Clingendael Asia Forum (The Hague: Clingendael Institute, April 20, 2012). See also Michito Tsuruoka, *Relocating Tactical Nuclear Weapons? A View from Japan* (Tokyo: Tokyo Foundation, May 2011).

30. A decade or so ago, such progress appeared unlikely. See for example Michael D. Swaine et al., *Japan and Ballistic Missile Defense* (Santa Monica, CA: RAND, 2001).

31. *Report of the Advisory Panel on Reconstruction of the Legal Basis for Security*, June 24, 2008. See also "What Is Abe's Real Motive for Collective Self Defense?" Editorial, *Asahi Shimbun*, February 9, 2013.

32. See, for example, Hideaki Kaneda et al., *Japan's Missile Defense: Diplomatic and Security Policies in a Changing Security Environment* (Tokyo: Japan Institute of International Affairs, March 2007); Shinichi Ogawa, "Missile Defense and Deterrence," *NIDS Security Reports*, No. 3 (March 2002), pp. 24–55; Sugio Takahashi, *Ballistic Missile Defense in Japan: Deterrence and Military Transformation*, Proliferation Papers #44 (Paris: IFRI, December 2012); and Tetsuya Umemoto, "Missile Defense and Extended Deterrence in the Japan–US Alliance," *Korean Journal of Defense Analysis*, Vol. 12, No. 2 (Winter 2000), pp. 135–152.

33. "Is Missile Defense Useful?" Commentary, *Japan Times*, May 13, 2013.

34. Song Sang-ho, "Korea, U.S. in Talks over THAAD," *Korea Herald*, October 1, 2014. See also Daniel Waserbly and James Hardy, "US Seeks Closer BMD Collaboration with Japan, South Korea," *Jane's Defence Weekly*, May 28, 2014.

35. See *Worldwide Ballistic Missile Inventories* (on-line data base) (Washington, DC: Arms Control Association), available at www.armscontrol.org/factsheets/missiles.

36. See Scott A Snyder, *South Korea's New Missile Guidelines and North Korea's Response*, Council on Foreign Relations Asia Unbound on-line blog, October 9, 2012, available at http://blogs.cfr.org/asia/2012/10/09/south-koreas-new-missile-guidelines-and-north-koreas-response/.

37. Sugio Takahashi, "Dealing with the Ballistic Missile Threat: Whether Japan Should Have a Strike Capability under Its Exclusively Defense-Oriented Policy," *NIDS Security Reports*, No. 7 (December 2006), pp. 79–94.

38. See "Japan Plans More Aggressive Defense," *Defense News*, May 16, 2013.

39. Michito Tsuruoka, *Why the NATO Nuclear Debate Is Relevant to Japan and Vice Versa*, Asia Program Policy Brief (Washington, DC: German Marshall Fund, October 2010).

Chapter 8

1. See Jeffrey W. Knopf, "Varieties of Assurance," *Journal of Strategic Studies*, Vol. 35, No. 3 (June 2012), pp. 375–399; Michael O. Wheeler, *The Changing Requirements of Assurance and Extended Deterrence*, Paper No. 4562 (Alexandria, VA: Institute for Defense Analyses, 2010); and Timothy W. Crawford, "The Endurance of Extended Deterrence: Continuity, Change, and Complexity in Theory and Policy," in T. V. Paul, Patrick M. Morgan, and James J. Wirtz, *Complex Deterrence: Strategy in the Global Age*, pp. 277–303 (Chicago: University of Chicago Press, 2009).

2. Choi Kang, Kim Jiyoon, Karl Friedhoff, Kang Chungku, and Lee Euicheol, *South Korean Attitudes on the Korea–US Alliance and Northeast Asia* (Seoul: ASAN Institute, April 2014).

3. Michael Green, *New Poll Shows Underlying Strength of U.S.-Japan Alliance, Need for Great Confidence* (Washington, DC: Center for Strategic and International Studies, December 16, 2013); and *Transatlantic Trends, 2014* (Washington, DC: German Marshall Fund of the United States, 2014).

4. Mira Rapp-Hooper, *Absolute Alliances: Extended Deterrence in International Politics*, Chapters 5 and 6 (PhD dissertation, Columbia University, forthcoming).

5. Jonathan Mercer, *Reputation and International Politics* (Ithaca, NY: Cornell University Press, 1996); Roger Powell, *Nuclear Deterrence Theory: The Search for Credibility* (Cambridge, UK: Cambridge University Press, 1990); and Daryl Press, *The Credibility of Power: How Leaders Assess Military Threats* (Ithaca, NY: Cornell University Press, 2005).

6. Andrew O'Neill, *Asia, the US and Extended Nuclear Deterrence* (New York: Routledge, 2013), p. 128.

7. For one analysis of nuclear hedge practices, see Alexis Blanc and Brad Roberts, *Nuclear Proliferation: A Historical Overview*, Paper No. 3447 (Alexandria, VA:

Institute for Defense Analyses, 2008). See also Van Jackson, "The Rise and Persistence of Strategic Hedging across Asia: A System-Level Analysis," in Ashley J. Tellis, Abraham M. Denmark, and Greg Chaffin, eds., *Strategic Asia 2014–2015: U.S. Alliances and Partnerships at the Center of Global Politics* (Seattle, WA: National Bureau of Asian Research, 2014).

8. Ibid.

9. Sinan Ülgen, *Turkey and the Bomb* (Washington, DC: Carnegie Endowment for International Peace, 2012).

10. Speaking on this subject in 2011, an influential member of the Japanese Diet and former defense minister, Shigeru Ishiba, argued that "it's important to maintain our commercial reactors because it would allow us to produce a nuclear warhead in a short amount of time . . . it's a tacit nuclear deterrent." See Chester Dawson, "In Japan, Provocative Case for Staying Nuclear," *Wall Street Journal*, October 28, 2011.

11. For further on this subject, see Ariel Levite, "Never Say Never Again: Nuclear Reversal Revisited," *International Security*, Vol. 27, No. 3 (Winter 2002/2003), pp. 59–88. See also Tristan Volpe, "Proliferation Blackmail: The Coercive Threat Advantages of Nuclear Latency" (PhD dissertation, George Washington University, forthcoming).

12. Martin A. Smith, "British Nuclear Weapons and NATO in the Cold War and Beyond," *International Affairs*, Vol. 87, No. 6 (2011), pp. 1393–1398.

13. Scott D. Sagan and Kenneth N. Waltz, *The Spread of Nuclear Weapons: A Debate Renewed* (New York: Norton and Co., 2003).

14. See, for example, Harvey M. Sopolsky and Christine M. Leah, "Let Asia Go Nuclear," *National Interest on-line*, April 14, 2014, available at http://nationalinterest .org/feature/let-asia-go-nuclear-10259.

15. Australia is another case study of interest. Although its security environment is quite different from that of Northeast Asia, it takes a strong interest in U.S. extended deterrence, factors affecting its credibility, and measures to strengthen the regional deterrence architecture. See O'Neill, *Asia, the US and Extended Nuclear Deterrence*.

16. On the tipping point argument, see *A More Secure World: Our Shared Responsibility*, Report of the Secretary General's High-Level Panel on Threats, Challenges, and Change (New York: United Nations, 2004), p. 40, para. 111. See also Kathleen J. McInnis, "Extended Deterrence: the U.S. Credibility Gap in the Middle East," *Washington Quarterly*, Vol. 28, No.3 (Summer 2005), pp. 169–186.

17. Quoted in Mark Landler and David E. Sanger, "Clinton Speaks of Shielding Mideast from Iran," *New York Times*, July 22, 2009.

18. *The Gulf Security Architecture: Partnership with the Gulf Cooperation Council*, A Majority Staff Report, Committee on Foreign Relations, United States Senate, June 19, 2012. See also Mira Rapp Hooper and Zachary Goldman, "Conceptualizing Containment: The Iranian Threat and the Future of Gulf Security," *Political Science Quarterly*, Vol. 128, No. 4 (Winter 2013–2014), pp. 589–616.

19. *Joint Communique from the Third Ministerial Meeting for the U.S–GCC Strategic Cooperation Forum*, September 26, 2013. See also Walter Pincus, "Hagel's Ver-

bal Assurances for Continued U.S. Presence in the Middle East Come with Action," *Washington Post*, December 11, 2013.

20. Norman Cigar, *Considering a Nuclear Gulf: Thinking about Nuclear Weapons in Saudi Arabia* (Maxwell Air Force Base, Ala.: USAF Counterproliferation Center, 2013), p. 22. See also HRH Prince Turki Al Faisal, "Saudi Arabia's New Foreign Policy Doctrine in the Aftermath of the Arab Awakening," public lecture to the Belfer Center for Science and International Affairs, Harvard University, April 25, 2013.

21. Cigar, *Considering a Nuclear Gulf*, pp. 106, 67.

22. Ibid., pp. 67, 95.

23. Ibid., p. 69.

24. Ibid., pp. 121, 114.

25. Ibid., p. vii.

26. Chemi Shalev, "Dennis Ross: Saudi King Vowed to Obtain Nuclear Bomb after Iran," *Haaretz*, May 30, 2012.

27. Colin H. Kahl, Melissa G. Dalton, and Matthew Irvine, *Atomic Kingdom: If Iran Builds the Bomb, Will Saudi Arabia Be Next?* (Washington, DC: Center for a New American Security, 2013); and Shashank Joshi and Michael Stephens, *An Uncertain Future: Regional Responses to Iran's Nuclear Programme*, Whitehall Report No. 4-13 (London: Royal United Services Institute, 2013).

28. Joseph F. Pilat, "Reassessing Security Assurances in a Unipolar World," *Washington Quarterly*, Vol. 28, No. 2 (Spring 2005), pp. 159–170; and Michael O. Wheeler, *Positive and Negative Security Assurances*, Project on Rethinking Arms Control Paper No. 9 (College Park, MD: University of Maryland, Center for International and Security Studies, February 1994).

29. Jeffrey W. Knopf, ed., *Security Assurances and Nuclear Nonproliferation* (Stanford, CA: Stanford University Press, 2012).

30. David S. Yost, "The Budapest Memorandum and Russia's Intervention in Ukraine," *International Affairs*, Vol. 91, No. 3 (May 2015), pp. 505–538.

31. Randy Rydell, "Looking Back: The 1995 Nuclear Non-Proliferation Treaty Review and Extension Conference," *Arms Control Today* (April 2005).

32. Thomas C. Schelling, *Arms and Influence* (New Haven, CT: Yale University Press, 1966), p. 74.

33. Lawrence Freedman, *Deterrence* (Cambridge, UK: Polity Press, 2004), p. 52.

34. Jeffrey Knopf has argued that *reassurance* is the better term for this particular function, on the argument that it is about addressing a fear or misperception that has taken hold. See Knopf, "Varieties of Assurance," pp. 383–387.

35. For an American argument that the United States can and should do more in the way in restraining its national ambitions for a liberal international order, see Barry F. Posen, *Restraint: A New Foundation for U.S. Grand Strategy* (Ithaca, NY: Cornell University Press, 2014).

36. For a recent elaboration of a comprehensive U.S. strategy for reassuring China, see James Steinberg and Michael E. O'Hanlon, *Strategic Reassurance and*

Resolve: U.S.–China Relations in the 21st Century (Princeton, NJ: Princeton University Press, 2014).

37. Karin Dawisha, *Putin's Kleptocracy: Who Owns Russia?* (New York: Simon and Schuster, 2014).

38. Clark A. Murdock and Jessica M. Yeats, *Exploring the Nuclear Posture Implications of Extended Deterrence and Assurance: Workshop Proceeding and Key Take-aways* (Washington, DC: Center for Strategic and International Studies, 2009).

39. At the Lisbon NATO summit, as cited in David Yost, "The US Debate on NATO Nuclear Deterrence," *International Affairs*, Vol. 87, No. 6 (2011), p. 1413.

40. Franklin Miller, "NATO's Nuclear Future: Self-Centered Policies Threaten Collective Security," remarks, Brookings Institution, Washington, DC, July 21, 2011.

41. The June 2012 Majority Staff Report of the Senate Committee on Foreign Relations cites this as a major risk of deeper U.S. integration with the Gulf Cooperation Council. See *The Gulf Security Architecture*. For a discussion of the potential negative effects on allies of U.S. security guarantees, see also Glenn Snyder and Paul Diesing, *Conflict among Nations: Bargaining, Decision Making, and System Structure in International Crises* (Princeton, NJ: Princeton University Press, 1978), p. 293.

42. James R. Schlesinger, "Nuclear Weapons in History," *Washington Quarterly*, Vol. 16, No. 4 (Autumn 1993), pp. 5–16.

Chapter 9

1. See *Concluding Report, the Trident Commission* (London: British-American Security Information Council, 2014), p. 7; and *A BASIC Guide to Interpreting the Trident Commission's Concluding Report* (London: British-American Security Information Council, 2014).

2. In order, Francis Fukuyama, *The End of History and the Last Man* (New York: Simon and Schuster, 1992); George Bush and Brent Scowcroft, *A World Transformed* (New York: Alfred Knopf, 1998); and Paul Schroeder, "The New World Order: A Historical Perspective," *Washington Quarterly*, Vol. 17, No. 2 (Spring 1994), pp. 367–384.

3. Henry Kissinger, *World Order* (New York: Penguin Press, 2014), p. 364. See also Richard N. Haass, "The Unraveling: How to Respond to a Disordered World," *Foreign Affairs*, Vol. 93, No. 6 (November/December 2014), pp. 70–79; and Charles Kupchan, *No One's World: The West, the Rising Rest, and the Coming Global Turn* (New York: Oxford University Press, 2012).

4. Thérèse Delpech, *Nuclear Deterrence in the 21st Century: Lessons from the Cold War for a New Era of Strategic Piracy* (Santa Monica, CA: RAND, 2012).

5. Carl von Clausewitz, *On War*, Michael Howard and Peter Paret, eds. (Princeton, NJ: Princeton University Press, 1989), especially book 7, chapter 21.

6. Sun Tzu, *The Art of War*, translated by Ralph D. Sawyer (New York: Basic Books, 1994).

7. Herman Kahn, among others, cautioned adversaries against expecting to persuade America to compromise by attacking it, arguing that the American tendency to see the world in terms of good and evil makes it inclined to apply "extravagant force" to expunge a hated enemy. Kahn, *On Escalation* (New York: Praeger, 1965), p. 17.

8. See also Bruno Tertrais, *In Defense of Deterrence: The Relevance, Morality and Cost-Effectiveness of Nuclear Weapons*, Proliferation Paper (Paris: IFRI, 2011).

9. Thérèse Delpech, *The Savage Century: Back to Barbarism* (Washington, DC: Carnegie Endowment for International Peace, 2007).

10. Milton Leitenberg, *Deaths in Wars and Conflicts in the 20th Century*, Peace Studies Program Occasional Paper No. 29 (Ithaca, NY: Cornell University, 2006).

Epilogue

1. Joseph I. Lieberman and Jon Kyl, "The Danger of Repeating the Cycle of American Isolationism," *Washington Post*, April 25, 2013; and Peter Beinart, "The Phantom Menace: The Myth of American Isolationism," *National Journal*, October 18, 2014.

2. Harvey M. Sapolsky and Christine M. Leah, "Let Asia Go Nuclear," *National Interest*, April 14, 2014.

3. Brent Scowcroft, Stephen J. Hadley, and Franklin Miller, "NATO-Based Nuclear Weapons Are an Advantage in a Dangerous World," *Washington Post*, August 17, 2014.

4. *Global Zero U.S. Nuclear Policy Commission Report, Modernizing U.S. Nuclear Strategy, Force Structure, and Posture* (Global Zero: A World without Nuclear Weapons, 2012), available at www.globalzero.org/files/gz_us_nuclear_policy_commission_report.pdf

5. The contrary case has been made in Hans Kristensen, Robert Norris, and Ivan Oelrich, *From Counterforce to Minimal Deterrence*, Occasional Paper No. 7 (Washington, DC: Federation of American Scientists and Natural Resources Defense Council, April 2009).

6. Keith B. Payne et al., *U.S. Force Posture Adaptability for Deterrence and Assurance* (Fairfax, VA: National Institute for Public Policy, 2014). See also Keith B. Payne et al., *Minimum Deterrence: Examining the Evidence* (Fairfax, VA: National Institute Press, 2013); and Payne et al., *Planning the Future U.S. Nuclear Force* (Fairfax, VA: National Institute Press, 2009).

7. For more on this topic, see David S. Yost, *Strategic Stability in the Cold War: Lessons for Continuing Challenges*, Proliferation Paper No. 36 (Paris: IFRI, 2011).

8. Keir Lieber and Daryl Press, "The Nukes We Need: Preserving the American Deterrent," *Foreign Affairs*, Vol. 88, No. 5 (November/December 2009); and Elbridge A. Colby, "The Need for Limited Nuclear Options," in David Ochmanek and Michael Sulmeyer, eds., *Challenges in U.S. National Security Policy*, pp. 141–168 (Santa Monica, CA: RAND, 2014).

Index

ABM Demarcation Agreement, 109
abolition of nuclear weapons. *See* disarmament
active defense, 162
Adamsky, Dmitry, 131–132
advisory groups and experts: on arms control, 13–14, 19, 27, 36, 38; on deterrence strategies, 19, 21, 185, 208, 210, 251, 267; on the Middle East, 92, 222–223, 320n41; on Northeast Asia, 69–70, 205–207, 209–210, 213; reduction in numbers of, 19; on stability with both Russia and China, 263–265; on U.S.–China strategies, 145, 152–159, 169; on U.S.–Russia strategies, 113, 120, 122, 131, 134, 191, 229, 251
Afghanistan, 110, 113, 126
Alagappa, Muthiah, 28
Albright, Madeleine, 185
allies, defense of; alternatives to reliance on U.S., 218–220, 254–255, 258; assurance in, *see* nuclear assurance; assurance of U.S. by allies, 231–233, 320n41; balanced approach and, 215, 254–256, 261–263; in case for U.S. nuclear weapons, 240–243; cost and risk sharing in, 190, 231, 249, 266; credibility of U.S. commitment in, 178–179, 199, 203, 209, 216–218; Crimea annexation by Russia and, 114–115, 120, 125, 189–192, 225; Deterrence and Defense Posture Review (2012), 185–192, 266, 311n25; disarmament advocacy and, 231–233, 237–238; forward-deployed nuclear weapons and, 93–94, 181–182, 184–189, 202, 223, 249–250, 258–260; hedge capabilities of allies and, 217–218, 238, 318n10; Non-Proliferation Treaty provisions and, 224–227, 259, 261–263; nuclear weapon substitutes in, 94–96; as potential restraint on U.S. action, 66–67, 139, 171–172; purpose of, 220; reduced role of nuclear weapons in, 32, 39, 179, 181–184, 188, 191; in Russian theory of victory, 135, 139; sole purpose formulation, 32–33, 201, 205–206, 262;

allies, defense of (*continued*)
  solidarity image in, 99, 101–102;
  Taiwan and, 162, 163–164, 171,
  208–209; U.S. declaratory policy on,
  201–202, 245, 315n13; U.S. homeland
  defense versus, 66–67, 90–92, 98,
  135, 178–179, 198–199. *See also*
  ballistic missile defense; credibility
  of deterrence; extended deterrence;
  NATO; nuclear assurance; regional
  deterrence architectures
antiaccess, area-denial (A2/AD)
  capabilities, 161, 208
Anti-Ballistic Missile Treaty (1972), 18,
  23, 109–111, 149
Arab Spring, 115, 188, 222. *See also* color
  revolutions
Arms Control and Disarmament
  Agency, 14, 19
arms control and reduction; advisory
  groups for, 13–14, 19, 27, 36, 38;
  benefits of, 122; bilateral, with
  Russia, 14–15, 36, 110–112, 122–124;
  China and, 151–152, 156–157, 158,
  216, 237; destabilizing attributes
  of, 122–123, 238; future reductions,
  216, 235–239, 257–261; Gang of
  Four on ultimate abolition, 26–27,
  29, 37, 46; minimum deterrence,
  35, 37, 48, 260–261; of nonstrategic
  nuclear weapons, 181–189, 191–192;
  reduced role of nuclear weapons
  in NATO, 179, 181–183, 184, 188,
  191; Russia–U.S. disagreements
  on, 122–125, 236–237, 257–260,
  271–272; unilateral, by U.S., 14,
  24, 33, 39, 140, 257–261, 272.
  See also arms control treaties;
  disarmament
arms control treaties: Anti-Ballistic
  Missile Treaty (1972), 18, 23,
  109–111, 149; Comprehensive
  Test Ban Treaty (CTBT), 17, 27,
  151, 226; Conventional Forces in
  Europe Treaty (CFE; 1990), 12;
  Intermediate-range Nuclear Forces
  Treaty (INF; 1987), 12, 94, 137,
  193, 211; Limited Test Ban Treaty
  (1963), 151; New START Treaty,
  see New START Treaty; Non-
  Proliferation Treaty; Strategic
  Arms Reduction Treaty (START;
  1991), 12, 15, 24, 33, 108, 113,
  121; Strategic Arms Reduction
  Treaty II (START II; 1993), 15,
  17, 108–109; Strategic Offensive
  Reductions Treaty (SORT; 2003), 24,
  33, 110–111
Aspin, Les, 16
assurance. *See* nuclear assurance
asymmetry of stake, 72–73, 82, 100–101,
  134, 169
Austin, Texas, as North Korean target,
  59
Australia, 27, 224, 318n15

balanced approach: allies and, 215,
  254–256, 261–263; case for and
  against, 254–256; under Obama, 3,
  30, 40, 90, 184–185, 204; in tailoring
  regional defenses, 92, 204
Ballistic Missile Defense Review
  (BMDR; 2010), 87
ballistic missiles; under Bush, George
  H. W., 14–15, 43; under Bush,
  George W., 23–25, 87, 112, 119;
  against China, 87–90, 149, 154–155,
  158, 163; in China, 149–150, 154–156,
  159–160, 166–170, 173, 209, 260;
  under Clinton, 18, 20; in the Cold
  War, 12; current arms control and
  deterrence issues on, 122–123,
  236–237, 259–260, 264–265,
  269; current state of, 86–87, 266;
  deterrence value of, 89–90, 101,
  122–123, 134–135; disarmament

and, 49; European phased adaptive approach, 119–120, 190; in geopolitical hedges, 232–233; in gray zone threats, 88, 97–98; ICBM retirement, 18, 38–39, 108, 269; in Iran, 82, 221–222, 236; Iskander missiles, 136–137; in Japan, 95, 201, 209–210; in the Middle East, 54–55, 221–222; MIRVd warheads, 150, 159, 298n53; missile proliferation; by regional actors, 20–21, 28, 52; modernization needs of, 43–44, 211, 269; in NATO, 184–185, 188–190, 193–195, 297n47; in North Korea, 53, 58–60; under Obama, 29–34, 87, 119–120; in Poland, 95, 112; in prenuclear deterrence, 134–135; prompt strike capabilities of, 211–212, 264, 266, 270; in red zone threats, 75, 88–90, 94; in regional deterrence architectures, 82–83, 86–90, 208, 232–233, 292nn10–11, 297n47; in Russia, 132, 134–138; Russia on NATO missiles, 112–114, 117–120, 123–125, 188, 297n45, 297n47, 298n53; in South Korea, 209–211; on submarines, 25, 35; as substitutes for nuclear deterrence, 95, 247; U.S.–China relationship and, 208, 264; in U.S. homeland defense, 90–92, 112; U.S.–Russia relationship and, 112–114, 123–124, 230, 236, 264, 297n47. See also cruise missiles

Baltic states, 111, 190, 193–194, 196
Bell, Robert, 18
Betts, Richard, 69
biological weapons; in deterrence, 184, 201, 262; Iraq and, 55; North Korea and, 59, 65–66, 76; protection against, 98, 184
black-and-white zone threats; deterrence of, 86, 100–102, 103; from North Korea, 75–77, 86; in Red theories of victory, 244, 245
blackmail: China and, 156, 158, 166; countering, 6, 96, 102–104, 246–247; dangers of precedents in use of, 81; missile defense and credibility of, 89–90, 101; North Korea and, 53, 65–69, 70, 80, 198; Russia and, 116, 192
Blair, Dennis, 72
Blank, Stephen, 128
Blue theory of victory, 96–104; in black-and-white zone threats, 100–102, 103; China and, 171–172; countering blackmail, 102–104, 246–247; in gray zone threats, 86, 97–99, 200; importance of, 7, 96–97, 216, 246; key assumptions in, 102; in red zone threats, 85–86, 95, 99–102; Russia and, 138–140; U.S. nuclear weapons in, 8–9, 245–249. See also deterrence strategies; extended deterrence; regional deterrence architectures
BMDR (Ballistic Missile Defense Review; 2010), 87
bombers: in deterrence strategies, 93–94, 223–224, 250, 269–270; replacement of, 43; taken off alert status, 14, 17, 35, 206
bottom-up review (BUR) of defense, 16
Bracken, Paul, 28
brinksmanship: China and, 163; countering, 96, 102–104, 246–247; Iran and, 57; in North Korean theory of victory, 53, 65–69, 70–72, 80; in Red theories of victory, 244–245; in Russian theory of victory, 135, 192
Britain. See United Kingdom
Brodie, Bernard, 13
Brown, Harold, 121
Bulgaria, 95
Bundy, McGeorge, 70, 71, 72

BUR (bottom-up review) of defense, 16
Bush (George H. W.) administration:
    China relationship with, 142;
    credibility of nuclear threat of, 73;
    forswearing regime removal in Iraq,
    227; nuclear policy in, 14–15, 43, 257,
    260; Russia relationship in, 108, 260
Bush (George W.) administration; China
    relationship in, 23, 143, 147–148,
    173; freedom agenda of, 111; nuclear
    policy in, 21–29, 41, 106, 147–148,
    154, 257; pursuit of regime change
    in Iraq, 227–228; Russia relationship
    in, 110–112; tailoring regional
    deterrence strategies, 93, 119

Changmai Initiative, 146
chemical weapons; China and, 151;
    NATO and, 184; in North Korea, 59,
    64, 66, 76; protection against, 98
Chemical Weapons Convention, 151
Cheney, Richard, 15
Cheonan, sinking of, 63, 75
chess analogy, 52–53; in North Korea,
    61, 67–68, 79; in the United States,
    97
China, 141–175: arms control and
    reduction and, 151–152, 156–157, 158,
    216, 237; ballistic missiles defense
    against, 87–90, 149, 154–155, 158,
    163; ballistic missiles of, 149–150,
    154–156, 159–160, 166–170, 173,
    209, 260; Bush, George H. W.,
    administration and, 142; Bush,
    George W., administration and,
    23, 143, 147–148, 173; Clinton
    administration and, 142–143,
    173; cyber warfare and, 144, 161,
    165–166, 170–172, 208; deterrence
    strategy, 37, 150–151, 153–155,
    166–169, 173; future of U.S.
    relationship, 159–160, 170–172;
    Japan and, 145, 158, 199; maritime

territorial claims, 147, 162, 199, 212;
    military planning in, 160–168; "no
    first use" policy of, 150–152, 154, 156,
    158, 169, 201–202, 305n31; North
    Korea and, 145, 162–163; nuclear
    assurances by U.S. to, 228–230,
    319n34; nuclear modernization by,
    148, 150, 154–160, 169–170; nuclear
    policy and strategy of, 58, 157–159,
    170–172; Obama administration
    and, 143–150, 173; perception of U.S.
    policies, 144–146, 153–156, 160,
    172–173, 175; regional alliances and,
    145–146, 154, 158, 170, 172, 208–212;
    as rising power, 143–144; Russia
    and, 128–129, 145; South Korea and,
    199; strategic stability with U.S.,
    148–150, 153, 157–158, 173–175, 237,
    263–265; Taiwan and, 162, 163–164,
    171, 208–209; theory of victory
    by, 62–69, 80, 164–170, 174–175,
    243–245. See also Red theories
    of victory; Tiananmen Square
    democracy movement, 142;
    transparency of, 148, 150, 152–153,
    157, 159, 173; unofficial nuclear
    dialogue with U.S., 152–159
Christensen, Thomas, 170
Cigar, Norman, 222–223
Clausewitz, Carl von, 7, 53, 68, 105, 244,
    247
clean assurance, NPT and, 32
Clinton, Hillary, 221, 231
Clinton administration; China
    relationship with, 142–143, 173;
    credibility of nuclear threat of, 73;
    nuclear policy in, 15–21, 42, 106, 257;
    Russia relationship in, 42, 108–110;
    tailoring regional deterrence
    strategies, 15–21, 92–93, 293n21
Cold War; as Eurocentric, 28; large
    standing conventional forces from,
    96; modernization during, 43–44;

nonstrategic weapons in Europe in, 181, 187, 194; in Northeast Asia, 197–198, 207, 219; nuclear threats made in, 69–70, 178; proliferation in, 220, 226; stability-instability paradox in, 63; strategic parity in, 127, 131; U.S. nuclear policy in, 11–14, 19–20, 93, 103, 246. *See also* Soviet Union

color revolutions; in Russian theory of victory, 133, 136, 138; Russia on U.S. support of, 111, 113–116, 125, 128–129, 133, 229–230

Commission on the Strategic Posture of the United States, 30

Comprehensive Test Ban Treaty (CTBT), 17, 27, 151, 226

Congress, U.S.; on arms control treaty ratifications, 17, 33, 45, 109; Bush (George W.) administration and, 21–22, 24–25, 43, 45; on money for modernization, 24–25, 40, 270–271; nuclear policy debates in, 3, 22, 26, 29–30; Obama administration and, 34, 39–40, 45; partisanship in, 44–45; responsibilities for deterrence strategy in, 34, 251, 255; Senate Arms Control Observer Group, 14, 19

containment policy; China's accusation of, 145, 153, 158, 170, 208; Russia's accusation of, 115–116, 128

conventional forces; in Blue theory of victory, 98, 100, 104; cost of, 83, 96; escalation and, 36, 73, 77, 85, 246–247, 267; Iran and, 57; Japan and, 205; in Middle East strategy, 222; in NATO, 12, 181, 183–185, 187, 190, 193–195; North Korea and, 59–60, 62–64, 66–68, 71, 75–77; in nuclear deterrence, 39, 83–86, 95–96, 98, 168, 247; prompt strike capabilities, 211–212, 264, 266, 270; in U.S.–China relationship, 154, 160, 162, 164–166, 168–171, 208–209; in U.S. modernization, 25, 44, 190, 211, 264; in U.S.–Russia relationship, 118–119, 129–130, 133–137, 140

Conventional Forces in Europe Treaty (CFE; 1990), 12

Conventional Prompt Global Strike (CPGS) system, 211–212

costs: allies sharing, 190, 231, 249, 266; of deterrence strategies, 44, 284n110; of large standing army, 83, 96; of modernization, 24–25, 40, 44, 270–271; of nuclear programs, 91

credibility of deterrence: arms control and, 36, 48, 179, 187; assurance versus credibility, 178–179; deployed weapons in, 181–183; in Europe, 178–180, 182–183, 187, 189–192, 200–212; importance of, 217–218; in Northeast Asia, 199, 203, 209, 216; in North Korea, 73; in nuclear blackmail, 89–90, 101; nuclear weapons of low yield and, 270–271; public opinion of, 216; U.S. homeland defense and, 90–91, 135, 178, 199

Crimea, Russian annexation of, 114–115, 120, 125, 189–192, 225

Cronin, Patrick, 69

cruise missiles; deterrence value of, 270; flown across U.S. by mistake, 25; of Iran, 221; of Russia, 135–137, 193; on submarines, 197–198; Tomahawk, 198, 202, 211; of U.S. allies, 211

CTBT (Comprehensive Test Ban Treaty), 17, 27, 151, 226

cyber warfare; China and, 144, 161, 165–166, 170–172, 208; defense against, 83, 85–86, 96, 98, 184, 266; North Korea and, 66, 68, 75; Russia and, 122, 132–133; in strategic stability, 122; U.S. attacks in crises, 98

Czech Republic, 109, 112

DDPR (Deterrence and Defense Posture
    Review), 185–192, 266, 311n25
defense counterproliferation initiative
    (DCI), 16
Defense Nuclear Agency, 13–14, 19
Defense Special Weapons Agency, 19
Defense Threat Reduction Agency, 19,
    279n26
delivery systems: bomber replacement,
    43; bombers in deterrence strategies,
    93–94, 223–224, 250, 269–270;
    bombers taken off alert status, 14,
    17, 35, 206; in China, 147; dual-
    capable aircraft, 181, 202, 223–224,
    249, 269; forward-deployable,
    93–94, 181, 202, 223, 249–250, 258;
    long-range high-precision, 134–136;
    modernization of, 12, 25, 43, 202,
    269; North Korea and, 59; reduction
    in, 18; Russia and, 132, 134, 136–137
Delpech, Thérèse, 27–28, 243, 251
Deng Xiaoping, 162
Department of Defense (DoD), 29–30
Deterrence and Defense Posture Review
    (DDPR), 185–192, 266, 311n25
Deterrence in the Second Nuclear Age
    (Payne), 20
deterrence strategies: advisory groups
    and experts, 19, 21, 185, 208,
    210, 251, 267; after Soviet Union
    demise, 108–109; arms control
    and, 122–123, 236–237, 259–260,
    264–265, 269; assured retaliation,
    167; ballistic missiles in, see ballistic
    missiles; biological weapons in,
    184, 201, 262; in black-and-white
    zone threats, 86, 100–102, 103;
    bombers in, 93–94, 223–224, 250,
    269–270; Bush (George H. W.)
    administration, 14–15; Bush
    (George W.) administration, 22–23;
    Clinton administration, 15–21,
    92–93, 293n21; comprehensive
    approach to, 82–86, 88–90, 232,
    272; conventional forces in, 39,
    83–86, 95–96, 98, 168, 247; cost of,
    44, 284n110; credibility of threat
    in, see credibility of deterrence;
    cross-domain deterrence, 102; cyber
    and space domain resilience as, 83,
    85–86, 98, 266; declaratory policy as,
    201–202, 245, 315n13; denial as, 20;
    geopolitical surprises and, 231–233;
    in gray zone threats, 86, 97–99,
    200; importance of, 81–83; intrawar
    deterrence, 103–104, 227–228, 233;
    limited nuclear response in, 99,
    103–104, 194; low-yield nuclear
    weapons in, 270–271; military core
    competencies in, 250–251; minimum
    deterrence, 35, 37, 48, 260–261;
    mutual deterrence, 14, 63, 82,
    121–124, 153, 173; nuclear arsenal
    size in, 249–251; nuclear weapons
    role in, 37, 247–248; Obama
    administration, 30–32, 33, 267,
    272–273; prenuclear deterrence,
    134–135, 168; Reagan administration,
    12–13; in red zone threats, 85–86,
    95, 99–100; safeguarding nuclear
    materials, 14; second centers of
    decision and, 219–220; shift from
    global to regional threats, 48;
    strategic stability in, 120–122, 140;
    substitutes for nuclear components
    in, 94–96, 247; unilateral weapons
    reductions and, 257–261, 272; U.S.
    homeland defense and, 90–92,
    94, 199; U.S. military supremacy
    as sole, 104. See also credibility of
    deterrence; extended deterrence;
    regional deterrence architectures
disarmament: advocacy mismatch in,
    46–47; case against, 238, 240–243;
    case for, 48–50, 239–240; China
    on, 151–152, 156–159; debate on,

2, 36–40, 46–47, 49, 182; future
likelihood of, 235–239; Gang
of Four and, 26–27, 29, 37, 46;
government advisory groups, 14, 19;
international movement for, 37–40;
modernization and, 46–47; moral
argument and, 248–249; NATO on,
184–189, 231–233; non-nuclear states
on, 233; Non-Proliferation Treaty
and, 24, 33–34, 226–227, 256–262;
Obama and, 26–27, 29–30, 33–34,
39–40, 47; organizations promoting,
26–27, 37, 39–40, 46; wedding ring
analogy, 187. *See also* arms control
and reduction
discrimination, principle of, 35, 101
Donilon, Tom, 145
DPRK. *See* North Korea
dual-capable aircraft, 181, 202, 223–224,
249, 269
Durkalec, Jacek, 189
Dworkin, Vladimir, 121

Eagleburger, Larry, 142
EDD (Extended Deterrence Dialogue),
202–203
EDPC (Extended Deterrence Policy
Committee), 202–203
Eisenstadt, Michael, 57
"the Elaine Bunn wedding ring
analogy," 187
electromagnetic pulse threats, 76, 165
England. *See* United Kingdom
escalation management: ballistic
missile defense in, 88–89; in
Blue theory of victory, 96–102,
246–247; China and, 163, 165–166,
168–169, 170–171; conventional
forces in, 36, 73, 77, 85, 246–247,
267; in cyber and space attacks,
85–86, 122; escalation thresholds,
103–104, 195; homeland defense
and, 90, 94; horizontal escalation,

66, 133; inadvertent escalation, *see*
inadvertent escalation; Iran and, 57;
Japan and, 203; lateral escalation,
66, 133; miscalculations in, 244–245,
321n7 (Ch. 9); in NATO–Russia
relationship, 192–193, 195, 258, 260;
North Korea and, 53, 65–68, 71–73,
74–78, 200; regime change assurance
in, 227–228, 233; role of nuclear
weapons in, 247–250, 258; Russia
and, 122, 131–135, 138, 192–193,
195; theory of escalation, 104;
vertical escalation, 66, 133. *See also*
brinksmanship
Europe, 176–196; credibility of extended
deterrence, 178–180, 182–183, 187,
189–192, 200–212; debate over
disarmament in, 184–189, 231–233;
phased adaptive approach in,
119–120, 190; regional deterrence
architectures in, 82–86, 93–94, 266.
See also allies, defense of; NATO;
names of specific countries
European Leadership Network, 186
European Phased Adaptive Approach,
119–120, 190
extended deterrence; assurance
of allies in, 36, 42, 90–91, 179,
215–219; credibility of threat
in, *see* credibility of deterrence;
definition and purpose of, 33,
177–180; disarmament and, 37,
49, 231–233, 239–240; homeland
defense and, 90–92, 94; minimum
deterrence and, 35, 37, 48,
260–261; modernization in, 202,
269; nonnuclear allies and, 89;
in Northeast Asia, 158, 198–213,
219, 266; nuclear weapons role in,
237–238, 240–243, 258–259. *See
also* allies, defense of; deterrence
strategies; regional deterrence
architectures; strategic stability

Extended Deterrence Dialogue (EDD),
    202–203
Extended Deterrence Policy Committee
    (EDPC), 202–203

fait accompli, military: in Chinese
    theory of victory, 164–165;
    deterrence of, 97–98; in North
    Korean theory of victory, 65, 67,
    75–76; in Russian theory of victory,
    133; similarities in Red theories of
    victory, 243–244
federally funded research and
    development centers (FFRDCs), 19
Federov, Yury, 130
Ford, Christopher, 24
forward-deployable nonstrategic nuclear
    weapons. See nonstrategic nuclear
    weapons
France: assurance to U.S., 231; nuclear
    weapons in, 38, 220, 256, 263; role in
    NATO, 34, 183, 206, 220
Freedman, Laurence, 20–21

Gang of Four, 26–27, 29, 37, 46
Gates, Robert, 25, 30, 112, 120
Gates-Bodman report (2001), 25
GCC (Gulf Cooperation Council), 92,
    222, 320n41
geopolitical surprises, 231–233
Georgia, 112
Gerson, Michael, 104
Global Zero movement: elimination of
    nuclear weapons in Europe, 186;
    formation of, 27; Gang of Four and,
    37; international disarmament
    movement and, 37–40; timeline for
    disarmament, 47, 48–49, 240; on
    unilateral reductions, 259–260
Gorbachev, Mikhail, 14–15
Gray, Colin, 13, 20
gray zone threats: ballistic missile
    defense in, 88, 97–98; China and,

162, 199; definition of, 75; deterrence
    in, 86, 97–99, 200; Japan and,
    291n84; North Korea and, 75, 82, 199
Gulf Cooperation Council (GCC), 92,
    222, 320n41

Hadley, Steve, 145
Healey theorem, 178–179, 214–215
hedging, geopolitical, 217–218, 232–233,
    238, 318n10
High Level Group (HLG), 186, 311n25
Hoffman, Stanley, 70–71
Holmes, James R., 62
homeland defense. See U.S. homeland
    defense
horizontal escalation, 66, 133
Hungary, 109
Huntley, Wade, 84
Hussein, Saddam, 52, 54–55, 73
Huth, Paul, 68, 177
hybrid (no-contact) warfare, 132–133,
    135, 193

IAEA (International Atomic Energy
    Agency), 54
Iklé, Fred, 20
inadvertent escalation: in attacks on
    the U.S., 90, 94, 321n7; China and,
    169, 170–171; definition of, 309n98;
    North Korea and, 78; Red theories
    of victory and, 102, 244–245, 321n7
    (Ch.9); Russia and, 122
India, 27, 51–52
Intermediate-range Nuclear Forces
    Treaty (INF; 1987), 12, 94, 137, 193,
    211
International Atomic Energy Agency
    (IAEA), 54
International Campaign to Abolish
    Nuclear Weapons, 27
International Commission on
    Nuclear Non-Proliferation and
    Disarmament, 27, 38

intrawar deterrence, 103–104, 227–228, 233

Iran: ballistic missiles in, 82, 221–222, 236; China and, 145; pursuit of nuclear weapons in, 55–57, 220–223; Russia on U.S. policy on, 111, 113–114; U.S. regional deterrence and, 220–222

Iraq: deterrence strategy of, 55; failure of "shock-and-awe" deterrence in, 95–96; as lesson in the need for nuclear weapons, 52–53, 61, 227–228; Persian Gulf War of 1990 and 1991, 15, 16; Russia on U.S. policy on, 111, 128; theory of victory of, 55; weapons of mass destruction in, 15, 16, 19, 54–55

Iskander missiles, 136–137

Islamic state, 57–58

isolationism, 82, 91, 231, 255–256

Israel: bombing of Syrian nuclear site, 54; Middle East regional strategy and, 221–222; nuclear weapons in, 51; security strategy for, 92

Japan: China and, 145, 158, 199; defense spending by, 266; missile defense in, 95, 201, 209–210; nonnuclear strike capabilities, 211–212; on non-proliferation and disarmament, 27; North Korea and, 64, 66, 76, 198–200; nuclear power as hedge strategy, 218, 318n10; nuclear weapons not deployed to, 197, 314n2; Russia and, 209, 316n29; security deficit in, 199–200; South Korea and, 201, 204–205; UN military bases in, 66; U.S. commitment fears, 199, 203, 209, 315n13, 316n29. See also Northeast Asia

Jiang Zemin, 151, 161

Kartchner, Kerry, 103, 104

Khan, A. Q., 54

Kim Jong Un, 59, 61, 69, 77, 199. See also North Korea

Kissinger, Henry, 26–27, 37, 56–58, 242–243. See also Gang of Four

Kokoshin, Andrei, 134–135, 137, 167, 301n102

Korea. See North Korea (DPRK); South Korea (RoK)

Kroenig, Matthew, 70

Lampton, David, 147

Larsen, Jeffrey, 73, 103

lateral escalation, 66, 133

Law of Armed Conflict, 35

"lead but hedge" strategy, 16, 25–26

legislature, U.S. See Congress, U.S.

Lewis, John, 168

Libya: invasion of, after giving up nuclear arms, 61; pursuit of nuclear weapons by, 54; Russia on NATO's actions in, 113–114

Lieber, Keir, 67, 71–72

Li Keqiang, 144–145

limited nuclear war: definition of, 103; in deterrence strategies, 99, 103–104, 194; in NATO theory of victory, 194; in North Korean theory of victory, 65–69, 80; in Red theories of victory, 245–246; in Russian theory of victory, 130–131

Limited Test Ban Treaty (1963), 151

Lisbon Protocol, 15

The Long Shadow (Alagappa), 28

Lukyanov, Fyodor, 113–114

Lunn, Simon, 185

Lyon, Rod, 207

MAD (mutual assured destruction), 16, 106, 124, 131, 264

"major theater wars," 18

"The Management of Savagery" training manual, 57–58

Mao Zedong, 305n31

MAS (Mutual Assured Safety), 16
McCain, John, 27
Medvedev, Dmitry Anatolyevich, 113
Middle East, regional deterrence in, 188,
    220–222. *See also names of specific
    countries*
Mies, Richard, 40
military planning: China and, 160–168;
    comprehensive strengthening
    approach, 266–267; core
    competencies in, 250–251; homeland
    defense, 90–92; Iran and, 56–57; in
    limited nuclear war, 193; in major
    theater wars, 18; military supremacy
    in deterrence, 104; North Korea
    and, 58–61, 64–69, 243–245; under
    Obama, 34–36; reduced reliance on
    nuclear deterrence in, 40, 95–96; for
    regional adversaries, 15–16, 84–86,
    266, 269; in Russia, 107, 125–126,
    128–138
Miller, Franklin C., 40, 231
minimum deterrence, 35, 37, 48,
    260–261
missile defense. *See* ballistic missile
    defense; cruise missiles
modernization: advocacy for, 44, 46–47;
    of ballistic missiles, 43–44, 211,
    269; under Bush, George H. W., 12;
    under Bush, George W., 24–25; by
    China, 148, 150, 154–160, 169–170;
    during the Cold War, 43–44; of
    conventional forces, 25, 44, 190, 211,
    264; of delivery systems, 12, 25, 43,
    202, 269; in Europe, 187, 190; low-
    yield nuclear weapons in, 270–271;
    money for, 24–25, 40, 44, 270–271;
    need for, 2, 43–44, 46–47, 268–271;
    under Obama, 33, 41–42, 44–45;
    partisanship and, 44–45, 46; in
    Russia, 137–138, 303n136
Morgan, Forrest, 131, 192
"mosaic" defense strategy, 56

Moscow Treaty (Strategic Offensive
    Reductions Treaty; 2003), 24, 33,
    110–111
multilateralism, 118, 123
mutual assured destruction (MAD), 16,
    106, 124, 131, 264
Mutual Assured Safety (MAS), 16
mutual assured security, 106, 124
mutual assured stability, 106, 124, 264
mutual deterrence, 14, 63, 82, 121–124,
    153, 173
mutual vulnerability, 153, 209, 229

NAC (North Atlantic Council), 186
National Missile Defense Act of 1999,
    18
National Nuclear Security
    Administration, 45
national security strategy: under
    Bush, George H. W., 142; under
    Bush, George W., 21–22, 110, 143,
    155; case for and against balanced
    approach, 254–256; case for U.S.
    nuclear weapons, 240–243, 262–263;
    under Clinton, 15–16, 142–143;
    geopolitical hedges in, 232–233, 238;
    modernization and, 268–271; moral
    argument and, 248–249; nuclear
    weapons and theory of victory,
    245–249; under Obama, 29–31, 143,
    272–273; optimism in, 241–243; in
    Red theories of victory, 244. *See also*
    Nuclear Posture Review
National Security Strategy of
    Engagement and Enlargement, 15–16
NATO: assurance of countries in,
    214–227; Baltic states defense, 111,
    190, 193–194, 196; conventional
    forces in, 12, 181, 183–185, 187, 190,
    193–195; credibility of deterrence
    in, 178–180, 182–183, 187; Crimea
    annexation response, 120, 125,
    189–192, 225; Deterrence and

Defense Posture Review (2012), 185–189, 311n25; on disarmament, 184–189, 231–233; escalation management, 192–193, 195, 258, 260; future deterrence adaptations, 192–195; future reductions of nuclear weapons, 257–258; missile defense in, 184–185, 188–190, 193–195, 297n47; as model for other regions, 184, 196, 206–207; nonstrategic nuclear weapons in, 180–182, 186–187, 195, 250; nuclear policy (1991 to 2009), 180–183; reduced role of nuclear weapons in, 179, 181–183, 184, 188, 191; Russian perception of threat from, 109–114, 116–117, 119, 124–131, 136, 190, 196; Russian theory of victory against, 129–139; shared decision making in, 183–185; support of, 17, 33, 34, 266; theory of victory of, 192–196; U.S. commitment questioned in, 186; Yugoslavia (former) action by, 109, 128. See also allies, defense of; Europe

NATO Nuclear Planning Group, 181

NATO–Russia Permanent Joint Council, 108, 120, 189, 194

New START Treaty (2010): expiration of, 258, 272; negotiations on, 33, 45, 113; proposed updates, 122–123, 140, 237; ratification of, 45

9/11 attack, 21, 110, 125

Nitze, Paul, 52, 53

"no first use" policy: of China, 150–152, 154, 156, 158, 169, 201–202, 305n31; Japan and, 201–202

nonproliferation policy: Bush (George W.) administration, 42; China's role in, 145–146; Clinton administration, 19; international consensus on, 38, 82, 261–263; NATO and, 185; North Korea and, 79, 204; Obama administration, 32, 106, 239–240, 254–256, 261–263. See also nuclear proliferation

Non-Proliferation Treaty (NPT; 1970): assuring non-nuclear weapon states in, 224–227, 238, 259, 261–263; Bush (George W.) administration, 24; China and, 145–146, 151; clean assurance and, 32; Clinton administration, 19; disarmament responsibilities under, 24, 33–34, 226–227, 256–262; lesson from Libya and Iraq on, 61; on members withdrawing from, 256; nuclear countries outside, 51; Obama administration, 32; Russia's annexation of Crimea and, 225; second centers of decision and, 219; Syria in, 54. See also nonproliferation policy; nuclear proliferation

nonstrategic nuclear weapons (NSNW): in Cold War, 181, 187, 194; delivery systems, 93–94, 181, 202, 223, 258; in NATO, 180–182, 186–187, 195, 250; reductions and removal of, 181–189, 191–192; in regional deterrence architectures, 93–94, 134–135; in risk-sharing by allies, 249; tactical versus nonstrategic, 93, 181

North Atlantic Council (NAC), 186

Northeast Asia, 198–213: changing security environment and, 198–200; Cold War and, 197–198, 207, 219; credibility of U.S. commitment, 199, 203; extended deterrence strengthening, 200–204, 266; nuclear component consensus and, 205–208; strategic stability and, 158, 208–212; theory of victory needed by, 200; trilateral cooperation and, 204–205. See also China; Japan; North Korea; South Korea

North Korea (DPRK), 58–79: balanced
approach to, 254; ballistic missiles
in, 53, 58–60; biological and
chemical weapons in, 59, 64–66,
76; case for nuclear weapons, 27,
60–62, 288n48; China and, 145,
162–163; conventional forces, 59–60,
62–64, 66–68, 71, 75–77; cyber and
space warfare, 66, 68, 75; deterrence
challenges, 74–79, 82, 94, 203–204,
254; escalation management, 53,
65–68, 71–73, 74–78, 200; Fatherland
Liberation War in, 69; Japan and,
64, 66, 76, 198–200; plausibility
of nuclear use, 69–74; political
objectives of, 60, 79; South Korea
threat from, 59–60, 64–65, 67, 76,
200; theory of victory by, 53, 61–69,
80, 198, 243–245, *see also* Red
theories of victory; U.S. homeland
threat from, 58–60, 64–67, 74, 199
NPR. *See* Nuclear Posture Review
NPT. *See* Non-Proliferation Treaty
NSNW. *See* nonstrategic nuclear
weapons
nuclear arsenal size: China and, 148,
151–152, 174; nonstrategic weapons
and, 123; reductions under Bush,
George H. W., 12, 14–15, 42;
reductions under Bush, George W.,
24, 42, 148, 257; reductions under
Clinton, 17–18, 42, 140; reductions
under Obama, 36, 42, 47–48,
257–263; required for deterrence,
249–251; in Russia after Soviet
Union demise, 17; safety margin
and, 135; in South Korea during
Northeast Asian Cold War, 197. *See
also* arms control and reduction
nuclear assurance, 214–234: of
adversaries in time of war, 103–104,
227–228, 233; of allies not under
U.S. nuclear umbrella, 220–224; of

allies under U.S. nuclear umbrella,
214–220; arms reduction and
disarmament and, 215–216;
assurance versus credibility,
178–179; to China, 228–230, 319n34;
clean assurance, 32; competing
agendas in, 233; Crimea annexation
effect on, 225; geopolitical surprises
and, 231–233; measures of success
in, 216–220, 318n10; minimum
and maximum requirements of,
225–226; of non-nuclear weapon
signers of the NPT, 224–227, 259;
positive versus negative, 225; of
regime stability and survival,
227–228, 233; to Russia, 228–230,
319n34; to the U.S., 230–233, 321n41
nuclear crisis, definition of, 70
nuclear materials, in Soviet Union
demise, 14, 15, 18, 108–109
Nuclear Non-Proliferation Treaty. *See*
Non-Proliferation Treaty
nuclear parity: in China, 23, 36, 156, 250;
in Russia, 36, 127, 131, 250; strategic
stability and, 250
nuclear policy history: Bush (George
H. W.) administration, 12, 14–15;
Bush (George W.) administration,
21–29; Clinton administration,
15–21, 42, 106, 257; in the Cold
War, 11–14, 19–20, 93, 103, 246;
congressional partisanship and,
44–45; continuity and change
in, 40–43; modernization and
disarmament debates, 47–50;
Obama administration, 29–40,
206, 267
Nuclear Posture Review (NPR): under
Bush, George W., 21–25, 147–148,
154; under Clinton, 16–18, 154;
continuity and change in, 40–43;
under Obama, 29–34, 48, 93, 148,
179, 183–184, 202, 205–206

"The Nuclear Posture Review: Setting the Record Straight" (Payne), 22
nuclear power industries, as hedges, 218, 318n10
nuclear proliferation: in Asia, 27–28; cascade of, 26, 51, 81–82, 242, 256; geopolitical hedges and, 232–233, 238; in the Middle East, 26, 223; in Northeast Asia, 26; plausible use of weapons in, 28–29; in U.S. disengagement, 256. *See also* Non-Proliferation Treaty
nuclear queens. *See* chess analogy
nuclear revolution, 118, 297n45
Nuclear Threat Initiative, 186–187
nuclear war: discrimination and proportionality principles in, 35, 101; escalation types in, 66; global versus regional, 36, 71, 103, 126, 129, 241–242; intrawar deterrence in, 103–104, 227–228, 233; nuclear crisis as substitute for, 70–71; plausible scenarios for, 28–29; role of, in Russian theory of victory, 130–131; role of conventional weapons in, 62–64, 68; U.S. and Russian views on likelihood of, 124–128; winning versus prevailing in, 12–13, 18. *See also* deterrence strategies; escalation management; nuclear weapons use; theory of victory
nuclear weapons maintenance: by allies with U.S. nuclear weapons, 95; under Bush, George W., 45; under Clinton, 22; costs of, 44; modernization and, 2, 43, 268–271; under Obama, 33, 43–44. *See also* modernization
nuclear weapons use: in asymmetry of stake, 72–73, 82, 100–101, 134, 169; authority of president in, 12, 35, 181, 273; in Blue theory of victory, 99–102; bluffing about, 78, *see also*

brinksmanship; break-out capability in, 123, 127, 137; chess analogy, 52–53, 61, 67–68, 79, 97; definition of, 52; in demonstration shots, 76; "first use," 150–152, 154, 156, 158, 169, 201–202, 305n31; incentives for weak states, 71–72; international humanitarian law and, 38; low-yield weapons and likelihood of, 270–271; in military fait accompli, 65, 75–76, 84, 164–165, 243–244; plausibility of, by North Korea, 69–74; plausibility of, by Russia, 130–131; precedents in, 81; for regime survival, 57, 71–72, 77, 138, 227–228; in regional conflicts, 36, 73; in retaliation, 35, 77, 100; sole purpose formulation, 32–33, 201, 205–206, 262; in state-sponsored terrorism, 41; substitutes for, 94–96; threats of, 52; U.S declaratory policy on, 201–202, 245, 315n13; World War II justification for, 40. *See also* nuclear war
Nunn, Sam, 26. *See also* Gang of Four
Nunn-Lugar Cooperative Threat Reduction program, 108

Obama administration; balanced approach in, 3, 30, 40, 90, 184–185, 204; ballistic missile defense review by, 87, 119–120; China relationship in, 143–147, 173; disarmament discussions and, 26, 29–30, 33–34, 39–40; national security strategy, 29–31, 143, 272–273; nuclear arsenal reductions in, 36, 42, 47–48, 257–263; nuclear policy in, 29–40, 206, 267; Nuclear Posture Review, 29–34, 48, 93, 148, 179, 183–184, 202, 205–206; on nuclear umbrella, 202, 315n13; nuclear weapons maintenance in, 33, 43–44; Russia relationship in, 112–117, 124–128;

Obama administration (*continued*)
    sole purpose formulation rejected
    by, 32–33, 201, 205–206, 262
Ochmanek, David, 72
O'Hanlon, Michael, 147

Pakistan: nuclear tests by, 27; outside
    the Non-Proliferation Treaty, 51;
    transfer of knowledge and weapons
    from, 54, 223
partisanship, nuclear policy and, 44–45
Payne, Keith, 20, 22
"peace dividend," 42–43, 110
Perry, William, 16, 26–27, 30, 33, 46. *See
    also* Gang of Four
Persian Gulf War of 1990 and 1991, 15,
    16
Piontkovsky, Andrei, 131
Poland: in arms control on nonstrategic
    weapons, 191–192; ballistic missile
    defenses in, 95, 112; entry into
    NATO, 109
political intent statements, 84, 86, 225
Pollack, Ken, 56
Powell, Colin, 149
Presidential Nuclear Initiatives, 14,
    42–43, 108, 257
Press, Daryl, 67, 71–72
prodemocracy movements, 142,
    229–230. *See also* color revolutions
proportionality, principle of, 35, 101
Purple Hearts for planned invasion of
    Japan, 40
Putin, Vladimir: on Crimea action, 120,
    125; legacy of, 117; Moscow Treaty
    and, 24; Munich speech (2007),
    111–112; on 9/11 attacks on the U.S.,
    110; worldview of, 113–114, 240. *See
    also* Russia

Qadhafi, Mu'ammar, 54
Quadrennial Defense Review (QDR), 18,
    36, 125, 160–161

Rauchhaus, Robert, 68
Reagan administration, 12–13
Red theories of victory, 53: China,
    62–69, 80, 164–170, 174–175,
    243–245; nonstrategic nuclear
    weapons and, 94; North Korea, 53,
    61–69, 80, 198, 243–245; risks in,
    243–245; Russia, *see* Russian theory
    of victory
red zone threats: ballistic missile defense
    in, 88–90, 94; China and, 200;
    deterrence of, 85–86, 95, 99–102;
    North Korea and, 75–76, 80, 82, 200
reflexive control, 132–133
regime stability and survival: intrawar
    assurances of, 227–228, 233; Iran
    and, 57; Libya and, 61, 113; North
    Korea and, 71–72, 77; Russia and,
    138
regional challengers: deterrence
    spectrum for, 74–79, 97–102; lessons
    from Iraq and Libya, 52–53, 61,
    227–228; in the Middle East, 54–58;
    North Korean case for nuclear
    weapons, 60–69; nuclear and
    missile proliferation in, 51–52, 54;
    plausibility of North Korean nuclear
    use, 69–74; U.S. homeland defense
    from, 58–60, 90–92, 94, 139–140,
    154–155, 165. *See also names of
    specific countries*
regional deterrence architectures,
    81–105: Australia and, 318n15;
    ballistic missile defense in, 82–83,
    86–90, 208, 232–233, 292nn10–11,
    297n47; for blackmail strategies,
    102–104; in Blue theory of victory,
    96–102; China and, 148–151,
    153–156, 166–169, 172–173, 208–209;
    competing agendas in, 233, 264;
    comprehensive approach to, 82–86,
    88–90, 232, 272; Europe and,
    82–86, 93–94, 266. *See also* NATO;

Middle East and, 55, 82–83, 95–96, 220–222; NATO model for, 184, 196, 206–207; nonnuclear components in, 94–96, 232–233; nonstrategic nuclear weapons in, 93–94, 134–135; Northeast Asia and, 74–79, 82, 94, 197–213, 254; political partnerships in, 83–84; progress in strengthening, 265–267; prompt strike capabilities in, 211–212, 264, 266, 270; Russia, 119, 122–128, 131–132, 254; tailoring to specific regions, 15–21, 92–94, 232–233, 293n21; U.S. homeland defense and, 90–92, 94. *See also* Blue theory of victory; extended deterrence

Reliable Replacement Warhead, 24–25

Republic of Korea (RoK). *See* South Korea

Rice, Condoleezza, 110, 315n13

Robust Nuclear Earth Penetrator, 24

"rogue states," 15

RoK. *See* South Korea

Rosen, Stephen, 28–29

Rumsfeld, Donald, 148

Russett, Bruce, 68

Russia, 106–140: arms control differences with U.S., 122–125, 236–237, 257–260, 271–272; Bush (George H. W.) administration and, 108, 260; Bush (George W.) administration and, 110–112; China and, 128–129, 145; Clinton administration and, 42, 108–110; on color revolution support by U.S., 111, 113–116, 128–129, 133, 229–230; Crimean annexation by, 114–115, 120, 125, 189–192, 225; escalation management, 122, 131–135, 138, 192–193, 195; Japan and, 209, 316n29; military confrontation deterrence by U.S., 124–128, 138–139; mismatch on threat from

NATO, 109–114, 116–11[ ] 124–131, 136, 190, 196; o[n] expansion, 109, 111–112, 116–117, 136; on NATO Kosovo operations, 128–129; on NATO missiles, 112–114, 117–120, 123–125, 188, 297n45, 297n47, 298n53; nuclear assurance by U.S. to, 228–230, 319n34; nuclear materials safety, 14, 15, 18, 108–109; Obama administration and, 112–117; "snap back hard" policy, 115–116, 128, 139, 190, 195–196; strategic stability disagreements with U.S., 120–122, 138–140, 254–255, 263–265. *See also* arms control and reduction; arms control treaties; Russian theory of victory

Russian theory of victory, 128–138: cyber and space warfare in, 122, 132–133; escalation management in, 133–135; fait accompli in, 133; implications for U.S., 139–140, 243–245; INF treaty and, 137–138, 190, 193; long-range nonnuclear precision strikes in, 136–137; military readiness in, 129–130, 137; mismatch with Blue theory of victory, 138–139; propaganda and misinformation in, 136; strategic attacks on U.S. homeland in, 135; substrategic nuclear operations in, 130–132, 134, 135–136; threat from NATO, 128–130. *See also* Red theories of victory

Saddam Hussein, 52, 54–55, 73

Satoh, Yukio, 201–202, 209, 316n29

Saudi Arabia, 222–223

Schelling, Thomas, 121, 178, 227

Schlesinger, James, 25, 30, 33, 231–232

Schulz, George, 26–27. *See also* Gang of Four

Schwartz, Lowell, 72
Scowcroft, Brent, 37, 142
"second nuclear age," 20–22, 27–28
Secretary of Defense Task Force on
    Nuclear Weapons Management,
    182–183
Senate Arms Control Observer Group,
    14, 19
September 11, 2001 attacks, 21, 110,
    125
Serbia, NATO bombing in, 109, 128
Shanghai Cooperation Organization,
    146
"Silent Contest" (documentary film),
    145
Single Integrated Operational Plan
    (SIOP), 12–13, 23
Sloss, Leon, 13
Snowden, Edward, 114
sole purpose formulation, 32–33, 201,
    205–206, 262
SORT (Strategic Offensive Reductions
    Treaty; 2003), 24, 33, 110–111
South Korea (RoK): China and, 199;
    defense spending by, 266; Japan
    and, 201, 204–205; missile defense
    in, 209–211; nonnuclear strike
    capabilities, 211; North Korea threat
    to, 59–60, 64–65, 67, 76, 200; nuclear
    weapons in Northeast Asian Cold
    War, 197; U.S. commitment fears
    by, 199, 203, 209. See also Northeast
    Asia; North Korea
Soviet Union, 11–15, 18, 108–109. See
    also Cold War; Russia
space warfare: China and, 144, 161,
    165–166, 170–172, 209; defense
    against, 85–86, 96, 246, 266; North
    Korea and, 66; Russia and, 119, 122,
    133
special forces, 98, 133, 193
stability-instability paradox, 63

state sponsored terrorism, 41
Steinberg, James, 147
Stent, Angela, 107–108, 109, 112–113
Stimson, Henry L., 49
Strategic Arms Reduction Treaty
    (START; 1991), 12, 15, 24, 33, 108,
    113, 121
Strategic Arms Reduction Treaty II
    (START II; 1993), 15, 17, 108–109
Strategic Arms Reduction Treaty III
    (START III), 17, 109. See also New
    START Treaty (2010)
Strategic Concept: of 1999, 180; of 2010,
    183–189
Strategic Cooperation Forum, 222
Strategic Offensive Reductions Treaty
    (SORT; 2003), 24, 33, 110–111
Strategic Posture Commission,
    33, 38, 45, 48, 238, 256. See also
    Commission on the Strategic
    Posture of the United States
strategic stability: assurance demands
    of, 228–233, 258; in Blue theory of
    victory, 247, 250; nuclear parity
    and, 250, 260; U.S. and China on,
    148–150, 153, 157–158, 173–175,
    237, 263–265; U.S. and Russia on,
    120–122, 138–140, 254–255, 263–265;
    U.S.–Northeast Asia alliances and,
    158, 208–212
submarines: China and, 260;
    maintenance of, 255; nonnuclear
    weapons on, 25; in Northeast Asia,
    197–198, 207; reduction of, on alert
    status, 35; reduction of numbers, 18,
    35, 269; removal of tactical nuclear
    weapons from, 14; Russia and,
    136
substrategic nuclear weapons: in NATO,
    181; in Russian theory of victory,
    130–132, 134, 136
Sundarji, General K., 52

Sun Tzu, 62, 105, 164, 244, 247
Sweden, 193
Syria: pursuit of nuclear weapons by, 51,
    54; Russia on U.S. policies in, 114;
    U.S. policy failures in, 222

tactical weapons. *See* nonstrategic
    nuclear weapons
Taiwan, 162–164, 171, 208–209
terrorism, nuclear, 41
theory of victory: in black-and-white
    zone, 86, 100–102; in blackmail
    strategies, 102–104, 244–247; Blue,
    see Blue theory of victory; by China,
    62–69, 80, 164–170, 174–175,
    243–245, *see also* Red theories
    of victory; definition of, 13; in
    gray zone threats, 86, 97–99, 200;
    importance of, 5–6, 96–97, 246;
    key assumptions in, 102; by NATO,
    192–196; by North Korea, 53, 61–69,
    80, 198, 243–245, *see also* Red
    theories of victory; Red, 53, *see also*
    Red theories of victory; in red zone,
    85, 86, 95, 99–102; by Russia, *see*
    Red theories of victory *and* Russian
    theory of victory; by U.S., 13, *see also*
    Blue theory of victory
Thomas, Timothy, 132–133
Tomahawk missiles, 198, 202, 211
Track 1.5 process, 205, 296–297n42
transparency: of China, 148, 150,
    152–153, 157, 159, 173; NATO and,
    191
Turkey, 218

Ukraine: Crimean annexation by
    Russia, 114–115, 120, 125, 189, 225;
    NATO membership invitation, 112
United Kingdom: assurance to U.S., 231;
    role in NATO, 180, 183, 211; role in
    nuclear umbrella, 220

United Nations Security Council, 225,
    241
United States: assurance to, 230–233;
    balanced approach debate, 254–256;
    case for disarmament in, 48–50,
    239–240; case for nuclear weapons
    in, 238, 240–243; containment
    policy, 115–116, 128, 145, 170, 208;
    current security environment,
    239–240; declaratory policy,
    201–202, 245, 315n13; future
    reductions in nuclear arsenal, 216,
    235–239, 257–261; geopolitical
    hedges of, 232–233; isolationism in,
    82, 91, 231, 255–256; large standing
    conventional forces of, 83, 96;
    maintenance and modernization
    needs, 2, 43–47, 268–271; 9/11 attack,
    21; nonproliferation responsibilities,
    261–263; nuclear threats made
    by, 69, 73; regional deterrence
    architecture progress, 265–267;
    Russian threat mismatch, 113–114,
    124–130, 133, 138–139; sole purpose
    formulation, 32–33, 201, 205–206,
    262; strategic stability needs with
    Russia and China, 263–265. *See also*
    national security strategy; Nuclear
    Posture Review
U.S. homeland defense: in Blue theory
    of victory, 100–102; China and,
    154–155, 165; credibility of extended
    deterrence and, 90–91, 199;
    modernization of nuclear forces and,
    269–271; North Korea and, 58–60,
    64–67, 74, 199; regional deterrence
    and, 90–92, 94; retaliation in, 100;
    Russia and, 135, 139–140
Utgoff, Victor, 72–73

Valdai Club, 115–116
vertical escalation, 66, 133

Waltz, Kenneth, 219
Warsaw Pact, 12, 14. *See also* Soviet
  Union
weapons of mass destruction: Bush
  (George W.) administration and,
  21, 41; Clinton administration
  and, 16, 20; in Iran, 56; in Iraq, 15,
  16, 19, 54–55; in North Korea, 64,
  68; Obama administration and,
  41; proliferation of, 41, 241; Putin
  administration and, 127–128. *See
  also* biological weapons; chemical
  weapons; nuclear weapons use

wedding ring analogy, 187
Wheeler, Michael, 72–73

Xi Jinping, 144–145, 157, 172
Xue Litae, 168

Yeltsin, Boris, 15, 110
Yeonpyeong Island, shelling of, 63, 75
Yoshihara, Toshi, 62
Yost, David, 182
Yugoslavia, NATO action in former,
  109, 128